I'd like to dedicate this book to the following special people . . .

My publisher, Judy Piatkus, and my editor, Gill Cormode, as this is my third book for them.

Jayne Cooper of Canon (UK) Ltd, and Mike and Christobel Spencer, for their technical help.

Mark H, William, Douglas, Marie, Keith, Brigitte, Ann, Gerald, Martino, Andrea, Bryan, Jennie, Tony, the Golder family in Devon, Hazel, Audrey, Peter, Ingrid, Aaron, Mike; and Rita, Sue and Pat, Dave, and, of course, my agents Alice and Mike Sharland.

With special thanks to Ken Ward for his cover idea, and to Luis Coelho who took my photograph. And to Joan Gay for some fascinating snippets of Moon lore.

Also to Penny and Tony Andrews in Alcalar, and Mark Gibbons in Ferragudo, for the use of their wonderful houses where *Moon Signs for Lovers* was written.

MOON SIGNS FOR LOVERS

Other books by Carole Golder
published by Henry Holt

Love Lives
The Seductive Art of Astrology

Moon Signs
for Lovers

An Astrological Guide
to Perfect Relationships

Carole Golder

An Owl Book
Henry Holt and Company New York

Copyright © 1992 by Carole Golder
All rights reserved, including the right to reproduce
this book or portions thereof in any form.
First published in the United States in 1992 by
Henry Holt and Company, Inc., 115 West 18th Street,
New York, New York 10011.
Originally published in Great Britain in 1992
by Judy Piatkus Ltd.

Library of Congress Cataloging-in-Publication Data
Golder, Carole.
Moon signs for lovers: an astrological guide to perfect
relationships / Carole Golder. — 1st American ed.
            p.   cm.
          "An Owl book."
1. Astrology.   2. Moon—Miscellanea.   3. Love—Miscellanea.
     4. Mate selection—Miscellanea.   I. Title.
            BF1723.G64   1992
133.5'3—dc20   92-20096
                                               CIP
        ISBN 0-8050-2121-3 (An Owl Book: pbk.)

Henry Holt books are available at special discounts
for bulk purchases for sales promotions, premiums,
fund-raising, or educational use. Special editions
or book excerpts can also be created to specification.

For details contact: Special Sales Director,
Henry Holt and Company, Inc., 115 West 18th Street,
New York, New York 10011.

First American/Owl Book Edition — 1992

Illustrations by Hanife Hassan O'Keeffe
Printed in the United States of America
Recognizing the importance of preserving
the written word, Henry Holt and Company, Inc.,
by policy, prints all of its first editions
on acid-free paper.∞

1   3   5   7   9   10   8   6   4   2

CONTENTS

INTRODUCTION

When I wrote *The Seductive Art of Astrology* I wanted to show how astrology could make a dream lover become a reality. I followed this up with *Love Lives*, showing you how it *is* possible to have a perfect relationship with the sign of your choice.

These two books were based on your Sun sign, but I have always been fascinated by the power of the Moon and its effect on our emotions. By understanding our inner selves, we are more easily able to communicate our thoughts, feelings and emotions to others – especially when it comes to love!

The Moon in your sign is the secret key to your inner life. Your Sun sign and Ascendant (often called the Rising sign and based on the exact moment of your birth) are only parts of you, and because the Moon has such a strong emotional effect on your being it can also tone down the effects of your basic Sun sign personality.

Moon sign astrology differs from Sun sign astrology in some very important ways. For a start you can be with a lot of people who are all born under the same Sun sign, say Gemini. But it's exceedingly unlikely that they will also have the same Moon Sign – hence their personalities will be very different. The reason for this is that the Moon takes only two and a half days to go through each sign, whereas the Sun takes between twenty-eight and thirty-one.

The Moon's effect on your horoscope is to highlight not only your emotions, but also your innermost needs. Whilst the Sun relates to self expression, the ego and the Father, the Moon represents your instincts, your emotions, and the Mother. It is also the female side of one's nature.

In a way the Sun is how you are by day, but the Moon is the night you, the part that is there but not shown, unless you are convinced the time and place is right.

Never under-estimate the importance of your Moon sign. It's been fascinating whilst writing this book to confirm my theories along the way through the new people I have met. And it's been a wonderful experience to watch the Moon herself waxing and waning in a brilliant and unforgettable night sky.

Somehow, it always seems to be Full Moons which create the most attention, excitement, fear – call it what you will – but there is something about this silvery white circle in the sky which has fascinated us throughout the ages.

There was an ancient belief that the Moon had her own menstrual cycle, that women were even impregnated by a Full Moon, and it is certainly true that medical studies carried out on women confirmed that the Moon does have a definite effect on the monthly cycles, and that menstruation more commonly coincided with both New and Full Moons than any other times. Gynaecologists also confirmed the rise in births at these times.

Since the Moon also has such a profound effect on tides, and since, like the Earth, we are composed of seventy percent water, is it any surprise that the Moon affects our bodies and our emotions? It has been said that there is often far more bleeding after operations around the time of the Full Moon, and that migraines and even epileptic attacks also occurred more then.

However, one of the most widely talked of correlations between the Moon and our emotions has often been connected with lunacy! Don't forget in Latin 'luna' meant Moon. Throughout the centuries, Full Moon time appeared to trigger off lunacy, a time when normally lucid people appeared to be taken over by some powerful emotion which turned them into 'lunatics'.

In America, many experiments have been carried out by psychiatrists as to the effects of the Moon. It appears that far more people are taken into mental hospitals around the time of the Full Moon, and that rapes, assaults, homicide, arson, violent behaviour and insanity all arise with greater frequency around both New and Full Moon times, whilst those suffering from manic depression become worse.

At one time, we lived by a lunar calendar, and the very word 'month' comes from 'Moon'. A month began at the time of the New Moon and lasted till the next, and each lunar quarter related to a week. In each year there were thirteen New Moons (and still are, although of course we don't operate by the lunar calendar any more). However, in this lunar calendar, Monday referred to the Moon's day. Sunday was the Sun's day, Tuesday the day of Mars, Wednesday the day of Mercury, Thursday the day of Jupiter, Friday the day of Venus, Saturday the day of Saturn. In Italian it is easier to link some of these: Lunedi for Monday Martedi for Mars, for Tuesday; Mercoledi, for Mercurio or Mercury, for Wednesday; Giovedi for Jove (Jupiter) for Thursday; Venerdi for Venere, Venus, corresponding to Friday.

If, therefore, the effect of the Moon on the tides, plants, animals and humans is so powerful, it cannot be any wonder that its effect on our ability to give and receive love can be equally powerful!

Think about your own emotions for a moment, regardless of your sign. Can you deny that there has never been a day when you have felt elated for no particular reason, or strangely low and depressed? You probably never thought of checking the Moon's phase at that time, but it might be interesting to do so, and to see whether it was New or Full Moon time. You don't have to suddenly become an astronomer or astrologer to do this — most diaries have the phases of the Moon clearly listed!

If the way you're feeling can be influenced in perhaps a fairly mundane way, think of the effects which can take place when love, platonic or passionate, friendly or fiery, is involved.

Because the Moon is a Feminine sign, and because it rules the fourth house of the Zodiac, corresponding to Cancer, the Crab — associated with the home and domesticity — it affects women particularly strongly. Depending on the strength of the Moon sign in a man, I've always felt it was the greatest pointer to his sensitivity. Cancer was the Moon's home, and ancient astrologers referred to it as the Mother sign.

Your Moon sign tends to be given far less importance than your Sun sign or Ascendant. Yet, considering the power given by the Ancients to the Moon in its various forms, this needs to be re-examined for, since it symbolizes the deeper, more private side of human nature, its power cannot be doubted.

The Moon's impact on your romantic life is considerable, and in the following chapters you will discover that lunar love can be the deepest, most soul-enhancing experience you have ever known. The feminine mystique of the moon which is inside each and every one of us heightens our perceptions and our feelings – and it truly is our own best friend when we learn how to use its mysterious influence – especially in love.

In this book I want to impress upon you the power of this silvery lady of the night, and show how, by taking advantage of her lunar influence, you can enhance your most important relationships in lots of fantastic ways.

Think how it will help you to understand why your lover can some-times be so coldly detached when he's also a passionately intense Scorpio. Once you've mastered the Moon tables at the back of the book you will realize he has a cool and detached Aquarius Moon! And that supposedly bossy Leo who seems so strangely vulnerable and dreamy – her Pisces Moon is the answer.

In *Moon Signs for Lovers* I will talk about your own Moon sign person-ality, with its inherent lunar influence, and also discuss your emotions, career, family, friends, and of course lunar love! There is a guide to lunar relationships to help you find your perfect soulmate. In the 'Lunar Lover' sections you will discover how to recognize each Moon sign, and learn how to captivate and live with your choice! There is also a checklist showing how the personality of the different Lunar Lovers will be modified by the position of the Sun in their horoscopes, plus tips on how to keep your very own Lunar Lover by your side!

This book will delve deeper into the mysteries of love by showing you how the magic of the Moon filters into your thoughts and feelings, right to the very depth of your emotions. It will show you how by learn-ing about Moon signs you will be able to ensure that your partner truly is the soulmate you have always yearned to have by your side.

It will put you in touch with the true emotional *you*. It will unfold some of the characteristics which perhaps have hitherto remained a secret, even to you, and it will show you that your Moon sign is just as important as your Sun sign, especially where relationships are involved.

However, I still insist on making the point that by learning more about yourself and about your partner, or the other people who are part of your life, you should be able to get on with everyone, and not just one or two specific signs.

Of course, depending on a person's individual chart, there could be exceptions to this – and I have to admit I do have may own personal *bêtes noires*, even though I *should* know better! But sometimes people born with both the Sun *and* the Moon in the same sign can be excessively impatient like Aries, or overly dominant in the case of Leo.

Nevertheless, if you really do your homework well on all the Moon signs (and don't forget that includes *yours* too!) you will discover that lunar love can be a whole new astrological way of dealing with your relationships.

You might never have realized it, but a little Moon magic in relationships also seems to work particularly strongly when one lover's Moon is in opposition to the other's Sun, ie an Aries Moon to a Libra Sun. Somehow you will often sense a karmic bond, a feeling you have known each other in other lives.

Lunar love is all about using the hidden power of your lunar intuition to the full – just try it and see. . .

MOON SIGNS

Almost everyone knows their star sign, which is the sign where the Sun was placed at the moment of birth. If you were born on March 26th, 1950 at 10.00 am Greenwich Mean Time, you know that you are an Aries. But you may not also know that the Moon was in the sign of Cancer on that day. Your typically Aries characteristics of enthusiasm, impulsiveness, and, dare I say, aggressiveness, will definitely be modified by the more sentimental, domesticated and sometimes moody Cancer Moon.

The Moon takes roughly two and a half days to travel through each sign, and the Moon tables at the back of this book will therefore be for the 1st, 3rd, 5th, 7th, etc dates of each month, giving the time of day the Moon entered each sign so that you are able to ascertain which Moon sign is applicable for you.

This makes the tables simple to follow, the only proviso being that since these times have been calculated in Greenwich Mean Time (GMT), it is necessary to adjust your own birth time to GMT if you were born in the United States, Canada, or anywhere else outside Great Britain. You will also need to make an adjustment if you were born in Great Britain during British Summer Time or in another country when Daylight Saving Time was in effect. (See page 182 for details on the correct formula to use to discover your Moon sign.)

Even if you don't know the exact GMT time of your birth, it should still be easy for you to discover your Moon sign and then you can begin to learn all about the hidden secrets of your personality!

If you discover that both the Sun and Moon were placed in the same sign, your basic Zodiac personality will be given even greater power. Both your outer personality and the 'inner you' will be strengthened considerably, and the depth of your emotions will be immense. Naturally, depending on the sign in which this occurs, the modifications to your personality can be very different. But a Sun/Moon Gemini is probably going to be even more of a social butterfly, flitting all over the place, than if the Moon alone is in Gemini; and a Sun/Moon Capricorn will definitely be a stickler for tradition and material security.

I have also often felt that people born on a New Moon, ie with the Sun and Moon in conjunction in the same sign, are born with an extra element of good fortune, and indeed to have a New Moon on your birthday often coincides with the start of something new and beneficial in your birthday year.

To be born on a Full Moon, ie the Sun in Scorpio and the Moon in Taurus, can lead to a real conflict between the outer and inner personalities, especially as there is supposed to be something of our opposite signs in each of us and this will naturally be magnified when Sun and Moon are placed in opposition at birth. Throughout my years of charting personal horoscopes I have also found that people born on a Full Moon often come from a split home, having experienced an early divorce between their parents or the death of a parent early on, or have had at least one divorce or major break-up in their own emotional lives.

Naturally, there are also other effects to be taken into consideration – the Ascendant sign and the position of the other planets in your own personal horoscope and the aspects they all make to each other. But in any astrology book one can only generalize, and to learn more about yourself you could have an individual birthchart prepared by a professional astrologer.

However, ascertaining your Moon sign, and thus being given the opportunity to unlock the door leading to your innermost feelings, can be a fascinating introduction to learning more about your emotions.

For most people, it is our emotions which tend to lead us helter-skelter into all sorts of situations, when perhaps, if we were to sit back and analyse what we were doing, it could result in something quite different. And nowhere does this tend to be more apparent than in our emotional lives. That is why I decided to explore the possibilities of achieving happier emotional relationships (or lunar loves!) by giving you the chance to fulfil the potential offered by your Moon sign.

This book certainly isn't about negating the power of your Sun sign, but it will advise you to allow both the Sun *and* the Moon to work together in a balanced way, so that your own life becomes more balanced and your relationships become even more fulfilling.

Balance is exceedingly important in relationships, and when one is comparing two horoscopes for compatibility, the aspects between the Sun, Moon and Ascendant are vital. When one party's Moon is in the same sign as the other's Sun it is a beneficial conjunction, as are having both parties' Moons in the same sign, or one party's Moon close to the Ascendant sign of his or her partner. Throughout the centuries this has been considered extremely important.

Carl Jung carried out some experiments with batches of horoscopes which confirmed the above in an extremely high number of cases. Jung believed that like alchemy, astrology originates in the collective unconscious, a layer of consciousness deep below waking thought which unites all human beings.

Jung's curiosity was aroused by the ancient traditional astrological and alchemical correspondences to marriage in terms of the three conjunctions described above. He carried out a study of the horoscropes of 483 married couples to see how often these conjunctions appeared.

The results showed an unusually high number of all three Moon conjunctions. Jung examined the horoscopes in batches. The first batch of 180 marriages (360 horoscopes) revealed 10.9 percent with Sun/Moon conjunctions – a probability of 1 in 10,000. The second batch of 220 marriages (440 horoscopes) revealed 10.9 percent of Moon/Moon conjunctions – another probability of 1 in 10,000. The third batch of 83 marriages (166 horoscopes) revealed a 9.6 percent Moon/Ascendant conjunction, or a probability of 1 in 3,000.

What is more, the probability that all three conjunctions would show up in the horoscopes studied was 1 in 3,000,000,000,000. Jung said that the improbability of this being due to mere chance 'is so enormous that we are forced to take into account the existence of some factor responsible for it'.

With a subject like astrology, which has been around for so many thousands of years, one is continually learning something new about its effects on our personalities. Your Moon sign is just one facet – but a fascinating and wonderful one too!

THE INFLUENCE OF
THE MOON ON YOU

As you can see, the influence of the Moon on you should never be under-stated. Whilst the Sun is your outward personality, the Moon is the inner you, and it has amazing influence on your feelings, instincts, reactions, and of course, your emotional life!

It's also the way you relate to *you*, the way you nurture yourself, the way you see yourself at the deepest possible level. Some Moon signs find it harder than others to recognize the soul level within, to get in touch with the Higher Self, to communicate on a more spiritual level and to reach that higher consciousness which is within all of us.

I have therefore compiled a quiz which, if you answer it truthfully, will show you just how strongly the power of the Moon can and does influence your life.

Some Moon signs are so strong that they will almost over-rule the Sun sign personality if that particular Sun sign portrays weaker basic characteristics. It will help you understand why a supposedly flirtatious Sun Gemini has such a romantic, idealistic personality – a Pisces Moon of course! Or your supposedly so sentimental Sun Pisces is amazingly tough, materialistic and ambitious – all due to a Capricorn Moon.

Some people are more typically Moon people than others. Cancer, for example, rules the Moon, and therefore Cancerians are invariably more sensitive to Moon phases. In America, Cancerians are often referred to by astrologers as 'Moon Children'. New Moons and Full Moons always seem to affect Cancerians more than any other sign.

The second part of the quiz gives some brief descriptions of each of the twelve Moon signs. Try to see which sounds most like you and see if you can indeed guess which Moon sign belongs to you. But it is advisable to check the Moon tables at the back of the book to verify your choice!

How much influence does the Moon have on your life?

The following questions will have an a, b, c or d answer which will relate to the Positive, Medium, Occasional and Weak influences of the Moon on you. Be totally honest with your answers, and when you tot up your score you will discover the effects of your lunar influence and how to make it even greater.

1 How emotional do you consider yourself?
   a Extremely so
   b It depends on the situation
   c Not usually
   d Never

2 Do you inwardly sense when the Moon is full or new?
   a Not at all
   b My moods sometimes seem to change
   c I have incredible highs and lows at those times
   d I feel more irritable at Full Moon time

3 When you meet a prospective lover, does your intuition:
   a Help you understand their character?
   b Usually lead you astray?
   c Work better at some times than others?
   d Prove to be the best guideline you ever had?

4   **Would you rather have a lover who:**
    a   Is romantic and tender but not necessarily practical?
    b   Cares more about the inner you than what's on the surface?
    c   Never fluctuates in his/her moods?
    d   Has a very material outlook on life?

5   **What appeals to you most when you're with a lover?**
    a   Going to a favourite restaurant
    b   Enjoying a cozy evening at home
    c   Watching a wonderful sunset together
    d   Getting together with some mutual friends

6   **How do you confront a problem in your daily life?**
    a   By getting into a panic first
    b   By trying to be very rational
    c   By being calm and still and listening to your inner voice
    d   By finding the right person who could advise you

7   **Have the Moon and stars always held a special fascination for you?**
    a   I've never really thought about it
    b   I sometimes love to look up at them when the night is clear
    c   Only when I'm with someone I love
    d   I always think how beautiful they are

8   **Do you keep in touch with family members even if you're miles away?**
    a   I'm not very good at keeping in touch
    b   I always feel very close to my family even if we are apart
    c   I need to talk every so often to a family member
    d   I'm not a terribly emotional person in that sense

9   **Would you say you're more of an extrovert than an introvert?**
    a   About half and half
    b   Definitely more extrovert
    c   I don't think I'm either really
    d   My introverted side is often stronger

10   **When you're in love, do you:**
   a Want everyone to know how you're feeling?
   b Indulge in romantic dreams of happiness ever after?
   c Become very secretive about how you're feeling?
   d Shower your lover with gifts?

11   **At work how are you influenced by your surroundings?**
   a I like to have lots going on around me
   b I need some peace and quiet so I can concentrate
   c I'm very sensitive to atmosphere
   d I just get on with what I have to do

12   **When it comes to health, do your emotions affect the way you feel?**
   a Very rarely
   b Emotional lows and highs definitely have negative and positive effects on my health
   c I've never really thought about it
   d I always seem to feel under the weather when it's Full Moon

13   **On holiday do you prefer to be:**
   a Near the sea, river or lakes?
   b In a busy resort?
   c Exploring somewhere new every time?
   d It doesn't matter where if you're with the love of your life?

14   **If you have a disagreement with your lover, do you:**
   a Lose your temper in a very emotional way?
   b Go off and sulk?
   c Write everything down even if you're living together?
   d Say 'I want to be alone' but in a jokey way?

15   **Would you say you're usually able to laugh at yourself?**
   a Most of the time
   b I'm usually far too embarrassed
   c I think I have a good sense of humour that way
   d It depends how good I'm feeling about myself

16 **How do you get in touch with your innermost feelings?**
    a By going for a long walk by myself
    b By sitting quietly and going into a meditative state
    c By talking silently to myself
    d By trying to analyse my thoughts

17 **Does your instinct lead you to the right lover?**
    a Nine times out of ten
    b About five times out of ten
    c You don't trust your intuition
    d Hardly ever

18 **Do you think it is a sign of weakness to be sensitive?**
    a It depends in what sense
    b It just means you get trodden on
    c No, it's immensely important
    d Isn't it more of a sign of strength?

19 **Do you get more emotional over:**
    a A tear-jerker film?
    b A beautiful painting?
    c A fantastic holiday romance?
    d A reunion with your favourite family members?

20 **Do your dreams often tell you something?**
    a I don't often remember my dreams
    b They tend to be mainly pre-cognitive
    c They seem to reflect all my romantic yearnings!
    d I dream about what's on my mind just before I go to sleep

Scores

	a	b	c	d
1	a 6	b 4	c 2	d 0
2	a 0	b 2	c 6	d 4
3	a 4	b 0	c 2	d 6
4	a 4	b 6	c 0	d 2
5	a 0	b 4	c 6	d 2

6	a 0	b 2	c 6	d 4
7	a 0	b 6	c 2	d 4
8	a 0	b 6	c 4	d 2
9	a 4	b 2	c 0	d 6
10	a 2	b 4	c 6	d 0
11	a 2	b 4	c 6	d 0
12	a 2	b 6	c 0	d 4
13	a 4	b 2	c 0	d 6
14	a 6	b 4	c 2	d 0
15	a 4	b 2	c 0	d 6
16	a 2	b 6	c 4	d 0
17	a 6	b 4	c 0	d 2
18	a 4	b 0	c 6	d 2
19	a 6	b 0	c 4	d 2
20	a 0	b 4	c 6	d 2

If you have 80 points or more, your lunar influence is very powerful, and you are therefore on the right path.

If you have over 60 and under 80 points your lunar influence is medium. You have probably begun to realize that your intuition can be a powerful guide, but why don't you start to trust it a little more?

Between 40 and 60 points your lunar influence works only occasionally, so that you're not completely sure whether to listen to your inner voice or not. You need to work on yourself more! Forget about being quite so realistic about life – your lunar influence can be a wonderful asset.

If you have less than 20 points, your lunar influence is weak, and it's definitely time to become more receptive to your innermost feelings and allow them to help you get more out of life. You're living too much on one plane and not allowing your sensitivity to shine through.

_____ *Which Moon sign are you?* _____

If you haven't already looked at your Moon tables, choosing one of the brief descriptions which sounds *most* like you out of the following twelve could give you your correct Moon sign – but don't forget to check the Moon tables to verify this!

a Sparkling, imaginative, quick-witted, though not always able to stick at things for too long. An emotional will-o-the-wisp.

b A fantastic memory, emotionally invincible and often very secretive. Able to overcome difficult challenges.

c Often restless, loving freedom, definitely a 'people person' but sometimes finds it hard to display true love.

d Very loving and usually lovable! Giving and idealistic, and very, *very* strong willed.

e Extremely romantic with a definitely sensual side, but also practical and concerned with status.

f Dedicated in everything they undertake, but tend to question their emotions a little too much and come across as rather cool.

g Invariably optimistic – if one love affair ends another is sure to take its place! Long distance relationships often appeal to this high-minded soul.

h Loves to talk, loves to chase, and hates to be tied down too much – one of the friendliest Moon signs around but can be exhausting . . .

i Can be very possessive and very psychic too. Needs stability in any relationship, definitely not a wanderer.

j Imaginative, romantic and artistic. If not careful can fall too easily for the wrong Lunar Lover if they *don't* listen to their inner voice.

k Tends to keep emotions under control, sometimes too much, and once true love comes along it's a serious business.

l Another true romantic and often tougher than first appears. Likes to see beauty in everything, not just a Lunar Lover.

Answers

a Gemini   b Scorpio   c Aquarius   d Leo   e Taurus   f Virgo
g Sagittarius   h Aries   i Cancer   j Pisces   k Capricorn   l Libra

Now go to the Moon tables (pages 182–222) for that double check!

THE MOON . . . AND YOU

Now that you've learnt that there is more to astrology than just your Sun sign, and you've checked the position of the Moon at your birth from the tables at the back of the book, it's time to find out more about just how your Moon sign influences your emotions.

We all have our good and bad points, our ups and downs, and there is no greater influence on our emotional feelings than the Moon. It's not just a question of perhaps acting strangely at Full Moon time, or feeling very up when there is a New Moon. It's understanding that your Moon sign personality is incredibly powerful, and that a lot of it is hidden away beneath the surface. The Moon represents what you feel as against what is shown outwardly by your Sun sign.

The first part of each of the following chapters will help you to discover more about yourself and get in touch with your lunar personality. This will enable you to understand the reasons why you often feel the way you do. By allowing the Moon's influence to heighten your perception and intuition, you will also be able to achieve a whole new depth of understanding in your most important relationships.

How you react to other people and to situations is activated by the Moon in your sign. It relates to your securities, insecurities, feelings about giving and receiving love, and how instinctively you perceive the world outside.

Reading the information on your particular Moon sign will help you to get in touch with the subconscious side of your nature and by learning more about the positive lunar influences of your particular Moon sign, and recognizing some of the more negative ones, you will be able to turn some of your deepest yearnings into reality and make your Lunar Lover feel you're irresistible!

THE LUNAR LOVER

Think how wonderful it could be to discover that hidden side of your Lunar Lover's personality, without resorting to dirty tricks like going through their pockets or opening their mail!

No, to really understand a Lunar Lover at deep soul level, it's necessary to realize that the Moon's influence has an extremely powerful bearing on their emotions.

On reading the second part of each chapter you will get an overall picture of the Moon's influence on the Lunar Lover of that sign and you will learn how to recognize him or her by the little give-aways which even they may not be aware of.

Captivating your Lunar Lover is something else – mind/body/soul relationships don't necessarily just happen with everyone. Some Moon signs also have feelings which they find excessively hard to show, and when you read these sections you will learn the best way to draw them out.

You will also learn how to be happy with your chosen Lunar Lover – and discover the things which will keep them by your side and the things which will possibly infuriate them.

Your Lunar Lover's personality will be modified by the position of the Sun in their sign and here I've compiled a guide to help you.

Discovering more about your Lunar Lover can be quite an illuminating and sometimes exciting experience. And if you are genuinely yearning for a deep, soul-level relationship, the secrets unfolded by your lover's lunar personality will mean that you will be able to communicate with each other in the most honest and understanding way.

By unlocking the door to your Lunar Lover's emotions, your love for each other will grow stronger all the time and truly be the mind, body and soul relationship you've dreamed of.

THE MOON . . . AND ARIES

YOUR LUNAR INFLUENCES

When you were born, the Moon was in Aries, first sign of the Zodiac, ruled by Mars, God of War, planet of energy and exuberance. Aries, sign of the Ram, is a Masculine, Positive, Fire and Cardinal sign, which means, in an astrological nutshell, that Ariens are basically energetic, assertive, enterprising and self-expressive.

You probably know already that the fiery Aries side of your personality tempts you to let your emotions take control of your life – especially when you're in love. You can be too quick to pick up the phone to plan that first date, too much inclined to show your interest, sometimes too passionate that much too soon!

The Moon relates to the inner you and the influence of your Aries Moon on your emotions is tremendous – it enhances your deepest feelings, draws you towards the spiritual side of life, and helps you to reach inward to that Higher Self. No matter what religion or creed you follow, your Aries Moon will help you, in the long run, to find greater inner peace. Its influence is just as important as the Sun and your Ascendant, perhaps even more so since it does relate so much to the subconscious.

If you're wondering what all this means, just think about the feminine, romantic, mystical Moon, and the effect she must be having on Aries, ruled by Mars, God of War, ready to go into battle at the slightest provocation. Your Aries Moon will make you a force to be reckoned with, an intensely motivated human dynamo of emotional passion, who will move heaven and earth to achieve your desire.

An Aries Moon person hates to take second place, in love, work or family life. You often have strong intuition which is a great asset and will be of immense value in leading you to that special inner place, deep within your anima. But it is still important to differentiate between your intuition and your impatient desire for results!

It's almost as if you came into the world saying 'me first', expecting (or at the very least hoping) that you could always achieve the maximum potential in the minimum of time, ie yesterday. Your Aries Moon enables you to tackle challenges with alacrity and enthusiasm, and it will stand you in good stead provided you don't let your ego take over lock, stock and barrel.

You may not know it, but deep down you want to be the best at every single thing you do, unless your particular Sun is a strong influence too. A Taurus Sun will make you sit back and evaluate the situation before rushing headlong, a Cancer Sun will help you to rely more on your intuition, Virgo will apply an analytical touch, whilst Libra will give you some necessary balance.

The New Age is very much with us, and in the times we live in we're being encouraged more and more to listen to our inner self, the voice deep within us all which can help and guide us if only we're prepared to take heed. When you have an Aries Moon it may be hard at first to do such a simple task. Your impatience could take over unless you're prepared to harness it from the start. But, if you learn more about the inner you, it can change you from being a typical rushing-about-all-over-the-place Moon Aries into a more tranquil one!

Why not resolve here and now that every time you feel yourself getting into a panic about something or someone, you will put on an invisible brake and go into neutral. Clear your mind of all the unnecessary garbage like making that unimportant phone call, checking what's on tonight's TV or running out to the shops for a non-essential item, and then write down whatever is making you so emotional. The very act of setting it all down on paper will then give you a chance to re-think, something an Aries Moon does not like to do, preferring to move on to the next thing without a second thought. This is where some form of meditation could be immensely helpful in allowing the feminine mystique of your Moon sign personality to shine through.

Positive and negative characteristics for Aries

Look at this checklist and see which characteristics apply to you:

The Positive Moon

- Enthusiastic
- Excitable
- Self-motivated
- Lively and outgoing
- Full of energy

The Negative Moon

- Very impatient
- Restless
- Inconsiderate
- Emotionally demanding
- Exhausting!

Your Aries emotions

It's often been said that to be born with the Moon in Aries means that early in life you learnt to fight for attention. Your mother could have been a strong character in her own right, perhaps with a career outside of motherhood. You might have learnt independence fast and this trait will have stayed with you throughout your life. You may also have had a competitive relationship with your father. As you are ruled so strongly by your emotions, you tend to come over as excessively aggressive to people who prefer slower, more diplomatic tactics. However, there's a wonderfully positive attribute about an Aries Moon. You never allow an emotional upset to last too long. You soon pull yourself together and are ready to move on to whatever life has in store for you next.

But one thing which many people don't know about an Aries Moon is that underneath your feisty exterior lurks a vulnerable and exceedingly idealistic romantic. There is often a deeply spiritual side to your bouncy personality. This also exists in Aries Sun people, though sometimes it's harder to believe because that 'me first' attitude is so much in evidence. But with an Aries Moon it can be a little easier to perceive for you often have a softer approach to everything, a more romantic view of the world, a greater desire to discover the inner you.

Your career

In your career, the influence of your Aries Moon will motivate you in the way you apply yourself, and it can be a Godsend. With your enthusiastic approach there is no stopping you when you want to get to the top. But there is also no way you will put up with any sort of boring routine either, which can sometimes mean you lose interest in projects half-way through – which considering how ambitious you are is not usually the best way to react! Patience is something which is often a necessity however difficult it may seem to you. You will also have to watch your emotions again – having very little respect for the way your boss handles his or her affairs may be understandable in certain circumstances, but an emotional outburst from you isn't going to go down terribly well.

An Aries career needs to involve lots of action. You're a people person even though you're not too good at taking orders! Your Martian energy will mean you are prepared to work very long hours for something you truly believe in and which really _does_ interest you! Success motivates you, but it is the creative buzz which attracts you more than financial gain. Aries careers include anything in which you can be a leader! The media, broadcasting, marketing and PR can be perfect occupations, and you'd enjoy running your own company.

Your family and friends

With your family you are invariably an affectionate and loving person, although perhaps a little keen to lay down the law as you see it sometimes. You can also be too insistent on trying to force on everyone around you your own often exhausting – to them – brand of energy.

Your're not always the greatest home-maker of all time – for whilst your home surroundings are very important to you, the domestic necessities of life, such as housework, don't really appeal to Lunar Aries people. Your excuse will invariably be that you simply don't have time and it's not that you don't want to do it! Both Moon and Sun Aries are more inclined to hide things under cushions if unexpected visitors arrive, rather than putting them tidily away in the correct place.

But you are a very loyal and affectionate person to have both as a relative and a friend, and relaxing with the people you care about is one of your happiest occupations.

Aries lunar love

In love you're a fire-ball, and I'm not sure quite how good or bad that is! One of the more positive effects of this is that you're prepared to do or die for the object of your affections – the only problem is that you're not necessarily prepared to accept defeat. Your Aries Moon helps you to throw yourself headlong into a challenge . . . you want him, or her *now*, why should anything or anyone stand in your way? Of course that means you can sometimes be a little bit too self-centred and selfish – a spot of altruism wouldn't go amiss in your character. Don't be quite so pushy, read up about the Libra Moon people and learn to be a little more laid back in your own approach. Love and romance need time to grow, and the trouble with you is that sometimes you're too concerned about an immediate display of fireworks and forget about the nitty-gritty which has to go into a relationship too.

Now that you've learnt something about your Moon sign it's time to delve into what you truly want out of life, to make the 'spiritual you' an almost equal partner with the 'outgoing you'. Exploring and disciplin-ing your whole personality will help you find the perfect soulmate in love, and the right relationships throughout the rest of your life.

You see, your Aries Moon may have given you a clear lead in the independence stakes, but deep down the emotional you isn't interested in all that. It's time to learn that love isn't simply a question of putting what *you* want first. Don't be so concerned with your outer desires and learn more about other people's emotional and spiritual needs too.

Lunar relationships

Try to find a Moon Lover whose personality can blend well with yours. The following will act as a guide:

ARIES MOON/ARIES MOON   A dynamic, exciting, emotional relationship which could burn out too fast unless you both slow down and let destiny also take a hand.

ARIES MOON/TAURUS MOON   Stop being quite so impatient if you've fallen for a Taurus Moon, for he, or she, prefers to take things step-by-step and let love grow slowly but surely.

ARIES MOON/GEMINI MOON   Remember that spiritual compatibility needs to be combined with mental stimulation when the power of your lunar influence is involved.

ARIES MOON/CANCER MOON   The Cancer Moon personifies true lunar mystique, but your Aries Moon is not too good at coping with anyone whose moods go up and down, unless they're your own!

ARIES MOON/LEO MOON   A fiery attraction which could burn out too soon if this combination becomes a battle between two powerful potentates vying for emotional dominance.

ARIES MOON/VIRGO MOON   Try not to be too over-emotional, even if you do find the Virgo Moon becoming super-analytical which somehow makes fiery Aries feel insecure!

ARIES MOON/LIBRA MOON   Your Aries flame will be subdued and perfectly balanced by this attraction of opposites. You have a lot to learn from Libra's tact and charm.

ARIES MOON/SCORPIO MOON   Rather like a moth to a flame you are attracted to the magnetic personality of a passionate Scorpio Moon, but you're somewhat wary too, and you're both very jealous!

ARIES MOON/SAGITTARIUS MOON   Don't try to tie down this happy-go-lucky personality too much. Sagittarius will cleverly side-step your tactics.

ARIES MOON/CAPRICORN MOON   Your fiery Aries Moon may have a hard time convincing this rational, down-to-earth sign that life with you doesn't have to be a battlefield!

ARIES MOON/AQUARIUS MOON   Your enthusiastic impulses will be confronted by somewhat cool detachment, which can be infuriating but also a worthwhile challenge too.

ARIES MOON/PISCES MOON   Be happy that you're both true romantics but don't throw Pisces into an emotional tizz by being too pushy and exuberant.

THE ARIES LUNAR LOVER
————————o————————

Male or female, the Aries Lunar Lover is an exciting combination of romantic idealism and enthusiastic ardour. This lover is no quiet little person, hiding away in the background. The Aries Lunar Lover is right out there, making his or her intentions very clear from the start.

There are many lovely sides to your Aries Lunar Lover's personality, and a genuine desire to please you. But the Moon in this sign also creates a somewhat restless individual. When you add restlessness to impatience and that Aries ego, you are certainly up against a strong individual who isn't terribly good at dealing with helplessness in other people. If you're rather submissive, the 'little woman' or 'hen-pecked husband' type, you won't last very long with this lunar mate who definitely respects and requires strength in a partner.

The emotional inner being of your Aries Lunar Lover is very much there, no matter how carefully it is being hidden. Underneath that outer strength, there are the same weaknesses we all have. Aries might like to think there is nobody else like Aries – but, you see, that's just one of those childish little thoughts which even an eighty-year-old Lunar Arien is unlikely to lose.

Always remember that the Moon represents the feminine side of our nature, which certainly doesn't mean that a male Aries Lunar Lover is going to lose any of his masculinity and present a less 'macho' image than he wants to project. But it does mean that he is likely to have more sensitivity than a man who has the Sun in this sign, and a female Aries Lunar Lover will have her often naturally aggressive tendencies toned down too if she has learnt to listen to her inner self!

Recognizing an Aries Lunar Lover

It might seem almost like a game at first, catching the eye of that attractive person across the room, enjoying a friendly flirtation with the eyes before even a word is spoken. At this moment it's important to remind you that Aries rules the head, and the Aries facial movements and expressions are vitally important, certainly as far as they are concerned, in making the right impression on their chosen prey. Prey might seem a rather unkind word, but it's not meant in that way. It's simply if Aries is the hunter, it follows on naturally that their chosen love is the prey, in the nicest possible way of course . . .

It really won't be very difficult to recognize the Aries Lunar Lover, unless you're unusually slow in realizing you've met someone who thrives on excitement, is amazingly impatient, and adores a challenge! Arrangements for a first date will have been suggested before you've even had time to think and you start to thrive on the enthusiasm you inspire.

Captivating an Aries Lunar Lover

Just like people with their Sun in this first sign of the Zodiac, the Aries Lunar Lover adores to be confronted by a challenge, but usually dislikes being chased. Aries the Ram is a hunter, but the hunting has to be on his, or her terms! It could even be said that this Lunar Lover is really rather selfish because of this, but don't expect Aries to see it that way!

One of the best ways to captivate an Aries Lunar Lover, and this will definitely apply to both sexes, is to try and keep an air of mystery in your behaviour. This may not seem easy if you're also a Sun or Moon

Aries, or if your Sun or Moon are in one of the other outgoing Fire signs, Leo or Sagittarius. But an Aries Lunar Lover needs to be kept guessing about the innermost aspects of your personality.

However, this definitely doesn't mean you should contemplate telling any lies, even little white ones! People with the Sun or Moon in Aries have a strict code of ethics, and honesty is extremely important to them. In fact, an Aries Lunar Lover can sometimes be almost as brutally honest as a somewhat tactless Sagittarius and tell you what you least want to hear, because it's all for your own good in Aries' eyes at least!

_____ *Life with an Aries Lunar Lover* _____

That fiery planet Mars, ruler of Aries, is bound to have a powerful effect on the romantic influence of the Moon, and if your special Lunar Lover has both the Sun and Moon in this sign you will discover that you've found yourself a powerful personality with whom your life will never be dull! Even if the Moon alone is in the sign of the Ram, it will sometimes feel like it's fireworks on Guy Fawkes night or the 4th of July!

An Aries Lunar Lover may have a quick temper. Both men and women of this sign will react at the speed of lightning to something which doesn't please them. But then, just the way the sun comes out after a violent thunder storm, the sunny sparkling side of the Aries Moon personality will shine through once again. This lover doesn't feel resentment or anger for long, and there is also a wonderfully childlike quality in his or her personality which can be refreshingly endearing. However, it can also be extremely irritating when a temper tantrum does appear!

There is certainly nothing childish in this lover's prowess when it comes right down to love in its physical sense though. The Aries Lunar Lover is definitely a sexy individual – passionate ardour is the name of the game. Aries intends to be the best lover you've ever had, for 'second best' simply doesn't exist in his or her vocabulary. Since being enthusiastic and energetic are natural parts of the Aries personality, it's no wonder that lots of energy and enthusiasm are an integral part of sex. But don't start worrying that your Aries Lunar Lover is going to be rough, ready and anything but gentle. If you did think that, you've obviously forgotten the romantic and idealistic side of Aries. An Aries

Moon will provide all the romanticism you could wish for, being almost as clever as Gemini at coming up with the perfect word at the right time and usually far more sensitive when it comes to the techniques of love.

Perhaps one of the main faults about an Aries Lunar Lover is that he or she always adores *falling* in love, but isn't quite so enamoured with the work which invariably has to go into bringing both parties the happiness they hoped for at the beginning.

But in an ideal relationship, your Aries Lunar Lover will be incredibly determined to protect and look after you in the best possible way. This, however, can also mean that jealousy and possessiveness arise. No-one could fairly accuse Aries of being as jealous and possessive as the average Scorpio, although some people who have been involved with an Aries Lunar Lover would probably have to admit that Aries comes a pretty close second.

Perhaps this is a characteristic which is rather appealing at first, but anyone involved with a very jealous Aries Lunar Lover might feel they've taken on more than they're prepared to cope with and decide that the relationship is just too heavy to handle. So if that fits *you*, then somehow you will have to let your Lunar Lover know right away that whilst you're flattered by a little jealousy from time to time, too much of it is impossible to cope with.

Just as with an Aries Sun person, your Aries Moon Lover possesses that inimitable Arien characteristic – Impatience with a capital I. Of course this can be wonderful when he or she is bombarding you with little tokens of love, spoken, physical or material, in the early days of your courtship. But after a while such impatience can be almost too much to take. Perhaps you even start to yearn for some peace and quiet, which I'm afraid you're not likely to have much of if your Aries Moon Lover is really typical.

One thing is certain, life with an Aries Lunar Lover need never be dull – and think what a challenge it can be for you, making sure that it doesn't ever have a chance to get that way . . .

_____ *Lunar Lovers and their Sun signs* _____

The personality of your Aries Lunar Lover will be modified by the position of the Sun in his or her horoscope:

ARIES SUN/ARIES MOON   This Lunar Lover's personality will be greatly magnified with the Sun in Aries too. A larger-than-life, impatient, enthusiastic and exuberant soul!

TAURUS SUN/ARIES MOON   Those fiery emotions are somewhat controlled and given more stability by that earth-ruled Taurus Sun whose feet are on the ground.

GEMINI SUN/ARIES MOON   There may be a certain emotional fickleness with this combination, but intellectually life will be stimulating and exciting too.

CANCER SUN/ARIES MOON   This Lunar Lover will be amazingly sensitive and will bring you lots of love and tenderness even if it is combined with a few up and down moods.

LEO SUN/ARIES MOON   The flamboyant, extrovert Leo Sun is accentuated by the Aries Moon and combines to make for a passionate and very exciting lover.

VIRGO SUN/ARIES MOON   The disciminating side of the Virgo personality helps to tone down the sometimes over-emotional side of your Aries Lunar Lover.

LIBRA SUN/ARIES MOON   The Sun in this diplomatic, tactful and laid-back sign can help to tame the somewhat impulsive Aries Lunar Lover and creates a good balance.

SCORPIO SUN/ARIES MOON   Jealousy could well be an understatement with Mars ruling both the Sun and the Moon of this Lunar Lover, and there will be plenty of passion!

SAGITTARIUS SUN/ARIES MOON   This Lunar Lover will be a happy-go-lucky soul, with a free and easy and wonderfully optimistic approach to relationships.

CAPRICORN SUN/ARIES MOON   The Capricorn Sun makes for an ambitious Lunar Lover who will not want to take second place in anything and demands lots of mutual respect.

AQUARIUS SUN/ARIES MOON   The cool detachment of the Aquarian Sun will make this Lunar Lover less impulsive than you might expect, and more unpredictable at the same time.

PISCES SUN/ARIES MOON   One of the most romantic Lunar Lovers of all, with a deep yearning to express those inner feelings to the perfect soulmate almost as soon as you meet!

To keep your Lunar Lover by your side

DO:
- Let there be a challenge when you first meet
- Show that you're independent with a mind of your own
- Be cool without being cold – at first!
- Then . . . be passionate, when it's the right time and place!
- Keep your sense of humour at all times
- Try to catch up on sleep when Aries is *not* around!

DON'T:
- Criticize this Lunar Lover's emotional tactics, especially in bed
- Accuse him or her of being childish once too often
- Let an Aries Lunar Lover think you're the two-timing sort
- Forget to keep a few mysteries about yourself
- Ever, ever become boring in any way at all!
- Let yourself be walked all over in an argument – stay strong!

THE MOON . . .
AND TAURUS

YOUR LUNAR INFLUENCES

When you were born, the Moon was in Taurus, second sign of the Zodiac. Taurus is a Feminine, Fixed, Negative, Earth sign, and anyone born with the Moon or Sun in Taurus is certain to have their feet very firmly on the ground from an early age.

The position of the Moon in your birthchart reflects your attitude from the inside, the deepest part of your inner being. With a Taurus Moon, the way you respond to people and situations will be in the main part fairly restrained, unless of course your Taurean patience is pushed to the limit and we see an exhibition of that famous 'bull in a china shop' routine!

I believe to have the Moon in Taurus is actually rather nice. It sits there very comfortably adding greater emphasis to the fact that you're someone to be relied upon, a dependable relative, lover and friend to all who need you.

Because of the astrological association between the Moon and the sign of Cancer, which is also a Feminine and Negative sign, Taurus Moon people are especially easy to be around. You can be very relaxing, you don't demand instant answers or results or put on airs and graces, wanting to lord it over everyone. You're happy to sit back and wait for whatever is in store. But that's where trouble can sometimes lie ahead, for just like Sun Taureans, you can also be a little *too* laid-back for your own good, spending just too long going along in the same old way when it is perhaps necessary to initiate a change.

Always remember that the influence of your Taurus Moon will aid and abet your instincts and intuition. Don't be afraid to listen to your inner voice, especially as the Taurus Moon sets out to stabilize your life, not weaken your resources in any way. Just like Sun Taureans you have a great deal of practical commonsense at your disposal, and you are prepared to persevere indefinitely to achieve your ideals, but always remember that your intuition is to be valued too.

The Moon in your sign will help you to achieve the security you desire by enabling you to be ever more resourceful in your day-to-day life. It will make you far more of a saver than a spender. (Although as Taurus is ruled by Venus, Goddess of Love, this will enhance your love of beauty and beautiful possessions.) It might also make you somewhat too concerned with security and status, and because of this you may commit yourself to someone or something for the wrong reasons. Again, allow your lunar intuition to guide you.

Positive and negative characteristics for Taurus

Look at this checklist and see which characteristics apply to you:

The Positive Moon

- Practical and perservering
- Unflagging energy
- Caring and sensitive
- Artistic
- Great inner strength

The Negative Moon

- Too fixed in opinions
- Unwilling to accept change
- Stubborn when challenged
- Can be too materialistic
- Too inclined to hang back

Your Taurus emotions

You are the first of the Earth signs, and whilst not possessing the fiery
passion of the Fire signs — Aries, Leo or Sagittarius — or the intensity of
your opposite sign of Scorpio (unless of course you have the Sun in one
of those signs!), there is definitely an earthy sensuality in your make-up
which is unmistakeable.

The Taurean emotions may be held in check at first. When you're
attracted to someone it's unusual for you to make an immediate move,
even if you do feel the stirrings of an inner passion! You're often accused
of being slow — but perhaps it's just that you'd rather be sure, or at least
try to be, before you let the object of desire know what you're thinking.

However, when you have made up that Taurean mind of yours there
is no doubt that you're amongst the most persistent suitors in the entire
Zodiac. The inner emotions of a Taurus Moon person are sincere and
lasting. When you're in love, you truly want a deep and meaningful
relationship, but you need to move at your own speed and in your own
time. Your Taurean Moon helps you to listen to your inner voice, for
unlike many of the other signs, you have the patience and willingness
to spend the necessary time to reach it. Perhaps your desire to create
permanence in your life, especially in your emotional life, is because
deep down there is an uncertainty which you are determined to overcome. You need to feel settled to feel completely whole in every area of
your life.

Your career

In your career, just like people with the Sun in Taurus, you're prepared
to work extremely hard for what you believe in. Your Taurus Moon
helps you to be very productive for it enhances your instinct with practical reality — no airy-fairy daydreams for you! The building instinct is
incredibly strong. The old saying 'Rome wasn't built in a day' is invariably unnecessary for you; you _know_ that it's worthwhile putting in
all the necessary hours, days, months, possibly years, to achieve your
highest aspirations. For with a Taurean Moon your aspirations are
high. They relate to security for you, your loved ones, and of course

your old age! That Taurus Moon, perhaps without you even realizing it, is always helping you to provide for the future!

The earthy side of your Moon sign can accentuate your love of nature and perhaps the desire to do some work in this field. The artistic side of the Taurean personality is also highlighted in your Moon sign. A love and appreciation of music can lead many of you into this area.

But whatever career you follow, you are invariably ambitious, and your Taurean Moon will enable you to cope with anything you set your heart on — even if you're *not* necessarily good at being an initiator!

Your family and friends

Taurus Moon people are friendly, reliable folk, and amongst your family and friends, you can usually be depended on for encouragement and support. But there is that other side of you which makes you dig your heels firmly into the ground and refuse to be pushed. Nonetheless there is a strong attachment to family and also to family traditions. You love to have the closeness of strong family ties, and you want the very best for them. Taurean Moon people make good parents because you do have that abundance of patience and understanding which endears you to your offspring, even if they do occasionally want to rebel against that sometimes stern and uncompromising attitude of yours.

Taurus lunar love

Sensual, earthy, passionate Taurus — who could wish for anything more! Your Taurus Moon helps to instil you with such depth of feeling, and it also makes you desire a strong and permanent relationship with the love of your life. Early on you search for a dependable partner. Your lunar aspirations lead you to look for someone who is a real soulmate. You're not someone who wants to play the field so divorce is definitely not a word you want to figure in your own vocabulary. Unlike Aries, the sign which precedes yours, you're quite prepared for love and romance to take its time to grow.

Since the Moon rules your emotions, its placement in your Venus-ruled sign is extremely important. As Venus was the Goddess of Love, it's hardly surprising that love and romance are so vital in your life. Being a practical Earth sign, you may think that you are unlikely to make mistakes in relationships and marriage. But the Moon *can* also create a deceptive influence, so that if you *are* initially swayed by your dreams of romance without any sense of reality, so break-ups and divorce could follow, just as they could for any other sign.

Lunar relationships

Try to find a Moon Lover whose personality can blend well with yours. The following will act as a guide:

TAURUS MOON/ARIES MOON   Your earthy sensuality is aroused by that fiery Aries passion, but your innate Taurean need for security bids you go slow.

TAURUS MOON/TAURUS MOON   Deep down you recognize a soulmate but somehow you may yearn to have a little more excitement in your life from someone a little more different from you.

TAURUS MOON/GEMINI MOON   You will have all the mental stimulation you could possibly desire, but Gemini's idea of security may be vastly different from yours.

TAURUS MOON/CANCER MOON   Both of you enjoy domesticity, but if your stubborness conflicts with one of Cancer's 'down moods' things may not be so great.

TAURUS MOON/LEO MOON   Inner strength belongs to both of you and love and respect will be an integral part of this relationship – mutual adoration could result!

TAURUS MOON/VIRGO MOON   This Earth combination means lots of work will be put into any relationship to ensure it goes smoothly, although Virgo may sometimes be overly critical.

TAURUS MOON/LIBRA MOON   Two Venus-ruled signs with the same inner search for peace, harmony, beauty, and plenty of tender loving care to keep you both happy.

TAURUS MOON/SCORPIO MOON   Two Moons opposing each other can be a powerful attraction arousing the deepest sensual feelings in both of you – but there could be a lot of jealousy too.

TAURUS MOON/SAGITTARIUS MOON   You almost envy the happy-go-lucky Sagittarian approach to life but deep down could be scared that you want more than they're able to give.

TAURUS MOON/CAPRICORN MOON   Two immensely pragmatic Earth signs both seeking the same kind of security out of life should certainly understand each other's secret yearnings too.

TAURUS MOON/AQUARIUS MOON   You might both be too fixed in your opinions to be real soulmates, and the Aquarian detachment could make your own passion cool.

TAURUS MOON/PISCES MOON   Romantic love is there in abundance, living up to your heart's innermost desires; but material security could be lacking with this more impractical sign.

THE TAURUS LUNAR LOVER

The Taurus Lunar Lover is someone well worth cultivating. If that sounds rather like talking about a vegetable patch, it's worth saying again that Taurus is an Earth sign, and a great many Taureans happen to be remarkably good at gardening, whether it's growing a pot of basil on their window sill, or tending a large garden.

But your Taurus Lunar Lover isn't going to be someone who has dirt ingrained in the finger nails, definitely not. Ruled by the Goddess of Love, Venus, your Lunar Lover will usually be far too concerned about creating the right appearance for that.

This Lunar Lover (especially when setting out to find the perfect partner) is a real charmer, and whilst not necessarily the most extrovert of souls will make a point of being very forthright when the occasion warrants it.

Male or female, the Taurus Lunar Lover can be quite a find, as well as quite a challenge too. Taurus the Bull is the second sign of the Zodiac, and whilst nowhere near as impetuous and impulsive as that first fiery sign of Aries, is far more determined to stand his or her ground when it comes to finding a mate.

A Taurus Lunar Lover is the sort of person who has an inbuilt horror of making mistakes, especially in the realms of love. Of course that doesn't mean to say that mistakes are never made – no-one said that Taureans are perfect! But it's probably fair to say that a Taurean Lunar Lover will work harder than most to ensure that a relationship is going to work, and work in the long term rather than just for a brief time.

If you're simply out for a quick fling with someone who has tickled your fancy, and if that someone has the Moon in Taurus, you should be warned. Their emotions are usually for real and they will be looking for a permanent relationship with a true soulmate.

There will always be someone who, perhaps at a party, when asking other guests which sign they are is going to emit a discouraging sort of sound when certain signs are mentioned. For some reason Taureans are considered by some people to be rather dull and boring, and since one's emotions are highly influenced by the Moon, this could throw Taurus Lunar Lovers into that category. This is quite unfair. Just because this warm and caring person may not want to leap headlong into a passionate relationship even if it *is* obvious that there may be not only mutual attraction but mutual compatability too, it does not make them boring!

One of the most important characteristics in the Taurus Lunar Lover's personality is that they tend to 'look before they leap'. This is especially true if they've suffered in their earlier life through difficulties at home, or had friends who have had a tricky time emotionally.

Your Taurus Lunar Lover has a steadfastness of purpose which is a valuable asset. What may sometimes seem like an unnecessary display of stubborness can simply be a deep belief in his or her inner feelings and therefore not to be laughed at.

_____ *Recognizing a Taurus Lunar Lover* _____

It would be easy if all Lunar Taureans had a preponderance for warbling something from the 'Top Ten' or a favourite Pavarotti number, thus confirming the Taurean love of music. But a good guideline for recognizing both Sun and Moon Taureans is that there is unlikely to be an instant move towards you! It's much more likely that you will experience the silent approach. Interest will be shown from the eyes – perhaps a handshake will last a shade longer than necessary – and you will see that there is a definite strength of character shining through. Even if you both recognize that there is a strong attraction between you, your Taurus Moon Lover, male or female, is unlikely to make the first move. The sensuality simmering below the surface is going to remain that way, for a while anyway. So be prepared to be satisfied with a long lingering look at the end of your very first meeting.

_____ *Captivating a Taurus Lunar Lover* _____

Firstly, make sure you remember from the start that this Lunar Lover is looking for stability. Both male and female Moon Taureans want a serene life (as much as can be possible in the hustle and bustle of today's frenetic world) and they definitely want to feel comfortable with the people closest to them.

If you're determined to behave like the current movie sex symbol, don't expect a Taurus Lunar Lover to feel you're the ideal partner! You might be thinking by now that if Taurus Lunar Lovers are full of sensuality and deep-rooted passion, then how could they fail to be attracted by a wonderfully sexy, attractive individual? The fact is that they might well be, but since their lunar emotions are inwardly search- ing for a deep, fulfilling and permanent relationship, too much showy behaviour is somehow a turn-off for them. Don't play the innocent, simply present yourself as a serious and sensitive being when it comes to love.

Don't be too pushy. This is one thing Lunar Taureans are definitely against. Even if you think this attractive being is the greatest person you've met in ages, play it cool. That doesn't mean implying you're totally uninterested – that is going too far the other way. Just cool will do.

Taurus Lunar Lovers believe in letting things grow slowly. Love is like planting a seed in the ground and revelling in the pleasure of watching it grow and flower. This is because Taurus is the first of the Earth signs and relates to the Spring and nature.

To captivate your Taurus Lunar Lover, above all you must be yourself. Putting on airs and graces would only have the wrong effect. Don't be extravagant in any way, and especially where finances are concerned. Never forget that Sun and Moon Taureans set great store by financial stability and wouldn't be too enamoured of someone who was terribly careless where cash was concerned – no matter how much they loved them!

Also, never forget, that the lunar influence represents the feminine side of our natures, the deeply sensitive inner yearnings which lurk below the surface of our personalities, and whilst your Taurean Lunar Lover might take a long time to let you peek beneath that surface, once you do reach the depths, your understanding of his or her personality will be even stronger and you will realize just how sincere this person's beliefs truly are.

——— *Life with a Taurus Lunar Lover* ———

If you've sometimes wondered whether life with a Taurus Lunar Lover might turn out to be a rather boring run-of-the-mill relationship that could end up anything but happy ever after, then you'd better start to think again.

Naturally an awful lot will depend on your chosen partner's particular horoscope, but you can be very happy together for a whole lot of different reasons.

The Taurus Lunar Lover will never purposely let you down – over anything. And whilst that might seem like quite a tall order, it really does seem to ring true. There is incredible loyalty, and a sense of fairness which is a joy to encounter.

Both Sun and Moon Taureans sometimes get accused of being too caught up with the material and practical sides of daily life. But don't worry that you'll lose out on the romantic side with your Lunar

Taurean. This Lunar Lover can be one of the most delightfully romantic of all the signs, and a special anniversary is unlikely ever to be forgotten. Taurus Lunar Lovers are the sort of people who like to find little cards for every special occasion, with the perfect words to go with the greetings.

Once your relationship has really taken off, no matter how long it took to start, you will realize just how powerful all that sensuality really is! Your Taurean Lunar Lover has as much passion as their opposite sign of the Zodiac — intense, emotional Scorpio — and no stone will be left unturned to ensure that your sexual compatability remains strong.

But what about that old 'bull in the china shop routine' you might be wondering? Are there going to be moments when your Taurean Lunar Lover behaves just like a spoilt child and throws a temper tantrum for no apparent reason? First of all, it usually takes a lot to make Taureans lose their temper — and can you honestly say that other Zodiac signs never get annoyed at times? At least life with your Taurean Lunar Lover can for the most part be serene and comfortable, romantic, passionate, and make you feel immensely secure in every possible way.

_____ Lunar Lovers and their Sun signs _____

The personality of your Taurus Lunar Lover will be modified by the position of the Sun in his or her horoscope:

ARIES SUN/TAURUS MOON   Your Taurus Lunar Lover's personality will show a more fiery, extrovert and enthusiastic approach to life.

TAURUS SUN/TAURUS MOON   The Taurean characteristics are magnified — an artistic, creative personality, incredibly loyal and loving.

GEMINI SUN/TAURUS MOON   A wonderful 'ideas' person, with the ability to carry them through. Needs mental stimulation and lots of loyalty from a lover.

CANCER SUN/TAURUS MOON   Cancer's love of home and family magnifies the Taurus Lunar Lover's desire for security. A very protective lover.

LEO SUN/TAURUS MOON   This Lunar Lover will be flamboyant, confident and immensely loyal and loving, but pretty stubborn too.

VIRGO SUN/TAURUS MOON   At times almost too practical and materialistic. Needs time to express those deep inner emotional feelings with a real soulmate.

LIBRA SUN/TAURUS MOON   This Lunar Lover has a great desire to find the perfect partner on every level. Art, beauty, peace and harmony are all important.

SCORPIO SUN/TAURUS MOON   An intensity of passion which is unlikely to be hidden for long! This Lunar Lover could be very possessive, and deep down slightly insecure.

SAGITTARIUS SUN/TAURUS MOON   The freedom loving Sagittarius Sun is given a somewhat more serious approach to life with the Moon in this persevering sign.

CAPRICORN SUN/TAURUS MOON   Security and tradition are immensely important to anyone influenced by these two signs which give great emotional strength.

AQUARIUS SUN/TAURUS MOON   This Lunar Lover might easily combine stubborness with unexpected unconventionality at certain times but they will never be dull!

PISCES SUN/TAURUS MOON   It's Valentine's Day all year round with this Lunar Lover who offers idealistic romanticism with more than a smattering of reality.

To keep your Lunar Lover by your side

DO:
- Let things grow slowly
- Give lots of tender loving care
- Be loyal and understanding
- Be sensual when the time and place are right!
- Try to share your Lunar Lover's taste in music
- Resolve never to be too extravagant

DON'T:
- Come on too strong
- Be flirtatious, fickle or flakey!
- Feel tired when your Lunar Lover feels passionate
- Ever laugh when your lover tells you their secret dreams
- Start talking about deep emotional experiences of the past
- Ever hide *your* real feelings

THE MOON . . .
AND GEMINI

YOUR LUNAR INFLUENCES

When you were born, the Moon was in Gemini, third sign of the
Zodiac and ruled by Mercury, planet of communication. Gemini is a
Masculine, Mutable, Positive, Air Sign, and it's that 'mutable' part
which is a major reason for your inherent ability to switch from one idea
to another at the drop of a hat. And if you thought it was only people
with the Sun in Gemini who were like that, you obviously don't know
yourself very well – yet!

Since the Moon is the inner you, and since you are such an extrovert
person, it is fair to say that there is a conflict of interests. It's not necessarily the easiest place for the Moon to be, as the inner you is the part
that even an immensely talkative Gemini will hide from others, and
often deny to themselves. You also have to admit that you're not the
quietest of people, even at the quietest of times! It would be especially
beneficial for you to learn about your lunar influences and how to make
the most of your lunar personality. If you also have the Sun in Gemini,
plus/or your Ascendant, this would be especially interesting to watch,
for your basic Gemini characteristics will be enhanced even more!

However, when you start to think about the positive characteristics
of the Moon in this sign, you could soon jump for joy, since you're

destined to be a wonderfully bright and quick-witted personality, brimming over with mental energy, full of imaginative ideas and curious about everyone and everything around you.

In fact if you combine all this with the inherent ability of the Moon to instil you with great instinct and intuition, you could concede that you're a real winner. People with the Moon in this sign are often brilliant at communication in all forms, and are drawn to the written and spoken word like a fish to water. You really have been given a head start in life!

Instinctively you will sense and feel things very quickly. It's not going to take you long to know if you like a person or not, or whether you feel comfortable in a certain spot. There is always going to be an immediate reaction, and you're usually in the fortunate position of being right with your first impressions.

Your Gemini Moon can also make you an intellectual dynamo, a very quick reader and someone who is naturally gifted at handling the latest high-tech gadgetry. (You were probably one of the very first people to buy a computer!) However, it can also make you almost as impatient as Aries – and sometimes even more so – usually when you're trying to cram a million and one things into a day which even modern technology can't make last longer than twenty-four hours.

Positive and negative characteristics for Gemini

Look at this checklist and see which characteristics apply to you:

The Positive Moon

- Imaginative and creative
- Mentally alert
- Interesting conversationalist
- Excitingly extrovert
- Fascinating and fun

The Negative Moon

- Restless and impatient
- Lacking in concentration!
- Too inclined to gossip
- Fickle and far too flirtatious!
- Two-faced and 'schizophrenic'!

There's also a rather irritating trait in your lunar pesonality. You tend to be exceedingly inquisitive about everyone else in your life, but enjoy being somewhat evasive yourself when you feel like it. Of course, you will say that is because your instinct tells you so – and you're right! Even so, it can still be annoying to those around you.

Your parents would have realized early on just how keen you were to learn everything possible, and your home would always have contained lots of books, encyclopaedias and other sources of knowledge.

_____ *Your Gemini emotions* _____

You are the first Air sign, and invariably an interesting and mentally stimulating companion. But emotionally you're not always the most stable of people. One reason for this is that the Moon, whose fluctuating nature is enhanced by its own relationship with the Feminine, Negative, Cardinal, Water sign of Cancer, adds greater emphasis on your Gemini personality – and you sometimes become *too* changeable in your feelings and emotions.

At least knowing there is a logical reason for this changeability should enable you to think more carefully from now on, and to try to control this difficulty in sticking to your feelings. Here, again, your intuition could be a great help if only you were prepared to sit still long enough to let your very best friend – your inner voice – guide you in its silent, beneficial way.

It's unlikely to come as any surprise to you that your Gemini emotions are sometimes thought of by others as being cold and unfeeling. This stems from your desire to come across as intelligent, sparkling and witty at all times, and sometimes because of this you don't put enough warmth and sensitivity into what you're saying.

The inner emotions of a Lunar Gemini can be just as sensitive and romantically idealistic as a Cancer or Pisces. You just have to have more faith in your own lunar being and let that hidden away sensitivity shine through. It will have a splendid effect on your personality.

Deep down you know that for a relationship to be truly meaningful for you, it needs to be mentally stimulating. Because you're the sign of The Twins, you're often thought of as someone who wants or needs more than one relationship on the go at the same time. But you know that if you find everything you want in a partner, you're not going to waste time playing around. Or are you? It's most important to be honest with yourself, to allow your Gemini Moon to probe gently below the surface of your mind and help you discover where your true happiness really lies. Not every Moon (or Sun) Gemini wants to spend their life playing the field, searching for that elusive dream lover who only seems to exist in their imagination!

Use your intuition properly, for deep down you will know when you're on the right track. Then you will feel more at peace with yourself and others.

Your career

In your career, just like Sun Geminis, you can be a one person band of creative activity from sunrise to sunset. But just like people with the Sun in Gemini, your attention span can be limited. In fact that may well be one of the understatements of all time! You would think that with your highly attuned intuition, you would be more aware than the rest of us when it's time to move on to something else – but no! There you are, your attention caught by something new and for no reason at all you lose interest in what you're supposed to be doing, and go racing off on tangents which appear to offer more stimulation.

Since the Moon influences your deep inner motives it's probably fairly clear to you by now that you need to work with people, and have lots of telephones, faxes and computers around. You're invariably brilliant at journalism, selling, and teaching and you love anything to do with travel. You tend to be very good with your hands, so some kind of artistic pursuit may also appeal. But if you're in any kind of partnership, your partner will need to have their feet firmly on the ground in order to provide the necessary stabilizing influence.

Your family and friends

Hopefully your family and friends have a sense of humour, for then they will be able to accept you as you are, a sort of will-o-the-wisp of the Zodiac. Of course you intend to be loyal and supportive and loving and caring and everying else towards them all, and certainly when it comes to telephone calls they couldn't wish for anyone more talkative. You're always ready to fill them in on all the latest news and gossip. But sometimes you're just a little too wrapped up in your priority of the moment to make the effort to be with your nearest and dearest in person.

You are always excellent company and around when its party time, but sometimes you're not good at dealing with rather more domestic responsibilities. As a parent you will enjoy imparting your knowledge to your offspring, but you will have to schedule your days with more discipline than you've probably been used to!

Gemini lunar love

Fun-loving, flirtatious Gemini – a love affair with you could definitely be one to remember! But it could sometimes be over almost before its begun.

Your Gemini Moon sends flashes of intuition your way to point you towards the perfect partner, but what is it about you that makes you doubt so much and makes you keep looking for someone with whom to spend your days and nights? One major possibility is that you have a logical side to your nature which refuses to let you trust your intuition. Since you're a person who probably yearns for the ideal soulmate just like every other Zodiac sign, why don't you resolve to listen to that inner voice a little more, and not be *quite* so logical in your behaviour when love is around?

If you get a reputation for being a flirt, you have only yourself to blame. You always think you're missing out on something. When you're at a cocktail party, for example, you go dashing from one side of the room to another, not even finishing one conversation with someone interesting before you're starting another with someone new.

You need a Moon Lover who is prepared to be a good listener, someone who can provide you with the mental stimulation that you crave in any emotional relationship. For you, passion alone will quickly pall.

Lunar relationships

Try to find a Moon Lover whose personality can blend well with yours. The following will act as a guide:

GEMINI MOON/ARIES MOON   The fiery emotions of Aries may find it hard to cope with the fickleness of your Gemini moods, and intellectual conversation alone will not be enough.

GEMINI MOON/TAURUS MOON   It's often hard for you to accept the down-to-earth approach of Lunar Taureans, so you may be scared that they expect too much security too soon.

GEMINI MOON/GEMINI MOON   There really ought to be a strong mutual bond between you – two like-minded people together – but since neither of you has much natural staying power the relationship could falter.

GEMINI MOON/CANCER MOON   The Lunar Cancerian might be very possessive and domesticated, so you'll have to change some of your tactics if you want this relationship to last!

GEMINI MOON/LEO MOON   Leo's flamboyance and sparkling personality are very attractive, but if you insist on being too flirtatious you'll be bossed around in no uncertain terms.

GEMINI MOON/VIRGO MOON   You're both ruled by Mercury, planet of the mind, so mental communication is there in abundance. But remember that romance isn't going to be *all* talk!

GEMINI MOON/LIBRA MOON   The Libran Lunar Lover is the sort dreams are made of, and two Air signs *should* understand each other, so do try to give this relationship time to work.

GEMINI MOON/SCORPIO MOON   A Scorpio Lunar Lover may seem intense and possessive to you, and you will need to let yourself go a little more emotionally if this is to last.

GEMINI MOON/SAGITTARIUS MOON   Two lunar opposites can be a big attraction, especially as you're both such freedom-loving souls with an immense thirst for knowledge.

GEMINI MOON/CAPRICORN MOON   If you're looking for material security, this is ideal. But convincing Capricorn that you're not as flighty as you're renowned to be may not be easy.

GEMINI MOON/AQUARIUS MOON   Two Air signs again, with lots of mental compatability, but both of you need to show your deepest emotions a little more if you are to be soulmates.

GEMINI MOON/PISCES MOON   Pisces yearns for sentimental affection so you will have to display a warmer personality and prove that you too can be an idealistic romantic given the chance.

THE GEMINI LUNAR LOVER
―――――――――――――o―――――――――――――

The very first thing to tell you about this Lunar Lover is that both the male and the female of the sign are going to be quite a challenge. If you are an Arien who adores challenges, a Taurean with plenty of staying power, or a Capricorn who knows that mountain tops exist to be conquered, this might not worry you in the slightest – but for most of the Zodiac it could just be a little daunting.

Your Gemini Lunar Lover, Air sign extraordinaire, is a vociferous talker. They will excel at cocktail party chat. He or she usually makes a beeline for the most interesting person in sight and is determined to make the best possible impression. Do not be surprised if you're totally captivated by this witty, intelligent, sparkling personality. Although a great talker, the talk may not always be what you'd like to hear from someone you've fallen in love with. There may be lots of intellectual talk, the latest gossip or simply inconsequential chat when you are longing desperately to receive compliments and words of love. But this Lunar Lover can also be charm personified and say all the right things at the right time, especially when you first meet at least.

Gemini wants to be at the centre of things, and enjoy a fascinating life meeting as many fascinating people as possible – even if lunar love does hit them right between the eyes! So it's advisable to hide away your jealous streak if you've set your heart on a Gemini Lunar Lover!

This Moon sign is always busy doing something, which is perhaps one reason why Gemini doesn't seem to have time for a really steady and enduring relationship. It's usually best to have an independent streak yourself if you are determined to make your Gemini Lunar Lover convinced that he or she can't live without you.

This Mercurial personality is often quite vulnerable emotionally. Due to that Gemini Moon, this Lunar Lover's feelings will be far more sensitive than appears on the surface but your Gemini won't want *you* to know that.

One of the most important characteristics in a Gemini Lunar Lover's personality is that mental stimulation and compatability are definitely just as important as suiting each other sexually. In fact the sexual side could come to nothing if the mental part isn't right. A Gemini Moon individual who appears to be playing the field left, right and centre might quite likely only be indulging in harmless flirtatious chats which really don't lead anywhere.

Your Gemini Lunar Lover will tease and tantalize you. Just when you think you're getting somewhere, you might feel they're about to flit away. It's almost like a game – but Gemini enjoys it that way!

_____ Recognizing a Gemini Lunar Lover _____

Someone who doesn't sit or stand still for more than a minute at a time and who has the ability to carry on about half-a-dozen conversations at once (two of them on mobile phones) might well describe the Gemini Lunar Lover. Expect the hands or arms to wave about too – this way of expressing oneself comes naturally to Italians and other Latins and it also seems to be a very distinct part of the Gemini lunar make-up.

Your Gemini Lunar Lover is also bound to have a good sense of humour, be spontaneous and have the ability to conduct a conversation about more or less anything. But be careful! If the Gemini you've set your heart on *wants* to get to know you better, the words you hear are bound to be the ones you want them to be. It's called the 'gift of the gab' and you're bound to recognize it in abundance in this Moon lover.

Something else you're almost sure to recognize in a Gemini man or woman is more than a touch of J. M. Barrie's Peter Pan. Your Gemini Lunar Lover often seems to flit through life with an irrepressible yet certainly amusing refusal to grow up!

_____ *Captivating a Gemini Lunar Lover* _____

A beginner's guide on how to catch a moonbeam or falling star might come in handy for there is a similarity in that all three could slip through your hands just as quickly.

It's no use being the sort of person who likes to hide away in a corner if you're out to captivate this Moon sign. On the other hand you don't necessarily want to cramp his or her style by being too strong a personality and wanting all the limelight for yourself.

Geminis are supposed to be intellectual, witty, flirtatious, quick-witted and mercurial, and they appreciate similar qualities in a partner. Make it an equal and balanced relationship without any strong ties too early on.

Don't let it appear that you're a hanger-on, an obsessively jealous type or someone who automatically starts planning for the future before you've had a chance to get to know each other properly.

People with the Moon in this sign really do appreciate the value of friends with whom there need be no holds barred. Resolve to be a good friend to your Lunar Lover before you get carried away with the seductive techniques which might appeal more to an earthily passionate Taurean or a sizzlingly sexy Scorpio.

The Gemini Lunar Lover likes to tease and be teased, so never be too serious if you want to make the right impression. It really is all down to the art of conversation, keeping right up-to-date with world events, new movies, the latest in-place in town and such like.

You want to captivate a Gemini Lunar Lover? My best advice is always ensure that he, or she, is never, *never*, bored! Be spontaneous – just like Gemini!

_____ *Life with a Gemini Lunar Lover* _____

Call it life in the fast lane or simply having a good time, being with a Gemini Lunar Lover can be a whole lot of fun.

However, depending on the age and situation of your Lunar Lover, there may be a fairly irresponsible side to his or her nature and you might be the one who has to be the problem solver if and when problems arise. Even so, living with a Lunar Lover born under this sign really can be like a magical mystery tour for ever and a day. In a Gemini Moon you will have a wonderful soulmate, provided that the sexual and mental sides are combined in just the right balance, and you are prepared to make the effort to learn how to understand Gemini's deepest thoughts.

If you are concerned that living with a Gemini Lunar Lover, a sign which is so dependent on mental stimulation, might mean that warm displays of affection will be missing from your life, then worry no more. Your Gemini can caress and cuddle and love just like any other sign. They simply have a horror of feeling smothered by someone's love.

Life with any Lunar Lover is bound to have its ups and downs, and there is certainly no reason to fear that Gemini is going to be more difficult than anyone else. Those flirtatious ways may not disappear overnight, but with the right soulmate by their side they are not likely to be anything more serious than party chat!

You will always receive your fair share of compliments from a Gemini. And if you have to be apart for any time at all you don't have to worry about not keeping in touch. Gemini is the communicator of the Zodiac, remember! The telephone will always ring. And your Gemini Lunar Lover won't be far away!

_____ *Lunar Lovers and their Sun signs* _____

The personality of your Gemini Lunar Lover will be modified by the position of the Sun in his or her horoscope:

ARIES SUN/GEMINI MOON   Your Gemini Lunar Lover's personality will be enhanced by the volatile, impetuous and outgoing Arien characteristics so expect to be swept off your feet *fast*.

TAURUS SUN/GEMINI MOON   This combination brings a more laid-back personality, the conversations will be deeper, more serious. The Taurus Lunar Lover wants to spend more time getting to know you better.

GEMINI SUN/GEMINI MOON   If Peter Pan really existed, his personality could be just like this. The Gemini Sun/Moon characteristics will be exaggerated and the intuition will be razor sharp.

CANCER SUN/GEMINI MOON   The Moon is the planetary ruler of Cancer, so the lunar influence will soften the fast-talking airy chat of Gemini, producing unexpected depths of sensitivity.

LEO SUN/GEMINI MOON   This Lunar Lover will be exceptionally affectionate and loving, and instinctively know what true romance is all about.

VIRGO SUN/GEMINI MOON   Both Sun and Moon are in Mutable signs, and this Lunar Lover is sure to have a flair for the right words at the right time, but physical gestures may be harder to draw out.

LIBRA SUN/GEMINI MOON   The Libran Sun will make this Lunar Lover even more charming and irresistible. Tender romantic touches will go hand-in-hand with the ability to whisper beautiful sweet nothings in your ears.

SCORPIO SUN/GEMINI MOON   The personality of this Lunar Lover will be doubly magnetic and invincible with the Sun in powerful Scorpio. This is one Gemini Moon Lover who *will* show jealousy *and* possessiveness.

SAGITTARIUS SUN/GEMINI MOON   This Lunar Lover may come from a broken home, or have had at least one big break-up in their own life. Therefore the freedom-loving nature of both these signs may, in this instance, produce someone who searches deep down for emotional security.

CAPRICORN SUN/GEMINI MOON   Whilst the influence of the Moon instinctively tells this Lunar Lover that freedom is wonderful, the Capricorn Sun produces a far more down-to-earth and realistic attitude to love!

AQUARIUS SUN/GEMINI MOON   This Lunar Lover could be brilliantly intellectual, with an interest in a great many subjects, and in some ways somewhat scared of deep emotional ties. So go slowly . . .

PISCES SUN/GEMINI MOON   The Pisces Sun makes this Gemini Lunar Lover far more of a romantic than would normally be expected, and a beautiful sense of humour may be part of the personality.

How to keep your Lunar Lover by your side

DO:

- Make sure that you are a good conversationalist
- AND . . . just as important . . . be a good listener too!
- Try to understand that this Lunar Lover needs to put logic alongside their intuition
- Be fascinating and good fun . . . but always keep an air of mystery too
- Be the best friend your Lunar Lover ever had, trustworthy in every way
- Bring out those hidden depths of passionate emotion, but not too fast!

DON'T:

- Ever try to pry into Gemini's deepest secrets
- Think that you can possess this Lunar Lover's mind
- Ever forget that mental stimulation is an essential part of love with this lover
- Lose your sense of humour
- Ever tell your Gemini Lunar Lover they're looking older!
- (On the whole) expect *big* displays of physical passion

THE MOON . . .
AND CANCER

YOUR LUNAR INFLUENCES

When you were born, the Moon was in Cancer, fourth sign of the Zodiac, and its natural house, for the Moon is the planetary ruler of this sign. Cancer is a Feminine, Negative, Cardinal, Water sign, which basically means that whilst there is an immensely sensitive and compassionate side to your nature, any Cardinal sign can be pretty tough at heart when necessary.

To have the Moon in Cancer, therefore, has an immense bearing on your personality, for the Moon shows you in a totally different way from the Sun sign personality. Your innermost being is highlighted by your lunar personality, all those subconscious feelings which you'd rather not transfer into words. The moon is your soul energy, something which may come over in your outward personality and characteristics without your being aware of it. With the Moon in this sign, you are sure to be even more emotional and sensitive than Sun Cancerians – so you can imagine what a receptive and empathetic soul you're going to be if the Moon *and* Sun or Ascendant or *both* happen to be there too.

In any event, as a Lunar Cancerian you are, without any doubt, one of the most caring and protective people around. The sign of Cancer is also associated with being extremely domesticated. It's not that you're always rushing around cleaning up in case any visitors arrive (that's more the way a Virgo would behave), but with the Moon in Cancer you are sure to be exceptionally sensitive to your surroundings. Your home has to be just right in every possible way, and that applies whether it's a studio flat or a mansion.

Your home is where you like to be when you're getting in touch with that inner voice which the Moon's influence bequeaths upon you. As a Water sign, being near the ocean, rivers or lakes is very appealing, especially with a silvery Moon above! But home is really where it all happens for you, where your subconscious comes into its own and where you often feel most at peace.

The Moon in this position means that you will always enjoy your domestic life, or at least make it a major concern to do so! It also means that you're likely to be someone who has incredible ups and downs in your emotional life. More than any other sign of the Zodiac you're extremely affected by the different phases of the Moon, especially the New and Full Moons, which if you think about it deeply will almost invariably coincide with your own highs and lows.

To say you feel things strongly is an understatement. The Moon in Cancer makes you very psychic. Everyone is born with psychic ability, which gets lost along the way unless we make a conscious effort to

Positive and negative characteristics for Cancer

Look at this checklist and see which characteristics apply to you:

The Positive Moon

- Protecting and nurturing others
- Immensely psychic
- Home-loving
- A marvellous parent
- A warm and sensitive lover

The Negative Moon

- Being ultra possessive
- Overly sensitive
- Too hermit-like
- Terribly possessive when kids grow up
- Moody and emotionally insecure

develop it. But, as a Lunar Cancerian, whether you make a real effort or not it's still firmly there in your subconscious and it doesn't take much effort to bring it to the surface. It can be of great help in your life.

Your Cancer Moon makes you very concerned with planning for the future, in other words being secure in your old age! It's not that you start to get paranoid about it, just that you want to enjoy your comforts throughout your life.

In the United States, many astrologers call people born under the sign of Cancer, the Moon Children – and after all this *is* what you are too!

_____ *Your Cancer emotions* _____

Born with the Moon in this sign, you're inclined to be very involved with your mother throughout your life, sometimes too much so. This is so regardless of whether the relationship is a good or bad one. Consequently this emotional part of your nature comes over in all your relationships. More than any other Zodiac sign you hang on to the past. It really is extremely difficult for you to let go of people or memories even when it would be much more positive to do so.

All the Water signs are emotional; it's one of the major effects that the Water element bequeaths upon you. Naturally when this effect is strengthened by the immensely powerful effect of the Moon, it is hardly any wonder that your emotions are so susceptible to those highs and lows which can make you either wonderful to be around or a real pain in the neck!

You're rather like a vortex, drawing everything into your innermost receptive being. With the aid of meditation you will be able to create something even more spiritually rewarding and soul-enhancing – and this will be so much more positive than hiding away in your shell or going off into a corner to sulk if something doesn't go your way.

Because you are such an emotional person, you will gain greater security within by coming to terms with your subconscious, your inner being, which as a Lunar Cancerian is such a vital life force in your personality.

As a Lunar Cancerian you hate the idea of any kind of disruption in your life, but sometimes disruptions have to arise and they are not all necessarily bad. When you do get into a state about something, or go into a real sulk, you're not making the best possible use of your lunar intuition which can be such an excellent help and inner guide if you will only let it.

Romantic dreams are an intrinsic part of your make-up, both your inner being and your outer one. And the influence of the Moon is not simply one that affects you inwardly. It's hardly surprising that moon-lit walks along a beach or river bank with the love of your life are emotionally so fulfilling for you.

Emotionally, only you know what you truly want out of life. You know that your emotions are the most important part of your whole make-up, and that somehow balancing them between the highs and lows is crucial too.

Using your lunar intuition will help you find your true self, greater inner peace and security. And in the process it will enable you to find even greater happiness with others.

Your career

With the Moon in Cancer you need a definite cause in life, and this is particularly true in the case of your career. No matter what you do, you have to believe totally in it, not only as work, but as a way to help other people. It's all down to that nurturing side of your personality.

As a Lunar Cancerian you are also affected by your working sur-roundings and atmosphere. It's very difficult for you to work in a situation to which you feel unsuited in any way, or unhappy because of the people around you. It's not that you want to work on your own – just that there have to be people around with whom you feel at ease and able to communicate. And whilst helping people is one thing, you also need to feel that you are financially secure through your work too. The 'helping' side will often come from voluntary work.

The Moon in your sign relates very much to the way you approach your job, and wherever possible it will draw you to something where you _can_ assist others, perhaps in teaching or social work. But Cancerian professsions also include hotel management, dealing in antiques, estate agency, veterinary work, banking – and your lunar instincts usually guide you in the right direction for you.

_____ *Your family and friends* _____

You're well aware of the importance of family ties, tradition, heritage and everything that goes with all of that. You sometimes have almost too much of a tendency to live for your family, or perhaps worse, live through them, not learning to let go when letting go is necessary – like when children have grown up and it's their time to leave home. Use your lunar intuition more, deep down you know what it's telling you even if sometimes you *don't* want to listen to it!

The same sort of attitude can apply to your friendships – not that your're jealously possessive like Scorpio can be – but you surely have to admit that you can get very sulky if you feel you're being left out.

But you do have incredible loyalty to both family and friends, and someone with you on their side will have plenty to be happy with.

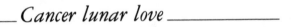

_____ *Cancer lunar love* _____

Warm, sensitive, loving Cancer, your sentimental ways can make you such a joy to be around. Your Cancerian Moon permeates your being with such strong psychic feelings that you feel you know instantly when you've met that ideal soulmate. But you'd probably be one of the first to admit that there is also such a strongly practical side to your nature (just like your opposite sign of Capricorn).

Living on red wine and cheese in a garret overlooking the roofs of Paris might seem wonderful if you're a nineteen-year-old art student, but love and poverty don't have to belong hand-in-hand for you! In fact lunar love could fly out of the window before too long if you found yourself in an emotional situation which was likely to be financially insecure. Of course, there will be Lunar Cancerians who disagree and say they would always give up everything for true love – but make sure you're being completely honest with yourself.

Watch out, however, that the influence of that beautiful, silvery Moon doesn't ever influence your emotions in a negative way– making you too dreamy-eyed, too much inclined to live on Cloud Nine and be swayed by romance.

Lunar relationships

Try to find a Moon Lover whose personality can blend well with yours. The following will act as a guide:

CANCER MOON/ARIES MOON   Your lunar sensitivity might initially be immensely appealing to the more vocal and exuberant Aries, but your fluctuating moods could dampen the Aries enthusiasm.

CANCER MOON/TAURUS MOON   You're in mutual agreement over domestic security, loving tenderness and having both feet on the ground. Passion may be slow to start but this relationship can grow to be immensely satisfying.

CANCER MOON/GEMINI MOON   It's important to curb your possessive qualities, for a Gemini Lunar Lover needs to feel mentally free. Always try to retain a sense of humour even if you are in one of your down moods!

CANCER MOON/CANCER MOON   This lunar love relationship will be wonderfully romantic, but perhaps sometimes too much like looking at a mirror image of yourself. Watch out for Full Moon when you may both behave a little crazily!

CANCER MOON/LEO MOON   Both of you have great charm and there will be incredible mutual attraction here. But since Leo can be bossy and you can be moody, it's necessary for both of you to work on your lunar personalities more.

CANCER MOON/VIRGO MOON   Resolve not to be quite so ultra-sensitive if Virgo has a few criticisms to make. Both of you desire perfection in your domestic set-up, so it's worth making a few concessions and showing less vulnerability.

CANCER MOON/LIBRA MOON   Romance, peace, and harmony, but fluctuating moods from you and indecision from Libra too. A lunar love affair which could be heaven sent if you're both prepared to balance yourselves more.

CANCER MOON/SCORPIO MOON   Two very emotional Water signs together. Both have a possessive streak and highly developed intuition bordering on the psychic – you should really understand each other's moods brilliantly.

CANCER MOON/SAGITTARIUS MOON   It's as though shafts of moonbeams have landed at your feet. The positive more outgoing Sagittarius Lunar Lover is very attractive, but your realms of fantasy may not be the same deep down.

CANCER MOON/CAPRICORN MOON   An interesting attraction of lunar opposites, both feeling the same way about traditional values and the ideal home. Drawing out Capricorn's deep inner feelings will be quite a challenge too!

CANCER MOON/AQUARIUS MOON   You're fascinated by this Lunar Lover's idealistic feelings, but not quite sure whether you can cope with someone whose moods are far more erratic than your own, and whose emotions can sometimes cool too fast.

CANCER MOON/PISCES MOON   Poetry in motion, a romantic dream made true – two of the most romantic signs in the whole Zodiac, both ruled by Water. In many ways a total blending of two kindred spirits, if you can get Pisces to be more practical too!

THE CANCER LUNAR LOVER
———————o———————

'Moonstruck' might be a perfect adjective to describe the Cancer Lunar Lover, or should it perhaps be the one who falls for this extremely attractive personality? No matter, for this Lunar Lover will certainly not be anyone you'd forget in a hurry no matter how brilliantly or disastrously your particular relationship turned out!

Your Cancer Lunar Lover, first of the Water signs, whose natural ruler of course just happens to be the Moon herself, is a force to be reckoned with because that lunar power is tremendously strong.

One of the very first things you should know about both male and female Moon Cancerians is that they are going to be incredibly sensitive, sometimes to the point of driving you crazy. Saying the wrong thing at the wrong moment isn't usually going to be the drama of all time to most people, but to a Lunar Cancerian it could be tantamount to a major tragedy. You see, this Lunar Lover's persona is delicately tuned and you need to be very gentle.

There is also another influence at work in your Cancer Lunar Lover's personality – and that is the mother influence. It is often very, very strong, especially in the case of a male (someone with the Sun in Cancer usually has a similar influence). In fact, deep down, the male Lunar Lover born under the sign of the Crab is very often subconsciously searching for someone who reminds him of his mother so you may have a lot to live up to if it's a male Lunar Cancerian you've fallen for!

Also, Cancerian Lunar Lovers of both sexes are extremely idealistic, especially when it comes to love. They are also both looking for someone with whom they can create a home, and then a family. Idle flirtations are not part of their make-up. The Cancerian Lunar Lover is all about nurturing, nurturing the relationship, the engagement, the marriage, the children. Family ties are what life is all about to him – or her.

This particular lunar personality is very vulnerable emotionally, but of course it won't take you long to realize that! And an excessively retentive memory means that even the smallest slight is unlikely to be forgotten.

One of the most important parts of a Cancer Lunar Lover's integral being is that warmth and tenderness are reciprocated. They look for total empathy, and affinity between two compassionate and sensitive beings who enjoy being together for a myriad of reasons and who intend to stay that way for a long time to come.

Your Cancer Lunar Lover will irritate you by being up one minute and down the next (not all the time, don't worry!) and sometimes fuss over you like crazy when all you've got is a sniffling cold. But their love will be genuine, and they'll give it with all they've got.

_____ *Recognizing a Cancer Lunar Lover* _____

Remember that Moon-faced description? It really can be a big give-away. Somehow with this Lunar Lover you often instinctively sense that they have to be a Water sign and you just *know* it isn't Scorpio. So with one down and two to go, the process of elimination isn't hard, especially because of those physical characteristics which can also include soft, sensitive eyes that seem to read you almost like a book. And that feeling of being protected you can perceive almost immediately.

If you meet a Cancer Lunar Lover at a particular phase of the Moon, New or Full, your task is made even easier. There'll be no mistaking the person you're with for they seem to be affected by lunar transits even if they won't admit it. And if you do happen to meet at a cocktail party or dinner, the Cancerian Lover could be the one who is perhaps enjoying their food just that little bit too much. Or lurking in the background because they're either in an excessively shy mood, or worse, a famous Cancerian sulk!

_____ *Captivating a Cancer Lunar Lover* _____

Always, but always, remember that the Cancer Lunar Lover is looking for a safe haven when it comes to emotional matters. Whether he or she comes from a secure family background or not, it's something that is always more than a dream to Moon Cancerians. So never come across as too strong, too flighty, too sexy – too anything in fact. Project a personality which is sensitive enough to attract this dreamy, romantic, tender and loving Lunar Lover.

And you'd better make sure you're not accustomed to eating too much junk food. The Lunar Cancerian, just like anyone born with the Sun in this sign, believes in healthy eating (even if they *are* tempted to eat too much!) which preferably means something which is home-cooked. Lunar Cancerians of both sexes are no mean hand in the kitchen – and it would certainly be a major added attraction if you're a good cook yourself!

Remember that your Lunar Lover was born with a protective shell around them, and don't start prying too deeply too soon. You have to learn to show interest without being nosy, but without appearing to be *too* disinterested either. Cool detachment may go down well with Lunar Lovers who like a challenge, but the Cancer Lunar Lover wants to suss out that they're with someone who is capable of lots of tender loving care which they're happy to share with the right soulmate. To captivate this Lunar Lover the relationship needs to go right down to soul level.

The Cancer Moon Lover doesn't like to be made fun of in any way, and especially not in public. If you truly want to captivate and keep your Lunar Lover by your side for ever more, always remember that a little gentle cajoling will work more miracles than trying to push them ever will.

_____ *Life with a Cancer Lunar Lover* _____

It is true that there will be more ups and downs with this particular sign than with others because of the strength of the lunar influence. And you might really be up against something if your Lunar Lover turned out to have the Sun and/or Ascendant also in Cancer. My advise is that, with a Moon Cancerian by your side, you'd be wise to become an avid follower of Moon phases, and be flexible when Full Moon time comes around. Hopefully your Lunar Lover will learn to cope with the negative aspects of his or her personality and being excessively moody at Full Moon time may become a thing of the past.

With Cancer Moon lovers, and Sun lovers too, life will be based on mutual understanding and respect for each other. This Lunar Lover does need a certain amount of privacy, not in the same way as Scorpio does, but the requirement is there all the same. And even if you *don't* get on particularly well with his/her parents, for heaven's sake try! It really will be worth the effort, because if you don't it's going to be a very big black mark against you. You already know that family and tradition are an inherent part of the Cancer make-up.

The Cancer Lunar Lover has this wonderful nurturing quality, but never forget it works both ways. Both male and female of the species want to live with someone who is going to look after them – in the way that, even if it hasn't been so in the past, they feel is their due! And never forget any important dates, for this Lunar Lover has an unbeliev-ably good memory, especially where sentiment is involved. This is perhaps a good moment to tell you that Moon Cancerians are never likely to throw away anything which holds special memories for them. This is just a warning in case you have a jealous streak and happen to come across a drawerful of old letters, cards or photographs. It probably doesn't mean a thing – other than that Cancerians (Sun *and* Moon) hate to throw away anything sentimental.

Life will be extremely comfortable and relaxed with a Cancer Lunar Lover. All the hugs, kisses and cuddles you could wish for will be a part of a normal day. This Lunar Lover can also be immensely sensual and you certainly won't have anything to complain about in your sex life. Also, their senses are so finely tuned that they instinctively know how you're feeling and what you need. It can be a marvellous, mystical lunar love affair all the way!

_____ *Lunar Lovers and their Sun signs* _____

The personality of your Cancer Lunar Lover will be modified by the position of the Sun in his or her horoscope:

ARIES SUN/CANCER MOON   The nurturing qualities of Cancer will still be there, but there will be an impatience and even aggressiveness which may take a while to get used to. The Cancer instinct is even more immediate.

TAURUS SUN/CANCER MOON   All the tender loving care you could want is contained in this combination, but that Taurus Sun might make this Lunar Lover fairly stubborn and self-opinionated too.

GEMINI SUN/CANCER MOON   The Gemini Sun makes this Lunar Lover more of an intellectual freedom-lover who is not quite so keen on settling down and being domesticated for ever more – so lots of mental stimulation is necessary here.

CANCER SUN/CANCER MOON   This conjunction of the Sun and Moon is beautiful for it is bound to infuse your Lunar Lover's personality with even greater tender loving care. On the other hand, fluctuations in mood could also be greater!

LEO SUN/CANCER MOON   Very, very emotional *and* very much a family-orientated person – the nurturing element is there in abundance. This Lunar Lover will be quite an extrovert, and have masses of pride too.

VIRGO SUN/CANCER MOON   Hopefully the fussy side of Virgo and the moody side of Cancer can both be toned down to produce a naturally caring and conscientious Lunar Lover.

LIBRA SUN/CANCER MOON   Someone who loves beauty, peace, harmony and a happy family home is often represented by this combination, although the Libran indecision could predominate.

SCORPIO SUN/CANCER MOON   This Lunar Lover will be incredibly intuitive but all that brooding intensity combined with fluctuating moods will keep you on your toes!

SAGITTARIUS SUN/CANCER MOON   Creativity blended with a good instinct abounds here. But the Sagittarius Sun gives a need for freedom which could come into conflict with the Moon's search for domestic security.

CAPRICORN SUN/CANCER MOON   A strong desire for settling down with the right person in the right place predominates. Emotional security is extremely important with this combination.

AQUARIUS SUN/CANCER MOON   Humanitarian principles come from the Aquarius Sun, but the emotional needs and feelings displayed by Cancer Lunar Lovers are somewhat more detached.

PISCES SUN/CANCER MOON   Warm, tender, romantic and full of care even if sometimes too much of a dreamer. A marvellous Lunar Lover as long as *you* can be the practical one in this duo!

How to keep your Lunar Lover by your side

DO:
- Learn about your own lunar personality to help it blend with his/hers
- Make your home surroundings a place where peace and tranquillity prevail
- Be romantic, sensitive and sentimental too
- Show you appreciate good food (and like cooking it too!)
- Remember all about those different phases of the Moon
- Remember *every* birthday, anniversary ad infinitum!

DON'T:
- Be too loud and over-powering – ever
- Spend a fortune on non-essential items
- Ever laugh at this Lunar Lover's sensitivity
- Be too fickle and fun loving
- Be emotionally cool – this Lunar Lover wants a soulmate in every way
- Ever criticise any of this Lunar Lover's family

THE MOON . . .
AND LEO

YOUR LUNAR INFLUENCES

When you were born, the Moon was in Leo, fifth sign of the Zodiac, and ruled by the Sun. So you are an interesting combination of Sun *and* Moon, plus of course all the other planets and planetary aspects which relate to your own particular horoscope.

Leo the Lion is a Masculine, Fixed, Positive, Fire sign – which, to put it mildly, means that most Leo Moon people are going to be sparkling, dynamic, generous, proud and often very bossy! It might occur to you that because the Moon is associated with the sign of Cancer (a Feminine, Negative, Cardinal, Water sign) there would be a definite conflict between your outer and inner personalities, but this doesn't necessarily apply. What it does mean is that you are sure to have an incredibly regal bearing deep inside, a definite nobility of demeanour which inevitably seems to come across. (Both Queen Elizabeth II and Prince Philip have the Moon in Leo, as did Mahatma Gandhi and Winston Churchill.) Since you are the proud possessor of a Leo Moon you are determined to be a star in one way or another. Apart from anything else you're sure to have more than an iota of star quality in your personality. And remember that the lunar influence represents what you feel inwardly even if you don't think you *are* showing it outwardly.

However, with a Leo Moon it's unlikely that even your supposedly deepest feelings remain completely hidden – it's not in your make-up to hide too much away.

The Moon in Leo is bound to create a flamboyant and dramatic sort of personality – perhaps overly so! Your Leo Moon is the emotional you, and you will gradually learn what that implies.

Since it is the Moon which endows you with your intuition, you have everything going for you to be a real winner. People with the Sun in Leo are great charmers, and with the Moon in Leo perhaps even more so. You seem to know *exactly* what to say at exactly the perfect time.

You react quickly to people and situations, but you're not terribly happy if someone else thinks they know better than you! You can be very stubborn, fixed in your opinions, and on occasions your pride can be your downfall! Therefore, it's important for you to get to know your inner self a little better and allow your lunar intuition to guide you in a positive way.

Your Leo Moon is a marvellous investment for the future. It can help to make you very successful in your emotional life and in business. But, it also means that you can be idealistic and if you're feeling too lazy to listen to your inner voice, you can be too impressionable and let down later by other people.

Positive and negative characteristics for Leo

Look at this checklist and see which characteristics apply to you:

The Positive Moon

- Lovable and generous
- Warm and witty
- Proud and dignified
- Glamorous and glorious!
- Lots of artistic flair

The Negative Moon

- Too showy and extravagant
- Bossy and domineering
- Snobbish
- Hates to take second place!
- Too conscious of status symbols

Both Moon and Sun Leos like to have authority and are not frightened of shouldering responsibility. With the Moon in Leo you take a great deal of pride in the kind of life-style you have, and it's bound to be one with lots of activity and lots of fun people to count as friends.

The Leo lunar influence will usually make you very striking, but a love of good food and expense account lunches can mean that you put on weight and are then too lazy to exercise. Listen to your inner voice – and remember that it's not good for you to be too inactive. The trouble is that Lunar Leos seem to have bursts of energy and then too many bursts of lazy idleness!

Your Leo emotions

Just like Aries and Sagittarius, Leo is a Fire sign, and as a Lunar Leo you're quite a firebrand as far as your emotions go. People with the Moon in Leo somehow always need to be in love. Since the Moon is the greatest possible influence on the way you feel inside, I think it's fairly true to say that you need to feel emotionally involved in _whatever_ you're doing.

But your Leo Moon can mean that because you have such incredibly proud feelings you also try not to reveal _too_ much of yourself in case it shows that even a Leo Moon can sometimes be weak. And weakness is not something you want to admit. From childhood you may have had the ability to smile at the world even if things behind the scenes are not too good at all. You also have a great depth of understanding for other people's moods and feelings, even if that bossy side of your personality does rear up from time to time.

There is also a lot of resilient inner strength to be gained from this position of the Moon, because you have the lunar feminine intuition combined with the positive outgoing sunny characteristics belonging to the sign of Leo. So you're quite a formidable force to face.

The deep innermost feelings of a Lunar Leo are also a force to be reckoned with and you need to keep in touch with your lunar emotions if you are to understand yourself well. You're just as emotional as any Water sign (Cancer, Scorpio, Pisces) and, at times, just as impatient as Aries. Sometimes, however, you put so much stock on outward appearances that you don't allow that voice deep inside you to help you find greater peace and tranquillity. You are inclined to want to live your life in the fast lane, and you forget about balancing your inner flow of energy. You need to nurture your inner being more, to concentrate on achieving greater peace and harmony within.

Sometimes people accuse you of being egotistical – but so often it is simply that you want to be appreciated and loved by the people *you* love and appreciate. Both Sun and Moon Leos love to give, often more than to receive. However, when you learn to understand your inner being better, you will probably find you don't need that confirmation of how other people see you, as your sense of self-worth will be enough. Allow the influence of your Leo Moon to give you the chance to know yourself better, perhaps through meditation.

Your career

The Moon also relates to your inner self professionally – the direction in which you want to go in life. If you're a typical Lunar Leo you need to be in a position of power in some way, high up in a company, or self-employed in a successful capacity. Often extremely creative, you want to exploit this to the full and you'll work full out to achieve your ambitions. Leo Moons often gravitate towards the worlds of show business or art; also fashion, PR or hotel management. But sometimes the lazy side of your nature can come to the fore all too easily and prevent you from fulfilling your dreams!

The famous Leo pride is evident in the way you tackle your work, and whilst no-one could say that you're as fussy as a Virgo, you certainly take great pains to ensure that everything is as perfect as possible. That also means that you're unlikely to face criticism, which a Lunar Leo never appreciates.

Your lunar influence is a very positive one as it inspires you to search for a career which is going to fulfil you in the best possible way. And it instils in you the ability to talk to people from all walks of life.

Your family and friends

The Cancerian influence of the Moon in sunny, sparkling Leo will imbue you with a very great desire to hold on to family ties and to be extremely loyal, lovable and supportive to all your relatives. You will invariably behave in the same way with your friends, but sometimes you are a little bit too impressed by who somebody is, and what they do, rather than just accepting them for themselves.

You may have believed that you had to live up to your parents' expectations of you, and sometimes felt that the amount of love you received was related to this. As a parent you are likely to be very loving yourself, but you may retain this need to feel proud of your offspring.

You are probably very receptive to the feelings of both family and friends and there could sometimes be an almost telepathic link between you.

Leo lunar love

To a lovable, generous Leo being in love is the most wonderful thing in the whole world. You positively sparkle with happiness and want to share that happiness with everyone around you.

Your Leo Moon means you want to give bucketfuls of love to the people you care for, and when you find the right soulmate it's caviar and champagne time!

The only snag is that whilst you want to put the object of your desire on a pedestal, you also like to be treated rather like a god or goddess yourself!

As much as you love *love*, you also enjoy the idea of being powerful, and out of all the lunar signs you are invariably the one who is most likely to be larger-than-life. Personally, I've always felt that you would do best with a Lunar Lover who is *not* going to give you star treatment all the time and will learn to deal with you gently, but firmly, when that sometimes inflated Lunar Leo ego gets out of hand.

Finally, remember to stay in touch with your inner being, the soul part of you which is the real, real you.

Lunar relationships

Try to find a Moon Lover whose personality can blend well with yours. The following will act as a guide:

LEO MOON/ARIES MOON   Both of you can be impatient, proud and sometimes a little too flirtatious – but you will also both work hard to show that true love between two strong Fire signs can be a brilliant combination.

LEO MOON/TAURUS MOON   A Taurean Lunar Lover may be slow to respond, but has real staying power when it comes to love relationships. You're both fixed in your opinions, both sometimes lazy – but lovable!

LEO MOON/GEMINI MOON   Life could be rather like being on a helter-skelter – lots of mental stimulation and certainly lots of activity. Both of you love parties but are not so good at dealing with the routine of everyday life.

LEO MOON/CANCER MOON   The Cancer Lunar Lover will be soft, sensitive and a beautiful soulmate as long as you're not averse to being overly protected by the one you love, *and* as long as you understand about Full Moons and Cancer Moon people!

LEO MOON/LEO MOON   Two Leo Lunar Lovers together will be incredibly loving and giving people, but you need to watch out for danger signals if you both want to be on top of that pedestal. A little more 'share and share alike' will help.

LEO MOON/VIRGO MOON   Since you don't appreciate being criticized, you need to be sure from the start that this Lunar Lover shares your *raison d'etre* and that there aren't too many bones of contention between you emotionally.

LEO MOON/LIBRA MOON   A warm and loving relationship can develop easily here, with both of you appreciating the little luxuries of life and finding beauty in each other and in the world of art.

LEO MOON/SCORPIO MOON   The flamboyance of your personality may be at odds with Scorpio's burning intensity, and a Scorpio Lunar Lover may also be overly jealous, even when there is no reason for mistrust.

LEO MOON/SAGITTARIUS MOON   With this relationship it could almost be a laugh a minute, but remember that although Sagittarius needs to feel inwardly free, it's also the sign of 'the higher mind'. Sagittarius needs to be in tune with that inner you.

LEO MOON/CAPRICORN MOON   The Capricorn Lunar Lover's approach to love is somehow more practical and philosophical than yours. Somehow that Capricorn Moon instils an inner belief that romantic love is what dreams are made of but that reality is a different thing.

LEO MOON/AQUARIUS MOON   Two opposing Moons, with Aquarius finding it much tougher than you to be spontaneously affectionate and physical when love comes along. Try to spend the time drawing out those deep-rooted Aquarian feelings – opposites *do* attract.

LEO MOON/PISCES MOON   Your idea of romantic love is very likely the same as Pisces who is the sort of person to worship every word you say and be quite happy to walk in your footsteps! But it often works better when the man is Leo and the woman Pisces. (Leo Moon ladies often feel they need a stronger personality.)

THE LEO LUNAR LOVER
———————o———————

The Leo Lunar Lover could be the most exciting person you've ever met in your entire life – an extrovert, a larger-than-life dynamo who will whirl you off your feet into a whole new wonderful way of living. This Lunar Lover truly believes that love really does make the world go round. Both male and female Moon Leos are happiest when they are in love!

Your Leo Lunar Lover is the second of the Fire signs, following on from Aries and preceding Sagittarius. The Leo Moon when combined with the power of the Sun, the natural ruler of Leo, will be a vital force. This Moon Lover not only loves to bequeath love, he or she wants to receive it in abundance, and to say that your Leo Lunar Lover likes to be given plenty of attention at all times is a huge understatement.

Since Leo is ruled by the Sun, the inner emotions of this personality will invariably be very positive. Even when this Lunar Lover goes through difficult times which might throw more sensitive Moon signs into a really down mood, your Leo Lunar Lover has the ability to throw off sadness or sulkiness and come up sparkling. That's not to say that their personality is insensitive and unfeeling – not at all – but just as the sun will shine again after a storm, so your Leo Lunar Lover's sunny personality will shine through again after a difficult patch.

One very important thing to remember if you've fallen for someone with the Moon in Leo is that there is a very idealistic side to the Leo Lunar nature, especially when it comes to love and romance. Sex alone is not enough, but it is definitely very important to both Sun and Moon Leos who can be just as sensual as they are sensitive!

They also need to feel proud, not only of their own prowess as lovers, but of yours too. Physical compatibility is very important and, because Leo Lunar Lovers have a deep and abiding sense of honour, so too is the sanctity of marriage or a deep long-lasting relationship.

The Leo Lunar Lover may appear on the surface to want and enjoy the good things of life too much to think of settling down, but deep down those lunar emotions are invariably yearning for an ideal soulmate with whom to share the beauties of sunrise and sunset. A lovely side to your Leo Lunar Lover's personality is the ability to sweep you off your feet with wonderful displays of tenderness, affection and romance which you will never forget. In return, this Moon Lover wants to be admired, respected, and – of course – adored!

_____ *Recognizing a Leo Lunar Lover* _____

In one way or another the Leo Lunar Lover will always be the centre of attention. Moon Leos invariably stand out in a crowd, and their regal bearing makes it even easier to guess their sign! This regal bearing is inherent in their make-up and impossible to hide. It is unlikely to be lessened by any other aspects in their own particular chart.

Very often, just as with Sun Leos, hairstyles can be a sign. The hair of Leo Moon ladies is often like a lion's mane, and often tawny too, whilst Leo Moon men can have not only quite a thick head of hair but also a beard!

But it's probably that flamboyant, extrovert, sparkling, dazzling personality, attracting an admiring entourage with the greatest of ease, which makes recognizing a Leo Lunar Lover such a simple procedure. It won't take you long to realize that the Leo Lunar Lover is also an incurable romantic with a proud and fiery disposition and lots of passion too.

_____ *Captivating a Leo Lunar Lover* _____

If you make it clear from the start that you're more than happy to place your Leo Lunar Lover on the pedestal to which he or she is convinced they belong, you're halfway there. You'd better make it known that you're also quite happy to be placed on a similar pedestal, for the Leo Lunar Lover wants to worship as well as be worshipped!

Be bright and sparkling, but use your own intuition too and try not to overshadow your Leo Lunar Lover. Whilst male and female Leo Moons love to see that the object of their affections is attractive to other people too, never forget that they can be very jealous and Leo pussycats can turn into roaring lions if they feel you're making a play for anyone but them.

Always be warm and loving, for a cool and unemotional personality would never fare too well with fiery Leo. Always be honest too, for love and honour go hand-in-hand with the Leo Moon.

First impressions mean a great deal and your Leo Lunar Lover is most likely to be attracted to your outer personality, the way you look and behave. But to captivate his or her Lunar emotions there has to be more than just physical attraction. Your Leo Lunar Lover is not simply searching for a captive audience, he or she needs to know that the two of you will be able to turn romantic dreams into reality, and that you're prepared to take the time and effort to understand the inner needs of the Leo Moon.

Therefore, to totally captivate the Leo Lunar Lover it's important to be warm, witty *and* wise. Always give praise when it's due but don't be afraid to criticize when you feel that the Leo Moon in your life is being unjust. Don't let yourself be bossed around, for proving that you're an equal and not about to be dominated by the regal ruler of the Zodiac will make you even more irresistible.

Life with a Leo Lunar Lover

Life is never *all* sunshine, even if you are living with this Lunar Lover whose sign of Leo is ruled by the Sun itself. However, there will be so many times when you can count your blessings that you won't moan too much the rest of time.

The most important thing to remember is that to both Sun and Moon Leos their home is their castle, and your Leo Lunar Lover is extremely sensitive to his or her home surroundings. Not only does it have to be pleasing to the eye, but it has to feel just right too.

Anyone with the Moon in Leo will have an intrinsic sense of beauty, an artistic flair that is bound to be reflected in their domestic ambience. The decor is sure to be interesting, and some Lunar Leos do tend to go rather over the top and make a show of opulence that can be a little hard to take. Status symbols tend sometimes to be too important to this sign!

Hopefully you will be someone who is ready, willing and able to entertain, for entertaining is something that anyone with a Leo Moon is usually justifiably proud of. If you intend sharing a Leo Lunar Lover's life, then it's bound to be expected that you do your fair share, and that you enjoy it too.

But think how great it is to be with someone who showers you with love and is one of the most generous signs of the whole Zodiac; and how enjoyable it is to know that the person you live with takes so much pride in making sure that your life together is the best it can possibly be.

Because your Leo Lunar Lover is such a proud person, he or she is unlikely to be incredibly dependent on you. In fact, the typical Lunar Lover born under this sign is much happier giving than receiving.

Life with a Leo Lunar Lover will mean that you're living with some-one who will invariably try to provide you with everything that money can buy, and sometimes it might be up to you to curb unnecessary bouts of extravagance.

Life with the lovable lion of the Zodiac can be full of so much sunshine and happiness, that you're bound to do everything you can to ensure that love doesn't fly out of the window, but becomes more soul-enhancing every day. You'll enjoy basking in the warmth of all that Leo has to give – and giving plenty in return as well.

_____ *Lunar Lovers and their Sun signs* _____

The personality of your Leo Lunar Lover will be modified by the position of the Sun in his or her horoscope:

ARIES SUN/LEO MOON   This Lunar Lover seeks the limelight but is an enthusiastic and enterprising personality, if at times a little too bossy! However, deep inside there is a sensitive soul too . . .

TAURUS SUN/LEO MOON   Two Fixed signs rule this Lunar Lover, and he or she will be pretty rigid in their opinions and ideals, but emotionally it's a secure combination.

GEMINI SUN/LEO MOON   Definitely a 'people person' who will always gravitate to where the action is. Once you pin them down you will have a chance to discover whether you share the same deep yearnings.

CANCER SUN/LEO MOON   The Moon's influence will be very strong here, and this Lunar Lover will be very emotional, strongly attached to home and family, but could be moody too!

LEO SUN/LEO MOON   This Lunar Lover could be a real extrovert, sparkly and sociable. It might be hard to draw them out on subjects like the meaning of life and spiritual matters.

VIRGO SUN/LEO MOON   The critical and analytical Virgo Sun could sometimes dampen this Lunar Lover's flamboyant freedom of expression and inhibit him or her from revealing deep emotions.

LIBRA SUN/LEO MOON   An irresistible charmer and an incredible romantic – two characteristics bound to be possessed by a Lunar Lover with the Libra/Leo combination.

SCORPIO SUN/LEO MOON   It could be really hard to refuse this Lunar Lover anything they might want. This is a very determined, intense, magnetic and unmistakably powerful personality.

SAGITTARIUS SUN/LEO MOON   Two Fire signs are highlighted here, and a Lunar Lover with this combination will be flamboyant, fiery and fun to be with. Trying to reach that inner personality may be hard at first, but exciting too.

CAPRICORN SUN/LEO MOON   This Lunar Lover will be a dominant personality determined to be the boss. It could be considered a weakness for them to reveal any emotional insecurities even if they do exist.

AQUARIUS SUN/LEO MOON   A freedom-loving individual who may be married more than once. Attractive and outgoing, but there could easily be a fairly stubborn side to this personality as well.

PISCES SUN/LEO MOON   It's love and romance all the way here. However, problems could arise if this Lunar Lover's compassion and tenderness coincide with a generosity that leads to financial extravagance!

How to keep your Lunar Lover by your side

DO:

- Remember a Leo Lunar Lover is always incredibly proud, especially of their deepest beliefs and feelings
- Show that you know how to appreciate the beautiful things in life
- Plan happy occasions for New Moon time (when the Moon is closest to Leo's planetary ruler, the Sun)
- Let your Lunar Lover feel he or she will always be Numero Uno in your life
- Be a good listener when Leo lets forth all their romantic inner yearnings
- Try to always retain a good sense of humour

DON'T:

- Ever try to dampen this Lunar Lover's natural zest for life
- Let yourself be bossed around too much!
- Be shy about showing gestures of affection or saying how you feel when you're in a relationship with this Lunar Lover
- Laugh at Leo if it's going to cause offence, especially in public!
- Be moody . . . Leo likes to show a sunny face to the world, and wants you to do the same
- Be neglectful about your Leo's needs – in any way at all

THE MOON . . .
AND VIRGO

YOUR LUNAR INFLUENCES

When you were born, the Moon was in Virgo, sixth sign of the Zodiac. Virgo is a Feminine, Mutable, Negative, Earth sign, and its plantetary ruler is Mercury, that winged messenger of the Gods.

Your Moon sign represents your gut reactions. With a Virgo Moon you try so hard to be perfect in every possible way, but don't be quite so insistent on extremely high standards for it could be hard for anyone else to live up to them. Besides, you can miss out on a lot of fun too!

Because of the astrological association between the Moon and the sign of Cancer (a Feminine, Negative, Cardinal, Water sign) there could sometimes be a problem. You are going to analyse your emotions so much that instead of getting on with whatever has to be done at the time, you tend to sit and worry.

Virgo is the sign of the critic and analyst, and to have the Moon in the sign of the Virgin will certainly ensure that criticism is definitely part of your make-up. But try to resolve not to be quite so critical of everyone, including yourself!

Virgo is also the sign of service, and the influence of your Moon will make you an incredibly caring person, willing to devote yourself untiringly to your chosen work and to looking after the people closest to you.

Because Mercury, planet of communication, rules Virgo, there is no doubt that you have a fantastic memory and that your mind is very alert. Your instinct is usually very good, so listen to your inner voice telling you to have more faith and learn to let go of that need to analyse every single little thing. Since the Moon relates to your inner needs, it really is important to know what yours are. Once you do, it will be time to stop questioning and to have confidence in what your higher self tells you in those quiet moments when you allow it to come through.

Your lunar influence can be incredibly positive for it gives you the ability to see through delusions. You attain fantastic insight when you trust what you feel and see and when you use the benefits of your discriminative powers. These bestow greater sagacity, sensitivity and perception on you and help you to avoid bias, prejudice and intolerance.

Your Virgo Moon endows you with a great sense of logic, and this, combined with the psychic ability which will certainly be developed by listening to that inner voice, can be a great asset in your life.

But people born with the Moon, or the Sun, in this sign often dwell on the need for perfection to such an extent that there is a chance of blaming themselves and feeling guilty for not achieving their ideals. When this happens, you can become much too introspective, and too much of a worrier. Try not to be one of those Lunar Virgo men or women who are continually falling prey to psychosomatic health problems.

With the Moon in Virgo it is almost certain that you do have a profound interest in health matters and in keeping fit, and that is fine when it is in a positive way! It's when you become obsessed by this or that new diet or fitness routine that you become your own worst enemy and invariably a bore to others.

There is an immense need for security in your make-up, perhaps more so than with any other Moon sign, and if that security is threatened in any way you really do get into a panic. That is just the time to allow your lunar influence to help you, and a few moments spent in quiet meditation will not only calm your mind but allow the right advice to filter through.

Positive and negative characteristics for Virgo

Look at this checklist and see which characteristics apply to you:

The Positive Moon

- Very hardworking
- Idealistic
- Health-conscious
- Discriminating
- Intellectually alert

The Negative Moon

- Too much of a workaholic
- A perfectionist – painfully so!
- Too obsessive about health matters
- Overly critical
- An abundance of self-doubt

Your Virgo emotions

Like Taurus and Capricorn, Virgo is an Earth sign, and as a Lunar Virgo your emotional feet will be firmly placed on the ground! There is a strongly practical side to your emotional nature for above all else you are searching for security in every possible way.

Enjoy being and accepting yourself for who you are, and *like* that person too! Everyone has imperfections of one kind or another, some can be changed and some cannot. Think about these words from Desiderata, 'God, grant me the serenity to accept the things I cannot change, the courage to change the things I can, and the wisdom to know the difference' and plan to use them in your own daily life.

The influence of your Virgo Moon instils you with wonderfully analytical abilities, which when used in a positive way can be immensely beneficial. And, your innermost feelings can be just as passionate as those of a Fire sign, or equally as tenderly romantic as any Water sign.

Learning more about your inner self can be a marvellously enlightening process and is worth every minute of the time you're prepared to give to it. So stop worrying and get on with the rest of your life!

Your career

As a Lunar Virgo you will be just as much of a workaholic as most people born with the Sun in this sign. But somehow the lunar influence can almost deceive you into thinking you're not good enough, not working hard enough, and will never achieve your objectives. Stop striving quite so hard, enjoy what you are doing, and always remember that even a Lunar Virgo is allowed to take a vacation.

The lunar influence in one's career relates to feeling motivated – and of course you are motivated by serving in the way you know best. With a Virgo Moon, you're often very good at accountancy, book-keeping and any kind of office work. Publishing, the field of health, and teaching will all suit the Virgo Moon, as would using your powers of criticism in the entertainment world as a theatre, film or TV critic.

But to be really successful, you must learn to have more confidence in your abilities, and also to have more faith in the abilities of those with whom you work.

Your family and friends

The Cancerian influence of the Moon in competent, critical Virgo is certain to have instilled in you a deep-rooted desire for a secure, comfortable home which is going to be exceedingly well-run if you have anything to say about it!

As a parent you certainly strive to be the ideal mother or father, but here again you need to listen to your inner voice, and allow yourself to be loved and respected for simply being you.

With friends you sometimes tend to worry about putting your foot in it by saying or doing the wrong thing, so try to let your hair down a little more often and relax and have fun!

Virgo lunar love

Virtuous, pensive Lunar Virgo, falling in love is invariably a serious business for you, but it doesn't have to be so serious that you continually analyse every aspect of it. 'Is this for real?', 'Will it last?', 'Is he or she really the right person for me?'. Sometimes you worry yourself silly about the most unnecessary things, and consequently diminish the beautiful, intrinsic parts of being in love. And that can mean being in love with life, with beauty, with art, nature, people, and not simply in a love relationship.

Listen seriously to your soul feelings, and stop trying to create difficulties for yourself. The influence of the Moon with its romantic hues can truly enhance your life if you allow it to do so.

Of course, the Moon can sometimes create an illusory influence too. But that's where your Moon in Virgo will use its discriminatory powers to ensure you don't need to be fooled. All the more reason to trust your instincts and enjoy being in love.

Lunar relationships

Try to find a Moon Lover whose personality can blend well with yours. The following will act as a guide:

VIRGO MOON/ARIES MOON   This relationship will need lots of initial nurturing for the Aries Lunar Lover may appear almost too aggressive, inconsiderate and impatient for you.

VIRGO MOON/TAURUS MOON   Two Earth signs both prepared to take their time for a good relationship to get off the ground, but all that Taurean sensuality may be unexpected.

VIRGO MOON/GEMINI MOON   Intellectually this is a sparkling combination, although the apparent flightiness of Gemini will no doubt give you something to worry about!

VIRGO MOON/CANCER MOON   A mutual desire for security will create a common bond. Cancer's moodiness combined with your somewhat pernickety ways will both need to be toned down to create true love!

VIRGO MOON/LEO MOON   Learn to relax more and enjoy the playfulness and enthusiasm of this Lunar Lover. Provided you're prepared to put Leo on a pedestal you will have lots of enjoyment in your life.

VIRGO MOON/VIRGO MOON   If you both manage to stop analysing your positive and negative characteristics, you should find plenty to like and understand in each other.

VIRGO MOON/LIBRA MOON   A Libran Lunar Lover can bring great peace and harmony into your life. So what if you do have to cope with a little indecision and a few extravagant ways?

VIRGO MOON/SCORPIO MOON   Both of you have a private side and don't like anyone to pry too much. Scorpio's stongly sexual personality could also be too intense for someone like you.

VIRGO MOON/SAGITTARIUS MOON   Here you definitely have to try and adopt a more free and easy approach to life. You can learn a lot from the positive optimism of Sagittarius.

VIRGO MOON/CAPRICORN MOON   The influence of Earth affects you both. Material desires combine with a practical approach to ensure that this relationship can work on all levels if you both unwind a little more.

VIRGO MOON/AQUARIUS MOON   You analyse your emotional feelings too much whilst the Aquarian feelings can be too coolly detached.

VIRGO MOON/PISCES MOON   Opposite signs of the Zodiac often do attract. Learn to be more romantic so that you can truly enjoy this Lunar Lover's tender caring ways.

THE VIRGO LUNAR LOVER
———————o———————

The Virgo Lunar Lover is definitely someone you are not going to forget in a hurry! At first you might feel that this Moon personality is just too much to take. You're not quite sure that you feel completely at ease with someone who is so obviously summing you up and analysing every little part of your personality.

However, you can invariably be sure that your Virgo Lunar Lover is not going to be a fly-by-night gallivanter who rushes from relationship to relationship like a moth to a flame. Always bear in mind that Virgo is an Earth sign, and even the ethereal, intangible Moon is not going to dilute this Lunar Lover's deep inner yearning for a genuine soulmate.

Virgo Lunar Lovers of both sexes have finely tuned senses. They abhor loud noises, people smoking in restaurants and untidiness! And they can be fairly obsessive about what is good, and not good, to eat. It's best to be warned about all this in advance so that you can decide whether it's all worthwhile.

But this is obviously the moment to tell you that it *can* be worthwhile and life with a Virgo Lunar Lover could easily turn into one of the most life-enhancing relationships you've ever known.

You see, far and above anything else, someone with the Moon in Virgo cannot help being an idealistic perfectionist. It is an intrinsic part of the Virgo nature, and since the Moon's influence on the emotions is so enormous, your Virgo Lunar Lover is desperately hoping that true love is here to stay every time he or she embarks on an emotional involvement.

Vulnerability can be very strong with the Virgo Moon, especially if this Lunar Lover has been hurt in the past. Anyone with the Moon in this sign has an extremely retentive memory. They can also have an over-abundance of guilt, often self-inflicted, if past relationships have gone disastrously wrong, even through no fault of their own.

There is another thing you will probably have to accept, which is that many Lunar Virgo Lovers have a major commitment to their work – in fact romance might often come a pretty poor second.

However, whatever you might have thought about Virgo being the sign of the Virgin, you don't really have to worry that Virgoans are going to be the biggest prudes of all time when it comes to sex! For Virgo is an Earth sign just like Taurus, and there is no doubt that sensuality is an integral part of an Earth sign's character. Besides, since Virgo the critic hates to be criticized, the Virgo Lunar Lover's actual love-making with the right partner will leave you with no cause for complaint!

_____ *Recognizing a Virgo Lunar Lover* _____

Even when this Lunar Lover is giving the most obvious come hither signs, there is bound to be a critically appraising look in those Virgo eyes.

The Virgo Lunar Lover isn't usually the most outgoing and extrovert soul, and it isn't really tremendously difficult to recognize the Virgo characteristics. Criticizing other people is invariably one of them, but so too is a tendency to undervalue themselves and be immensely self-critical too.

It probably won't take you too long to realize also that this Lunar Lover is a worrier, perhaps a workaholic, often overly fussy about health, food and diet, and whose eye for detail is surpassed by none. So, always remember to give praise when it's due – there's nothing like it for bringing a smile to this Lunar Lover's face.

You won't find a shoelace dangling, or a missing button on a Virgo Lunar Lover! Usually impeccably dressed themselves, you'll know you've met someone with the Moon in Virgo when their eyes seem to bore straight on to that tiny mark you hoped no-one would notice when you put on a favourite outfit.

Yes, the Virgo Lunar Lover is a bit of a nit-picker, but although a few disapproving looks at the start might be rather off-putting, it's worth persevering and not allowing yourself to be discouraged.

You'll soon discover that this Lunar Lover might not on the surface seem to be the jolliest person you've ever met, but there is a bright and sparkling humour lurking below the surface, and they are a great sparring partner when it comes to intellectual debates.

_____ *Captivating a Virgo Lunar Lover* _____

If the object of your desires was born with the Moon in Virgo, the very first thing you need to do is read up on this sign's lunar personality. It isn't the easiest in the world, but then anything worth having is worth working for – something with which a Virgo Lunar Lover will be in total agreement.

If being the centre of attention, flirting outrageously with all and sundry is something you can't live without, perhaps you'd better stop right here and aim to captivate a different Moon lover, for that sort of behaviour is something that is usually not only alien to Virgo but unacceptable too.

But, if you had started to worry that the average Virgo Lunar Lover is perhaps going to turn out a bore – forget it. Richard Burton had a Virgo Moon, as do Robert Redford and Shirley MacLaine!

One of the most important things to remember is to always be yourself, for anyone with the Moon in Virgo hates airs and graces of any kind, *and* can invariably see right through them anyway.

You need to cultivate the sort of humour that proves you keep up with what is going on in the world. The Virgo Lunar Lover doesn't suffer fools terribly easily!

It's also essential to show that you are a genuinely caring person who dislikes playing around with other peoples' feelings and emotions, for a Virgo Lunar Lover is looking for a soulmate and not simply a few nights of passion!

———— Life with a Virgo Lunar Lover ————

By now, the more faint-hearted amongst you might have started to wonder if you would have to live with a paragon of virtue whose painstaking and analytical ways would somehow make life hell. No way – deep down the Virgo Lunar Lover just wants to love and give love as much as every other sign, so don't give up.

However, it's probably true to say that since your Virgo Lunar Lover does set him or herself impeccably high standards in just about everything, it's worth making a bit of an effort if you do happen to be excessively untidy, lazy and too much of a party-goer.

Once you've settled into a routine with a Virgo Moon you don't have to fear you're in for a boring life though.

The Virgo Lunar Lover can be amazingly sentimental, once you've got down to those soul depths. Mutual trust and understanding will lead to a depth of feeling between you that will continue to grow ever stronger, and you certainly don't have to fear that because this Moon personality is often so coolly intelligent, love, romance and earthy passion are going to be lacking in your relationship.

This Lunar Lover may be an expert at laying down the laws on vice and virtue, but will be no shrinking violet when it comes to a mentally and physically compatible involvement with a soulmate.

Of course, living with anyone with the Moon (or Sun) in Virgo does mean that you will probably need to keep a well-stocked medicine cabinet. It's not that this Lunar Lover is going to be ill a lot, just that he or she might easily worry about the possibility! And Virgo does like to know the ingredients in new recipes . . .

But life with a Virgo Lunar Lover means you will be with someone who will prove their dedication in a myriad of different ways once you've reached below the surface and communicated with their inner being.

Don't ever forget that this Earth-ruled sign can also be very passionate, and if you thought that someone who appears to analyse emotions so much could never be jealous – forget it! The Virgo Lunar Lover might not necessarily like to admit it, but jealousy can figure quite strongly in the make-up of a Virgo Moon.

However, once you've both agreed to compromise a little on your own particular faults and foibles which irritate the other – why would you want to make your Virgo Lunar Lover jealous in the first place? For, as you'll discover, you can have a very loving and emotionally rewarding relationship for many moons to come!

_____ *Lunar Lovers and their Sun signs* _____

The personality of your Virgo Lunar Lover will be modified by the position of the Sun in his or her horoscope:

ARIES SUN/VIRGO MOON   Aries tends to act in an enthusiastic and impulsive way, so that this Lunar Lover won't spend quite so much time analysing the personality of others, or indeed themselves, but may still feel emotionally insecure!

TAURUS SUN/VIRGO MOON   There is a strong earthy rationality here, and emotionally this Lunar Lover will have great depths of feeling that they yearn to express.

GEMINI SUN/VIRGO MOON   A Mercury-ruled combination giving rise to an intellectual, a mentally communicative personality, who is sometimes slow in allowing any form of passion to show.

CANCER SUN/VIRGO MOON   This is a very caring personality, with a deep-rooted need for a soulmate to share a domestic nest. Sentimental with an amazingly retentive memory.

LEO SUN/VIRGO MOON   A proud and powerful personality who will leave no stone unturned to achieve his or her objectives. This combination will produce a deeply loyal and loving Lunar Lover.

VIRGO SUN/VIRGO MOON   Encourage this Lunar Lover to have more faith and belief in his or her inner voice and in you too! But be prepared for lots of analysing along the way.

LIBRA SUN/VIRGO MOON   A love of peace and harmony will prevent this Lunar Lover from being inordinately critical, and there might even be a few welcome traits of laziness!

SCORPIO SUN/VIRGO MOON   An intensity of purpose is magnified and the emotions of this personality run extremely deep. Never play around with this Lunar Lover's sensitive feelings.

SAGITTARIUS SUN/VIRGO MOON   The open, frank and optimistic personality bequeathed by a Sagittarius Sun will soften the Virgo Moon. But this Lunar Lover could be quite a 'know-it-all'!

CAPRICORN SUN/VIRGO MOON   Two Earth signs combine once more to create a 'feet firmly on the ground' Lunar Lover with a deep inner need for stability and security, both romantically *and* materially.

AQUARIUS SUN/VIRGO MOON   The humanitarian Aquarian and the Virgo who wants to serve merge here. However both influences can create a Lunar Lover who finds it hard to say 'I love you' and will need drawing out with care.

PISCES SUN/VIRGO MOON   Opposite Zodiac signs, opposite personalities. But the romantic and instinctive Pisces Sun can soften the more
analytical Virgo Moon in a truly beautiful way.

How to keep your Lunar Lover by your side

DO:
- Make it plain that you want to understand your Lunar Lover's personality through and through
- Resolve to be perfect, at least once a week
- Be prepared to cultivate tidy and well-organized ways
- Learn to rise above any criticism with a smile
- Be faithful
- Admire Virgo's dedication to duty

DON'T:
- Create any embarrassing situations when you're with this Lunar Lover
- Be too much of a critic yourself, one out of two is enough!
- Be too flirtatious with other people, Virgo will be off
- Ever forget a promise made to this Lunar Lover
- Be lazy and let yourself go
- Accuse him or her of hypochondria or fussiness over food

THE MOON . . .
AND LIBRA

YOUR LUNAR INFLUENCES

When you were born, the Moon was in Libra, seventh sign of the Zodiac, and house of marriage and partnerships. Libra is a Masculine, Cardinal, Positive, Air sign, and its planetary ruler is Venus, Goddess of Love.

To have the Moon in Libra is to have an inherent desire for romance in your life. Giving and receiving love is an absolute must for a Lunar Libran. You can be one of the most caring souls in the whole Zodiac, but since Libra is the sign of relationships, you do expect to be treated the same way in return.

Because of the astrological association between the Moon, and the sign of Cancer, as a Lunar Libran you are not only a person who needs partners and companions in order to feel truly fulfilled, but you deeply desire a secure home base too.

More than most of the other Lunar signs, you long for a safe domestic haven, which will aim to be a place of peace and harmony for yourself and those you love.

Since Venus is the planetary ruler of Libra, you will be endowed with the Venusian qualities of love and beauty. Somehow your lunar instincts will always be to search for the beauty in each and every situation. Also, diplomacy and the ability to mediate brilliantly will be amongst your most positive qualities.

However, before you start to bask in the glory of all these compliments, it is also necessary to warn you that the vacillating quality which is common to both Sun and Moon Librans is of essence especially strong in the Lunar Libran since the Moon affects your very deepest feelings and emotions.

It is really important for you to have more trust in your Higher Self, to meditate in those peaceful and harmonious surroundings so essential for our wellbeing, and – once you feel you have the answers to your silent questions – to have the faith and perhaps courage to act upon them.

Your Lunar Moon also bestows upon you a strong sense of self-preservation. There is, surprisingly, a toughness within your make-up which usually belies your appearance and your outward attitude. All the more reason to allow your inner voice to guide and direct you.

For all your tactful, charming and diplomatic ways, there comes a moment when, having allowed your lunar intuition to shine through, you will refuse to be swayed from your decision or point of view.

Positive and negative characteristics for Libra

Look at this checklist and see which characteristics apply to you:

The Positive Moon

- Charm personified
- Diplomatic and tactful
- Loving and romantic
- Love of art and beauty
- An ideal partner
- Inwardly ambitious

The Negative Moon

- Manipulating through your charm!
- Vacillating through indecision
- Emotionally insecure
- Can have very extravagant tastes
- Feels inadequate alone
- Sometimes outwardly lazy

As a Lunar Libran it's definitely safe to say that you have immense personal appeal. It's also important though for you to admit to yourself that you do sometimes feel unnecessarily insecure and out of balance without a partner who you are convinced could balance your Libran scales correctly.

Sometimes you can become too dependent on a partner for this very reason, whereas if you genuinely ask that voice deep within for support you will become surprisingly resilient and a great deal more adept at controlling your own destiny.

It will certainly mean that you don't feel you have to stick with someone simply because you feel you cannot cope alone.

Your Libra emotions

Just like Gemini and Aquarius, Libra is an Air sign, and as a Lunar Libran you are, without any doubt, a communicator. In fact you have no qualms over communicating about almost anything, but most especially if you see, or feel, that injustice is being done. It's all to do with those Libran scales (the symbol of Libra) which you desperately want to keep balanced.

But, unfortunately, being a Lunar Libran, trouble can arise if you become convinced that life without a soulmate is almost no life at all. You already know that Libra relates to the seventh house of marriage and partnerships, but there is no hard and fast astrological ruling which says that emotionally you're no good if you don't have the right partner by your side. Be a partner to yourself, to that inner you, which, influenced by the instinctive powers of the Moon, can endow you with a sense of self-worth possibly greater than any other person could do anyway!

It really is worth the time and trouble to nurture yourself a little more, instead of being quite so preoccupied in giving love to someone else or continually searching for a romantic crock of gold at the end of the rainbow.

Besides, craving for love and romance and emotional security all in one beautiful combination can sometimes lead you into trouble. Lunar Librans can sometimes be far too inclined to stay with the wrong partner just because you fear the thought of life without them.

Your lunar intuition and instincts will be an invaluable guide when your help is needed by the people closest to you. These inner voices can be your best friends if you let them, and will help you to balance those Libran scales in the best possible way.

Your career

The lunar influence relates to your innermost motivations, and as a Lunar Libran you will be drawn most strongly to anything of a creative and artistic nature. Your natural sense of charm could make you an ideal salesperson as long as you believe in what you are selling. And that Libran sense of justice would make you a good lawyer. Other Lunar Libran careers might include diplomat, musician, hairdresser, public relations, fashion and personnel.

Your surroundings are important to you – dusty, noisy and generally unpleasing surroundings offend your aesthetic senses and you invariably enjoy working in a partnership far more than working on your own. Of course there are Lunar Librans who are perfectly happy being self-employed, but as the seventh sign of the Zodiac, you really do prefer to work alongside someone you both like and respect.

Sometimes the vacillating quality of your nature can prevent you from achieving your highest potential, for whilst being as ambitious as any other sign, there does exist within your personality the ability to succumb to a lazy streak.

Your family and friends

'Share and share alike' would be a good Libran motto. Your charm has been with you since the moment you entered this world, and it's sure to be lavished on both family and friends throughout your life, unless of course you feel you have a genuine reason to withhold it!

Your family will probably be quite a close-knit group, since there are few moments when you feel like being a loner.

As a parent you are usually especially kind and loving, sometimes a little lax with necessary criticism or rebukes, but with a wonderful ability to instil a sense of right and wrong, and the ability to ascertain the difference, in your offspring.

As a friend you're invariably a delightful, charming companion who enjoys discussing a variety of different subjects, but can sometimes be a little loth to entertain in more energetic activities. You're probably one of the most fair-minded friends one could possibly find and you possess a lovely sense of humour too.

Libra lunar love

Romantic, tender Libra, with your touching words and charming gestures. Who could wish for anyone better! The trouble is that whilst you're not in the same league as Gemini when it comes to outrageous flirtation, you are inclined to add an amazing amount of guile to your naturally endowed Lunar intuition, and this can make you quite a schemer in your own way.

Your lunar aspirations send you in search of a soulmate on the physical and spiritual level, someone who will fulfil your fantasy of that perfect partner for ever more.

And since the Moon is ruling your emotions, and is also placed in a sign ruled by Venus, the Goddess of Love herself, it's not surprising that you are so dedicated to the cause of true love. You will do everything you can to find it, and having found it keep it for as long as you possibly can.

So use your lunar intuition and the power that it gives you. Don't be swayed this way and that, taking so long to make up your mind that you could miss out on someone perfect – but naturally remember to be realistic too.

Lunar relationships

Try to find a Moon Lover whose personality can blend well with yours. The following will act as a guide:

LIBRA MOON/ARIES MOON   Your Libran love of peace and harmony could be at odds with the impatient Arien Lunar Lover, but this opposite Zodiac sign will prove a strong attraction.

LIBRA MOON/TAURUS MOON   With romantic Venus ruling you both, your could discover the ideal soulmate here. Make sure you take the time and trouble to get to know each other well.

LIBRA MOON/GEMINI MOON   Two Air signs together, able to communicate on many different levels and both possessed with indisputable charm, even though Gemini may be somewhat too flighty for you.

LIBRA MOON/CANCER MOON   Finding the perfect partner and domestic security in harmonious surroundings is a mutual priority. Just remember to be diplomatic when Cancer is in one of those Cancerian moods!

LIBRA MOON/LEO MOON   Love makes the world go round for both of you, and you're probably quite content to let Leo take the limelight most of the time, as long as you can enjoy it once in a while!

LIBRA MOON/VIRGO MOON   The nit-picking ways of Virgo will sometimes irritate, whilst your famed indecisiveness will be Virgo's reason to question your compatibility.

LIBRA MOON/LIBRA MOON   This should be the perfect blend of soulmate, best friend, and lover. At least you will know exactly what to expect in such a mirror image!

LIBRA MOON/SCORPIO MOON   Both of you are searching for eternal love, so don't let Scorpio's sexual intensity scare you off, before you've discovered the sensitive side too.

LIBRA MOON/SAGITTARIUS MOON   Both of you possess bags of charm, but the free-and-easy Sagittarian approach to life may somewhat daunt you if you try to tie them down too soon.

LIBRA MOON/CAPRICORN MOON   You may inwardly yearn for a more sensitive soul, but the protective caring qualities of the Capricorn Moon will grow on you as time goes by.

LIBRA MOON/AQUARIUS MOON   Mentally you're in perfect harmony, and can be the best of friends, so it's up to you to charm Aquarius into revealing those emotional feelings a little more.

LIBRA MOON/PISCES MOON   The romantic tenderness of Pisces combined with your own delightfully romantic ways could make this pairing perfect bliss, if both of you can keep your feet on the ground too!

THE LIBRA LUNAR LOVER
———————— o ————————

The Libra Lunar Lover is one of the most attractive personalities in the whole Zodiac. And an especially nice thing about him or her is that they truly are searching deep down for the perfect relationship to enhance their lives. They crave a spiritual and sensual soulmate with whom to enjoy the beauty which life has to offer, and naturally to share the sadness too.

For a Libra Lunar Lover, sharing is what life is all about, and whilst on the surface someone born with the Moon in Libra might seem almost too charming, personable and diplomatic for their own good, all these characteristics are an inherent part of their personality. I'm sure you will concede that they are all certainly worthwhile.

Male, or female, the Libra Lunar Lover is someone you will usually want to show off proudly to your family and friends. If you are prepared to put up with a certain amount of dithering whilst the Libra Moon wavers this way and that before deciding whether you can be soulmates, it will all be worth it.

However, it's best to be prepared to wait an awfully long time sometimes before your Lunar Lover actually decides that you're pretty good yourself. Since you will already know that people born with the Moon in Libra are indecisive, *that* probably won't come as much of a surprise, but it is infuriating all the same. Especially as there is something perverse in a person who searches so persistently for true love to come along, and even when it does, in a person who is ideal in a million and one different ways, the vacillating quality of your Libra Lover can often mean you're left wondering what on earth is going on in the Libra Moon's mind.

One thing you will learn early on is that this Lunar Lover is as much of a perfectionist as Virgo, for in that inimitable Libran way their quest for everlasting love goes hand in hand with the search for a lover who is going to live up to their appreciation of beauty and good taste. A Libra Lunar Lover cannot cope with anyone or anything conceivably thought of as being tacky. As pernickety as Virgo, but certainly as tenderly romantic as Pisces, your Libra Lunar Lover may appear to be a harder nut to crack than first you thought!

What you will also note early on is that anyone with the Moon in Libra can sometimes be as fickle and flirtatious as that other Air sign Gemini. There is an inconsistency in their behaviour which on the surface really does seem to negate their definitely deep-rooted desire for a perfect soulmate.

But since Libra does relate to the house of marriage and partnership, it follows that your Libra Lunar Lover really does want to share their life with someone, even finding it inconceivable to think of doing otherwise. Once that perfect love exists, and the Libran mind *is* made up, your Lunar Lover will be one of the most attractive, tender lovers you could ever wish to meet.

_____ *Recognizing a Libra Lunar Lover* _____

It's not that there is necessarily a wistful look in those eyes, or a dimple in your Lunar Lover's chin, but there is always an abundance of that Libran charm which it is impossible to mistake. The romantic, gentle qualities of this Moon sign will be very appealing and in many instances quite irresistible. Somehow it won't be difficult to sense that the Libran Lunar Lover is the kind of person for whom the perfect soulmate is the ultimate joy in life.

The Libra Lunar Lover invariably spends a great deal of time making him or herself look as attractive as possible. It isn't even that an exorbitant amount of money is spent on clothes, although you will often recognize an extravagant streak in many Librans when they see something especially pleasing to the eye! There is also an amazing ability to hide the passage of time! The Libran Lunar Lover may be quite a few years older than you might think on first sight.

The Libran Lunar Lover does not necessarily have the sort of flamboyant personality which stands out in a crowd, but there is definitely something in the way this Moon sign projects him or herself quietly, often unassumingly, but always charmingly, which makes it easy to guess that you've met a Libran Lunar Lover.

_____ *Captivating a Libra Lunar Lover* _____

One of the most important things to remember is that the Libra Lunar Lover is, without any doubt, always inwardly searching for a soulmate with whom to live happily ever after.

This Moon sign invariably functions better in a partnership, and if you're setting out to captivate a Libra Moon, you'd better be serious in your intentions, and not just out for a casual flirtation. That's not to say that people with the Moon in Libra don't enjoy a gentle flirtation. They do. However they definitely want to be sure that you're not simply playing around with their feelings and only out for a good time.

Never make dramas in public, or in private either! Your Libra Lunar Lover's peaceful and tranquil personality cannot cope with raised voices and arguments. Don't ever be too critical, judge anyone unfairly, or be too long making up your mind as to whether the Libran Lunar Lover is for you (this Moon sign is indecisive enough for both of you!).

Something also to remember is that both male and female Libran Lovers adore knowing they are appreciated. They respond happily to affection and are one of the most romantic and lovable Moon signs in the Zodiac. If you can prove that you'll be an ideal companion, a loyal and supportive friend, and someone who can be warm, witty and wonderful, you'll be well on the way.

Captivating this Moon sign definitely doesn't mean aggressive pursuit, nor does it mean too much cool indifference. Ruled by the Scales, your Libran Lunar Lover searches for balance in all things, and especially so in a partner to share his or her life.

_____ *Life with a Libra Lunar Lover* _____

By all rights, living with a Libra Lunar Lover should be one of the most beautiful experiences you could possibly have. Imagine living with such a charming, diplomatic sensitive soul who wants nothing better than for the two of you to live well, and to love well too!

There can be many beautiful moments in your relationship together. Problems, however, can arise when you start to realize that this lovable, romantic soul often has a problem when it comes to making instant decisions (*even if they are urgent*). Balancing scales can sometimes be a fine art, and there may be moments when you begin to feel that those Libran scales have some hidden weights which make it almost impossible to make them equal.

However, everyone has up and down moods, and at least your Libran Lunar Lover isn't someone who gets horribly depressed or spends hours sulking in a corner. The best part of living with a Libran Lunar Lover is that Libra can see beauty and happiness in so many different things, and truly wants you to share them.

Life with this Moon sign can be blissfully warm and cozy. Your domestic surroundings will often give off an aura of that special peace and harmony which is so important to this Lunar Lover.

It won't take you long to realize that your Libran Lunar Lover is one of the most generous signs of all, and very sentimental about anniversaries of any kind.

As a lover, both male and female Libran Moons are sensual and seductive. Don't forget that Venus, Goddess of Love, is the plantetary ruler of their sign. The Libra Lunar Lover is especially considerate of your needs and desires, and you can look forward to a perfect blending of mind, body and soul in your life together.

It won't take you very long to understand that, whilst a man or woman with the Moon in Libra does enjoy the company of the opposite sex, their gentle flirting with another doesn't mean your Lunar Lover is going to stray from the fold!

Always try to be the person your Lunar Lover fell for in the beginning, and enjoy your life together.

_____ *Lunar Lovers and their Sun signs* _____

The personality of your Libra Lunar Lover will be modified by the position of the Sun in his or her horoscope.

AIRES SUN/LIBRA MOON   This Lunar Lover's personality will be fiery on the surface, but amazingly soft and sensitive once you've discovered those yearnings for someone to share life and love with.

TAURUS SUN/LIBRA MOON   With both Sun and Moon ruled by Venus, this Libran Lover will be a real romantic, brimming with sensuality, but sometimes both stubborn *and* indecisive!

GEMINI SUN/LIBRA MOON   Intellectually stimulating and tenderly romantic as a lover, with one of the most attractive personalities you could ever hope to meet!

CANCER SUN/LIBRA MOON   This combination creates an inherent desire for peace and harmony in a perfect domestic atmosphere. The only snag would be those Cancerian moods combined with Libra's vacillation.

LEO SUN/LIBRA MOON   A Lunar Lover with great *joie de vivre*. Extravagant gestures combine with masses of sentimental romance.

VIRGO SUN/LIBRA MOON   The Virgo Sun will make this Libran Lover a real perfectionist who needs to be doubly sure that he or she has found the perfect partner.

LIBRA SUN/LIBRA MOON   A perfectly balanced Lunar Lover? Or someone who finds it totally impossible to commit because it's totally impossible to decide? Either way you could still be bowled over by their charms.

SCORPIO SUN/LIBRA MOON   Broodingly intense and deeply passionate, this Lunar Lover will have the sort of magnetic personality you just can't resist – even if you are a little scared!

SAGITTARIUS SUN/LIBRA MOON   An open-minded free-thinker with a wonderfully optimistic personality which makes them very appealing to your romantic dreams.

CAPRICORN SUN/LIBRA MOON   Don't worry about indecisiveness with this Lunar Lover. There is a very practical streak combined with all that tenderness which won't allow the right soulmate to get away.

AQUARIUS SUN/LIBRA MOON   This Lunar Lover may be hard to pin down to a permanent relationship, as a free-and-easy involvement often appeals to a Sun and Moon both ruled by the element of Air.

PISCES SUN/LIBRA MOON   You couldn't wish for a more lovable idealistic, caring and devoted Lunar Lover, but there could be a very impractical side too. One of you will need to have their feet on the ground!

How to keep your Lunar Lover by your side

DO:
- Show that you're keen to have a peaceful and relaxed life
- Let your Lunar Lover know you're a marvellous friend as well as their lover
- Cultivate an interest in the arts
- Be understanding and decisive too
- Always look as attractive as you can
- Remember to pay your Lunar Lover compliments when they're due

DON'T:
- Raise your voice to argue unless it's truly unavoidable!
- Accuse your Lunar Lover of being lazy
- Go on about people who can't make decisions, even if it's true
- Give your Lunar Lover reason to think you're not the perfect soulmate
- Ever get sloppy in your dress
- Forget this Lunar Lover believes in 'share and share alike'

THE MOON . . . AND SCORPIO

YOUR LUNAR INFLUENCES

When you were born, the Moon was in Scorpio, eighth sign of the Zodiac and ruled by both Mars, God of War, and Pluto, God of the Underworld. Scorpio is a Feminine, Fixed, Negative, Water sign, and the Moon relates to Cancer, which is also Feminine, Negative and Water but a Cardinal sign. Astrologically, the Moon should be very much at ease in Scorpio although the intensity bestowed upon you can sometimes be very daunting for others. It's strange but often true that whenever anyone hears the word 'Scorpio' they tend to back off, or immediately murmur about that sting in the Scorpion's tail.

With the Moon in Scorpio it means that the basic Scorpio characteristics of intensity, power, the ability to heal and to research will be even more accentuated. It's as though with a Scorpio Moon you really *are* invincible, especially if you develop plenty of self-discipline which is important. It's certainly true that your instincts and intuition are so highly attuned that it is almost impossible to hide anything from you.

However, since the Moon *is* the Inner You, and since its Scorpio effect is going to be so strong, it is also very likely that the deep intensity of your feelings will be hidden deep, deep below the surface, and that the typically Scorpio characteristic of needing a private space will be magnified to such an extent that if you're not careful you could even come across as excessively brooding and intense. Of course, *you* know that you're probably deep inside your own private little world where only that special soulmate is ever allowed, and that's not likely to happen all that often.

It's actually a wonderful bonus to have the Moon in Scorpio if you use its powerful influences in a really positive way. But if you also have the Sun in Scorpio, plus/or your Ascendant, perhaps you shouldn't blame people if they do back away when you tell them so, for to describe you as a frighteningly magnetic personality is probably the understatement of all time.

With both Mars and Pluto ruling the sign of Scorpio, your magnetism is combined with a deep sense of motivation and sometimes even a power complex. Your sense of authority seems to come from the very depths of your being, and your energy is infallible. However, as a Scorpio Moon personality, you must learn to control your inner power as otherwise it has a very destructive quality about it, which can be towards yourself just as much as to others. Remember how the Scorpion stings itself to death when it can see no way out from a dangerous situation, and be resolved that, unlike that Scorpion, you will let your

Positive and negative characteristics for Scorpio

Look at this checklist and see which characteristics apply to you:

The Positive Moon

- Magnetic and irresistible
- Amazingly intuitive
- Very sensual
- Brilliant at research
- Never forgets anything

The Negative Moon

- Overly powerful and dominating
- Unnecessarily secretive
- Too passionate about sex!
- Sometimes pries too much
- But may never forgive either!

instinct (which invariably borders on the psychic) guide you. Be constructive, *not* destructive.

As a Lunar Scorpio you have sometimes had a difficult childhood, which has made you even tougher and more resilient, although at the same time left you on occasion finding it hard to place complete trust in someone, even when your instinct does tell you it's okay to do so. Because you tend to have a fantastic memory, emotional scars of any kind take a very long time to heal.

For a Moon in Scorpio person, no challenge is too great, and nothing in the world ever impossible!

_____ *Your Scorpio emotions* _____

Second of the Water signs, you are indubitably the most powerful emotionally, but you are certainly as romantic and idealistic as Cancer and Pisces, and often a great deal more so.

However, the depth of your lunar emotions is often a deep, dark secret, never allowed to see the light of day. Sometimes you are even scared by the power of your feelings, and there are bound to have been occasions in your life when you know you have scared off someone who attracted you by coming on just that much too strong. Both male and female Scorpio Moons possess this particular characteristic, but it's definitely true that your magnetic personalities are often without comparison when it comes to arousing romantic and passionate dreams in others. Interestingly enough, James Dean and Elizabeth Taylor were both born with the Moon in this sign.

But what you need to realize is that your strong emotions can also be a turn-off because you start to become immensely possessive and jealous when you meet someone you really care for, regardless of whether the object of your desires is giving you any cause to doubt their faithfulness or not.

This is where you must listen to that inner voice, your Higher Self, and allow it to calm you down and become more rational. Sometimes you're too inclined to go over the top with your emotions.

Also, for someone who is so insistent on having their own space, their own privacy, their own little silent world, you appear to be awfully reticent at granting similar possibilities to anyone with whom you become involved! Often people with the Moon in this position need to give and take a little more and not be quite so 'heavy' in their approach.

The inner emotions of a Scorpio Moon sometimes create a duality of feeling. It's as though you want to be the dominant one especially in a relationship, and yet at the same time you then sometimes resent having anyone dependent on you.

Resentment is sometimes a very strong feeling with you, especially when it relates to things which went wrong in the past and which, of course, you simply cannot forget.

Use your intuition properly, learn to let go of the things which have no bearing on what is happening today. You do need to remember that you have the power to transcend the negativity in life and, just like the grey eagle which is the other symbol of the sign of Scorpio, soar to the heights.

Your career

Since it is the Moon which motivates you, it follows that your intensity of feelings will be applied equally to your career and working life. You are often very determined to be powerful and for that power to bring you wealth, so you don't mind how hard and how long you work to achieve your objectives.

The Scorpio influence often leads you to law, reporting (especially anything of an investigative nature), selling, science, and spiritual healing. Becoming a psychiatrist or a surgeon is also a possibility. Your determination to get to the top can sometimes make you jealous and resentful of others who get there before you. Once again, it is necessary to use the positive influence of the Moon to awaken the hidden potential within you, that creative ability which is bursting to get out. When you have real faith in that and in the knowledge that you don't have to feel jealous of anyone else but simply move on up that ladder to success at your very own speed because you're certain to get there in the end, all will go smoothly.

Your family and friends

There is an old astrological tale that when a Moon (or Sun) Scorpio is born, it might coincide with a sudden death in the family, but perhaps this is because one of the qualities associated with Scorpio is the regenerative power of Pluto.

If, as is often the case with the Moon in Scorpio, your childhood wasn't always an easy one, you will be very determined that your own family don't experience the same sort of situation. You are very loyal and loving to both family and friends but it's certainly true that even with those closest to you it is very hard for you to condone mistakes and forgive even the smallest slight.

It's important to learn how to deal with this aspect of your personality by having more faith and trust and not being quite so quick to rise to any imagined slights.

Because of your psychic sensitivity, however, it is important that you feel truly at home in your surroundings and in the company of others.

Scorpio lunar love

Fascinating, exciting, amazingly sensitive and awe-inspiringly sensual, a love affair with you is unlikely to be forgotten. Your Scorpio Moon heightens your senses, and puts your intuition into the major league. There is often an almost frightening intensity about your personality and when you fall for someone it is unlikely to be lightly.

The interesting thing about you is that people always tend to go on about Scorpio being the sex symbol of the Zodiac, and that all you care about in a love affair is sex. But the truth is usually far less obvious. Deep down your Scorpio Moon is instilling inside you the need for a truly compatible soulmate. In your youth, casual affairs may be both stimulating and satisfying, but even more than the Scorpio Sun, a Scorpio Moon is searching deep down for that mind/body/soul relationship which you're convinced is in your destiny.

You can be one of the most romantic and idealistic Moon signs, but sometimes you're almost scared to show it. You often prefer to live on your reputation as the Scorpion with the sting so that no-one can get too close to you and discover the vulnerability lurking in your heart, especially if you've been hurt in the past.

You need a Lunar Lover who will understand your need to block off certain parts of your inner self until you are ready to talk about them. Deep down you do want to talk about them, but you have to totally trust your chosen partner before you will admit that even a Scorpio can be vulnerable.

You need your Lunar Lover to be passionate yet sensitive, strong but not pushy, soft but not weak – with that perfect blending of mind, body and soul.

Lunar relationships

Try to find a Moon Lover whose personality can blend well with yours. The following will act as a guide:

SCORPIO MOON/ARIES MOON   You're excited by the challenge of taming the Aries fire-brand, and two Mars-ruled signs together will definitely create more than a few sparks!

SCORPIO MOON/TAURUS MOON   The earthy passion of Taurus can be very fulfilling, but on a true soul level you may feel that the vital ingredients of a good love relationship are slightly lacking.

SCORPIO MOON/GEMINI MOON   This will-o-the-wisp of the Zodiac can all too easily arouse your jealousy, and may in turn be more than slightly fazed by your often possessive and intense personality.

SCORPIO MOON/CANCER MOON   Two Water signs, both romantic and yearning for a perfect partner, but if Cancer is the clinging sort you may feel your privacy is too threatened.

SCORPIO MOON/LEO MOON   This can be quite a power struggle, but your strength lies in different areas, and emotionally you could be just what bossy Leo needs!

SCORPIO MOON/VIRGO MOON   With Virgo's famed ability to analyse, plus your depths of intuition, this could be a very magnetic combination as you'll enjoy delving into each other's soul.

SCORPIO MOON/LIBRA MOON   Libra's gentle ways will be very attractive, but he or she could be frightened away by the strength of your feelings if you show them too soon.

SCORPIO MOON/SCORPIO MOON   Battling for supremacy in the emotional stakes can be an amazingly sensual and soul-enhancing experience – and exhausting too!

SCORPIO MOON/SAGITTARIUS MOON   Always remember that Sagittarius needs to feel free to roam the universe, even if it's only in their mind. This can be a very happy-go-lucky relationship.

SCORPIO MOON/CAPRICORN MOON   The Capricorn strength is less emotional than yours but equally powerful. However, the Mountain Goat's concept of a soulmate tends to be on a more practical level.

SCORPIO MOON/AQUARIUS MOON   You can be possessive and jealous whilst Aquarius can be totally unpredictable and unconventional. This can be tricky unless you're both prepared to bend a little.

SCORPIO MOON/PISCES MOON   You'll both adore gazing into each other's eyes and at wonderful sunrises and sunsets. This can be romantic bliss if your chosen Pisces Moon Lover isn't too dreamy-eyed.

THE SCORPIO LUNAR LOVER

The Scorpio Lunar Lover will be like no-one else you have ever known (other than someone with a Scorpio Sun or Ascendant, and even then *they* won't have the same depth of emotion, since it is the Moon which represents the feelings and emotions). If you're looking for a calm and peaceful relationship, this almost certainly *won't* be it!

A Scorpio Lunar Lover has incredibly strong and passionate feelings, not necessarily only about love. They are not always spoken about, but you can often sense those feelings simmering away below the surface of this Zodiac personality.

Male or female, the Scorpio Lunar Lover has immense power and despite 'the sting of the Scorpion's tale' and the heavy duty sarcasm which can sometimes occur, there is quite a vulnerable human being beneath who is longing for the perfect soulmate as much as anyone else.

Sometimes it's awfully hard to know where you stand with a lover with the Moon in Scorpio. His or her moods can be almost as changeable as any Cancerian, as dictatorial as any Leo, and as critical as Virgo. It's almost as though there are times when the Scorpio Lunar Lover prefers to negate their emotions, hide them away in the deepest recesses of their mind, and get on with whatever else is to hand.

For Scorpio, this is probably a very constructive and positive attitude, but it's not necessarily so for the recipient of a Scorpio glare or cold word! However, it's important to remind you that since Scorpio is also one of the most loyal signs around and someone with a great deal of sensitivity, it's worth putting up with a few black moods and simply getting on with your own thing. Never show too many signs of weakness, for strength is always admired by the Scorpio Lunar Lover, and although he or she hates to admit it, they have more than enough weakness of their own.

A Scorpio Lunar Lover is a very tactile person. They are quick to give little affectionate gestures, plus the more sensual touches which can send shivers down your spine. It's best to try to lose all your inhibitions, forget about being too shy or sensitive, and allow yourself to open up to the passion of your Scorpio Lunar Lover if you want to achieve a truly fulfilling relationship.

A word of warning, if you didn't know it already, the Scorpio Lunar Lover can be immensely jealous, and definitely dislikes hearing about past lovers, for whilst there is definitely a great deal more in their personality than that 'famed sex-symbol of the Zodiac' tag, both male and female Lunar Scorpios are usually (and often justifiably) proud of their sexual prowess.

The Scorpio Lunar Lover yearns for a true soulmate, but strangely enough sees there is a threat of danger in that very thing, and may take quite a while to admit that you could be it!

Your Scorpio Lunar Lover may sometimes appear to be a daunting adversary rather than a perfect partner. But don't give up the challenge too soon, for you could be missing out on the thousand and one delights of a spiritually rewarding relationship.

_____ *Recognizing a Scorpio Lunar Lover* _____

It's not as though every Scorpio Lunar Lover is going to conform with the classic text-book descriptions of dark hair, flashing eyes, a brooding intensity, simmering sexuality. But in a funny way, apart from the dark hair, the other characteristics are usually there in one form or another. The Scorpio Lunar Lover takes great pride in looking sexy (although many of them may strongly deny it).

What is invariably true is that you can sense the hidden power lurking inside this Lunar Lover and mentally you may even feel yourself wanting to back away.

In both male and female Scorpios you will often feel that they have the ability to reach deep into the furthest recesses of your mind and to know just what you're thinking. That sometimes makes you more than a little uneasy until you're able to get used to it.

_____ *Captivating a Scorpio Lunar Lover* _____

If you honestly don't feel that there is a mutual chemistry between you, it is really rather pointless trying to captivate this Lunar Lover. Even a Scorpio who gets his or her kicks in trying to play the field has got to feel something deep inside before embarking on a love affair, however brief it may be.

This Moon sign will invariably know before you do that there *is* that mutual chemistry and then you probably won't even have to worry much about how you are going to conduct your captivating – for that too will often be mutual!

Show that you have a warm and loving personality, a good sense of humour, an ability to communicate on the things which interest your Lunar Lover, and no matter what you've heard about him or her, try very very hard not to pry into what went on before you came along.

Perhaps to be truly irresistible to anyone with the Moon in Scorpio, you should also endeavour to retain an air of mystery about you. Scorpio loves to unravel mysteries and it will make getting to know each other even more fun!

You also need to be that little bit different from everyone else. That doesn't mean coming across in an excessively extrovert and flamboyant way, dressing up to the nines, making the first move, or some of the other seductive little ploys which can work well with many signs. Scorpio doesn't fall for all of that. You have to prove there is something very special below the surface for Scorpio to want to know you better. Don't make it all too easy – Scorpio wants to be a loyal friend as well as being a passionate and exhilarating lover. Always be honest, never hide how you feel, but for heaven's sake try to combat any streaks of jealousy (not too easy if you're another Scorpio!) and never let your Scorpio Lunar Lover doubt that you genuinely care for him or her.

_____ Life with a Scorpio Lunar Lover _____

An immensely fulfilling emotional experience or a lunar nightmare? In some ways that will be up to you, for your Scorpio Lunar Lover is not always the easiest of partners. Possibly because without even realizing it, he or she is inwardly searching for something which has a strong spiritual connotation, and if your relationship ever falters on the deep soul level, problems can arise.

It may sometimes take a while for your Scorpio Lunar Lover to reveal the true depth of his or her emotions, and when you're living together you may continually discover little facets of his or her personality which will often fascinate, but sometimes puzzle you. The puzzling bit is that suddenly your Lunar Lover may seem to cut off, to retreat into a private little space to be alone with their thoughts, and entry is not allowed, not even to you. Your Scorpio Lunar Lover is actually very wise for times of silence and solitude are very necessary to the inner self. Don't begrudge your Lunar Lover what can be the very food of life, but learn to value your own private space too for there is a lot to gain from this.

As a _lover_, both male and female Scorpio Moons are certainly extremely passionate – look no further to find an ardent, but never usually selfish, lover who seems to have an uncanny knowledge of you and your body, your needs and your desires. This sixth sense of the

Scorpio Lunar Lover can lead to an incredibly satisfying relationship for someone who can really appreciate it.

Life with a partner with the Moon in Scorpio can be one of the most perfect mind, body and soul relationships, soaring to the heights of ecstacy at the best of times, and sometimes throwing you into a flat spin. Intense it might be, but it will certainly never be dull!

Don't waste precious time worrying about whether your Scorpio Lunar Lover might stray – just be the ideal soulmate, and your fears will disappear.

_____ Lunar Lovers and their Sun signs _____

The personality of your Scorpio Lunar Lover will be modified by the position of the Sun in his or her horoscope.

ARIES SUN/SCORPIO MOON   This Lunar Lover will be intensely passionate, amazingly enthusiastic and enterprising. A real firebrand of energy – almost too much to handle at times!

TAURUS SUN/SCORPIO MOON   A deep desire for security goes hand-in-hand with strongly sensual needs and a very possessive and jealous nature.

GEMINI SUN/SCORPIO MOON   Intellectual stimulation plus plenty of passion is vital for this interesting and highly intuitive Lunar Lover who has immense appeal.

CANCER SUN/SCORPIO MOON   The Cancer Sun adds a certain vulnerable quality to the powerful Scorpio Moon, although a Cancerian 'down' mood combined with so much brooding intensity is tricky!

LEO SUN/SCORPIO MOON   A bright and sparkling personality with immense intuition and the desire to be the best in every possible way. A powerful Sun/Moon combination.

VIRGO SUN/SCORPIO MOON   This Lunar Lover is sure to be critical and analytical and brilliant at research, but may find it hard to let emotional feelings show through.

LIBRA SUN/SCORPIO MOON   Charm personified with a fascinating hint of ruthlessness when it comes to captivating his or her chosen soulmate.

SCORPIO SUN/SCORPIO MOON   This Lunar Lover believes in being invincible and plays life that way. Watch out when those powerful emotions are released!

SAGITTARIUS SUN/SCORPIO MOON   The Sagittarius Sun makes this Lunar Lover a freedom-loving personality and tones down the Scorpio jealous streak in a big way.

CAPRICORN SUN/SCORPIO MOON   It's really hard for this Scorpio Moon to show their emotions as they often think this shows a weakness in a sign whose feet are entrenched on terra firma.

AQUARIUS SUN/SCORPIO MOON   Stubborn and also unconventional. Cool and detached on the surface but often burning with passion underneath, although they won't admit it.

PISCES SUN/SCORPIO MOON   A romantic dreamer who can be incredibly sensual in a very tender and loving way.

How to keep your Lunar Lover by your side

DO:
- Make sure your Lunar Lover knows you love their sensual touch
- Retain that little air of mystery
- Learn to appreciate the smouldering intensity of their passion
- Remember that Scorpio Moons can be emotionally sensitive too
- Resolve to love, cherish and obey as long as it lasts!
- Encourage your Lunar Lover to listen to their instincts

DON'T:
- Try to invade the private space which Scorpio needs
- Start accusing this Lunar Lover of disloyalty – not without proof anyway!
- Find faults when you're making love . . .
- Forget that Scorpio wants your mind, body and your soul
- Ever play around with anyone else – this Lunar Lover could be off fast
- Be frightened to show your own sexuality!

THE MOON . . .
AND SAGITTARIUS

YOUR LUNAR INFLUENCES

When you were born, the Moon was in Sagittarius, ninth sign of the Zodiac. Sagittarius is ruled by Jupiter, planet of good fortune and expansion, and is a Masculine, Mutable, Positive, Fire sign, whereas the Moon is associated with Cancer, a Feminine, Cardinal, Negative, Water sign, which in basic terms actually means that your Sagittarius Moon is slightly out of place in the sign of the Archer.

As you know, the Moon relates to the inner you, the part one invariably tends to keep hidden from the rest of the world, but the Sagittarius influence makes it harder for you to keep *anything* hidden, sometimes to the extent that you can be unbelievably tactless when you let your emotions get the better of you.

However, since Sagittarius is the sign of the Sage and Counsellor, the Higher Mind, and Long Distance Traveller of the Zodiac, it shouldn't be too difficult for you to devise a philosophical approach to help you to understand the workings of your inner mind and develop your intuition at the same time.

The Moon in Sagittarius instils in you a deep need for independence, the freedom to lead your life as and where you choose it. You cannot be tied down, mentally or physically. Your Sagittarian Moon inspires your mind to search for new avenues of learning, new fields to conquer, and you invariably put a great deal of energy and enthusiasm into your search which often encompasses both religion and philosophy. Your thirst for knowledge is unquenchable so that you are determined not to rest until you have found the answers you need.

Your search for inner identity can be a great source of pleasure because it will be conducted in the happy-go-lucky and optimistic manner bequeathed to you by your Sagittarian Moon.

Jupiter, ruling planet of Sagittarius, also has a profound effect on your spiritual development, and interestingly enough this planet is called 'Guru' in Hindu astrology. The combined influence of Jupiter and your Sagittarian Moon will give you the ability to expand your consciousness and your awareness. By taking the time to meditate silently and communicate with your Higher Self it won't be long before you find that you can discover even more about the wonders of life and transcend many of the problems which do arise.

The Cancerian influence of your Moon will not produce many bouts of depression or even particularly down moods. Your basic enthusiasm and zest for life are so strong that you refuse to wallow in misery! However, do make sure that you are not so optimistic that you end up becoming careless, not taking enough time and trouble to carry your thoughts and ideas through to the finishing line.

The Moon's influence can create too much restlessness and sometimes even self-delusion in your nature. Combined with the feeling that 'Lady Luck' is on your side (the Jupiter influence again) this can turn you into one of those people who always think that the grass is greener on the other side. There is also a gambling tendency bestowed on Lunar Sagittarians, and it is advisable to use moderation or it can lead you into trouble!

The best part of having a Sagittarian Moon is that even when you have to endure unavoidably difficult situations, the ability to pick yourself up and start all over again never loses its powerful impact on your life. Just think how much more powerful this could become if you allow your lunar influence to heighten your perception and enable you to grow in even more directions.

In some ways your Sagittarian Moon makes you a visionary, a visionary with a good sense of humour, someone who doesn't mind how many times they make mistakes if they are going to learn from them, and someone who definitely has a story to tell!

However, do listen well to your inner voice, and don't continually insist on telling other people how to run their lives. Concentrate on your search for your *own* inner identity – that is more than enough to keep you busy.

Positive and negative characteristics for Sagittarius

Look at this checklist and see which characteristics apply to you:

The Positive Moon

- Optimistic and enthusiastic
- Great thirst for knowledge
- Adventurous
- Philosophical
- Great sense of humour

The Negative Moon

- Careless and over-indulgent
- A know-it-all
- Too much of a gambler
- Tactless and overly frank!
- Surprisingly insensitive at times

Your Sagittarius emotions

The third and last of the Fire signs, you are the sort of person who can easily be the life and soul of any party. You are genuinely interested in people and keen to expound on your thoughts and ideas related to just about everything and everywhere.

But the inherent watery sensitivity of the Moon is somewhat at odds with your often restless Sagittarius emotions. This restless side can far too easily create problems for you since it does make it difficult for you to settle down and conform to what, perhaps, is expected of you – perhaps even what you, deep down, expect of yourself. This is where some quiet moments of reflection, asking for inner guidance over your desires and objectives, can be of immense benefit both mentally and emotionally.

Your Sagittarius emotions sometimes come across as having very little depth to them. That open honest approach is fine in certain situations, but on a more intimate level could give the impression that you don't have the inclination, or won't spend the time, to let the depth of your emotions show through. And this is strange because when you believe totally in something or someone you often want the whole world to know and are prepared to shout it from the highest roof top.

Since Sagittarius is a Fire sign there is no doubt that you possess qualities of fiery passion which you do give in to when you are sure the time is right. But perhaps it is because you have the wanderlust spirit so firmly entrenched within your soul that you are sometimes scared to let yourself go in the fear that you could be trapped, and thus lose the opportunity to indulge yourself in your wandering ways.

You are well aware that a relationship has to leave you a certain amount of freedom but that doesn't mean you are necessarily the sort of person who wants to play around with other people when you're in a partnership. It's simply that to feel *inwardly* free is such an integral part of any Moon or Sun Sagittarian make-up that it is something which would be very hard to lose.

But don't miss out on the chance of achieving a good relationship simply because you are worried about this. Let your intuition shine through and point you in the right direction. Use that hidden power of the Moon to guide your emotions and enable you to find a soulmate who understands how you feel and will never let you feel trapped or a prisoner of love.

Whilst so many people need to feel completely secure in a love relationship, *you* need something in addition to that – the ability to keep your own identity at all times. Your spirit sometimes needs to fly alone.

Your career

The Moon relates to your inner motivations, which inspire you in relation to your career and working life, not necessarily the type of career you choose. But inevitably you will do best in something which is not a dead-end routine occupation that makes you feel imprisoned. Both Sun and Moon Sagittarians often gravitate to fields where communication is essential, as your ability to communicate on so many levels is often unsurpassed. Such careers include philosophy, law, teaching, politics, interpreting, writing, broadcasting, the travel business, and promoting sport.

Often you're drawn to the outdoor life, and with your Sagittarian Moon inspiring you to expand your consciousness ever more, you would make a wonderful explorer or could become very involved in ecology.

Your thirst to impart your knowledge to others is usually unquenchable, and it can even make you a hard taskmaster. But you're not terribly good at being given orders yourself and can sometimes be a rather outspoken and tactless employee.

Your inherent optimism and enthusiasm enable you to have great belief in your talents and abilities, and if anyone can succeed at their chosen objective, it's you!

Your family and friends

Lunar Sagittarians often come from a family who encouraged them to learn about life from an early age, and you tend to behave the same way when you have a family of your own.

Your own free and easy approach to life is often passed on to your offspring, although you do have a tendency to air your views as though they are always, always right. It's necessary once again to allow your lunar instincts to guide you, for sometimes you can upset someone unnecessarily by going about your views for far too long.

As a friend you're one of those people who can be the life and soul of any party, and a welcome addition to any group. Sometimes you're not too good at keeping constantly in touch with people, but with your natural ability for making friends you are never likely to be alone for very long, no matter where you go. And since travelling is something you usually adore, you're sure to have a cosmopolitan selection from all over the world.

Sagittarius lunar love

Freedom-loving, frolicsome, full of fun Sagittarius – you sometimes tend to be too wary of being trapped into a relationship, and even though you're also a passionate Fire sign, you're definitely going to look before you leap!

However, once you allow your lunar intuition to work to its full potential you'll know when you've met your ideal soulmate and you can concentrate on some wonderful fantasies instead of dwelling on unnecessary fears! Since you tend to think you know best anyway, why should you even hazard the notion that you could be involved in the wrong relationship? Trust yourself a little more and you will enjoy yourself more too.

You do, though, need a Moon Lover who enjoys freedom as much as you do and who wants a mate who is a good companion as well as sharing mutual feelings about love, sex and an ongoing relationship. Someone who is terribly jealous and possessive would find you very difficult to take, and for you it would be disaster!

You can be as romantic as anyone else, but perhaps deep down you're scared of responsibility, and having someone else to care for aside from yourself. And yet when you do find that perfect partner you suddenly start to discover that hidden part of yourself which recognizes that even Sagittarians are destined to have a soulmate! When that moment comes along for you, that's when you can quietly ask your Higher Self for guidance, listening to the still, deep voice. Suddenly all the reasons you've been giving for not wanting to become really involved will disappear – and you won't regret it for a moment!

Lunar relationships

Try to find a Moon Lover whose personality can blend well with yours. The following will act as a guide:

SAGITTARIUS MOON/ARIES MOON   You find the Aries impatience unsettling but exciting, and Aries probably enjoys having a lover who can also be their best friend.

SAGITTARIUS MOON/TAURUS MOON   Taurus stubbornly insists on security which you're afraid to promise, but you have to admit you enjoy all that tender loving care.

SAGITTARIUS MOON/GEMINI MOON   A true attraction of opposites in the Zodiac, both with a yearning for mental freedom and mental stimulation. A totally compatible soulmate.

SAGITTARIUS MOON/CANCER MOON   The sensitivity of Cancer's touch, and all that cozy domesticity seems wonderful at first, but you'll both have to change some of your ways for this to work well.

SAGITTARIUS MOON/LEO MOON   Two strong Fire signs together, both enjoying many mutual interests, including the party scene. But you will refuse to be bossed around by Leo the Lion.

SAGITTARIUS MOON/VIRGO MOON   You think you know all the answers, whilst Virgo is determined to criticize. This may not be the free and easy sort of love affair you've been hoping for.

SAGITTARIUS MOON/LIBRA MOON   You truly enjoy the peace and harmony which Libra brings your way. Suddenly real romance seems worth giving up a little freedom for, and is worth the try!

SAGITTARIUS MOON/SCORPIO MOON   Scorpio's intensity needs to be toned down and possessive jealousy will have to be a no-no if this is to be as happy-go-lucky as you would want.

SAGITTARIUS MOON/SAGITTARIUS MOON   Now you really know what it feels like to be involved with someone like you! You could both be so busy learning about life you almost forget each other . . .

SAGITTARIUS MOON/CAPRICORN MOON   If all that freedom has begun to pall, you're looking at the right person to give you material and emotional security in a big way.

SAGITTARIUS MOON/AQUARIUS MOON   Surely two such highly evolved souls can stay put long enough to realize that mental stimulation and an unconventional way of life can be a whole lot of fun.

SAGITTARIUS MOON/PISCES MOON   Just think – you could travel the world together on a perpetual honeymoon looking for romantic places where no-one has ever been before!

THE SAGITTARIUS LUNAR LOVER

With a Sagittarius Lunar Lover, you will have a wonderfully relaxed, free and easy relationship, with not too many strings attached. That's all very well if you're not looking for something more permanent. If you *are*, it's going to take more than just a sprinkling of gentle persuasion on your part to convince this Lunar Lover that you're that ideal soulmate that subconsciously they have been searching for!

Your Sagittarius Lunar Lover is the third and last of the Fire signs, and is more laid-back when it comes to love than either Aries or Leo with their fiery, passionate natures. Perhaps it's just that anyone with their Moon in Sagittarius instinctively feels that when the time and place are right, everything else will automatically fall into place.

'Lucky in love' could easily be a description of the Sagittarius Lunar Lover, and for the reason why, you need probably look no further than the influence of Jupiter, ruling planet of Sagittarius. How often have you read in horoscope columns about the 'lucky planet Jupiter'? Its planetary influence on this Lunar Lover certainly seems to be immensely beneficial in making both male and female Lunar Sagittarians attractive to would-be suitors, who are often bowled over by the open, friendly and humorous charm displayed by anyone with the Moon in Sagittarius.

Sagittarius wants to be everyone's best friend, and isn't terribly concerned necessarily about being their best lover! That's not to say that this Lunar Lover isn't interested in sex, but sex alone isn't going to keep a Sagittarian Lunar Lover by your side.

This Moon sign also has one rather irritating fault – being convinced that he, or she, knows best, not just occasionally, but most of the time! And this will be pointed out to you, in no uncertain tones. The Sagittarian Lunar Lover has probably spent a great deal of time and energy finding the right answers, and woe betide you if you doubt their word! Sensitivity when it comes to how you might feel could be sadly lacking.

However, don't be put off or start to think that the Sagittarian Lunar Lover could be disaster with a capital D! Who else has the ability to lift your spirits so wittily when you're feeling down? Who else always manages to see the silver lining behind the darkest cloud? And who else has the most positive and optimistic personality you've ever known? Who else could make you feel so relaxed and comfortable from the start of your relationship but your Sagittarius Lunar Lover?

The Sagittarian Lunar Lover may not admit (at least not at first) that a true soulmate could be just what is needed to make life even more bright and sparkling. But since it's not always easy to see below the surface of Sagittarius the Archer's outer personality, you will simply have to believe that whilst no Sagittarian Lunar Lover wants to feel fenced-in, they also don't want to miss out on their fair share of romance and tender loving care.

___ Recognizing a Sagittarius Lunar Lover ___

People with both the Sun and Moon in Sagittarius tend to enjoy an outdoor life, and often a very sporty one. Even a Lunar Lover who doesn't fit into this category is almost sure to be a gregarious, life-and-soul-of-the-party type. Male Lunar Lovers could come across as womanizers, whilst the female of the species may be more flirtatious than many of the other eleven signs.

Meanwhile, if you meet a man with irresistible boyish charm or a woman with an infectious sense of humour and a friendly, open smile, you might discover that you've just encountered a Sagittarius Moon.

Another of the most recognizable traits of a Sagittarius Lunar Lover is the warmth and generosity which flows from this sign. Sagittarius genuinely wants to make people happy and have fun, and is the perfect person to have around on those days when life seems awfully dull.

However, if you're beginning to wonder if you *have* met a Sagittarius Lunar Lover (and haven't liked to ask), perhaps the most obvious give-away of all is if the conversation veers towards travel, and you start to hear about all the places this Moon sign has visited or intends to go. The Sagittarian wanderlust is insatiable, and unmistakable!

___ Captivating a Sagittarius Lunar Lover ___

Resolve to project a personality as up-beat and interesting as the Lunar Lover you want to captivate. Show that you're an independent free spirit who would never be possessive or painfully jealous, as that would probably send Sagittarius running fast. Make sure you're not lacking in energy, for even Sagittarians who don't like sport still enjoy going on long walks, and keep busily on the go with a host of different activities.

Don't be ultra-sensitive. Your Sagittarian Lunar Lover is bound to put his or her foot right in it by saying something thoughtless or too brutally honest, at some point. It's not meant to hurt, but can often happen that way!

Try to be patient, even if you're dying to make the first move. You will achieve far more by letting things take their own pace, discovering that you have mutual interests, gradually becoming good buddies and then wanting to see each other more, and more and more.

Never give the Sagittarius Lunar Lover any reason to doubt your loyalty, and certainly never to think you could be the type of person to play around with anyone else. Deeply loyal themselves when with the perfect partner, Lunar Sagittarians often have strong religious beliefs and demand mutual respect alongside love.

Resolve to try very hard to understand the Sagittarian need to feel mentally free and not loaded down with responsibilities. Show that you're the sort of person who will make every effort to enjoy the good things life has to offer, and that, like your Sagittarian Lunar Lover, you will also retain your sense of humour and look for the positive in everything.

Be someone whose mind, body and soul can be just what Sagittarius needs to feel truly whole – a partner, helpmate, lover and friend. Encourage his or her dreams, share their Sagittarian enthusiasm, and enjoy discovering the wanderlust part of *your* nature too!

_____ *Life with a Sagittarius Lunar Lover* _____

Sometimes you may feel that your Lunar Lover's insistence on being right so very often is just too much, for no-one can be right all the time. There is a preaching side to the Sagittarian Moon which can sometimes make you feel you're on trial, but you'll soon begin to realize that your Lunar Lover probably isn't even aware of this particular characteristic, and has sufficient sense of humour to see the funny side of any quarrels you may have about it.

Be prepared for a home which isn't always easy to keep tidy, could often contain an animal or two, and which will usually have a marvellously relaxed atmosphere. It will be the sort of place where friends can pop in at any time of day or night.

Once you've settled into the sort of open, easy-going relationship which Sagittarius enjoys, you won't have very much to complain about where love and affection are concerned. Your Sagittarian Lunar Lover genuinely wants to make you happy, in every possible way, and although he or she isn't thought of as the most sensual of souls, the Lunar Sagittarian's heart will beat as fast as any other.

Don't start worrying that because your Sagittarian Lunar Lover has enjoyed being a free spirit before you came along, the thought of settling down to live with you could be a daunting experience and he or she will want to roam again. Just because a Sagittarian Moon likes to converse with everyone in sight, imparting a myriad of thoughts and ideas to anyone who cares to listen, and just because a little gentle flirtation can be fun, it doesn't have to affect your life together. Once you've shown you are Sagittarian's true soulmate you can have a perfect relationship.

A happy love relationship combined with a really good friendship is something which can take a long time to find, so enjoy life with your very own Sagittarius Lunar Lover.

_____ *Lunar Lovers and their Sun signs* _____

The personality of your Sagittarius Lunar Lover will be modified by the position of the Sun in his or her horoscope:

ARIES SUN/SAGITTARIUS MOON   An adventurous explorer with an active mind and pasionately enthusiastic nature. This Lunar Lover will be ardently emotional and won't be tamed!

TAURUS SUN/SAGITTARIUS MOON   This Lunar Lover professes to yearn for security, but deep down an inner restlessness creates a wanderlust and fear of settling down too soon.

GEMINI SUN/SAGITTARIUS MOON   The true traveller of the Zodiac, flirtatious, fun, but hard to pin down. Mental stimulation *must* go hand-in-hand with physical attraction here.

CANCER SUN/SAGITTARIUS MOON   This Lunar Lover will have more of a domesticated side than most Sagittarian Moons, but will fight inwardly against being fenced in!

LEO SUN/SAGITTARIUS MOON   A wonderful, larger-than-life personality with a heart of gold. Being in love with love is fantastic, but the adventurous spirit of this Lunar Lover needs to roam too.

VIRGO SUN/SAGITTARIUS MOON   Sometimes this Lunar Lover analyses and criticizes just *too* much. But a wonderful warmth and generous, friendly nature invariably comes across.

LIBRA SUN/SAGITTARIUS MOON   Unbeatable charm and a lazy, easy-going sense of humour combined with a positive aspect on what living with an ideal soulmate *really* should be like!

SCORPIO SUN/SAGITTARIUS MOON   Brilliantly intuitive, this Lunar Lover can read you like a book but will be infinitely more possessive than any other Sagittarius Moon!

SAGITTARIUS SUN/SAGITTARIUS MOON   An unmistakable free-spirit with a *joie de vivre* which is unquenchable. Wonderful to be with if you can pin them down for long enough!

CAPRICORN SUN/SAGITTARIUS MOON   Material security will be important to this Lunar Lover who has a positive and optimistic view of life.

AQUARIUS SUN/SAGITTARIUS MOON   An unconventional love affair with an unpredictable, adventurous happy-go-lucky soulmate will be yours with this Lunar Lover.

PISCES SUN/SAGITTARIUS MOON   Highly intuitive, bordering on the psychic, with a deep desire to explore the world and share the sights with a true soulmate.

How to keep your Lunar Lover by your side

DO:
- Be their best friend in the world as well as their lover
- Enjoy sharing adventures with this free-spirited Moon sign
- Be positive, optimistic and have a good sense of humour
- Allow Sagittarius to know best – sometimes!
- Try to be interested in what interests Sagittarius
- Enjoy the outdoor life

DON'T:
- Ever show too much of a possessive or jealous streak
- Be too critical too often
- Stay in a bad mood for too long!
- Encourage this Lunar Lover to gamble (Lady Luck isn't always around)
- Try to make your life together seem too much like routine
- Criticize your Lunar Lover's adventurous spirit

THE MOON . . .
AND CAPRICORN

YOUR LUNAR INFLUENCES

When you were born, the Moon was in Capricorn, tenth sign of the Zodiac, and ruled by Saturn, the taskmaster of the Zodiac – old Father Time or 'Chronos', as he was known in the mythology of the ancient Greeks. Capricorn is a Feminine, Cardinal, Negative, Earth Sign, whilst the Moon is associated with your opposite sign of Cancer, also Feminine, Cardinal and Negative but a Water sign. In many ways to have your Moon in Capricorn is a fairly compatible placing, although because Capricorn is actually the opposition sign to Cancer, and because the Moon rules your emotions, the Capricorn tendency to repress feelings may be exaggerated.

A Capricorn Moon placing often means you will be exceptionally practical, capable and organized. Since the Moon represents the inner you, the side of your personality that you guard with a very special reverence, it is almost inevitable that you will be subconsciously determined to keep control of your feelings at all times. And if you're a typical Capricorn Moon person this characteristic could stick with you throughout your life.

However, whilst the Capricorn influence creates your outer search for security in all its possible forms, the idealistic and impressionable qualities bestowed on you by the Moon's influence cannot be negated. Having your feet on the ground is all very well, but it isn't a sin to have romantic and idealistic dreams, to want to soar to the heights and allow your feelings to express themselves naturally.

To be born with the Moon in Capricorn can often mean you have had a difficult early life, perhaps due to problems in your childhood and this has often left you with a surprisingly timid side to your nature which is a contrast to the personality you probably project to the outside world.

There is a tendency to bottle up your emotions to such an extent that you can come across as cold and unfeeling, materialistic and insensitive. It is therefore very important for you to make contact with your Higher Self, to establish a relationship with the spiritual side of your nature and to understand that far from being punished for showing greater sensitivity, the rewards you will gain from reaching down to the soul level of your personality will be immeasurable in your daily life, and particularly in your relationships with other people.

Whilst you feel totally at home on 'earth' you tend to be extremely unsure of yourself in the spiritual world, and you need to allow the influence of the Moon to help your deep-rooted instincts and intuition to shine through and enable you to conquer your deepest fears and insecurities.

The trouble with having a Capricorn Moon is that often when you do feel something instinctively, the practical and materialistic side of the Capricorn personality takes over and you somehow link your intuition with being unrealistic and impractical. Saturn gives you great powers of concentration, so why don't you harness those powers towards a more positive awareness of what your inner self can teach you.

To be unsentimentally practical and realistic is fine on one level, but on a deeper soul level it can mean you miss out on many of the beautiful aspects of life by controlling your feelings to excess.

Your Capricorn Moon can also make you somewhat too judgmental in your approach to others. You may not be able to help having a serious nature, but very often you possess a wonderfully dry sense of humour which can make you a lively and amusing companion.

With a Capricorn Moon it's almost as though you were an adult before you were a child. Emotions were something you didn't talk about, let alone show. But now that you know you can communicate with your inner being and let your intuition be your best friend instead

of something you turn away from, you will reach new heights of awareness, not only related to your own personality, but to the way you jour-
ney through life.

Positive and negative characteristics for Capricorn

Look at this checklist and see which characteristics apply to you:

The Positive Moon

- Practical and organized
- Serious and sensible
- Down-to-earth
- Searching for security
- Ambitious and hardwork-
  ing

The Negative Moon

- Too materialistic and
  pragmatic
- Overly serious and insensi-
  tive!
- Lacking in idealism
- Can be unromantic
- Can be too much of a
  workaholic

———— *Your Capricorn emotions* ————

Never contrived but inevitably controlled, you can miss out on the
sheer joy of being alive, of experiencing passionate ecstasy, of simply
letting your hair down and having fun – all because you have been so
determined to hide away your emotions for ever and a day.

Whether it's because of your childhood, your present situation, your
inner fear of letting go, is all immaterial. The point is that you can be as
romantic and passionate as anyone else, and if you will just resolve to let
your inhibitions fade, to let the Moon help you unleash your romantic
dreams and turn them into beautiful reality, you will soon surprise
yourself and the people you love by becoming a much warmer and softer
human being. It doesn't mean you have to lose your outer strength, it
just means that your sensitivity will start to be your guiding light, your

intuition will be magnified to such great heights that you will wonder how on earth you reached where you are now without it.

Relationships will always be a serious business for you. Putting down roots with the perfect soulmate is not something you will undertake in a lighthearted way. But think how much easier it's going to be to know if you're on the right track if the power of your Capricorn Moon is allowed to shine through to guide you.

Often you need to overcome an almost pessimistic attitude to love and romance, an inner fear that things aren't going to work out the way you want them to. This is because you worry about old age and survival, especially if you have already suffered any kind of hardship in your life. You desperately yearn for security on all levels, and are an immensely caring, loyal and supportive partner when you are involved with someone. It's time you allowed yourself to have a little more faith in the ability of others to behave in the same way. Sometimes you can be as critical and analytical as Virgo.

You hate rejection in any form, it makes you withdraw further into yourself. But do you honestly think that anyone likes to be rejected? Believe in the hidden powers of your mind, and you'll learn to believe even more in others too, which will make you stronger emotionally and happier too.

Your career

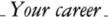

Your attitude to your career is usually identical to that of a Sun Capricorn. Just like the Mountain Goat, symbol of Capricorn, you are determined to reach the top of the mountain, to have the greatest possible success in your chosen field so that you can at the same time reap the benefits of material security which are so essential to you.

The inspirational force of the Moon will be immensely beneficial in pointing you in the right direction to achieve your highest potential. Capricorn careers tend to include science, administration, politics, banking, teaching, the civil service, building, farming – indeed any profession where organization plays a key role. The business world and any form of management are especially appealing to Moon Capricorns.

You are prepared to put in exceptionally long hours (hence your 'workaholic' description) so that you can climb higher up that ladder to success, and you are immensely painstaking over your work. Out of all the Moon signs you are possibly the most career-minded at heart with a devotion to duty which is to be admired, and there can actually be quite a ruthless quality (which you may not even be aware of!) whereby you may even take advantage of a relationship in order to advance your own career!

_____ *Your family and friends* _____

There may have been a difficult relationship with your family, perhaps an early loss, or an inability to communicate on all levels. This all adds up to your own feeling of inadequacy or timidity in expressing love and affection because it was not necessarily handed out in the way or amount you yearned for.

This is one of the main reasons why it is often so hard for Capricorn Moon people to let themselves go totally and relax and enjoy a loving relationship with relatives and friends. Inwardly you almost seem to feel it truly is a sin to show what you *are* feeling.

But you are immensely devoted to both family and friends, if a little too inclined to bow to tradition and conservative approaches to life, and you can be a hard taskmaster when you have children of your own. However, you are always there when you're needed (except of course when you are working late!) and you really do try to create enduring and loving ties with your relatives and friends.

_____ *Capricorn lunar love* _____

Cool, calm, controlled Capricorn! Yes, even someone as serious and hard-working as you can participate in the bliss of falling in love with that perfect partner, even though it might be a little more difficult for you to recognize and accept the feeling at first!

In a funny way you hate the idea of becoming emotionally dependent on anyone else although you are usually perfectly happy for your partner to feel emotinally dependent on you. But for things to work well you function best in the sort of equal relationship where there is mutual respect, trust and enjoyment in each other's company, without any possessive jealousy (be it over a person or your job).

When you do allow your emotions to show through you can be just as passionately romantic as anyone else, but it can certainly take an awfully long time to draw you out. You're not usually a tactile sort of person which can be a bit offputting for somone who loves cozy cuddles and other little affectionate gestures.

It's almost as though you have an inferiority complex, fearing that your overtures might be rebuffed. Just try to let yourself go. Forget about any past mistakes or hurts, and enjoy letting the loving side of your nature shine through. Listen to your lunar intuition and you will know when you're with the right soulmate who will help you lose your inhibitions and find love!

Lunar relationships

Try to find a Moon Lover whose personality can blend well with yours. The following will act as a guide:

CAPRICORN MOON/ARIES MOON   Emotionally you're far more restrained than impulsive Aries who could really knock you for six in the romance stakes!

CAPRICORN MOON/TAURUS MOON   Both ruled by the element of Earth, the sensuality of Taurus could soon break down your defences and since both of you yearn for security – why not!

CAPRICORN MOON/GEMINI MOON   Flirtatious Gemini might stimulate your mind but you're not at all sure this could be a long-lasting relationship as your ideals are invariably diverse.

CAPRICORN MOON/CANCER MOON   An interesting attraction of opposites which could work wonderfully on a deep soul level – or be a total disaster. No in-betweens here!

CAPRICORN MOON/LEO MOON   Two dominant signs, but whilst Leo loves to be in love and show it, you're far more fearful of letting that Capricorn emotion shine through.

CAPRICORN MOON/VIRGO MOON   Another Earthy combination, sharing many mutual interests, and both reticent about expressing deep emotions until the time and place are really right.

CAPRICORN MOON/LIBRA MOON   If you're after a warm loving relationship with someone who has masses of charm and diplomacy, Libra could be perfect. But you'll have to be more romantic if it's going to work.

CAPRICORN MOON/SCORPIO MOON   Invincible Scorpio with all that powerful passion might send you scurrying for safety. One look from those brooding eyes which read you like a book will excite you all the same!

CAPRICORN MOON/SAGITTARIUS MOON   Sagittarius is probably just too free and easy for someone who puts material security above all else – but at least you'd have lots of fun.

CAPRICORN MOON/CAPRICORN MOON   It takes one to know one! You'll understand each other really well and probably have the same life ambitions but don't let it be all work and no play.

CAPRICORN MOON/AQUARIUS MOON   There is no doubt that this would be an unpredictable relationship but perhaps it's just what you need to lighten your life in a truly unconventional way.

CAPRICORN MOON/PISCES MOON   It's impractical, it's sentimental, it's not what you thought you wanted – but Pisces will be the most romantic lover you've ever known.

THE CAPRICORN LUNAR LOVER

A Capricorn Lunar Lover is not someone to be taken lightly. Life for anyone strongly influenced by the sign of Capricorn is a serious business, and since the Moon rules one's emotions, it stands to reason that love and romance are no laughing matter for the Mountain Goat of the Zodiac.

The Capricorn Lunar Lover is a person whose feet are so firmly placed upon the ground, even more so than the other two Earth signs Taurus and Virgo, that the thought of basking in idyllic, romantic passion could send many a Capricorn running away very fast.

However, before you start to wonder whether a Capricorn Lunar Lover is capable of love and passion, let me reassure you that you won't actually have too much to complain about once this Moon sign has realized you are an ideal soulmate and has fallen for you hook, line and sinker.

Capricorn wants to be totally sure of someone before committing him or herself totally. This could be because of childhood memories and family difficulties, or perhaps because of a deep-rooted need for material and emotional security. Second best will just not do for this sign.

Your Capricorn Lunar Lover is not going to play the field, and one night stands are a total anathema. People with the Moon in this sign are often quite late starters where love is concerned. They are far more pre-occupied with creating a secure base and establishing themselves professionally, for your Capricorn Moon personality is one of the most ambitious signs of the Zodiac, and there is no way emotional hassles are going to stand in their way when it comes to achieving their objectives.

The Capricorn Lunar Lover simply doesn't have time for little dalliances, no matter how delightful they might be! Somehow the conviction that love and happiness with the ideal mate cannot happen until success on other levels has been obtained seems to be ingrained within this Lunar Lover's personality – and can be hard to overcome.

The effect of Saturn, Capricorn's ruling planet, can also be a bit of a damper on your Lunar Lover. Saturn can cast a melancholy hue, making a Capricorn Moon person far too pessimistic to believe that a perfect soulmate could truly fall for them.

But don't despair that you're not going to get anywhere if you've just met a Capricorn Lunar Lover! There will be lots of other signs, planets and aspects which affect his or her horoscope, and since the Moon has to have a powerful effect on anyone's emotions, even someone who appears to have a cool approach to the possibilities of romantic bliss will soon unwind when someone wonderful comes their way!

The Capricorn Lunar Lover is a somewhat comlex personality, for it's almost as though they have trained themselves to withhold emotion for so long that it's become second nature. It's therefore a marvellous challenge to meet them and convince them that love and security can go hand-in-hand.

Recognizing a Capricorn Lunar Lover

Anyone with the Moon or the Sun in Capricorn is sure to some across as being an undemonstrative, serious soul for whom taking time off from work is almost a mortal sin. Of course this is a slight exaggeration, but most Capricorn Lunar Lovers convey the appearance that they should be continually working away like beavers (or Mountain Goats!) until the late hours of the evening when it's time to have a quick bite, and sleep a while until it's time to start all over again the next day.

So, if you meet someone who seems to find it hard to relax and enjoy themselves, who continually checks a watch, and tends to dress more formally than most of the other folk around, it won't come as any surprise to find you've met a Lunar Capricorn. If the talk tends to veer towards work, and the financial worries besetting the world, you can be almost sure you've hit the nail on the head.

Sexual compatibility is exceedingly important to the Capricorn Lunar Lover, and the deepening of a relationship on a mind/body/soul level can be a beautiful experience, for once your Capricorn Lunar Lover is convinced you're a perfect partner, he or she will do everything possible to ensure you won't want to find anyone else.

Captivating a Capricorn Lunar Lover

Perhaps an old-fashioned approach would be best if you're out to captivate a Lunar Lover whose own approach is hardly likely to be the most forward you're ever known!

Always remember that your Capricorn Lunar Lover is often very shy, no matter how powerful and successful they might be in their professional life. They need to be drawn out gently, carefully, and certainly won't like anyone who comes over too strongly, who is too extrovert, too blatantly sexual (and even if they do like it deep down, they certainly would never admit it).

To be truly captivating it's almost best to give off an air of aloofness, a sense of power, of total confidence in your own being, and have an aura of success about you (even if you happen to be out of work at the time!). Don't ever be too loud or ostentatious – this Lunar Lover can be quiet a snob. And hopefully there won't be too many black sheep in your family background!

Your Capricorn Lunar Lover certainly doesn't want to think that you are a flirt, someone who is only looking for a casual affair, so make sure that if you are dressed to kill it's done in an understated way! Capricorn appreciates elegance. You need to be able to converse well on serious subjects, never indulge in idle gossip and at the same time have a good sense of humour. Whilst this might be slightly lacking in the Capricorn Lunar Lover it is certainly appreciated in others, for Capricorn well knows that being too serious all the time isn't such a good thing even if for him or her it often appears to be inevitable.

Show that you're someone who is prepared to put a great deal of work into making a relationship succeed on every possible level. Capricorn wants an equal partner, never a 'yes' man or woman. And take the time to reach those Capricorn Lunar emotions which are buried so very far down. They are well worth discovering if you want a loyal and loving soulmate by your side.

_____ Life with a Capricorn Lunar Lover _____

If you're looking for domestic security, with as many material comforts as is reasonably possible, in the right sort of neighbourhood, and with the right sort of neighbours around you, you may not have to look any further than a Capricorn Lunar Lover.

However, you'd best prepare yourself for living with someone who is going to upset a great many of your arrangements, whether they be a cozy dinner for two in front of the fire, or a dinner party given for some of your closest friends. The reason for this, as if you haven't already guessed, is that your Capricorn Lunar Lover will probably still be working when everyone else is on their way home. It isn't that

Capricorn dislikes social activities, just that it is very hard to find the time to fit them in.

Moon Capricorns of both sexes can actually make life rather too much like hard work. Even the housework is a serious business and hopefully you won't be someone who is incredibly untidy if you're going to live with a Capricorn Lunar Lover.

Living with a Lunar Capricorn may not appear to be a continuous round of jollity, with parties every other night. However, it will certainly give you a great deal of emotional security, for your Capricorn Lunar Lover, having found you and having been convinced that you're the ideal partner, is going to be quite content to leave things that way. You won't have to worry about this partner feeling that the grass is greener on the other side, continually on the lookout for an ideal flirtation. With the Capricorn Lunar Lover a relationship is for life, or at least that is how they want things to be, and probably the only cause for jealousy will be your Capricorn's job!

The Capricorn Lunar Lover appreciates beauty and elegance, tradition and the good things of life, but is never likely to be unduly extravagant financially (he or she has usually worked too hard to consider squandering any of their earnings).

Romantic passion may not appear to be there in abundance – but it is there, never fear!

_____ *Lunar Lovers and their Sun signs* _____

The personality of your Capricorn Lunar Lover will be modified by the position of the Sun in his or her horoscope:

ARIES SUN/CAPRICORN MOON   This Lunar Lover will enjoy challenges in both personal and professional situations. A *very* determined personality this!

TAURUS SUN/CAPRICORN MOON   Security is immensely important to this Earth-ruled Lunar Lover. Loyal and supportive but sometimes shy about showing any really deep feelings.

GEMINI SUN/CAPRICORN MOON   A talkative workaholic, who will take a lot of time to convince that a perfect soulmate is one of the best things in life!

CANCER SUN/CAPRICORN MOON   A somewhat materialistic Lunar Lover who is sometimes almost afraid to admit that they yearn for emotional security above all else.

LEO SUN/CAPRICORN MOON   Definitely a strong-willed individual who doesn't want to take second place to anyone! But a side of this personality is incredibly loving and quite a romantic.

VIRGO SUN/CAPRICORN MOON   Steeped in tradition and with their feet firmly on the ground, this Lunar Lover may be too serious and needs to cultivate a sense of fun.

LIBRA SUN/CAPRICORN MOON   Somewhat cool on the surface but with a sensitive inner core, this Lunar Lover will always be a charming and diplomatic companion.

SCORPIO SUN/CAPRICORN MOON   An invincible partner! If this Lunar Lover sets their sights on you it may be hard to walk away if there truly is a mutual attraction.

SAGITTARIUS SUN/CAPRICORN MOON   An adventurer with an inner yearning for a secure life with the perfect soulmate. More optimistic than most Capricorn Lunar Lovers!

CAPRICORN SUN/CAPRICORN MOON   Yes, there really are deep emotional feelings beneath the surface of this seemingly so controlled and disciplined Lunar Lover.

AQUARIUS SUN/CAPRICORN MOON   A conflict between the unpredictable and the traditional creates an interesting individual who will never leave you feeling bored.

PISCES SUN/CAPRICORN MOON   Serious but sensitive, realistic but intensely intuitive – this Lunar Lover's personality is more romantic than you might first expect.

How to keep your Lunar Lover by your side

DO:
- Be patient whilst Capricorn's emotions slowly start to show
- Understand how important tradition is with this Lunar Lover
- Be loyal, loving and supportive
- Be serious about what Capricorn considers serious in life
- Appreciate this Lunar Lover's dedication to work – but try encouraging them to have some time off too!
- Remember that Capricorn needs emotional and material security

DON'T:
- Be too flirtatious when you first meet – especially not with anyone else!
- Ever become jealous of their work – at least it's not another person . . .
- Be financially extravagant or impractical, Capricorn cannot cope with either
- Embarrass this Lunar Lover in any way
- Criticize their family or friends
- Expect an excess of passion unless the time and place is really right!

THE MOON . . .
AND AQUARIUS

YOUR LUNAR INFLUENCES

When you were born, the Moon was in Aquarius, eleventh sign of the Zodiac, and ruled by Uranus, planet of invention and inspiration. Aquarius is a Masculine, Fixed, Positive, Air sign, and it's that Fixed quality which can sometimes make you almost as stubborn as Taurus, although by nature your emotions are often unpredictable, to say the least! The Moon itself is associated with Cancer – a Feminine, Cardinal, Negative, Water sign – and its influence in Aquarius will usually mean that you can be even *more* cool and detached than someone with the Sun or Ascendant in this sign.

The Moon in your horoscope relates to the inner you, to the secret part of you which you like to keep to yourself. You are probably quite a unique individual, one who doesn't like to follow the same path as most other people. Sometimes others may find you difficult, describing you as anything from a 'wayward genius' or 'irritating time-keeper' to an 'unfeeling and unsympathetic character'. Naturally this is going to hurt you, because you are also one of the friendliest people in the whole Zodiac and you never consciously want to hurt anyone.

There is actually an eccentric side of your personality which can be unbelievably infuriating to anyone who has anything at all to do with you. Just like Sun Aquarians you can be wonderful when you're expected to be in a horrible mood, and impossible when everything should be sweetness and light. Perhaps you feel that unconventionality is your birthright, but if you use the power of your lunar influence to become more in touch with your Higher Self you will discover that your intuition can be immensely valuable in helping you to avoid unnecessary contretemps with the people you care for! Being the original rebel without a cause, as far as your emotions are concerned, might be fine for a while but it can be awfully boring and time consuming for everyone else.

Since Aquarius is so often an intellectual free-thinker, it naturally stands to reason that your thoughts and feelings could lead you into realms of philosophy, new political reasonings and cleverly thought out reasons for just about everything.

Because you *are* such an unpredictable Air sign, some of you almost refuse to admit that you *have* emotional feelings, deep ones that is. Sometimes this can relate back to your childhood and disruptions you experienced whilst you were growing up, either because of the situation between your parents or simply because you seemed to be on the move a great deal.

It is often because of this that your Aquarian Moon instils deep within you an even greater need to develop your individuality and independent, freedom-loving approach to life. But don't miss out on the chance of meeting that ideal soulmate because you refuse to understand your own emotions.

Since personal growth needs to come from within, to have an Aquarian Moon can be a great blessing, for if you are prepared to sit silently and meditate upon the questions you hold most dear, you will probably be surprised just how soon you could receive the answers. Since the element of Aquarius is Air, and since Uranus relates to space age inventions, why not visualize yourself in space when you do meditate and enjoy what you experience.

The Aquarian tendency is to be friendly to all but close to very few. It's wonderful to be a humanitarian, but don't lose out on meeting your very own soulmate by blocking your emotions to the extent of coming across as too cool and detached for your *own* good, let alone as someone's possible ideal partner!

Restless and often creative, it's almost as though you like to shock other people into awareness of what is going around them. But how about using your lunar intuition to wake up your own feelings and discover interesting new facets about your own personality and your own little world?

Positive and negative characteristics for Aquarius

Look at this checklist and see which characteristics apply to you:

The Positive Moon

- Imaginative and inspirational
- Exciting and charismatic
- Humanitarian
- A pace-setter
- Idealistic

The Negative Moon

- Cold and unfeeling
- Unpredictable and rebellious
- Difficult to get close to
- *Too* unconventional
- Overly radical

Your Aquarius emotions

From reading about your lunar influences you will already realize that your Aquarian emotions are not just laid-back or even non-existent, they are simply buried deep below the surface of the somewhat extrovert personality you prefer to present to the world.

Anyone who doubts whether indeed you do have emotions need have no fear. It's simply that they are also not always what is expected from you, and as if you feel that daring to show them could possibly be construed as a display of weakness – something to which you would definitely never admit!

This is probably why you tend to gravitate towards relationships which do not appear (at first, anyway) that they could be 'heavy'! It is why you are such a great friend to have around but not necessarily always the perfect lover.

Even if this is because of your childhood, as it's often said that Aquarians tend to sometimes have a disruptive early life, don't let past emotional disappointments or an inner fear prevent you from realizing that the intuitive and instinctive powers of the Moon can be your guiding light. Try to allow your emotions to break through the clouds when you are with someone with whom you feel a special affinity.

There is no need to hide what you are feeling. Sometimes it may have seemed hard for you to make even an affectionate gesture. You may not be the most tactile of signs, but even when you are sensually aroused it's as though you are determined to put up your own little notice 'Keep away, don't touch'.

However, since it's very unlikely that the idea of a soulmate totally fills you with abject horror, why not try that much harder to get in touch with your emotions? Enjoy the fulfilling pleasure of loving not just the world in general − but a partner of your own!

Because you are deeply idealistic you have very strong ideas about what a perfect soulmate should be. That's fine as long as you are prepared to allow yourself to grow spiritually, so that you can also be a perfect soulmate to that other person and thus completely aware of the existence of your inner self. As your emotions become easier to express, the whole of your emotional life will become easier too.

Your career

With the motivation of the Moon, it is almost inevitable that your Aquarian qualities will lead you to seek work which enables you to have a certain freedom to follow the dictates of your mind.

It would be hard for you to stick to a routine nine-to-five sort of deskbound job where you were totally tied to authoritarian rules and regulations, although having said this you are invariably equally determined to follow through to the end anything you have started especially when it is for the benefit of others.

Both Sun and Moon Aquarians are often drawn to radio, TV, cinema, science, politics, social work, astrology, astronomy, archaeology, aviation, inventing, electronics and anything to do with space.

The inspirational and inventive characteristics of your Aquarian Moon are a great asset, so that the more prepared you are to spend the time and trouble getting in touch with your inner senses, the greater both your emotional and professional fulfilment will be.

——————— *Your family and friends* ———————

If your own family were not terribly demonstrative in showing love and affection, this could add to your Lunar Aquarian difficulty in giving these out to nearest and dearest. It's certainly not that you don't care about family and friends, far from it. It's just your inability to express outwardly what you are feeling inside and because you've repressed those Aquarian emotions for so long, you prefer to continue in the same way.

However, do try to remember that you can come across as unfeeling, and resolve that the more you discover about the depth of your lunar emotions, the more you will try to give a greater part of yourself to the people you care for most, especially if and when you have children of your own.

It's not simply enough to say that your family and friends know you well enough by now, and that this detached aura is an integral part of your personality – to be really true to yourself you have to stop being quite so self-contained and controlled.

——————— *Aquarius lunar love* ———————

Unpredictable, unconventional, unemotional Aquarius, how will you behave when you fall head-over-heels in love? Or do you actually believe that such a situation could never happen to someone as coolly detached as you? Don't fool yourself by giving in to that last belief, for whilst the influence of the Moon can sometimes create a feeling of delusion, you must by now have realized that it also enhances intuition and instinct in an extremely powerful manner.

One of the most important things for you to remember when you meet that perfect soulmate is to try harder than usual to be less cool and detached. You don't have to change overnight into a fireball of passion, but it would be nice to see that you care!

Perhaps the major problem is that out of all the lunar signs you are the least influenced by the Moon herself, and it's almost as though you refuse to listen to your inner voice when you fall in love!

What is certainly true is that you need a soulmate who is intellectually stimulating. Sometimes your most important relationships will result from a good platonic friendship, developing slowly into something of a more physical nature.

You're definitely not bound by any hidebound convention. When you do find that perfect partner they don't have to fit into any preconceived notion of what a soulmate should be – for when you truly want to use your lunar intuition – it really does work!

_____ *Lunar relationships* _____

Try to find a Moon Lover whose personality can blend well with yours. The following will act as a guide:

AQUARIUS MOON/ARIES MOON   Aries provides you with a fiery challange which is quite overpowering, but you may feel a threat to your independence which is hard to take.

AQUARIUS MOON/TAURUS MOON   You won't have much to complain about if it's tender loving care you're after. But remember that Taurus has a very stubborn streak at times.

AQUARIUS MOON/GEMINI MOON   Both ruled by the element of Air, you have lots to talk about and make an interesting duo. But this might work best on a platonic rather than physical level.

AQUARIUS MOON/CANCER MOON   Domestic bliss may not be exactly what you have in mind, but if it is, and you're prepared to put up with a few Cancerian moods, it's fine!

AQUARIUS MOON/LEO MOON   An interesting attraction of opposites – poles apart in some ways but Leo's sunny, sparkling personality is very fascinating.

AQUARIUS MOON/VIRGO MOON   If you dislike criticism in any form, it's probably best to choose a different Lunar Lover – or try to change some of *your* ways fast!

AQUARIUS MOON/LIBRA MOON   A beautiful duo if you make the effort to be more romantic and affectionate towards this peaceful and lovable Air sign, who will charm you in a multitude of ways.

AQUARIUS MOON/SCORPIO MOON   Call it playing with fire if you like! Scorpio's emotional intensity could send shivers down even the most cool and detached Aquarian spine.

AQUARIUS MOON/SAGITTARIUS MOON   A casual, enjoyable friendship with someone who shares similar interests and is equally independent could develop into something more.

AQUARIUS MOON/CAPRICORN MOON   You're both serious about many things in life, but Capricorn is more concerned with material security than you.

AQUARIUS MOON/AQUARIUS MOON   Two highly motivated free-thinkers together, both unpredictable and unconventional – a real mirror-image relationship.

AQUARIUS MOON/PISCES MOON   If you're prepared to believe in romantic dreams, then Pisces is the perfect person with whom to share beautiful sunrises and sunsets – but perhaps too sentimental for you!

THE AQUARIUS LUNAR LOVER

Before an Aquarius Lunar Lover really does become a lover, there is probably a long way to go! This Moon sign doesn't believe in rushing into a tempestuous affair, even if they do find the idea appealing and are strongly attracted to you.

It's probably best to advise you at the outset, that you may not even *know* that this particular Lunar Lover is even the slightest little bit interested in you. Don't expect any of the usual giveaways you can get from other signs. No, the Aquarian Lunar Lover is often so aloof and diffident that you'd need your own lunar intuition working overtime to discover what is happening beneath the surface.

In some ways it's almost as though this Lunar Lover has been trained from birth to reveal nothing, or certainly as little as possible, about his or her emotional feelings. This means you can be in for quite a challenging time ahead of you, so hopefully you possess plenty of patience and already share some mutual interests with your chosen soulmate!

Aquarius loves to meet new people, become involved in new interests, and above all to help those in need. A champion of the under-dog, of lost causes, of ways to save the environment, this Lunar Lover is nevertheless often unbelievably shy or just plain stubborn about admitting to the need for a partner. Your best bet at the outset is to concentrate on being a friend, an ideal friend, an irreplaceable friend – and let things grow slowly. Believing in destiny will also help – tell yourself if it's meant to be, it will be, and that meanwhile you'll do everything you can to prove your worth!

With an Aquarian Lunar Lover, it's nice to know that philandering is not usually the name of the game. When Aquarius does fall for someone, they feel no urge to search around for anyone else. Just make sure that the mental stimulation which existed in the beginning doesn't slip, as sexual compatibility alone will never satisfy Aquarius for very long.

Very idealistic, the Aquarian Lunar Lover is inwardly searching for someone to share the same goals, so this is the moment to warn you that if your ideals are very different it is probably much better to accept the limitations that this would create. Aquarius can be almost as stubborn as Taurus, and is unlikely to change.

Last of the Air signs, and in many ways the most unusual of the three, this Lunar Lover is simply never going to conform to many people's standards of how someone should live their life. But if you are attracted to such an unconventional personality it will no doubt be worth your while to find out more.

The Aquarian Lunar Lover is usually incredibly proud of being independent but always enjoys sharing too. And never forget that admitting they need someone special in their life isn't always easy for this charismatic personality.

Recognizing an Aquarius Lunar Lover

If you come across someone expounding their views about humanity, who doesn't appear to fit into the normal run-of-the-mill personality you're used to – either in dress or behaviour – it's quite likely you've met an Aquarius Moon personality.

The Aquarian Lunar Lover isn't usually a tremendous flirt, although he or she is obviously an incredibly friendly and gregarious sort of person. Somehow you may feel there is something slightly eccentric about their behaviour, that emotionally they are holding back, not wanting anyone to know that they even _have_ feelings.

You immediately sense that you've met an immensely independent character who is going to be more interested in whether you are intellectually stimulating than whether you're going to be great in bed! You soon realize that even if your physical attributes are being sized up and appreciated in a sensual way, it's unlikely there will be anything more than the slightest flicker of awareness that there is some chemisty between you.

Amusing, charming and definitely unusual – it shouldn't be very hard to discover that you've just met an Aquarius Lunar Lover!

Captivating an Aquarius Lunar Lover

Needless to say it will be a whole lot easier if you happen to be a Sun or Moon Aquarian yourself! If not, you may have to learn how to project a whole new personality, holding back if you're an impulsive Fire sign, showing a little less sentimentality if you're born under the Water element, and being less stubborn, materialistic or critical if you're one of the Earth signs.

Above all, it's best to appear as though you are equally independent and free-thinking, and to have at least one favourite charity or cause to which you give your whole-hearted support.

Once you've managed to establish that you share more than a few common interests and have held this Aquarian Lunar Lover spellbound for an entire evening, just play it really cool and be very nonchalant as to when it will be possible to meet again.

Some of the best and longest lasting relationships take a long while to grow, and to captivate the Aquarius Lunar Lover you really do need to be their true friend before you become their lover. Don't ever try to put sentimental words into this Moon Lover's mouth, even if you're dying to know what they really feel about you. By now you must have learnt that Aquarius often simply hates having to express any terms of endearment, and to try to push them into talking about emotions is definitely taboo!

Don't let it appear as though you're searching for someone to depend on. Although your Aquarian Lunar Lover might not want to admit it, deep down his or her lunar intuition is saying that being dependent on someone or having someone become dependent on them is just not the right thing.

Be loving without being jealous or possessive. It might appear that Lunar Aquarians don't even want to be loved, but just like every other sign of the Zodiac they are often inwardly searching for that special soulmate to make life truly worthwhile.

Always remember that whilst a passionately sexy affair which doesn't necessarily involve being in love might suit some Aquarians, most of them need to know that love *is* the major and intrinsic factor.

_____ *Life with an Aquarius Lunar Lover* _____

Don't expect an ordinary 'every day's more or less the same' type of life if you're embarking on this particular voyage of a lifetime! Life with an Aquarius Lunar Lover will never be boring but sometimes you might concede that it can be infuriating.

Perhaps one of the most irritating little facets of your Aquarian Lunar Lover's personality is an apparent inability to be a good time keeper. This might not appear to be such a dramatic problem, until the times when there is an important dinner party, a night out at the theatre or a plane to catch. It's not that Aquarius means to be difficult, just that he or she usually has so many other important things in their mind that the time just goes by, and by, and by . . .

Your Aquarian Lunar Lover isn't necessarily the most organized of people, and is also invariably someone who takes pity on lame dogs of both the human *and* animal variety.

Whilst being loving and supporting as much as possible, it's no use expecting great displays of affection unless you're in the most intimate of situations. By now you know very well that your Aquarian Lunar Lover is very far from being amongst the most demonstrative signs of the Zodiac, and if you've got this far, you've obviously become used to it, and even become convinced that it will be you, and you alone, who possesses the power to bring those deep-rooted emotions to the surface.

At least you shouldn't have to worry that your Aquarian Lunar Lover is going to play the field, for once he or she has settled into an easy-going relationship with an ideal partner, they won't start to think that the grass might be greener on the other side.

Just remember the importance of mental communication, of sharing the same ideals and never lose your own independent way of thinking.

_____ *Lunar Lovers and their Sun signs* _____

The personality of your Aquarius Lunar Lover will be modified by the position of the Sun in his or her horoscope:

ARIES SUN/AQUARIUS MOON   An enthusiastic supporter of innumerable causes, with a friendly, outgoing and lovable personality. Not afraid to express how he, or she really feels!

TAURUS SUN/AQUARIUS MOON   An artistic and creative Lunar Lover, whose inner need for freedom is tempered by the Taurean desire for emotional security with a loving partner.

GEMINI SUN/AQUARIUS MOON   Mentally you couldn't wish for a more stimulating Lunar Lover, but you'll have to really work hard to convince someone with this combination that it's going to be you, and only you, for ever more!

CANCER SUN/AQUARIUS MOON   Seemingly concerned with seeking cozy domestic bliss, this Lunar Lover will have an unpredictable side to his or her personality which will invariably keep you guessing.

LEO SUN/AQUARIUS MOON   On the surface this bright and sparkling and sometimes bossy personality has lots of love to give – but somehow they always seem to hold something back so you're not sure where you stand.

VIRGO SUN/AQUARIUS MOON   Not only shy about revealing their emotions, but often extremely self-critical at the same time. This Lunar Lover is sure to think for a long time before giving up their freedom!

LIBRA SUN/AQUARIUS MOON   This combination of two Air elements creates an idealistic romantic full of irresistible charm, who is torn between life with a perfect soulmate and fulfilling their adventurous dreams.

SCORPIO SUN/AQUARIUS MOON   A Lunar Lover with incredible insight and intuition, and a passionate intensity which really is hidden way, way beneath the surface.

SAGITTARIUS SUN/AQUARIUS MOON   A broad-minded individualist who will stand out in any crowd but may be hard to pin down if you're looking for a permanent partner in your life!

CAPRICORN SUN/AQUARIUS MOON   Very materialistic in some ways and amazingly unconventional in others, this Lunar Lover will keep you guessing as to their intentions till the very last minute, but you'll then feel very secure.

AQUARIUS SUN/AQUARIUS MOON   Definitely a unique individual, freedom-loving and adventurous, idealistic and unpredictable – if you're ready for the unexpected in your life, this could be it!

PISCES SUN/AQUARIUS MOON   A romantic dreamer who sometimes finds it strangely difficult to believe that true love really can exist. But this Lunar Lover can be amazingly intuitive and sensitive too.

How to keep your Lunar Lover by your side

DO:

- Prove that you can also be cool, detached and unemotional!
- Listen to and support your Lunar Lover's idealistic aspirations
- Remember that mental stimulation is a vital part of your relationship
- Retain the independent streak which first captivated this Lunar Lover
- Be your Lunar Lover's best friend as well as lover
- Try to be a humanitarian too . . .

DON'T:

- Be clinging, cloying or overly sentimental
- Be upset if your Lunar Lover isn't as demonstrative as you'd like
- Try to push your Aquarian Lunar Lover into something they're really set against
- Ever start being passionate in public – it's a real turn-off
- Try to plan too orderly a life with this Lunar Lover – it won't work!
- Criticize your Lunar Lover's time keeping!

THE MOON . . .
AND PISCES

YOUR LUNAR INFLUENCES

When you were born, the Moon was in Pisces, twelfth and last sign of the Zodiac, ruled by Neptune, planet of imagination and inspiration. Pisces, sign of the Fish, is a Feminine, Mutable, Negative, Water sign and, since Piscean emotions tend to be so sensitive anyway, it stands to reason that as a Moon Pisces *you* will be particularly influenced by everything you feel deep inside. The Moon itself is astrologically associated with Cancer, which is a Feminine, Cardinal, Negative, Water sign and is very much at home when placed in Pisces.

Your Pisces Moon helps to make you one of the most sensitive, compassionate and spiritual signs of the Zodiac. Often very psychic you might even be called a true visionary, and many people with the Moon in this sign are extremely artistic and creative. (People with the Moon in Pisces include Audrey Hepburn, Paul Newman, Frank Sinatra and Michael Jackson.) And no matter *how* strong you may appear on the outer surface, you are sure to be very soft inside!

Your Pisces Moon instils within you not only an interest in spiritual matters, but often an interest in religion too. You will always be drawn to helping others less fortunate than yourself, but sometimes you can be too much of an idealistic, romantic dreamer, and if you intend to use your lunar influence to its full potential it will be necessary to listen well to those finely-tuned senses when they warn you to keep your feet a little more firmly on the ground. Universal empathy is very much a Piscean password, but you do need to protect yourself too and not give out so much emotion that you end up feeling completely drained. Your inner sensitivity is a great bonus but as with any other bonus it needs to be used well and not wasted!

With a Pisces Moon, it really is very important to listen to your intuition and not simply brush it aside. You will also find that by spending some time quietly on your own, in a meditative state, your inner voice will come through even stronger and be a fantastic guiding light for you in your everyday life.

This doesn't mean you have to become so wrapped up in the unworldly and mystical side of life that you start to lose touch with the so-called 'real world'. You need to balance things properly for there is sometimes a tendency for Lunar Pisceans to become so steeped in fantasy that they are living up in the clouds more often than down on earth, which can lead to material problems.

You must also remember that with the Moon in Pisces you tend to be so impressionable and empathetic that your psychic senses can become like a sponge, mopping up everyone else's worries and problems, again at the cost of your own strength. And with those Piscean fish swimming in opposite directions, and the sometimes deceptive influence of Neptune, your own emotions can sometimes lead you astray.

In many ways it's a wonderful blessing to have so much instinct and intuition bestowed upon you by the influence of the Moon. But, it really is extremely important to keep in continual touch with your Higher Self and ask for guidance for those moments when emotionally you want to believe one thing and yet instinctively know that a rational approach is needed.

This is especially necessary when you start to feel you've met a soul-mate. It's not that you're as impulsive as Aries or emotionally intense as Scorpio – but just like Sun Pisceans you do tend to view the world with those beautiful rose-coloured spectacles which enhance someone who attracts you in an often quite amazing way! That is when you have to be totally truthful with your inner self, for your romantic dreams may be leading you away from your instincts!

Use the strength of your lunar influence in a positive way and it will make you aware of all the nuances of your personality and the personalities of the people with whom you come into contact. It will help you to become more independent too.

Positive and negative characteristics for Pisces

Look at this checklist and see which characteristics apply to you:

The Positive Moon

- Sensitive and imaginative
- Creative and artistic
- Spiritual
- Compassionate
- A true visionary

The Negative Moon

- Ultra-sensitive and escapist
- Too much of a dreamer
- Emotionally insecure
- Too much of a soft touch
- Becomes easily confused

Your Pisces emotions

One thing is for sure, you are probably the most emotional of all the Moon signs, and in some ways you find this confusing. Because you're such a compassionate and sympathetic soul it's very hard for you to turn away from anyone who needs your help. When your help is needed you invariably give it with love. But somehow you always seem to find yourself in situations where you are having to be responsible for the welfare of others, sometimes to the detriment of your own wellbeing.

Starry-eyed when it comes to romance, you believe strongly in the ideal of a true soulmate, someone whose personality will blend with yours in a total mind, body and soul relationship. However, your highly-attuned psychic ability seems to let you down quite often, and you have to watch out you're not attracted to someone because you also feel they need emotional support. Do try to learn to understand your emotions a little better and realize that you also need someone you can depend on, for if your own emotions start to get shot to pieces because of everything you're giving out, you can become dependent far too easily on alcohol or even drugs. There is often an emotional weakness which goes hand-in-hand with your sensitivity.

Sometimes this weakness can in turn lead you into depression or despair when things go wrong, and you can really make yourself ill. However, this must mean that you're not using the power of your lunar intuition in the best possible way. Deep down you really *do* know when something is right for you, so stop insisting on putting a rosy glow on it all and get out there in that real world!

There is a fey quality about you which is wonderfully refreshing, and you certainly don't need to lose that. But stop being like those two fishes swimming in different directions, and benefit from the inspirational qualities of Neptune and your Pisces Moon. Always remember that looking after your mind and spirit are just as important as looking after your body, and when the three are in total harmony you will feel on top of the world.

Your career

The influence of your Pisces Moon will motivate you in the way you apply yourself to your chosen career, and both Sun and Moon Pisceans are often drawn to the arts where they can use their creativity. Careers which appeal include being a poet, writer, actor, dancer, photographer, sailor, musician, or psychic. Since you truly want to help other people, professions such as teaching, nursing, social work and preaching will also be right for you.

Hopefully, you have learnt to use your lunar intuition well enough not to land yourself in a sort of dead-end job which is terribly boring, for as far as you're concerned liking what you are doing is possibly more important than the salary you receive! Ambitious in a creative sense, you are sometimes much too impractical when it comes to the state of your finances, and need to harness your energies *and* your intuition and resolve that you will start to take better care of yourself financially.

Your lunar intuition *can* make you a star in your chosen field if you follow through on what it tells you, and don't allow yourself to indulge in a state of apathy – which I'm afraid can happen from time to time!

Your family and friends

Since you *are* such a sympathetic and compassionate soul, you should be very much loved by your family and friends. But you do have to be careful that you don't let people depend on you too much, for occasionally you simply don't know what to do. Sometimes, just like your opposite sign of Virgo, you can be too much of a worrier and hate to think of the people you care for having any problems. But your sensitivity can become a weakness, so listen to your inner voice for it will tell you when it really is time to step back.

You love to have people around, and your home is probably not only full of people, but will invariably have a few dogs and cats too (possibly ones that you have rescued from trouble!).

You are wonderfully supportive to your family and your friends and are especially good with children as you understand just what they need from you.

Sometimes you are a little too concerned about whether everyone really likes you – and hopefully you have relatives and friends who bolster up your self-confidence when you are in that sort of mood.

Pisces lunar love

Romantic, sentimental, dreamy-eyes Pisces, surveying the world through your rose-coloured spectacles, wondering whether it's time to take them off and if you've really met the soulmate of your fantasies.

You are possibly the most romantic of all the signs, and when you're truly in love you're on Cloud Nine, oblivious of everything else that is going on around you. However, you can be far too inclined to wallow in self-pity if emotional problems arise.

Use the power of the Moon in a positive way, don't let it cloud your emotions so that you're simply in love with love. Let Neptune's inspiration enhance your intuition so that you truly know when you've met a partner who fulfils your dreams in a total mind, body and soul way. And even then, don't let yourself become so completely involved emotionally that everything else falls by the wayside.

Combine romance with a more realistic approach to life and you'll be delighted to find that your most important relationships become even more fulfilling.

The lovely thing about you is that you genuinely want to make your partner happy in every possible way, and you'll continually search for new ideas, sentimental gestures of affection with your words, your actions and very often little gifts as well.

Lunar relationships

Try to find a Moon Lover whose personality can blend well with yours. The following will act as a guide:

PISCES MOON/ARIES MOON   You're strongly attracted to this fiery Moon who will probably sweep you off your feet with the greatest of ease – but you need to make it a challenge for Aries!

PISCES MOON/TAURUS MOON   A cozy, comfortable relationship with lots of cuddles on cold winter nights from lovable Taurus. Both of you enjoying feeling so emotionally secure.

PISCES MOON/GEMINI MOON   Your intuition fascinates Gemini and you may have lots to talk about together. But Gemini's dislike of being in any one place too long may worry you!

PISCES MOON/CANCER MOON   There can be a strong bond between two such intuitive sensitive signs. Both of you are extremely sentimental and can enjoy a good relationship together.

PISCES MOON/LEO MOON   Love and romance flow in abundance and you feel protected by magnanimous Leo. Of course Leo wants to take the limelight, but that doesn't usually bother you.

PISCES MOON/VIRGO MOON   An attraction of opposites which can only work if the Virgo Lunar Lover stops being quite so picky and lets you be your dreamy but impractical self!

PISCES MOON/LIBRA MOON   Both of you seek romance, and Libra's charm can be quite overwhelming, although at times their indecision may have you wondering if your instinct was way off course.

PISCES MOON/SCORPIO MOON   Psychically you can't help but realize this attraction is very strong and you enjoy the magnetic charisma of this other Water Sign.

PISCES MOON/SAGITTARIUS MOON   You feel very comfortable with this friendly happy-go-lucky Moon Lover, but sometimes fear your own personality is far too introvert in comparison.

PISCES MOON/CAPRICORN MOON   If you're looking for material security, look no further. But Capricorn may sometimes seem too concerned with practicalities to be able to send shivers of excitement down your spine.

PISCES MOON/AQUARIUS MOON   On an intellectually stimulating level, this could be good. But the Aquarius inability to communicate very easily emotionally could make romance difficult.

PISCES MOON/PISCES MOON   This is a real soul level involvement and you can easily read each other's minds. Love and romance work beautifully, but on a more practical level you may not be so good for each other.

THE PISCES LUNAR LOVER
—————————— o ——————————

'Fly me to the Moon' could be the appropriate vocals, describing how you will feel if you've found yourself a Pisces Lunar Lover. This Moon sign is just about the most romantic person you could ever meet, and if the eyes are truly the windows of soul, you will know you've encountered a real soulmate when you embark on a relationship with a Pisces Lunar Lover of either sex and you gaze into each other's eyes!

However, you'd best be warned that the Pisces Lunar Lover is definitely not the most practical of souls (unless their personal horoscope contains evidence to the contrary!), and whilst not meaning to deceive, there is a quality in the Pisces Moon personality which makes them rather too good at avoiding the total truth. You see when Pisces falls in love, he or she can rather too conveniently forget about everything else, including a current relationship! It's not that Pisces wants to play the field, simply that romantic love is the be all and end all of life to this Moon sign, and those Piscean lunar emotions are so incredibly strong that they overshadow everything else.

Therefore I'd like to suggest that one of the first things to do if you've met a Pisces Moon is ascertain promptly his or her marital status in the most tactful way possible, hoping that you'll also be able to check up on it in an equally tactful way later on.

Once you know that your Pisces Lunar Lover is definitely a free agent you can look forward to a blissfully happy involvement with someone who is sure to be one of the most tender and caring lovers you have ever known and who has the most endearing charm imaginable.

A romantic idealist to the end, champion of lame dogs and lost causes, at worst a Pisces Lunar Lover can sometimes become too dependent emotionally on his or her partner, and unrequited love is also an idea too terrible to entertain for a Pisces Moon. It is very often unrequited love which can in fact create their need to turn to alcohol or even drugs as a solace for their sorrows.

It is therefore important to tread very carefully with the highly sensitive emotions of the Pisces Lunar Lover. Never play around with their feelings for the hurt you create will be enormous.

One of the most important characteristics in the Pisces Lunar Lover's personality is that they appreciate the joys of having the perfect soulmate more than most of the other Lunar Lovers, and they believe that sharing happiness makes it an even greater joy.

Building castles in the air may be like escaping from reality, but building a castle in the air with an adorably unworldly Pisces Dream Lover who is also capable of putting their feet on the ground will be pure magic!

_____ Recognizing a Pisces Lunar Lover _____

There is often a fey, mysterious and elusive quality to the Pisces Lunar Lover, plus a soulful look in those big, deep eyes which can almost appear to be like round pools of water in which you could lose yourself for ever. You sense a deep aura of spirituality within many Pisces Lunar Lovers, some of whom may also have deep religious beliefs too.

The Pisces Lunar Lover isn't often jumping around being the life and soul of a party (unless he or she has a Leo or Sagittarius Ascendant or planetary configurations which create a more extrovert personality), and is much more likely to be found sitting alone reading a book of poetry or listen to music with a rapt expression on their face.

You immediately know that the Pisces Lunar Lover is brimming over with sympathy and compassion, and if you're going to see a movie you've heard is sad, make sure you take a stock of Kleenex along too!

Listen to the Pisces Lunar Lover talk, and it won't be long before you also know that you've met the true dreamer of the Zodiac, who is sure to be artistic and creative, but overly sensitive to criticism of any kind.

_____ *Captivating a Pisces Lunar Lover* _____

If you've just met this most romantic sign of the Zodiac, there are several things for you to learn.

First of all, remember that the Pisces Lunar Lover is very psychic, and will soon see through any seductive wiles. In fact both male and female Pisces Moons will see through anything which doesn't smack of total honesty. Secondly, if you're lacking in romantic dreams and ideals yourself, it's probably best to find yourself a Lunar Lover born under a different sign. Being cool, calm and collected with a detached manner might be a challenge to some people, but the Pisces Moon is far too sensitive to cope with someone who appears to be uncaring.

To truly captivate this Lunar Lover, show that you have lots of tenderness and compassion; it doesn't have to be as much as Pisces who possesses it in abundance – but it does have to be there!

Try not to carry on too much about how important it is to be practical and continually save for the future, especially not at the beginning, for most Piscean Moons simply don't understand this kind of philosophy. Kind and generous to extremes, financial practicality is not one of their virtues. So don't imply you only enjoy expensive trendy restaurants and shopping in the best stores for it can be disastrous for such a generous sign.

Get out all your old photos of sunrises and sunsets to show your Pisces Lunar Lover (as long as you're not pictured with someone else!) and be ready to talk about your own dreams and ideals.

Your Moon in Pisces Lover definitely yearns for massive amounts of tender loving care from a sensitive soulmate who will share life on Cloud Nine, and only you know if that's for you!

_____ *Life with a Pisces Lunar Lover* _____

Your Pisces Lunar Lover ideally wants a life full of romance and free of problems. The 'real world' needless to say doesn't necessarily fulfil these wishes, but certainly life with a Pisces Moon of either sex could easily fulfil many of your own most romantic dreams and bring you a great deal of happiness. Because your Pisces Lunar Lover is such a tender compassionate human being, nothing ever seems to be too much for him or her to do for you.

Always remember that your Pisces Lunar Lover is very vulnerable emotionally. Being so sentimental, he or she will be very upset if you forget about those special anniversaries which always mean so much to Pisces. Even once you've been married or lived together for years, it's a cardinal sin to be forgetful in this way!

Because a castle in the air is a very comfortable place for the Pisces Lunar Lover, living in the day-to-day world brings them down to earth with a great big bang. Don't expect an unworldly Pisces Moon to be amazingly handy around the house, or to be especially brilliant at remembering to pay the bills (and having enough money in the bank to do so). But the artistic creative side of this Moon sign's personality can show in many different ways, and your home is sure to be a warm, comfortable place of refuge for everyone who wants to be there.

Life can be very cozy with Pisces, as long as the love is kept alive in your relationship so that those rose-coloured spectacles aren't slipped on once again in a search for another perfect soulmate! However, whilst the Pisces Lunar Lover is always the romantic idealist, playing around is not what Pisces wants – sailing off into the sunset together for ever more is much more agreeable . . .

_____ *Lunar Lovers and their Sun signs* _____

The personality of your Pisces Lunar Lover will be modified by the position of the Sun in his or her horoscope:

ARIES SUN/PISCES MOON   Impulsive, hot-headed, but amazingly intuitive with a sensitivity not always found in fiery Aries! Romance is a definite necessity for this Lunar Lover.

TAURUS SUN/PISCES MOON   Another romantic but one whose feet are usually firmly on the ground and whose castles in the air usually require solid bricks and mortar. Material security is essential.

GEMINI SUN/PISCES MOON   This Lunar Lover is great fun to be with, but could lead your heart a merry dance. Gemini is nervous of too much sentimentality for fear of being trapped!

CANCER SUN/PISCES MOON   Watch those Cancerian moods, but revel in blissful domesticity with someone who is definitely sensitive and sentimental but can also be practical too.

LEO SUN/PISCES MOON   A wonderfully lovable personality with a heart of gold and deep, deep emotions. This Lunar Lover wants to be the star of the show, and why not!

VIRGO SUN/PISCES MOON   It might be hard for this Lunar Lover to reveal their emotions without worrying that they're giving just too much away. Expect some criticism from time to time too.

LIBRA SUN/PISCES MOON   A perfect mind/body/soul Lunar Lover if indecision doesn't get in the way. But with this combination, sharing ideals together is beautiful.

SCORPIO SUN/PISCES MOON   A combination of two emotional Water signs, the Scorpio Sun will create a charismatic and highly intuitive Lunar Lover who may be irresistible!

SAGITTARIUS SUN/PISCES MOON   The urge to travel the world is tempered with a fascinating blend of romanticism and philosophical 'other worldliness'. An attractively exciting lover at true soul level!

CAPRICORN SUN/PISCES MOON   Somehow this Lunar Lover may be too steeped in traditional ways and almost too practical for you. But search below the surface and you'll find lots of idealism too.

AQUARIUS SUN/PISCES MOON   Intuitive, mystical, romantic but definitely one of the most unpredictable Lunar Lovers you could ever meet. A positive whirlwind of original thoughts and ideas.

PISCES SUN/PISCES MOON   Amazingly psychic, there won't be a thing you can keep secret from this Lunar Lover, but you probably wouldn't want to anyway. A very old soul lurks deep inside this Lover's personality.

How to keep your Lunar Lover by your side

DO:
- Always show your Pisces Lunar Lover how much you care
- Be tender, loving and compassionate – even if you *have* had a bad day!
- Remember all those special anniversaries, and I mean *all*
- Make sure you enjoy seeing 'weepy' films together
- Be encouraging and supportive towards this Lunar Lover's idealistic aims
- Enjoy some good old fashioned romance!

DON'T:
- Ever be cold and calculating
- Go on and on about your Lunar Lover's impracticality – help them combat it gently
- Be with this romantic idealist unless you're truly in love
- Let them get depressed because of you – they can't cope well with feeling bad
- Ever laugh at them, especially when other people are around
- Be too busy for love . . .

THE MAGICAL, MYSTERIOUS MOON

Throughout history the power of the Moon has always been respected, and in ancient days it was worshipped by people all over the world, and revered both as a God and most often as a Goddess, and there are still those today who share the same beliefs. It is as a Goddess that the Moon has represented the Great Mother, Mother Earth, the fruits of the Earth, and fertility.

So many names were bestowed upon the Moon by different races and in different times that it would be impossible to give them all – but amongst the best known are:

- **Artemis** (called Diana by the Romans) who was one of the most important Greek divinities and sister of the Sun God.
- **Hecate**, who was a Moon Goddess, also thought to be a Goddess of the Earth, and a mysterious divinity of the Greeks. Her great powers were honoured by all the immortal Gods and because of these she was also identified with Selene or Luna in heaven, Diana or Artemis on Earth, and Persephone or Proserpina in the lower world.
- **Isis**, Egyptian wife of Osiris and mother of Horus. She was originally the Earth Goddess and afterwards the Moon Goddess.
- **Metztli** was the Aztec Moon Goddess.
- **Parvati** was the Moon Goddess of the Hindus.

- **Shing-Moo** was the Chinese Moon Goddess – the Queen of the Heavens.
- **Thoth** was the Egyptian Moon God of wisdom and learning, who was also the inventor of magic.
- **Ur** was an Oriental Moon God and also an Assyrian Fire God.

In the days before Christianity was the major religion, we know that people worshipped many Gods, but the worship of the Moon apparently surpassed all others. This is not surprising when you consider the Moon's connection with fertility, childbirth and crops.

Rituals and ceremonies were held at Full Moon time, when the Moon's power was considered at its peak, and still are today. But although there are many who consider worshipping the Moon as witchcraft and scorn it out of hand, it was really an understanding of the Moon's relationship to plants, to humans, to animals, and of course, to the tides of the seas.

I have always been fascinated by the Moon, and it seems that, just as with Astrology as a whole, there is always something new to learn. Whilst writing this book, I read an especially interesting article with some fascinating little snippets of Moon lore. In certain cultures, particularly among tribes in Mexico and Australia (the Bushmen), and even among the Chinese, lunar beings are represented in mythology as being endowed with special functions and abilities, and one character common to all these cultures is represented with only one foot and one hand. Its special magical power causes the rain to fall. Apparently the Australians have a story that the Moon one day asked for some possum skins to wear on chilly nights – but man selfishly refused. The Moon, to avenge itself, caused torrents of rain to fall on the Earth, indicating the believe that rainfall somehow has a lunar connection.

Many fishermen are convinced that their catch is far greater two days before and up to three days after the Full Moon, and I have often read about oysters that have been taken from the ocean and placed in tanks, and which open and close for feeding depending on the Moon's rhythms.

The Moon waxes and wanes but it's always there, casting its silvery light down from the heavens, and likewise, its magical, mysterious power upon our emotions never falters.

You've learned about your Moon sign, and that of your Lunar Lover, and now it's time to let you in on the few remaining little secrets which can help to enhance your mind/body/soul relationship with your perfect partner even more.

Since the Moon acts so strongly upon your subconscious mind, why not start to pay a little more attention to your dreams, for whilst you sleep there is much going on beneath the surface of your conscious reality. Your lunar intuition and instincts really can help you to decipher your dreams, so why not put a pad and pencil beside your bed so that upon waking you can quickly make notes. So often we remember dreams too briefly, and yet they can unlock the door to so much in our unconscious natures if we allow them.

It's a wonderful feeling to be on Cloud Nine, and whilst I don't want to discourage anyone from keeping their feet on the ground and being in touch with the 'real world', a little extra lunar enchantment can help to bring even more love and happiness your way.

Take advantage of New Moons to initiate new beginnings in your life. Don't immediately think that a Full Moon is going to create the end of something however, or bring were-wolves creeping up on you in the night. Likewise you don't need to get yourself into a panic if you've read that you need to be careful because the Moon is Void of Course, a term which seems to be used more frequently in the United States than in Great Britain, and which relates to the time just before the Moon changes signs and which can be disorientating if you allow it. A Moon is Void of Course from the time of the last important lunar aspect until it enters the next sign.

Therefore if you or your Lunar Lover possess a Moon sign which has an especially powerful influence, always remember to be aware of the above pointers.

Everyone can benefit from a little extra Moon magic – and whilst writing this book I was fortunate enough to be in an amazing house in Ferragudo in Portugal, whose garden and roof terrace were overlooked by a wonderful old church. To gaze up at the illuminated cross, the bell tower and the changing cycle of the Moon was one of the most magical experiences I have known. At Full Moon time it was exceptionally beautiful, and to magnify the immense power one felt from this shining Lady of the Night, close by was bright, bright Venus, close to Jupiter and Mars – the first time they had been this close for many years.

To become more in tune with the Moon, try walking in the moonlight – even the most detached and unemotional soul will feel a surge of romanticism rising up within! Buy yourself a Moonstone, perhaps wear one in a ring, as I have done for many years. Sit quietly sometimes in the moonlight and meditate deeply, asking those questions of your Higher Self that you would not dare to ask another human being. Remember that at New Moon time your intuition and instincts are highlighted – and benefit from what they will teach you. But remember also that the Moon can create illusion and delusion, and in her silvery light and her magnificent presence it can also be rather like surveying the world through a pair of rose-coloured spectacles, although in this case silver-hued ones!

All sorts of happenings are associated with the New Moon – it's said that psychic powers are heightened, and seeds should be planted with a suitable blessing. Full Moons can create conflicts, with emotions running high, but can also stimulate ovulation. Waxing Moons help to awaken consciousness and inspire one to start new projects, whilst Waning Moons mean it's time for a greater concentration of energy, to prepare to receive what has been grown.

I've talked a lot about mind, body and soul relationships in *Moon Signs for Lovers* and the symbol of the Moon herself, those two curved lines which represent the Crescent Moon (half way between the New Moon and the First Quarter) represents the soul in its purest form, the inner personality.

Always continue to allow your lunar intuition to guide *your* inner personality so that it can reach its highest level. Worries and disappointments will take on less importance in your life, and you will be able to achieve a serenity and peace within that is surely helped along by more than a little Moon magic . . .

MOON TABLES

The following tables are easy to follow. Simply choose the appropriate formula to adjust your birth time to GMT: If you were born in Eastern Standard Time, add five hours to your birth time. If you were born in Central Standard Time, add six hours to your birth time. If you were born in Mountain Standard Time, add seven hours to your birth time. If you were born in Pacific Standard Time, add eight hours to your birth time.

Suppose you were born at 5:10 pm on July 12, 1965 in Eastern Standard Time. Add five hours to your birth time, making it 10:10 pm (GMT) on July 12. Since the Moon was in Capricorn from 10:30 pm on July 11th until 11:07 am on July 14th, your Moon sign is Capricorn.

If you were born at 11:00 pm on November 24, 1966 in *Pacific* Standard Time, at first glance it might appear that your Moon sign is Aries. However, by following the formula and adding eight hours, your birth time becomes 7:00 am (GMT) on November 25th. The chart shows that your Moon sign is actually Taurus.

In addition, you must also remember that Daylight Saving Time can affect how you calculate your GMT birth time. See page 223 for more details.

January 1925	February 1925	March 1925	April 1925
1st 3:01 am Aries	2nd 5:35 am Gemini	1st 1:29 am Gemini	2nd 10:33 pm Leo
3rd 11:36 am Taurus	4th 6:11 pm Cancer	4th 1:37 am Cancer	5th 9:52 am Virgo
5th 10:54 pm Gemini	7th 6:49 am Leo	6th 2:22 pm Leo	7th 6:02 pm Libra
8th 11:34 am Cancer	9th 5:60 pm Virgo	9th 1:24 am Virgo	9th 11:04 pm Scorpio
11th 0:14 am Leo	12th 3:05 am Libra	11th 9:42 am Libra	12th 2:06 am Sagittarius
13th 11:51 am Virgo	14th 9:51 am Scorpio	13th 3:36 pm Scorpio	14th 4:33 am Capricorn
15th 9:31 pm Libra	16th 2:24 pm Sagittarius	15th 7:51 pm Sagittarius	16th 7:25 am Aquarius
18th 4:08 am Scorpio	18th 5:00 pm Capricorn	17th 11:07 pm Capricorn	18th 11:04 am Pisces
20th 7:29 am Sagittarius	20th 6:21 pm Aquarius	20th 1:51 am Aquarius	20th 3:46 pm Aries
22nd 8:20 am Capricorn	22nd 7:37 pm Pisces	22nd 4:34 am Pisces	22nd 10:01 pm Taurus
24th 8:11 am Aquarius	24th 10:22 pm Aries	24th 8:06 am Aries	25th 6:35 am Gemini
26th 8:50 am Pisces	27th 4:07 am Taurus	26th 1:39 pm Taurus	27th 5:47 pm Cancer
28th 12:05 pm Aries		28th 10:09 pm Gemini	30th 6:35 am Leo
30th 7:03 pm Taurus		31st 9:44 am Cancer	

May 1925	June 1925	July 1925	August 1925
2nd 6:35 pm Virgo	1st 12:24 pm Libra	1st 3:29 am Scorpio	1st 5:42 pm Capricorn
5th 3:24 am Libra	3rd 6:17 pm Scorpio	3rd 6:50 am Sagittarius	3rd 5:39 pm Aquarius
7th 8:19 am Scorpio	5th 8:31 pm Sagittarius	5th 7:22 am Capricorn	5th 5:24 pm Pisces
9th 10:27 am Sagittarius	7th 8:45 pm Capricorn	7th 6:51 am Aquarius	7th 6:50 pm Aries
11th 11:32 am Capricorn	9th 8:56 pm Aquarius	9th 7:10 am Pisces	9th 11:24 pm Taurus
13th 1:11 pm Aquarius	11th 10:41 pm Pisces	11th 9:59 am Aries	12th 8:00 am Gemini
15th 4:26 pm Pisces	14th 3:06 am Aries	13th 4:10 pm Taurus	14th 7:40 pm Cancer
17th 9:35 pm Aries	16th 10:19 am Taurus	16th 1:39 am Gemini	17th 8:41 am Leo
20th 4:42 am Taurus	18th 7:58 pm Gemini	18th 1:35 pm Cancer	19th 9:12 pm Virgo
22nd 1:53 pm Gemini	21st 7:38 am Cancer	21st 2:33 am Leo	22nd 8:03 am Libra
25th 1:07 am Cancer	23rd 8:30 pm Leo	23rd 3:15 pm Virgo	24th 4:42 pm Scorpio
27th 1:59 pm Leo	26th 9:19 am Virgo	26th 2:28 am Libra	26th 10:49 pm Sagittarius
30th 2:34 am Virgo	28th 8:11 pm Libra	28th 10:51 am Scorpio	29th 2:17 am Capricorn
		30th 3:50 pm Sagittarius	31st 3:40 am Aquarius

September 1925
2nd   4:02 am Pisces
4th   5:03 am Aries
6th   8:31 am Taurus
8th   3:43 pm Gemini
11th 2:36 am Cancer
13th 3:29 pm Leo
16th 3:55 am Virgo
18th 2:14 pm Libra
20th 10:17 pm Scorpio
23rd 4:16 am Sagittarius
25th 8:34 am Capricorn
27th 11:27 am Aquarius
29th 1:19 pm Pisces

January 1926
3rd   11:24 am Virgo
5th   11:42 am Libra
8th   9:13 am Scorpio
10th 2:56 pm Sagittarius
12th 5:05 pm Capricorn
14th 5:06 pm Aquarius
16th 4:51 pm Pisces
18th 6:07 pm Aries
20th 10:17 pm Taurus
23rd 5:59 am Gemini
25th 4:33 pm Cancer
28th 4:52 am Leo
30th 5:48 pm Virgo

May 1926
1st   11:34 pm Capricorn
4th   3:30 am Aquarius
6th   6:31 am Pisces
8th   8:55 am Aries
10th 11:36 am Taurus
12th 3:50 pm Gemini
14th 10:54 pm Cancer
17th 9:22 am Leo
19th 9:54 pm Virgo
22nd 10:01 am Libra
24th 7:40 pm Scorpio
27th 2:14 am Sagittarius
29th 6:23 am Capricorn
31st 9:19 am Aquarius

September 1926
1st   1:49 am Cancer
3rd   1:03 pm Leo
6th   1:41 am Virgo
8th   2:23 pm Libra
11th 2:15 am Scorpio
13th 12:17 pm Sagittarius
15th 7:33 pm Capricorn
17th 11:21 pm Aquarius
20th 0:05 am Pisces
21st 11:19 pm Aries
23rd 11:12 pm Taurus
26th 1:50 am Gemini
28th 8:38 am Cancer
30th 7:11 pm Leo

January 1927
2nd   10:49 am Capricorn
5th   2:09 am Aquarius
7th   4:06 pm Pisces
9th   6:01 am Aries
11th 8:59 am Taurus
13th 1:33 pm Gemini
15th 8:01 pm Cancer
18th 4:32 am Leo
20th 3:10 pm Virgo
23rd 3:26 am Libra
25th 3:51 pm Scorpio
28th 2:18 am Sagittarius
30th 9:06 am Capricorn

October 1925
1st   3:06 pm Aries
3rd   6:21 pm Taurus
6th   0:34 am Gemini
8th   10:34 am Cancer
10th 11:09 pm Leo
13th 11:40 am Virgo
15th 9:56 pm Libra
18th 5:09 am Scorpio
20th 10:09 am Sagittarius
22nd 1:56 pm Capricorn
24th 5:11 pm Aquarius
26th 8:14 pm Pisces
28th 11:22 pm Aries
31st 3:30 am Taurus

February 1926
2nd   6:08 am Libra
4th   4:35 pm Scorpio
7th   0:02 am Sagittarius
9th   3:46 am Capricorn
11th 4:34 am Aquarius
13th 3:57 am Pisces
15th 3:50 am Aries
17th 6:14 am Taurus
19th 12:28 pm Gemini
21st 10:29 pm Cancer
24th 11:01 am Leo
26th 12:00 pm Virgo

June 1926
2nd   11:54 am Pisces
4th   2:47 pm Aries
6th   6:30 pm Taurus
8th   11:44 pm Gemini
11th 7:18 am Cancer
13th 5:31 pm Leo
16th 5:49 am Virgo
18th 6:16 pm Libra
21st 4:38 am Scorpio
23rd 11:31 am Sagittarius
25th 3:15 pm Capricorn
27th 5:01 pm Aquarius
29th 6:15 pm Pisces

October 1926
3rd   7:47 am Virgo
5th   8:27 pm Libra
8th   7:57 am Scorpio
10th 5:52 pm Sagittarius
13th 1:46 am Capricorn
15th 6:58 am Aquarius
17th 9:25 am Pisces
19th 9:55 am Aries
21st 10:04 am Taurus
23rd 11:54 am Gemini
25th 5:11 pm Cancer
28th 2:31 am Leo
30th 2:43 pm Virgo

February 1927
1st   12:17 pm Aquarius
3rd   1:05 pm Pisces
5th   1:22 pm Aries
7th   2:54 pm Taurus
9th   6:57 pm Gemini
12th 1:51 am Cancer
14th 11:14 am Leo
16th 10:17 pm Virgo
19th 10:31 am Libra
21st 11:08 pm Scorpio
24th 10:29 am Sagittarius
26th 6:51 pm Capricorn
28th 11:12 pm Aquarius

November 1925
2nd   9:47 am Gemini
4th   7:07 pm Cancer
7th   7:15 am Leo
9th   8:06 pm Virgo
12th 6:48 am Libra
14th 2:01 pm Scorpio
16th 6:10 pm Sagittarius
18th 8:38 pm Capricorn
20th 10:48 pm Aquarius
23rd 1:38 am Pisces
25th 5:32 am Aries
27th 10:48 am Taurus
29th 5:53 pm Gemini

March 1926
1st   12:02 pm Libra
3rd   10:28 pm Scorpio
6th   6:37 am Sagittarius
8th   12:03 pm Capricorn
10th 2:37 pm Aquarius
12th 3:02 pm Pisces
14th 2:53 pm Aries
16th 4:11 pm Taurus
18th 8:44 pm Gemini
21st 5:33 am Cancer
23rd 5:37 pm Leo
26th 6:36 am Virgo
28th 6:25 pm Libra
31st 4:16 am Scorpio

July 1926
1st   8:16 pm Aries
3rd   12:00 pm Taurus
6th   6:00 am Gemini
8th   2:21 pm Cancer
11th 0:50 am Leo
13th 1:08 pm Virgo
16th 1:52 am Libra
18th 1:02 pm Scorpio
20th 9:07 pm Sagittarius
23rd 1:27 am Capricorn
25th 2:47 am Aquarius
27th 2:47 am Pisces
29th 3:16 am Aries
31st 5:51 am Taurus

November 1926
2nd   3:20 am Libra
4th   2:34 pm Scorpio
6th   11:51 pm Sagittarius
9th   7:09 am Capricorn
11th 12:38 pm Aquarius
13th 4:20 pm Pisces
15th 6:26 pm Aries
17th 7:54 pm Taurus
19th 10:10 pm Gemini
22nd 2:56 am Cancer
24th 11:14 am Leo
26th 10:36 pm Virgo
29th 11:12 am Libra

March 1927
3rd   0:05 am Pisces
4th   11:18 pm Aries
6th   11:07 pm Taurus
9th   1:30 am Gemini
11th 7:33 am Cancer
13th 4:55 pm Leo
16th 4:23 am Virgo
18th 4:50 pm Libra
21st 5:21 am Scorpio
23rd 5:04 pm Sagittarius
26th 2:37 am Capricorn
28th 8:34 am Aquarius
30th 10:48 am Pisces

December 1925
2nd   3:19 am Cancer
4th   3:13 pm Leo
7th   4:12 am Virgo
9th   3:48 pm Libra
12th 0:04 am Scorpio
14th 4:20 am Sagittarius
16th 5:58 am Capricorn
18th 6:37 am Aquarius
20th 7:55 am Pisces
22nd 11:01 am Aries
24th 4:28 pm Taurus
27th 0:19 am Gemini
29th 10:29 am Cancer
31st 10:25 pm Leo

April 1926
2nd   12:06 pm Sagittarius
4th   6:02 pm Capricorn
6th   10:00 pm Aquarius
9th   0:03 am Pisces
11th 1:02 am Aries
13th 2:32 am Taurus
15th 6:25 am Gemini
17th 1:59 pm Cancer
20th 1:07 am Leo
22nd 1:58 pm Virgo
25th 1:53 am Libra
27th 11:17 am Scorpio
29th 6:19 pm Sagittarius

August 1926
2nd   11:30 am Gemini
4th   8:11 pm Cancer
7th   7:14 am Leo
9th   7:39 pm Virgo
12th 8:26 am Libra
14th 8:15 pm Scorpio
17th 5:35 am Sagittarius
19th 11:17 am Capricorn
21st 1:25 pm Aquarius
23rd 1:12 pm Pisces
25th 12:33 pm Aries
27th 1:30 pm Taurus
29th 5:43 pm Gemini

December 1926
1st   10:38 pm Scorpio
4th   7:28 am Sagittarius
6th   1:48 pm Capricorn
8th   6:20 pm Aquarius
10th 9:44 pm Pisces
13th 0:32 am Aries
15th 3:23 am Taurus
17th 7:02 am Gemini
19th 12:23 pm Cancer
21st 8:18 pm Leo
24th 7:03 am Virgo
26th 7:29 pm Libra
29th 7:24 am Scorpio
31st 4:45 pm Sagittarius

April 1927
1st   10:28 am Aries
3rd   9:39 am Taurus
5th   10:31 am Gemini
7th   2:48 pm Cancer
9th   11:01 pm Leo
12th 10:21 am Virgo
14th 10:53 pm Libra
17th 11:19 am Scorpio
19th 10:49 pm Sagittarius
22nd 8:32 am Capricorn
24th 3:40 pm Aquarius
26th 7:34 pm Pisces
28th 8:42 pm Aries
30th 8:29 pm Taurus

May 1927
2nd 8:54 pm Gemini
4th 11:51 pm Cancer
7th 6:42 am Leo
9th 5:05 pm Virgo
12th 5:28 am Libra
14th 5:51 pm Scorpio
17th 4:56 am Sagittarius
19th 2:09 pm Capricorn
21st 9:15 pm Aquarius
24th 2:01 am Pisces
26th 4:36 am Aries
29th 5:51 am Taurus
30th 7:05 am Gemini

June 1927
1st 9:56 am Cancer
3rd 3:42 pm Leo
6th 0:55 am Virgo
8th 12:50 pm Libra
11th 1:16 am Scorpio
13th 12:14 pm Sagittarius
15th 8:50 pm Capricorn
18th 3:03 am Aquarius
20th 7:25 am Pisces
22nd 10:28 am Aries
24th 12:54 pm Taurus
26th 3:28 pm Gemini
28th 7:06 pm Cancer

July 1927
1st 0:50 am Leo
3rd 9:31 am Virgo
5th 8:48 pm Libra
8th 9:16 am Scorpio
10th 8:35 pm Sagittarius
13th 5:03 am Capricorn
15th 10:28 am Aquarius
17th 1:42 pm Pisces
19th 3:59 pm Aries
21st 6:25 pm Taurus
23rd 9:47 pm Gemini
26th 2:33 am Cancer
28th 9:04 am Leo
30th 5:45 pm Virgo

August 1927
2nd 4:45 am Libra
4th 5:16 pm Scorpio
7th 5:10 am Sagittarius
9th 2:18 pm Capricorn
11th 7:43 pm Aquarius
13th 10:04 pm Pisces
15th 10:58 pm Aries
18th 0:13 am Taurus
20th 3:10 am Gemini
22nd 8:23 am Cancer
24th 3:42 pm Leo
27th 0:57 am Virgo
29th 12:05 pm Libra

September 1927
1st 0:37 am Scorpio
3rd 1:08 pm Sagittarius
5th 11:28 pm Capricorn
8th 5:45 am Aquarius
10th 8:11 am Pisces
12th 8:17 am Aries
14th 8:06 am Taurus
16th 9:32 am Gemini
18th 1:53 pm Cancer
20th 9:15 pm Leo
23rd 7:04 am Virgo
25th 6:32 pm Libra
28th 7:07 am Scorpio
30th 7:54 pm Sagittarius

October 1927
3rd 7:10 am Capricorn
5th 3:01 pm Aquarius
7th 6:45 pm Pisces
9th 7:13 pm Aries
11th 6:18 pm Taurus
13th 6:15 pm Gemini
15th 8:52 pm Cancer
18th 3:09 am Leo
20th 12:45 pm Virgo
23rd 0:26 am Libra
25th 1:09 pm Scorpio
28th 1:48 am Sagittarius
30th 1:19 pm Capricorn

November 1927
1st 10:25 pm Aquarius
4th 3:51 am Pisces
6th 5:50 am Aries
8th 5:37 am Taurus
10th 5:06 am Gemini
12th 6:18 am Cancer
14th 10:54 am Leo
16th 7:15 pm Virgo
19th 6:41 am Libra
21st 7:26 pm Scorpio
24th 7:51 am Sagittarius
26th 6:58 pm Capricorn
29th 4:04 am Aquarius

December 1927
1st 10:33 am Pisces
3rd 2:16 pm Aries
5th 3:44 pm Taurus
7th 4:11 pm Gemini
9th 5:13 pm Cancer
11th 8:32 pm Leo
14th 3:27 am Virgo
16th 1:57 pm Libra
19th 2:30 am Scorpio
21st 2:56 pm Sagittarius
24th 1:35 am Capricorn
26th 9:51 am Aquarius
28th 3:57 pm Pisces
30th 8:17 pm Aries

January 1928
1st 11:14 pm Taurus
4th 1:20 am Gemini
6th 3:28 am Cancer
8th 6:55 am Leo
10th 12:57 pm Virgo
12th 10:17 pm Libra
15th 10:25 am Scorpio
17th 11:04 pm Sagittarius
20th 9:44 am Capricorn
22nd 5:23 pm Aquarius
24th 10:22 pm Pisces
27th 1:47 am Aries
29th 4:42 am Taurus
31st 7:49 am Gemini

February 1928
2nd 11:24 am Cancer
4th 3:55 pm Leo
6th 10:10 pm Virgo
9th 7:06 am Libra
11th 6:41 pm Scorpio
14th 7:29 am Sagittarius
16th 6:49 pm Capricorn
19th 2:44 am Aquarius
21st 7:01 am Pisces
23rd 9:08 am Aries
25th 10:44 am Taurus
27th 1:10 pm Gemini
29th 5:07 pm Cancer

March 1928
2nd 10:39 pm Leo
5th 5:53 am Virgo
7th 3:08 pm Libra
10th 2:31 am Scorpio
12th 3:23 pm Sagittarius
15th 3:30 am Capricorn
17th 12:25 pm Aquarius
19th 5:15 pm Pisces
21st 6:51 pm Aries
23rd 7:06 pm Taurus
25th 7:55 pm Gemini
27th 10:43 pm Cancer
30th 4:06 am Leo

April 1928
1st 11:55 am Virgo
3rd 9:47 pm Libra
6th 9:29 am Scorpio
8th 10:20 pm Sagittarius
11th 10:53 am Capricorn
13th 9:05 pm Aquarius
16th 3:16 am Pisces
18th 5:37 am Aries
20th 5:35 am Taurus
22nd 5:11 am Gemini
24th 6:17 am Cancer
26th 10:16 am Leo
28th 5:30 pm Virgo

May 1928
1st 3:36 am Libra
3rd 3:39 pm Scorpio
6th 4:32 am Sagittarius
8th 5:07 pm Capricorn
11th 3:55 am Aquarius
13th 11:30 am Pisces
15th 3:25 pm Aries
17th 4:23 pm Taurus
19th 3:56 pm Gemini
21st 4:01 pm Cancer
23rd 6:20 pm Leo
26th 0:08 am Virgo
28th 9:39 am Libra
30th 9:41 pm Scorpio

June 1928
2nd 10:37 am Sagittarius
4th 11:00 pm Capricorn
7th 9:38 am Aquarius
9th 5:51 pm Pisces
11th 11:13 pm Aries
14th 1:45 am Taurus
16th 2:24 am Gemini
18th 2:36 am Cancer
20th 4:06 am Leo
22nd 8:33 am Virgo
24th 4:46 pm Libra
27th 4:18 am Scorpio
29th 5:14 pm Sagittarius

July 1928
2nd 5:23 am Capricorn
4th 3:30 pm Aquarius
6th 11:23 pm Pisces
9th 5:02 am Aries
11th 8:47 am Taurus
13th 10:50 am Gemini
15th 12:21 pm Cancer
17th 2:10 pm Leo
19th 5:56 pm Virgo
22nd 1:04 am Libra
24th 11:50 am Scorpio
27th 0:34 am Sagittarius
29th 12:43 pm Capricorn
31st 10:33 pm Aquarius

August 1928
3rd 5:33 am Pisces
5th 10:32 am Aries
7th 2:18 pm Taurus
9th 5:23 pm Gemini
11th 8:05 pm Cancer
13th 10:59 pm Leo
16th 3:10 am Virgo
18th 9:59 am Libra
20th 7:59 pm Scorpio
23rd 8:28 am Sagittarius
25th 8:58 pm Capricorn
28th 6:52 am Aquarius
30th 1:26 pm Pisces

September 1928
1st 5:25 pm Aries
3rd 8:08 pm Taurus
5th 10:44 pm Gemini
8th 1:54 am Cancer
10th 5:53 am Leo
12th 11:05 am Virgo
14th 6:16 pm Libra
17th 4:06 am Scorpio
19th 4:24 pm Sagittarius
22nd 5:14 am Capricorn
24th 3:57 pm Aquarius
26th 11:01 pm Pisces
29th 2:30 am Aries

October 1928
1st 3:59 am Taurus
3rd 5:10 am Gemini
5th 7:24 am Cancer
7th 11:21 am Leo
9th 5:17 pm Virgo
12th 1:15 am Libra
14th 11:32 am Scorpio
16th 11:46 pm Sagittarius
19th 12:50 pm Capricorn
22nd 0:34 am Aquarius
24th 8:45 am Pisces
26th 12:50 pm Aries
28th 2:14 pm Taurus
30th 2:13 pm Gemini

November 1928
1st 2:43 pm Cancer
3rd 5:17 pm Leo
5th 10:42 pm Virgo
8th 7:07 am Libra
10th 5:55 pm Scorpio
13th 6:20 am Sagittarius
15th 7:25 pm Capricorn
18th 7:38 am Aquarius
20th 5:15 pm Pisces
22nd 11:14 pm Aries
25th 1:30 am Taurus
27th 1:23 am Gemini
29th 0:43 am Cancer

December 1928
1st 1:30 am Leo
3rd 5:20 am Virgo
5th 12:56 pm Libra
7th 11:46 pm Scorpio
10th 12:30 pm Sagittarius
13th 1:29 am Capricorn
15th 1:33 pm Aquarius
17th 11:48 pm Pisces
20th 7:10 am Aries
22nd 11:20 am Taurus
24th 12:37 pm Gemini
26th 12:17 pm Cancer
28th 12:10 pm Leo
30th 2:18 pm Virgo

January 1929
1st   8:11 pm Libra
4th   6:11 am Scorpio
6th   6:50 pm Sagittarius
9th   7:49 am Capricorn
11th   7:30 pm Aquarius
14th   5:19 am Pisces
16th   1:04 pm Aries
18th   6:34 pm Taurus
20th   9:42 pm Gemini
22nd 10:52 pm Cancer
24th 11:16 pm Leo
27th   0:48 am Virgo
29th   5:23 am Libra
31st   1:50 pm Scorpio

February 1929
3rd   1:58 am Sagittarius
5th   2:58 pm Capricorn
8th   2:32 am Aquarius
10th 11:39 am Pisces
12th   6:39 pm Aries
15th   0:02 am Taurus
17th   4:00 am Gemini
19th   6:44 am Cancer
21st   8:42 am Leo
23rd 11:02 am Virgo
25th   3:20 pm Libra
27th 10:54 pm Scorpio

March 1929
2nd 10:03 am Sagittarius
4th 10:53 pm Capricorn
7th 10:39 am Aquarius
9th   7:40 pm Pisces
12th   1:50 am Aries
14th   6:03 am Taurus
16th   9:22 am Gemini
18th 12:24 pm Cancer
20th   3:28 pm Leo
22nd   7:05 pm Virgo
25th   0:11 am Libra
27th   7:52 am Scorpio
29th   6:28 pm Sagittarius

April 1929
1st   7:02 am Capricorn
3rd   7:14 pm Aquarius
6th   4:48 am Pisces
8th 10:53 am Aries
10th   2:13 pm Taurus
12th   4:11 pm Gemini
14th   6:04 pm Cancer
16th   8:51 pm Leo
19th   1:04 am Virgo
21st   7:16 am Libra
23rd   3:37 pm Scorpio
26th   2:16 am Sagittarius
28th   2:44 pm Capricorn

May 1929
1st   3:18 am Aquarius
3rd   1:46 pm Pisces
5th   8:48 pm Aries
8th   0:16 am Taurus
10th   1:21 am Gemini
12th   1:44 am Cancer
14th   3:04 am Leo
16th   6:35 am Virgo
18th 12:56 pm Libra
20th   9:55 pm Scorpio
23rd   9:05 am Sagittarius
25th   9:34 pm Capricorn
28th 10:17 am Aquarius
30th   9:36 pm Pisces

June 1929
2nd   5:53 am Aries
4th 10:29 am Taurus
6th 11:54 am Gemini
8th 11:35 am Cancer
10th 11:28 am Leo
12th   1:25 pm Virgo
14th   6:42 pm Libra
17th   3:34 am Scorpio
19th   3:05 pm Sagittarius
22nd   3:45 am Capricorn
24th   4:23 pm Aquarius
27th   3:57 am Pisces
29th   1:16 pm Aries

July 1929
1st   7:29 pm Taurus
3rd 10:12 pm Gemini
5th 10:20 pm Cancer
7th   9:38 pm Leo
9th 10:12 pm Virgo
12th   1:55 am Libra
14th   9:49 am Scorpio
16th   9:02 pm Sagittarius
19th   9:48 am Capricorn
21st 10:20 pm Aquarius
24th   9:37 am Pisces
26th   7:12 pm Aries
29th   2:24 am Taurus
31st   6:40 am Gemini

August 1929
2nd   8:13 am Cancer
4th   8:12 am Leo
6th   8:27 am Virgo
8th 11:02 am Libra
10th   5:27 pm Scorpio
13th   3:45 am Sagittarius
15th   4:20 pm Capricorn
18th   4:48 am Aquarius
20th   3:44 pm Pisces
23rd   0:46 am Aries
25th   7:53 am Taurus
27th 12:50 pm Gemini
29th   4:02 pm Cancer
31st   5:27 pm Leo

September 1929
2nd   6:29 pm Virgo
4th   8:45 pm Libra
7th   2:22 am Scorpio
9th 11:42 am Sagittarius
11th 11:44 pm Capricorn
14th 12:14 pm Aquarius
16th 11:06 pm Pisces
19th   7:28 am Aries
21st   1:43 pm Taurus
23rd   6:24 pm Gemini
25th   9:52 pm Cancer
28th   0:29 am Leo
30th   2:53 am Virgo

October 1929
2nd   6:14 am Libra
4th 11:45 am Scorpio
6th   8:21 pm Sagittarius
9th   7:52 am Capricorn
11th   8:26 pm Aquarius
14th   7:38 am Pisces
16th   3:59 pm Aries
18th   9:27 pm Gemini
21st   0:54 am Gemini
23rd   3:23 am Cancer
25th   5:56 am Leo
27th   9:11 am Virgo
29th   1:42 pm Libra
31st   8:05 pm Scorpio

November 1929
3rd   4:50 am Sagittarius
5th   4:00 pm Capricorn
8th   4:34 am Aquarius
10th   4:28 pm Pisces
13th   1:42 am Aries
15th   7:15 am Taurus
17th   9:51 am Gemini
19th 10:53 am Cancer
21st 12:00 pm Leo
23rd   2:35 pm Virgo
25th   7:24 pm Libra
28th   2:41 am Scorpio
30th 12:11 pm Sagittarius

December 1929
2nd 11:26 pm Capricorn
5th 11:59 am Aquarius
8th   0:28 am Pisces
10th 10:53 am Aries
12th   5:45 pm Taurus
14th   8:47 pm Gemini
16th   9:03 pm Cancer
18th   8:35 pm Leo
20th   9:23 pm Virgo
23rd   1:03 am Libra
25th   8:15 am Scorpio
27th   6:13 pm Sagittarius
30th   5:56 am Capricorn

January 1930
1st   6:30 pm Aquarius
4th   7:03 am Pisces
6th   6:24 pm Aries
9th   2:56 am Taurus
11th   7:29 am Gemini
13th   8:31 am Cancer
15th   7:38 am Leo
17th   7:01 am Virgo
19th   8:51 am Libra
21st   2:30 pm Scorpio
23rd 11:56 pm Sagittarius
26th 11:53 am Capricorn
29th   0:34 am Aquarius
31th 12:58 pm Pisces

February 1930
3rd   0:23 am Aries
5th   9:45 am Taurus
7th   4:05 pm Gemini
9th   6:52 pm Cancer
11th   6:58 pm Leo
13th   6:15 pm Virgo
15th   6:54 pm Libra
17th 10:46 pm Scorpio
20th   6:52 am Sagittarius
22nd   6:13 pm Capricorn
25th   6:55 am Aquarius
27th   7:11 pm Pisces

March 1930
2nd   6:07 am Aries
4th   3:16 pm Taurus
6th 10:15 pm Gemini
9th   2:33 am Cancer
11th   4:25 am Leo
13th   4:54 am Virgo
15th   5:46 am Libra
17th   8:51 am Scorpio
19th   3:27 pm Sagittarius
22nd   1:40 am Capricorn
24th   2:03 pm Aquarius
27th   2:22 am Pisces
29th 12:56 pm Aries
31st   9:22 pm Taurus

April 1930
3rd   3:40 am Gemini
5th   8:08 am Cancer
7th 11:06 am Leo
9th   1:10 pm Virgo
11th   3:19 pm Libra
13th   6:47 pm Scorpio
16th   0:49 am Sagittarius
18th 10:10 am Capricorn
20th   9:57 pm Aquarius
23rd 10:20 am Pisces
25th   9:08 pm Aries
28th   5:05 am Taurus
30th 10:22 am Gemini

May 1930
2nd   1:51 pm Cancer
4th   4:30 pm Leo
6th   7:10 pm Virgo
8th 10:29 pm Libra
11th   3:07 am Scorpio
13th   9:42 am Sagittarius
15th   6:41 pm Capricorn
18th   6:05 am Aquarius
20th   6:34 pm Pisces
23rd   5:52 am Aries
25th   2:09 pm Taurus
27th   7:03 pm Gemini
29th   9:24 pm Cancer
31st 10:44 pm Leo

June 1930
3rd   0:36 am Virgo
5th   4:04 am Libra
7th   9:33 am Scorpio
9th   4:58 pm Sagittarius
12th   2:21 am Capricorn
14th   1:41 pm Aquarius
17th   2:11 am Pisces
19th   2:11 pm Aries
21st 11:36 pm Taurus
24th   4:56 am Gemini
26th   6:54 am Cancer
28th   7:06 am Leo
30th   7:30 am Virgo

July 1930
2nd   9:51 am Libra
4th   2:59 pm Scorpio
6th 10:50 pm Sagittarius
9th   8:50 am Capricorn
11th   8:24 pm Aquarius
14th   8:57 am Pisces
16th   9:24 pm Aries
19th   7:49 am Taurus
21st   2:33 pm Gemini
23rd   5:17 pm Cancer
25th   5:17 pm Leo
27th   4:36 pm Virgo
29th   5:22 pm Libra
31st   9:07 pm Scorpio

August 1930
3rd   4:27 am Sagittarius
5th   2:37 pm Capricorn
8th   2:37 am Aquarius
10th   3:02 pm Pisces
13th   3:31 am Aries
15th   2:34 pm Taurus
17th 10:45 pm Gemini
20th   2:59 am Cancer
22nd   3:56 am Leo
24th   3:15 am Virgo
26th   3:00 am Libra
28th   5:15 am Scorpio
30th 11:09 am Sagittarius

September 1930
1st 8:37 pm Capricorn
4th 8:27 am Aquarius
6th 9:06 pm Pisces
9th 9:19 am Aries
11th 8:17 pm Taurus
14th 4:58 am Gemini
16th 10:38 am Cancer
18th 1:15 pm Leo
20th 1:45 pm Virgo
22nd 1:46 pm Libra
24th 3:13 pm Scorpio
26th 7:38 pm Sagittarius
29th 3:52 am Capricorn

January 1931
1st 11:30 am Gemini
3rd 3:17 pm Cancer
5th 4:31 pm Leo
7th 5:08 pm Virgo
9th 6:51 pm Libra
11th 10:41 pm Scorpio
14th 4:52 am Sagittarius
16th 1:04 pm Capricorn
18th 11:05 pm Aquarius
21st 10:57 am Pisces
23rd 11:56 pm Aries
26th 12:06 pm Taurus
28th 9:16 pm Gemini
31st 2:09 am Cancer

May 1931
1st 11:27 am Scorpio
3rd 1:18 pm Sagittarius
5th 5:40 pm Capricorn
8th 1:38 am Aquarius
10th 1:04 pm Pisces
13th 1:57 am Aries
15th 1:51 pm Taurus
17th 11:24 pm Gemini
20th 6:23 am Cancer
22nd 11:24 am Leo
24th 3:04 pm Virgo
26th 5:49 pm Libra
28th 8:07 pm Scorpio
30th 10:47 pm Sagittarius

September 1931
1st 8:57 pm Taurus
4th 8:39 am Gemini
6th 5:10 pm Cancer
8th 9:46 pm Leo
10th 11:03 pm Virgo
12th 10:44 pm Libra
14th 10:41 pm Scorpio
17th 0:40 am Sagittarius
19th 5:52 am Capricorn
21st 2:21 pm Aquarius
24th 1:28 am Pisces
26th 2:09 pm Aries
29th 3:06 am Taurus

January 1932
2nd 12:24 pm Scorpio
4th 3:17 pm Sagittarius
6th 6:39 pm Capricorn
8th 11:46 pm Aquarius
11th 7:54 am Pisces
13th 7:10 pm Aries
16th 8:02 am Taurus
18th 7:45 pm Gemini
21st 4:21 am Cancer
23rd 9:37 am Leo
25th 12:46 pm Virgo
27th 3:08 pm Libra
29th 5:45 pm Scorpio
31st 9:08 pm Sagittarius

October 1930
1st 3:10 pm Aquarius
4th 3:48 am Pisces
6th 3:51 pm Aries
9th 2:13 am Taurus
11th 10:26 am Gemini
13th 4:27 pm Cancer
15th 8:18 pm Leo
17th 10:26 pm Virgo
19th 11:44 pm Libra
22nd 1:34 am Scorpio
24th 5:28 am Sagittarius
26th 12:33 pm Capricorn
28th 10:55 pm Aquarius
31st 11:24 am Pisces

February 1931
2nd 3:24 am Leo
4th 2:58 am Virgo
6th 2:57 am Libra
8th 5:07 am Scorpio
10th 10:27 am Sagittarius
12th 6:41 pm Capricorn
15th 5:16 am Aquarius
17th 5:24 pm Pisces
20th 6:20 am Aries
22nd 6:52 pm Taurus
25th 5:10 am Gemini
27th 11:42 am Cancer

June 1931
2nd 3:09 am Capricorn
4th 10:28 am Aquarius
6th 9:03 pm Pisces
9th 9:44 am Aries
11th 9:53 pm Taurus
14th 7:17 am Gemini
16th 1:33 pm Cancer
18th 5:34 pm Leo
20th 8:32 pm Virgo
22nd 11:21 pm Libra
25th 2:35 am Scorpio
27th 6:27 am Sagittarius
29th 11:38 am Capricorn

October 1931
1st 3:00 pm Gemini
4th 0:37 am Cancer
6th 6:46 am Leo
8th 9:31 am Virgo
10th 9:49 am Libra
12th 9:20 am Scorpio
14th 9:57 am Sagittarius
16th 1:24 pm Capricorn
18th 8:42 pm Aquarius
21st 7:35 am Pisces
23rd 8:20 pm Aries
26th 9:10 am Taurus
28th 8:46 pm Gemini
31st 6:24 am Cancer

February 1932
3rd 1:40 am Capricorn
5th 7:53 am Aquarius
7th 4:19 pm Pisces
10th 3:19 am Aries
12th 4:06 pm Taurus
15th 4:25 am Gemini
17th 1:58 pm Cancer
19th 7:47 pm Leo
21st 10:25 pm Virgo
23rd 11:23 pm Libra
26th 0:22 am Scorpio
28th 2:40 am Sagittarius

November 1930
2nd 11:34 pm Aries
5th 9:34 am Taurus
7th 4:55 pm Gemini
9th 10:04 pm Cancer
12th 1:44 am Leo
14th 4:41 am Virgo
16th 7:28 am Libra
18th 10:39 am Scorpio
20th 3:04 pm Sagittarius
22nd 9:45 pm Capricorn
25th 7:27 am Aquarius
27th 7:35 pm Pisces
30th 8:05 am Aries

March 1931
1st 2:21 pm Leo
3rd 2:20 pm Virgo
5th 1:35 pm Libra
7th 2:07 pm Scorpio
9th 5:34 pm Sagittarius
12th 0:38 am Capricorn
14th 11:04 am Aquarius
16th 11:26 pm Pisces
19th 12:22 pm Aries
22nd 0:44 am Taurus
24th 11:16 am Gemini
26th 7:02 pm Cancer
28th 11:29 pm Leo
31st 0:58 am Virgo

July 1931
2nd 6:59 pm Aquarius
4th 5:11 am Pisces
6th 5:40 pm Aries
9th 6:12 am Taurus
11th 4:09 pm Gemini
13th 10:28 pm Cancer
16th 1:40 am Leo
18th 3:21 am Virgo
20th 5:07 am Libra
22nd 7:58 am Scorpio
24th 12:20 pm Sagittarius
26th 6:24 pm Capricorn
29th 2:26 am Aquarius
31st 12:48 pm Pisces

November 1931
2nd 1:35 pm Leo
4th 6:05 pm Virgo
6th 8:02 pm Libra
8th 8:22 pm Scorpio
10th 8:41 pm Sagittarius
12th 10:54 pm Capricorn
15th 4:44 am Aquarius
17th 2:37 pm Pisces
20th 3:09 am Aries
22nd 3:58 pm Taurus
25th 3:10 am Gemini
27th 12:07 pm Cancer
29th 7:03 pm Leo

March 1932
1st 7:09 am Capricorn
3rd 2:03 pm Aquarius
5th 11:16 pm Pisces
8th 10:37 am Aries
10th 11:19 pm Taurus
13th 12:01 pm Gemini
15th 10:45 pm Cancer
18th 5:53 am Leo
20th 9:15 am Virgo
22nd 9:56 am Libra
24th 9:37 am Scorpio
26th 10:12 am Sagittarius
28th 1:14 pm Capricorn
30th 7:33 pm Aquarius

December 1930
2nd 6:30 pm Taurus
5th 1:31 am Gemini
7th 5:30 am Cancer
9th 7:52 am Leo
11th 10:05 am Virgo
13th 1:07 pm Libra
15th 5:21 pm Scorpio
17th 10:55 pm Sagittarius
20th 6:15 am Capricorn
22nd 3:48 pm Aquarius
25th 3:37 am Pisces
27th 4:29 pm Aries
30th 3:49 am Taurus

April 1931
2nd 0:49 am Libra
4th 0:51 am Scorpio
6th 2:54 am Sagittarius
8th 8:25 am Capricorn
10th 5:42 pm Aquarius
13th 5:48 am Pisces
15th 6:46 pm Aries
18th 6:47 am Taurus
20th 4:53 pm Gemini
23rd 0:41 am Cancer
25th 6:00 am Leo
27th 9:07 am Virgo
29th 10:34 am Libra

August 1931
3rd 1:09 am Aries
5th 2:02 pm Taurus
8th 1:00 am Gemini
10th 8:05 am Cancer
12th 11:26 am Leo
14th 12:24 pm Virgo
16th 12:46 pm Libra
18th 2:13 pm Scorpio
20th 5:50 pm Sagittarius
22nd 11:58 pm Capricorn
25th 8:40 am Aquarius
27th 7:28 pm Pisces
30th 7:56 am Aries

December 1931
2nd 0:16 am Virgo
4th 3:43 am Libra
6th 5:43 am Scorpio
8th 7:07 am Sagittarius
10th 9:22 am Capricorn
12th 2:16 pm Aquarius
14th 10:52 pm Pisces
17th 10:52 am Aries
19th 11:46 pm Gemini
22nd 10:56 am Gemini
24th 7:20 pm Cancer
27th 1:16 am Leo
29th 5:39 am Virgo
31st 9:16 am Libra

April 1932
2nd 5:06 am Pisces
4th 4:53 pm Aries
7th 5:43 am Taurus
9th 6:26 pm Gemini
12th 5:45 am Cancer
14th 2:17 pm Leo
16th 7:19 pm Virgo
18th 8:58 pm Libra
20th 8:34 pm Scorpio
22nd 7:50 pm Sagittarius
24th 9:18 pm Capricorn
27th 2:06 am Aquarius
29th 10:59 am Pisces

May 1932
1st 10:47 pm Aries
4th 11:45 am Taurus
7th 0:20 am Gemini
9th 11:32 am Cancer
11th 8:45 pm Leo
14th 3:10 am Virgo
16th 6:29 am Libra
18th 7:13 am Scorpio
20th 6:49 am Sagittarius
22nd 7:17 am Capricorn
24th 10:37 am Aquarius
26th 6:02 pm Pisces
29th 5:11 am Aries
31st 6:04 pm Taurus

September 1932
2nd 8:30 am Libra
4th 10:07 am Scorpio
6th 12:03 pm Sagittarius
8th 3:14 pm Capricorn
10th 8:18 pm Aquarius
13th 3:32 am Pisces
15th 1:02 pm Aries
18th 0:32 am Taurus
20th 1:13 pm Gemini
23rd 1:12 am Cancer
25th 10:28 am Leo
27th 4:03 pm Virgo
29th 6:20 pm Libra

January 1933
2nd 3:19 pm Aries
5th 2:38 am Taurus
7th 3:20 pm Gemini
10th 3:16 am Cancer
12th 1:25 pm Leo
14th 9:41 pm Virgo
17th 4:01 am Libra
19th 8:22 am Scorpio
21st 10:53 am Sagittarius
23rd 12:19 pm Capricorn
25th 1:50 pm Aquarius
27th 5:35 pm Pisces
30th 0:21 am Aries

May 1933
1st 11:06 pm Leo
4th 8:36 am Virgo
6th 2:12 pm Libra
8th 4:04 pm Scorpio
10th 3:44 pm Sagittarius
12th 3:20 pm Capricorn
14th 4:51 pm Aquarius
16th 9:36 pm Pisces
19th 5:47 am Aries
21st 4:28 pm Taurus
24th 4:32 am Gemini
26th 5:11 pm Cancer
29th 5:31 am Leo
31st 4:03 pm Virgo

September 1933
1st 7:01 am Aquarius
3rd 9:46 am Pisces
5th 2:19 pm Aries
7th 9:35 pm Taurus
10th 8:03 am Gemini
12th 8:26 pm Cancer
15th 8:28 am Leo
17th 6:10 pm Virgo
20th 0:51 am Libra
22nd 4:58 am Scorpio
25th 7:48 am Sagittarius
26th 10:24 am Capricorn
28th 1:27 pm Aquarius
30th 5:28 pm Pisces

June 1932
3rd 6:29 am Gemini
5th 5:18 pm Cancer
8th 2:13 am Leo
10th 9:02 am Virgo
12th 1:37 pm Libra
14th 3:57 pm Scorpio
16th 4:45 pm Sagittarius
18th 5:34 pm Capricorn
20th 8:16 pm Aquarius
23rd 2:28 am Pisces
25th 12:38 pm Aries
28th 1:09 am Taurus
30th 1:33 pm Gemini

October 1932
1st 6:44 pm Scorpio
3rd 7:05 pm Sagittarius
5th 9:02 pm Capricorn
8th 1:44 am Aquarius
10th 9:30 am Pisces
12th 7:37 pm Aries
15th 7:23 am Taurus
17th 8:03 pm Gemini
20th 8:24 am Cancer
22nd 6:54 pm Leo
25th 2:02 am Virgo
27th 5:13 am Libra
29th 5:29 am Scorpio
31st 4:42 am Sagittarius

February 1933
1st 10:43 am Taurus
3rd 11:05 pm Gemini
6th 11:12 am Cancer
8th 9:16 pm Leo
11th 4:42 am Virgo
13th 9:57 am Libra
15th 1:46 pm Scorpio
17th 4:42 pm Sagittarius
19th 7:23 pm Capricorn
21st 10:29 pm Aquarius
24th 2:58 am Pisces
26th 9:47 am Aries
28th 7:22 pm Taurus

June 1933
2nd 11:15 pm Libra
5th 2:23 am Scorpio
7th 2:32 am Sagittarius
9th 1:35 am Capricorn
11th 1:43 am Aquarius
13th 4:55 am Pisces
15th 11:56 am Aries
17th 10:13 pm Taurus
20th 10:27 am Gemini
22nd 11:07 pm Cancer
25th 11:15 am Leo
27th 9:50 pm Virgo
30th 6:06 am Libra

October 1933
2nd 10:50 pm Aries
5th 6:19 am Taurus
7th 4:19 pm Gemini
10th 4:29 am Cancer
12th 5:00 pm Leo
15th 3:22 am Virgo
17th 10:02 am Libra
19th 1:24 pm Scorpio
21st 2:53 pm Sagittarius
23rd 4:15 pm Capricorn
25th 6:51 pm Aquarius
27th 11:18 pm Pisces
30th 5:42 am Aries

July 1932
3rd 0:06 am Cancer
5th 8:15 am Leo
7th 2:30 pm Virgo
9th 7:10 pm Libra
11th 10:27 pm Scorpio
14th 0:37 am Sagittarius
16th 2:35 am Capricorn
18th 5:47 am Aquarius
20th 11:39 am Pisces
22nd 8:53 pm Aries
25th 8:55 am Taurus
27th 9:26 pm Gemini
30th 8:03 am Cancer

November 1932
2nd 4:58 am Capricorn
4th 8:11 am Aquarius
6th 3:11 pm Pisces
9th 1:26 am Aries
11th 1:34 pm Taurus
14th 2:13 am Gemini
16th 2:31 pm Cancer
19th 1:34 am Leo
21st 10:02 am Virgo
23rd 3:02 pm Libra
25th 4:35 pm Scorpio
27th 3:59 pm Sagittarius
29th 3:21 pm Capricorn

March 1933
3rd 7:18 am Gemini
5th 7:42 pm Cancer
8th 6:16 am Leo
10th 1:39 pm Virgo
12th 6:02 pm Libra
14th 8:28 pm Scorpio
16th 10:19 pm Sagittarius
19th 0:48 am Capricorn
21st 4:41 am Aquarius
23rd 10:19 am Pisces
25th 5:52 pm Aries
28th 3:33 am Taurus
30th 3:15 pm Gemini

July 1933
2nd 10:50 am Scorpio
4th 12:27 pm Sagittarius
6th 12:16 pm Capricorn
8th 12:09 pm Aquarius
10th 2:08 pm Pisces
12th 7:35 pm Aries
15th 4:52 am Taurus
17th 4:46 pm Gemini
20th 5:24 am Cancer
22nd 5:17 pm Leo
25th 3:34 am Virgo
27th 11:41 am Libra
29th 5:17 pm Scorpio
31st 8:24 pm Sagittarius

November 1933
1st 1:54 pm Taurus
3rd 12:00 pm Gemini
6th 12:05 pm Cancer
9th 0:56 am Leo
11th 12:19 pm Virgo
13th 8:10 pm Libra
15th 11:52 pm Scorpio
18th 0:35 am Sagittarius
20th 0:24 am Capricorn
22nd 1:21 am Aquarius
24th 4:53 am Pisces
26th 11:16 am Aries
28th 8:04 pm Taurus

August 1932
1st 3:54 pm Leo
3rd 9:13 pm Virgo
6th 0:56 am Libra
8th 3:50 am Scorpio
10th 6:32 am Sagittarius
12th 9:40 am Capricorn
14th 1:57 pm Aquarius
16th 8:15 pm Pisces
19th 5:19 am Aries
21st 4:57 pm Taurus
24th 5:33 am Gemini
26th 4:47 pm Cancer
29th 1:03 am Leo
31st 5:55 am Virgo

December 1932
1st 4:53 pm Aquarius
3rd 10:10 pm Pisces
6th 7:39 am Aries
8th 7:43 pm Taurus
11th 8:26 am Gemini
13th 8:27 pm Cancer
16th 7:10 am Leo
18th 4:04 pm Virgo
20th 10:31 pm Libra
23rd 1:52 am Scorpio
25th 2:41 am Sagittarius
27th 2:33 am Capricorn
29th 3:26 am Aquarius
31st 7:23 am Pisces

April 1933
2nd 3:49 am Cancer
4th 3:13 pm Leo
6th 11:34 pm Virgo
9th 3:50 am Libra
11th 5:31 am Scorpio
13th 5:54 am Sagittarius
15th 6:58 am Capricorn
17th 10:07 am Aquarius
19th 3:58 pm Pisces
22nd 0:13 am Aries
24th 10:32 am Taurus
26th 10:18 pm Gemini
29th 10:58 am Cancer

August 1933
2nd 9:40 am Capricorn
4th 10:22 am Aquarius
7th 0:10 am Pisces
9th 4:44 am Aries
11th 12:49 pm Taurus
13th 11:58 pm Gemini
16th 12:32 pm Cancer
19th 0:23 am Leo
21st 10:04 am Virgo
23rd 5:28 pm Libra
25th 10:44 pm Scorpio
28th 2:20 am Sagittarius
30th 4:51 am Capricorn

December 1933
1st 6:45 am Gemini
3rd 6:53 pm Cancer
6th 7:56 am Leo
8th 7:56 pm Virgo
11th 5:14 am Libra
13th 10:20 am Scorpio
15th 11:45 am Sagittarius
17th 11:09 am Capricorn
19th 10:42 am Aquarius
21st 12:21 pm Pisces
23rd 3:21 pm Aries
26th 1:45 am Taurus
28th 12:46 pm Gemini
31st 1:07 am Cancer

January 1934		February 1934		March 1934		April 1934	
2nd	1:55 pm Leo	1st	7:59 am Virgo	3rd	0:04 am Libra	1st	1:34 pm Scorpio
5th	2:08 am Virgo	3rd	5:58 pm Libra	5th	6:57 am Scorpio	3rd	5:37 pm Sagittarius
7th	12:15 pm Libra	6th	1:31 am Scorpio	7th	11:56 am Sagittarius	5th	8:46 pm Capricorn
9th	7:06 pm Scorpio	8th	6:11 am Sagittarius	9th	3:20 pm Capricorn	7th	11:43 pm Aquarius
11th	10:16 pm Sagittarius	10th	8:22 am Capricorn	11th	5:35 pm Aquarius	10th	2:53 am Pisces
13th	10:37 pm Capricorn	12th	8:57 am Aquarius	13th	7:27 pm Pisces	12th	6:42 am Aries
15th	9:57 pm Aquarius	14th	9:30 am Pisces	15th	10:01 pm Aries	14th	11:59 am Taurus
17th	10:19 pm Pisces	16th	11:44 am Aries	18th	2:48 am Taurus	16th	7:44 pm Gemini
20th	1:30 am Aries	18th	5:08 pm Taurus	20th	10:56 am Gemini	19th	6:30 am Cancer
22nd	8:32 am Taurus	21st	2:18 am Gemini	22nd	10:14 pm Cancer	21st	7:11 pm Leo
24th	6:57 pm Gemini	23rd	2:24 am Cancer	25th	11:02 am Leo	24th	7:18 am Virgo
27th	7:25 am Cancer	26th	3:15 am Leo	27th	10:45 pm Virgo	26th	4:29 pm Libra
29th	8:12 pm Leo	28th	2:45 pm Virgo	30th	7:35 am Libra	28th	10:08 pm Scorpio

May 1934		June 1034		July 1934		August 1934	
1st	1:03 am Sagittarius	1st	11:59 am Aquarius	3rd	0:41 am Aries	1st	1:32 pm Taurus
3rd	2:55 am Capricorn	3rd	2:11 pm Pisces	5th	6:52 am Taurus	3rd	9:51 pm Gemini
5th	5:08 am Aquarius	5th	6:35 pm Aries	7th	3:59 pm Gemini	6th	9:17 am Cancer
7th	8:29 am Pisces	8th	1:17 am Taurus	10th	3:22 am Cancer	8th	10:10 pm Leo
9th	1:10 pm Aries	10th	10:17 am Gemini	12th	4:07 pm Leo	11th	10:58 am Virgo
11th	7:26 pm Taurus	12th	9:15 pm Cancer	15th	5:06 am Virgo	13th	10:33 pm Libra
14th	3:40 am Gemini	15th	9:53 am Leo	17th	4:44 pm Libra	16th	7:48 am Scorpio
16th	2:20 pm Cancer	17th	10:51 pm Virgo	20th	1:28 am Scorpio	18th	2:06 pm Sagittarius
19th	2:55 am Leo	20th	9:54 am Libra	22nd	6:22 am Sagittarius	20th	5:24 pm Capricorn
21st	3:33 pm Virgo	22nd	5:20 pm Scorpio	24th	8:01 am Capricorn	22nd	6:16 pm Aquarius
24th	1:42 am Libra	24th	8:47 pm Sagittarius	26th	7:44 am Aquarius	24th	6:08 pm Pisces
26th	7:47 am Scorpio	26th	9:25 pm Capricorn	28th	7:24 am Pisces	26th	6:46 pm Aries
28th	10:26 am Sagittarius	28th	9:04 pm Aquarius	30th	8:51 am Aries	28th	9:56 pm Taurus
30th	11:13 am Capricorn	30th	9:41 pm Pisces			31st	4:59 am Gemini

September 1934		October 1934		November 1934		December 1934	
2nd	3:43 pm Cancer	2nd	11:45 am Leo	1st	8:34 am Virgo	1st	4:36 am Libra
5th	4:33 am Leo	5th	0:30 am Virgo	3rd	7:39 pm Libra	3rd	1:00 pm Scorpio
7th	5:15 pm Virgo	7th	11:17 am Libra	6th	3:30 am Scorpio	5th	5:50 pm Sagittarius
10th	4:22 am Libra	9th	7:31 pm Scorpio	8th	8:31 am Sagittarius	7th	8:08 pm Capricorn
12th	1:17 pm Scorpio	12th	1:32 am Sagittarius	10th	11:56 am Capricorn	9th	9:34 pm Aquarius
14th	8:03 pm Sagittarius	14th	6:03 am Capricorn	12th	2:52 pm Aquarius	11th	11:32 pm Pisces
17th	0:36 am Capricorn	16th	9:31 am Aquarius	14th	5:57 pm Pisces	14th	2:53 am Aries
19th	3:05 am Aquarius	18th	12:08 pm Pisces	16th	9:27 pm Aries	16th	8:00 am Taurus
21st	4:14 am Pisces	20th	2:29 am Aries	19th	1:47 am Taurus	18th	3:01 pm Gemini
23rd	5:15 am Aries	22nd	5:37 pm Taurus	21st	7:51 am Gemini	21st	0:12 am Cancer
25th	7:50 am Taurus	24th	10:58 pm Gemini	23rd	4:28 pm Cancer	23rd	11:39 am Leo
27th	1:38 pm Gemini	27th	7:49 am Cancer	26th	3:55 am Leo	26th	0:32 am Virgo
29th	11:15 pm Cancer	29th	7:43 pm Leo	28th	4:51 pm Virgo	28th	12:54 pm Libra
						30th	10:39 pm Scorpio

January 1935		February 1935		March 1935		April 1935	
2nd	4:23 am Sagittarius	2nd	6:23 pm Aquarius	2nd	5:14 am Aquarius	2nd	3:32 pm Aries
4th	6:41 am Capricorn	4th	5:48 pm Pisces	4th	5:12 am Pisces	4th	4:23 pm Taurus
6th	7:04 am Aquarius	6th	5:53 pm Aries	6th	4:43 am Aries	6th	7:39 pm Gemini
8th	7:20 am Pisces	8th	8:26 pm Taurus	8th	5:48 am Taurus	9th	2:52 am Cancer
10th	9:08 am Aries	11th	2:39 am Gemini	10th	10:18 am Gemini	11th	1:55 pm Leo
12th	1:31 pm Taurus	13th	12:29 pm Cancer	12th	6:55 pm Cancer	14th	2:48 pm Virgo
14th	8:45 pm Gemini	16th	0:37 am Leo	15th	6:50 am Leo	16th	3:00 pm Libra
17th	6:40 am Cancer	18th	1:33 pm Virgo	17th	7:52 pm Virgo	19th	1:10 am Scorpio ·
19th	6:28 pm Leo	21st	2:03 am Libra	20th	8:07 am Libra	21st	9:05 am Sagittarius
22nd	7:19 am Virgo	23rd	1:01 pm Scorpio	22nd	6:44 pm Scorpio	23rd	3:11 pm Capricorn
24th	7:57 pm Libra	25th	9:39 pm Sagittarius	25th	3:23 am Sagittarius	25th	7:42 pm Aquarius
27th	6:42 am Scorpio	28th	3:03 am Capricorn	27th	9:46 am Capricorn	27th	10:41 pm Pisces
29th	2:04 pm Sagittarius			29th	1:39 pm Aquarius	30th	0:26 am Aries
31st	5:43 pm Capricorn			31st	3:13 pm Pisces		

May 1935		June 1935		July 1935		August 1935	
2nd	2:11 am Taurus	2nd	8:46 pm Cancer	2nd	2:15 pm Leo	1st	9:08 am Virgo
4th	5:30 am Gemini	5th	6:22 am Leo	5th	2:10 am Virgo	3rd	9:54 pm Libra
6th	11:56 am Cancer	7th	6:26 pm Virgo	7th	2:51 pm Libra	6th	9:53 am Scorpio
8th	9:56 pm Leo	10th	6:58 am Libra	10th	2:14 am Scorpio	8th	7:21 pm Sagittarius
11th	10:27 am Virgo	12th	5:32 pm Scorpio	12th	10:22 am Sagittarius	11th	1:08 am Capricorn
13th	10:48 pm Libra	15th	0:57 am Sagittarius	14th	2:59 pm Capricorn	13th	3:20 am Aquarius
16th	8:52 am Scorpio	17th	5:20 am Capricorn	16th	4:52 pm Aquarius	15th	3:19 am Pisces
18th	4:11 pm Sagittarius	19th	7:56 am Aquarius	18th	5:32 pm Pisces	17th	2:58 am Aries
20th	9:21 pm Capricorn	21st	9:58 am Pisces	20th	6:36 pm Aries	19th	4:12 am Taurus
23rd	1:10 am Aquarius	23rd	12:25 pm Aries	22nd	9:24 pm Taurus	21st	8:31 am Gemini
25th	4:14 am Pisces	25th	3:57 pm Taurus	25th	2:46 am Gemini	23rd	4:22 pm Cancer
27th	6:50 am Aries	27th	9:08 pm Gemini	27th	10:47 am Cancer	26th	3:02 am Leo
29th	10:01 am Taurus	30th	4:29 am Cancer	29th	9:07 pm Leo	28th	3:22 pm Virgo
31st	2:15 pm Gemini					31st	4:08 am Libra

September 1935
2nd 4:21 pm Scorpio
5th 2:46 am Sagittarius
7th 10:03 am Capricorn
9th 1:39 pm Aquarius
11th 2:12 pm Pisces
13th 1:22 pm Aries
15th 1:15 pm Taurus
17th 3:52 pm Gemini
19th 10:29 pm Cancer
22nd 8:53 am Leo
24th 9:20 pm Virgo
27th 10:05 am Libra
29th 10:07 pm Scorpio

October 1935
2nd 8:39 am Sagittarius
4th 4:59 pm Capricorn
6th 10:19 pm Aquarius
9th 0:26 am Pisces
11th 0:19 am Aries
12th 11:54 pm Taurus
15th 1:18 am Gemini
17th 6:24 am Cancer
19th 3:38 pm Leo
22nd 2:45 am Virgo
24th 4:30 pm Libra
27th 4:14 am Scorpio
29th 2:16 pm Sagittarius
31st 10:31 pm Capricorn

November 1935
3rd 4:35 am Aquarius
5th 8:17 am Pisces
7th 9:52 am Aries
9th 10:30 am Taurus
11th 11:57 am Gemini
13th 4:01 pm Cancer
15th 11:50 pm Leo
18th 11:13 am Virgo
20th 11:52 pm Libra
23rd 11:33 am Scorpio
25th 9:08 pm Sagittarius
28th 4:27 am Capricorn
30th 9:57 am Aquarius

December 1935
2nd 2:01 pm Pisces
4th 4:52 pm Aries
6th 7:04 pm Taurus
8th 9:38 pm Gemini
11th 1:55 am Cancer
13th 9:10 am Leo
15th 7:34 pm Virgo
18th 7:57 am Libra
20th 8:00 pm Scorpio
23rd 5:41 am Sagittarius
25th 12:24 pm Capricorn
27th 4:44 pm Aquarius
29th 7:42 pm Pisces
31st 10:15 pm Aries

January 1936
3rd 1:12 am Taurus
5th 5:06 am Gemini
7th 10:32 am Cancer
9th 6:04 pm Leo
12th 4:06 am Virgo
14th 4:11 pm Libra
17th 4:36 am Scorpio
19th 3:06 pm Sagittarius
21st 10:17 pm Capricorn
24th 1:60 am Aquarius
26th 3:34 am Pisces
28th 4:37 am Aries
30th 6:40 am Taurus

February 1936
1st 10:43 am Gemini
3rd 5:02 pm Cancer
6th 1:27 am Leo
8th 11:51 am Virgo
10th 11:46 pm Libra
13th 12:23 pm Scorpio
15th 11:54 pm Sagittarius
18th 8:15 am Capricorn
20th 12:40 pm Aquarius
22nd 1:52 pm Pisces
24th 1:36 pm Aries
26th 1:55 pm Taurus
28th 4:35 pm Gemini

March 1936
1st 10:27 am Cancer
4th 7:23 am Leo
6th 6:20 pm Virgo
9th 6:28 am Libra
11th 7:05 pm Scorpio
14th 7:03 am Sagittarius
16th 4:48 pm Capricorn
18th 10:51 pm Aquarius
21st 0:58 am Pisces
23rd 0:31 am Aries
24th 11:38 pm Taurus
27th 0:32 am Gemini
29th 4:56 am Cancer
31st 1:08 pm Leo

April 1936
3rd 0:08 am Virgo
5th 12:32 pm Libra
8th 1:06 am Scorpio
10th 1:01 pm Sagittarius
12th 11:24 pm Capricorn
15th 6:45 am Aquarius
17th 10:33 am Pisces
19th 11:18 am Aries
21st 10:39 am Taurus
23rd 10:43 am Gemini
25th 1:28 pm Cancer
27th 8:06 pm Leo
30th 6:25 am Virgo

May 1936
2nd 6:44 pm Libra
5th 7:17 am Scorpio
7th 6:55 pm Sagittarius
10th 4:55 am Capricorn
12th 12:44 pm Aquarius
14th 5:50 pm Pisces
16th 8:12 pm Aries
18th 8:49 pm Taurus
20th 9:14 pm Gemini
22nd 11:21 pm Cancer
25th 4:45 am Leo
27th 1:52 pm Virgo
30th 1:39 am Libra

June 1936
1st 2:12 pm Scorpio
4th 1:37 am Sagittarius
6th 11:01 am Capricorn
8th 6:15 pm Aquarius
10th 11:28 pm Pisces
13th 2:46 am Aries
15th 4:49 am Taurus
17th 6:32 am Gemini
19th 9:14 am Cancer
21st 2:11 pm Leo
23rd 10:17 pm Virgo
26th 9:26 am Libra
28th 9:53 pm Scorpio

July 1936
1st 9:24 am Sagittarius
3rd 6:32 pm Capricorn
6th 0:56 am Aquarius
8th 5:10 am Pisces
10th 8:11 am Aries
12th 10:48 am Taurus
14th 1:42 pm Gemini
16th 5:31 pm Cancer
18th 11:00 pm Leo
21st 6:58 am Virgo
23rd 5:33 pm Libra
26th 5:53 am Scorpio
28th 5:54 pm Sagittarius
31st 3:22 am Capricorn

August 1936
2nd 9:21 am Aquarius
4th 12:34 pm Pisces
6th 2:23 pm Aries
8th 4:15 pm Taurus
10th 7:15 pm Gemini
12th 11:53 pm Cancer
15th 6:24 am Leo
17th 2:49 pm Virgo
20th 1:18 am Libra
22nd 1:37 pm Scorpio
25th 2:09 am Sagittarius
27th 12:30 pm Capricorn
29th 7:08 pm Aquarius
31st 10:05 pm Pisces

September 1936
2nd 10:44 pm Aries
4th 11:05 pm Taurus
7th 0:55 am Gemini
9th 5:19 am Cancer
11th 12:17 pm Leo
13th 9:22 pm Virgo
16th 8:16 am Libra
18th 8:34 pm Scorpio
21st 9:24 am Sagittarius
23rd 8:51 pm Capricorn
26th 4:49 am Aquarius
28th 8:35 am Pisces
30th 9:08 am Aries

October 1936
2nd 8:28 am Taurus
4th 8:41 am Gemini
6th 11:34 am Cancer
8th 5:49 pm Leo
11th 3:02 am Virgo
13th 2:21 pm Libra
16th 2:48 am Scorpio
18th 3:38 pm Sagittarius
21st 3:37 am Capricorn
23rd 12:55 pm Aquarius
25th 6:24 pm Pisces
27th 8:06 pm Aries
29th 7:35 pm Taurus
31st 6:52 pm Gemini

November 1936
2nd 8:03 pm Cancer
5th 0:37 am Leo
7th 9:03 am Virgo
9th 8:16 pm Libra
12th 8:51 am Scorpio
14th 9:35 pm Sagittarius
17th 9:19 am Capricorn
19th 7:08 pm Aquarius
22nd 2:03 am Pisces
24th 5:33 am Aries
26th 6:28 am Taurus
28th 6:14 am Gemini
30th 6:44 am Cancer

December 1936
2nd 9:48 am Leo
4th 4:36 pm Virgo
7th 2:56 am Libra
9th 3:28 pm Scorpio
12th 4:06 am Sagittarius
14th 3:24 pm Capricorn
17th 0:43 am Aquarius
19th 7:42 am Pisces
21st 12:23 pm Aries
23rd 3:03 pm Taurus
25th 4:24 pm Gemini
27th 5:37 pm Cancer
29th 8:15 pm Leo

January 1937
1st 1:46 am Virgo
3rd 10:58 am Libra
5th 10:57 pm Scorpio
8th 11:41 am Sagittarius
10th 10:52 pm Capricorn
13th 7:22 am Aquarius
15th 1:26 pm Pisces
17th 5:47 pm Aries
19th 9:06 pm Taurus
21st 11:55 pm Gemini
24th 2:40 am Cancer
26th 6:10 am Leo
28th 11:34 am Virgo
30th 7:51 pm Libra

February 1937
2nd 7:10 am Scorpio
4th 7:57 pm Sagittarius
7th 7:30 am Capricorn
9th 3:55 pm Aquarius
11th 9:08 pm Pisces
14th 0:12 am Aries
16th 2:35 am Taurus
18th 5:24 am Gemini
20th 9:07 am Cancer
22nd 1:54 pm Leo
24th 8:06 pm Virgo
27th 4:29 am Libra

March 1937
1st 3:26 pm Scorpio
4th 4:07 am Sagittarius
6th 4:19 pm Capricorn
9th 1:34 am Aquarius
11th 6:46 am Pisces
13th 8:57 am Aries
15th 9:35 am Taurus
17th 11:22 am Gemini
19th 2:29 pm Cancer
21st 7:38 pm Leo
24th 2:45 am Virgo
26th 11:50 am Libra
28th 10:52 pm Scorpio
31st 11:34 am Sagittarius

April 1937
3rd 0:16 am Capricorn
5th 10:34 am Aquarius
7th 4:54 pm Pisces
9th 7:25 pm Aries
11th 7:39 pm Taurus
13th 7:35 pm Gemini
15th 9:04 pm Cancer
18th 1:12 am Leo
20th 8:18 am Virgo
22nd 5:54 pm Libra
25th 5:22 am Scorpio
27th 6:06 pm Sagittarius
30th 6:56 am Capricorn

May 1937
2nd   6:06 pm Aquarius
5th   1:57 am Pisces
7th   5:44 am Aries
9th   6:31 am Taurus
11th 5:58 am Gemini
13th 6:03 am Cancer
15th 8:33 am Leo
17th 2:23 pm Virgo
19th 11:35 pm Libra
22nd 11:21 am Scorpio
25th 0:10 am Sagittarius
27th 12:51 pm Capricorn
30th 0:13 am Aquarius

June 1937
1st   8:54 am Pisces
3rd   2:17 pm Aries
5th   4:34 pm Taurus
7th   4:46 pm Gemini
9th   4:34 pm Cancer
11th 5:49 pm Leo
13th 10:04 pm Virgo
16th 6:11 am Libra
18th 5:34 pm Scorpio
21st 6:26 am Sagittarius
23rd 6:58 pm Capricorn
26th 5:52 am Aquarius
28th 2:35 pm Pisces
30th 8:50 pm Aries

July 1937
3rd   0:35 am Taurus
5th   2:17 am Gemini
7th   2:55 am Cancer
9th   4:03 am Leo
11th 7:22 am Virgo
13th 2:09 pm Libra
16th 0:36 am Scorpio
18th 1:21 pm Sagittarius
21st 1:51 am Capricorn
23rd 12:17 pm Aquarius
25th 8:21 pm Pisces
28th 2:15 am Aries
30th 6:31 am Taurus

August 1937
1st   9:30 am Gemini
3rd 11:35 am Cancer
5th   1:39 pm Leo
7th   4:59 pm Virgo
9th 10:59 pm Libra
12th 8:41 am Scorpio
14th 8:59 pm Sagittarius
17th 9:36 am Capricorn
19th 8:03 pm Aquarius
22nd 3:27 am Pisces
24th 8:23 am Aries
26th 11:57 am Taurus
28th 3:03 pm Gemini
30th 6:06 pm Cancer

September 1937
1st   9:24 pm Leo
4th   1:36 am Virgo
6th   7:53 am Libra
8th   5:03 pm Scorpio
11th 5:01 am Sagittarius
13th 5:51 pm Capricorn
16th 4:48 am Aquarius
18th 12:14 pm Pisces
20th 4:28 pm Aries
22nd 6:49 pm Taurus
24th 8:46 pm Gemini
26th 11:26 pm Cancer
29th 3:17 am Leo

October 1937
1st   8:31 am Virgo
3rd   3:36 pm Libra
6th   0:57 am Scorpio
8th 12:47 pm Sagittarius
11th 1:47 am Capricorn
13th 1:35 pm Aquarius
15th 10:02 pm Pisces
18th 2:32 am Aries
20th 4:09 am Taurus
22nd 4:41 am Gemini
24th 5:49 am Cancer
26th 8:46 am Leo
28th 2:05 pm Virgo
30th 9:48 pm Libra

November 1937
2nd   7:51 am Scorpio
4th   7:48 pm Sagittarius
7th   8:51 am Capricorn
9th   9:18 pm Aquarius
12th 7:04 am Pisces
14th 12:55 pm Aries
16th 3:08 pm Taurus
18th 3:09 pm Gemini
20th 2:50 pm Cancer
22nd 4:00 pm Leo
24th 7:59 pm Virgo
27th 3:23 am Libra
29th 1:49 pm Scorpio

December 1937
2nd   2:06 am Sagittarius
4th   3:07 pm Capricorn
7th   3:40 am Aquarius
9th   2:18 pm Pisces
11th 9:53 pm Aries
14th 1:49 am Taurus
16th 2:42 am Gemini
18th 2:03 am Cancer
20th 1:50 am Leo
22nd 4:01 am Virgo
24th 9:58 am Libra
26th 7:46 pm Scorpio
29th 8:13 am Sagittarius
31st 9:17 pm Capricorn

January 1938
3rd   9:29 am Aquarius
5th   8:06 pm Pisces
8th   4:26 am Aries
10th 10:02 am Taurus
12th 12:47 pm Gemini
14th 1:20 pm Cancer
16th 1:11 pm Leo
18th 2:17 pm Virgo
20th 6:32 pm Libra
23rd 2:57 am Scorpio
25th 2:52 pm Sagittarius
28th 3:57 am Capricorn
30th 3:57 pm Aquarius

February 1938
2nd   1:57 am Pisces
4th   9:53 am Aries
6th   3:56 pm Taurus
8th   8:07 pm Gemini
10th 10:25 pm Cancer
12th 11:34 pm Leo
15th 0:57 am Virgo
17th 4:32 am Libra
19th 11:42 am Scorpio
21st 10:39 pm Sagittarius
24th 11:26 am Capricorn
26th 11:34 pm Aquarius

March 1938
1st   9:10 am Pisces
3rd   4:14 pm Aries
5th   9:29 pm Taurus
8th   1:33 am Gemini
10th 4:46 am Cancer
12th 7:24 am Leo
14th 10:07 am Virgo
16th 2:13 pm Libra
18th 8:56 pm Scorpio
21st 6:06 am Sagittarius
23rd 7:32 pm Capricorn
26th 7:52 am Aquarius
28th 5:48 pm Pisces
31st 0:33 am Aries

April 1938
2nd   4:41 am Taurus
4th   7:32 am Gemini
6th 10:08 am Cancer
8th   1:06 pm Leo
10th 4:52 pm Virgo
12th 10:03 pm Libra
15th 5:24 am Scorpio
17th 3:22 pm Sagittarius
20th 3:33 am Capricorn
22nd 4:09 pm Aquarius
25th 2:51 am Pisces
27th 10:03 am Aries
29th 1:57 pm Taurus

May 1938
1st   3:43 pm Gemini
3rd   4:50 pm Cancer
5th   6:43 pm Leo
7th 10:17 pm Virgo
10th 4:07 am Libra
12th 12:19 pm Scorpio
14th 10:41 pm Sagittarius
17th 10:52 am Capricorn
19th 11:38 pm Aquarius
22nd 11:05 am Pisces
24th 7:32 pm Aries
27th 0:17 am Taurus
29th 1:51 am Gemini
31st 1:52 am Cancer

June 1938
2nd   2:10 am Leo
4th   4:24 am Virgo
6th   9:40 am Libra
8th   6:03 pm Scorpio
11th 4:58 am Sagittarius
13th 5:22 pm Capricorn
16th 6:07 am Aquarius
18th 6:01 pm Pisces
21st 3:38 am Aries
23rd 9:44 am Taurus
25th 12:21 pm Gemini
27th 12:26 pm Cancer
29th 11:48 am Leo

July 1938
1st 12:29 pm Virgo
3rd   4:14 pm Libra
5th 11:49 pm Scorpio
8th 10:49 am Sagittarius
10th 11:23 pm Capricorn
13th 12:05 pm Aquarius
15th 11:56 pm Pisces
18th 9:50 am Aries
20th 5:28 pm Taurus
22nd 9:42 pm Gemini
24th 10:55 pm Cancer
26th 10:27 pm Leo
28th 10:19 pm Virgo
31st 0:35 am Libra

August 1938
2nd   6:54 am Scorpio
4th   5:05 pm Sagittarius
7th   5:33 am Capricorn
9th   6:14 pm Aquarius
12th 5:43 am Pisces
14th 3:33 pm Aries
16th 11:27 pm Taurus
19th 4:50 am Gemini
21st 7:38 am Cancer
23rd 8:27 am Leo
25th 8:47 am Virgo
27th 10:33 am Libra
29th 3:33 pm Scorpio

September 1938
1st   0:28 am Sagittarius
3rd 12:31 pm Capricorn
6th   1:10 am Aquarius
8th 12:26 pm Pisces
10th 9:41 pm Aries
13th 4:54 am Taurus
15th 10:22 am Gemini
17th 2:08 pm Cancer
19th 4:27 pm Leo
21st 6:03 pm Virgo
23rd 8:23 pm Libra
26th 0:59 am Scorpio
28th 9:08 am Sagittarius
30th 8:23 pm Capricorn

October 1938
3rd   8:57 am Aquarius
5th   8:27 pm Pisces
8th   5:20 am Aries
10th 11:40 am Taurus
12th 4:09 pm Gemini
14th 7:31 pm Cancer
16th 10:20 pm Leo
19th 1:10 am Virgo
21st 4:46 am Libra
23rd 10:05 am Scorpio
25th 5:59 pm Sagittarius
28th 4:42 am Capricorn
30th 5:09 pm Aquarius

November 1938
2nd   5:09 am Pisces
4th   2:32 pm Aries
6th   8:40 pm Taurus
9th   0:03 am Gemini
11th 1:59 am Cancer
13th 3:52 am Leo
15th 6:40 am Virgo
17th 11:06 am Libra
19th 5:28 pm Scorpio
22nd 1:58 am Sagittarius
24th 12:42 pm Capricorn
27th 1:01 am Aquarius
29th 1:29 pm Pisces

December 1938
2nd   0:04 am Aries
4th   6:57 am Taurus
6th 10:15 am Gemini
8th 11:07 am Cancer
10th 11:20 am Leo
12th 12:42 pm Virgo
14th 4:31 pm Libra
16th 11:14 pm Scorpio
19th 8:34 am Sagittarius
21st 7:39 pm Capricorn
24th 7:50 am Aquarius
26th 8:42 pm Pisces
29th 8:10 am Aries
31st 4:44 pm Taurus

January 1939
2nd 9:18 pm Gemini
4th 10:19 pm Cancer
6th 9:33 pm Leo
8th 9:10 pm Virgo
10th 11:12 pm Libra
13th 4:57 am Scorpio
15th 2:13 pm Sagittarius
18th 1:45 am Capricorn
20th 2:16 pm Aquarius
23rd 2:51 am Pisces
25th 2:40 pm Aries
28th 0:30 am Taurus
30th 6:45 am Gemini

February 1939
1st 9:17 am Cancer
3rd 9:05 am Leo
5th 8:06 am Virgo
7th 8:35 am Libra
9th 12:28 pm Scorpio
11th 8:26 pm Sagittarius
14th 7:43 am Capricorn
16th 8:21 am Aquarius
19th 8:51 am Pisces
21st 8:23 am Aries
24th 6:17 am Taurus
26th 1:44 pm Gemini
28th 6:04 pm Cancer

March 1939
2nd 7:28 pm Leo
4th 7:17 pm Virgo
6th 7:29 pm Libra
8th 10:01 pm Scorpio
11th 4:26 am Sagittarius
13th 2:38 pm Capricorn
16th 3:00 am Aquarius
18th 3:29 pm Pisces
21st 2:38 am Aries
23rd 11:55 am Taurus
25th 7:13 pm Gemini
28th 0:19 am Cancer
30th 3:14 am Leo

April 1939
1st 4:39 am Virgo
3rd 5:50 am Libra
5th 8:26 am Scorpio
7th 1:52 pm Sagittarius
9th 10:46 pm Capricorn
12th 10:33 am Aquarius
14th 11:04 pm Pisces
17th 10:10 am Aries
19th 6:53 pm Taurus
22nd 1:14 am Gemini
24th 5:41 am Cancer
26th 8:52 am Leo
28th 11:26 am Virgo
30th 2:03 pm Libra

May 1939
2nd 5:39 pm Scorpio
4th 11:11 pm Sagittarius
7th 7:37 am Capricorn
9th 6:42 pm Aquarius
12th 7:08 am Pisces
14th 6:38 pm Aries
17th 3:26 am Taurus
19th 9:02 am Gemini
21st 12:19 pm Cancer
23rd 2:33 pm Leo
25th 4:51 pm Virgo
27th 8:06 pm Libra
30th 0:47 am Scorpio

June 1939
1st 7:18 am Sagittarius
3rd 3:52 pm Capricorn
6th 2:42 am Aquarius
8th 3:05 pm Pisces
11th 3:10 am Aries
13th 12:37 pm Taurus
15th 6:28 pm Gemini
17th 9:04 pm Cancer
19th 9:57 pm Leo
21st 10:56 pm Virgo
24th 1:30 am Libra
26th 6:28 am Scorpio
28th 1:41 pm Sagittarius
30th 10:54 pm Capricorn

July 1939
3rd 9:56 am Aquarius
5th 10:17 pm Pisces
8th 10:47 am Aries
10th 9:25 pm Taurus
13th 4:17 am Gemini
15th 7:12 am Cancer
17th 7:30 am Leo
19th 7:10 am Virgo
21st 8:14 am Libra
23rd 12:08 pm Scorpio
25th 7:12 pm Sagittarius
28th 4:52 am Capricorn
30th 4:16 pm Aquarius

August 1939
2nd 4:42 am Pisces
4th 5:21 pm Aries
7th 4:45 am Taurus
9th 1:01 pm Gemini
11th 5:17 pm Cancer
13th 6:07 pm Leo
15th 5:20 pm Virgo
17th 5:08 pm Libra
19th 7:24 pm Scorpio
22nd 1:15 am Sagittarius
24th 10:36 am Capricorn
26th 10:10 pm Aquarius
29th 10:43 am Pisces
31st 11:16 pm Aries

September 1939
3rd 10:45 am Taurus
5th 8:00 pm Gemini
8th 1:51 am Cancer
10th 4:11 am Leo
12th 4:09 am Virgo
14th 3:42 am Libra
16th 4:47 am Scorpio
18th 9:08 am Sagittarius
20th 5:15 pm Capricorn
23rd 4:24 am Aquarius
25th 4:59 pm Pisces
28th 5:21 am Aries
30th 4:27 pm Taurus

October 1939
3rd 1:38 am Gemini
5th 8:14 am Cancer
7th 12:07 pm Leo
9th 1:44 pm Virgo
11th 2:18 pm Libra
13th 3:22 pm Scorpio
15th 6:40 pm Sagittarius
18th 1:24 am Capricorn
20th 11:44 am Aquarius
23rd 0:06 am Pisces
25th 12:27 pm Aries
27th 11:10 pm Taurus
30th 7:28 am Gemini

November 1939
1st 1:39 pm Cancer
3rd 5:50 pm Leo
5th 8:56 pm Virgo
7th 11:03 pm Libra
10th 1:15 am Scorpio
12th 4:46 am Sagittarius
14th 10:48 am Capricorn
16th 8:04 pm Aquarius
19th 8:02 am Pisces
21st 8:35 pm Aries
24th 7:19 am Taurus
26th 3:05 pm Gemini
28th 8:10 pm Cancer
30th 11:34 pm Leo

December 1939
3rd 2:22 am Virgo
5th 5:23 am Libra
7th 8:60 am Scorpio
9th 1:35 pm Sagittarius
11th 7:54 pm Capricorn
14th 4:47 am Aquarius
16th 4:17 pm Pisces
19th 5:02 am Aries
21st 4:30 pm Taurus
24th 0:37 am Gemini
26th 5:02 am Cancer
28th 7:05 am Leo
30th 8:30 am Virgo

January 1940
1st 10:47 am Libra
3rd 2:40 pm Scorpio
5th 8:14 pm Sagittarius
8th 3:31 am Capricorn
10th 12:46 pm Aquarius
13th 0:04 am Pisces
15th 12:56 pm Aries
18th 1:16 am Taurus
20th 10:27 am Gemini
22nd 3:30 pm Cancer
24th 5:09 pm Leo
26th 5:14 pm Virgo
28th 5:46 pm Libra
30th 8:20 pm Scorpio

February 1940
2nd 1:37 am Sagittarius
4th 9:30 am Capricorn
6th 7:23 pm Aquarius
9th 7:01 am Pisces
11th 7:49 pm Aries
14th 8:33 am Taurus
16th 7:08 pm Gemini
19th 1:47 am Cancer
21st 4:17 am Leo
23rd 4:12 am Virgo
25th 3:31 am Libra
27th 4:17 am Scorpio
29th 7:59 am Sagittarius

March 1940
2nd 3:07 pm Capricorn
5th 1:07 am Aquarius
7th 1:08 pm Pisces
10th 1:60 am Aries
12th 2:44 pm Taurus
15th 1:53 am Gemini
17th 9:53 am Cancer
19th 2:11 pm Leo
21st 3:18 pm Virgo
23rd 2:49 pm Libra
25th 2:38 pm Scorpio
27th 4:36 pm Sagittarius
29th 10:02 pm Capricorn

April 1940
1st 7:15 am Aquarius
3rd 7:11 pm Pisces
6th 8:09 am Aries
8th 8:38 pm Taurus
11th 7:29 am Gemini
13th 4:01 pm Cancer
15th 9:43 pm Leo
18th 0:34 am Virgo
20th 1:23 am Libra
22nd 1:34 am Scorpio
24th 2:50 am Sagittarius
26th 6:54 am Capricorn
28th 2:44 pm Aquarius

May 1940
1st 1:55 am Pisces
3rd 2:51 pm Aries
6th 3:11 am Taurus
8th 1:29 pm Gemini
10th 9:31 pm Cancer
13th 3:20 am Leo
15th 7:15 am Virgo
17th 9:39 am Libra
19th 11:12 am Scorpio
21st 1:03 pm Sagittarius
23rd 4:39 pm Capricorn
25th 11:21 pm Aquarius
28th 9:42 am Pisces
30th 10:18 pm Aries

June 1940
2nd 10:41 am Taurus
4th 8:46 pm Gemini
7th 3:59 am Cancer
9th 8:58 am Leo
11th 12:38 pm Virgo
13th 3:41 pm Libra
15th 6:31 pm Scorpio
17th 9:33 pm Sagittarius
20th 1:45 am Capricorn
22nd 8:19 am Aquarius
24th 5:59 pm Pisces
27th 6:14 am Aries
29th 6:51 pm Taurus

July 1940
2nd 5:11 am Gemini
4th 12:05 pm Cancer
6th 4:09 pm Leo
8th 6:43 pm Virgo
10th 9:07 pm Libra
13th 0:07 am Scorpio
15th 4:06 am Sagittarius
17th 9:19 am Capricorn
19th 4:24 pm Aquarius
22nd 1:59 am Pisces
24th 2:02 pm Aries
27th 2:54 am Taurus
29th 1:59 pm Gemini
31st 9:30 pm Cancer

August 1940
3rd 1:20 am Leo
5th 2:50 am Virgo
7th 3:51 am Libra
9th 5:48 am Scorpio
11th 9:32 am Sagittarius
13th 3:17 pm Capricorn
15th 11:07 pm Aquarius
18th 9:12 am Pisces
20th 9:14 pm Aries
23rd 10:15 am Taurus
25th 10:12 pm Gemini
28th 6:49 am Cancer
30th 11:25 am Leo

September 1940
1st 12:54 pm Virgo
3rd 12:55 pm Libra
5th 1:20 pm Scorpio
7th 3:41 pm Sagittarius
9th 8:47 pm Capricorn
12th 4:53 am Aquarius
14th 3:27 pm Pisces
17th 3:43 am Aries
19th 4:45 pm Taurus
22nd 5:03 am Gemini
24th 2:54 pm Cancer
26th 9:07 pm Leo
28th 11:42 pm Virgo
30th 11:47 pm Libra

October 1940
2nd 11:12 pm Scorpio
4th 11:53 pm Sagittarius
7th 3:31 am Capricorn
9th 10:48 am Aquarius
11th 9:18 pm Pisces
14th 9:50 am Aries
16th 10:49 pm Taurus
19th 10:57 am Gemini
21st 9:17 pm Cancer
24th 4:47 am Leo
26th 9:06 am Virgo
28th 10:35 am Libra
30th 10:26 am Scorpio

November 1940
1st 10:26 am Sagittarius
3rd 12:29 pm Capricorn
5th 6:08 pm Aquarius
8th 3:49 am Pisces
10th 4:14 pm Aries
13th 5:12 am Taurus
15th 4:58 pm Gemini
18th 2:51 am Cancer
20th 10:35 am Leo
22nd 4:07 pm Virgo
24th 7:22 pm Libra
26th 8:45 pm Scorpio
28th 9:20 pm Sagittarius
30th 10:52 pm Capricorn

December 1940
3rd 3:16 am Aquarius
5th 11:41 am Pisces
7th 11:28 pm Aries
10th 12:26 pm Taurus
13th 0:08 am Gemini
15th 9:17 am Cancer
17th 4:14 pm Leo
19th 9:34 pm Virgo
22nd 1:36 am Libra
24th 4:30 am Scorpio
26th 6:37 am Sagittarius
28th 9:02 am Capricorn
30th 1:15 pm Aquarius

January 1941
1st 8:38 pm Pisces
4th 7:38 am Aries
6th 8:29 pm Taurus
9th 8:25 am Gemini
11th 5:31 pm Cancer
13th 11:40 pm Leo
16th 3:46 am Virgo
18th 7:00 am Libra
20th 10:05 am Scorpio
22nd 1:18 pm Sagittarius
24th 5:03 pm Capricorn
26th 10:07 pm Aquarius
29th 5:38 am Pisces
31st 4:05 pm Aries

February 1941
3rd 4:41 am Taurus
5th 5:08 pm Gemini
8th 2:55 am Cancer
10th 9:05 am Leo
12th 12:20 pm Virgo
14th 2:08 pm Libra
16th 3:54 pm Scorpio
18th 6:39 pm Sagittarius
20th 10:55 pm Capricorn
23rd 5:03 am Aquarius
25th 1:21 pm Pisces
27th 11:54 pm Aries

March 1941
2nd 12:24 pm Taurus
5th 1:12 am Gemini
7th 11:59 am Cancer
9th 7:17 pm Leo
11th 10:52 pm Virgo
13th 11:52 pm Libra
16th 0:03 am Scorpio
18th 1:09 am Sagittarius
20th 4:27 am Capricorn
22nd 10:36 am Aquarius
24th 7:32 pm Pisces
27th 6:41 am Aries
29th 7:14 pm Taurus

April 1941
1st 8:05 am Gemini
3rd 7:42 pm Cancer
6th 4:23 am Leo
8th 9:17 am Virgo
10th 10:52 am Libra
12th 10:32 am Scorpio
14th 10:12 am Sagittarius
16th 11:45 am Capricorn
18th 4:36 pm Aquarius
21st 1:07 am Pisces
23rd 12:36 pm Aries
26th 1:21 am Taurus
28th 2:09 pm Gemini

May 1941
1st 1:55 am Cancer
3rd 11:29 am Leo
5th 6:02 pm Virgo
7th 9:10 pm Libra
9th 9:33 pm Scorpio
11th 8:51 pm Sagittarius
13th 9:07 pm Capricorn
16th 0:16 am Aquarius
18th 7:39 am Pisces
20th 6:36 pm Aries
23rd 7:25 am Taurus
25th 8:09 pm Gemini
28th 7:34 am Cancer
30th 5:13 pm Leo

June 1941
2nd 0:37 am Virgo
4th 5:14 am Libra
6th 7:10 am Scorpio
8th 7:23 am Sagittarius
10th 7:36 am Capricorn
12th 9:47 am Aquarius
14th 3:40 pm Pisces
17th 1:32 am Aries
19th 2:04 pm Taurus
22nd 2:43 am Gemini
24th 1:48 pm Cancer
26th 10:54 pm Leo
29th 6:00 am Virgo

July 1941
1st 11:13 am Libra
3rd 2:30 pm Scorpio
5th 4:11 pm Sagittarius
7th 5:22 pm Capricorn
9th 7:38 pm Aquarius
12th 0:43 am Pisces
14th 9:38 am Aries
16th 9:31 pm Taurus
19th 10:08 am Gemini
21st 9:13 pm Cancer
24th 5:45 am Leo
26th 12:00 pm Virgo
28th 4:39 pm Libra
30th 8:08 pm Scorpio

August 1941
1st 10:49 pm Sagittarius
4th 1:16 am Capricorn
6th 4:34 am Aquarius
8th 9:55 am Pisces
10th 6:14 pm Aries
13th 5:33 am Taurus
15th 6:09 pm Gemini
18th 5:34 am Cancer
20th 2:11 pm Leo
22nd 7:51 pm Virgo
24th 11:21 pm Libra
27th 1:49 am Scorpio
29th 4:14 am Sagittarius
31st 7:20 am Capricorn

September 1941
2nd 11:40 am Aquarius
4th 5:54 pm Pisces
7th 2:28 am Aries
9th 1:33 pm Taurus
12th 2:05 am Gemini
14th 2:06 pm Cancer
16th 11:36 pm Leo
19th 5:26 am Virgo
21st 8:14 am Libra
23rd 9:23 am Scorpio
25th 10:27 am Sagittarius
27th 12:48 pm Capricorn
29th 5:19 pm Aquarius

October 1941
2nd 0:17 am Pisces
4th 9:39 am Aries
6th 8:51 pm Taurus
9th 9:22 am Gemini
11th 9:52 pm Cancer
14th 8:25 am Leo
16th 3:31 pm Virgo
18th 6:51 pm Libra
20th 7:24 pm Scorpio
22nd 7:02 pm Sagittarius
24th 7:43 pm Capricorn
26th 11:02 pm Aquarius
29th 5:54 am Pisces
31st 3:40 pm Aries

November 1941
3rd 3:19 am Taurus
5th 3:52 pm Gemini
8th 4:24 am Cancer
10th 3:45 pm Leo
13th 0:29 am Virgo
15th 5:18 am Libra
17th 6:38 am Scorpio
19th 5:54 am Sagittarius
21st 5:15 am Capricorn
23rd 6:52 am Aquarius
25th 12:16 pm Pisces
27th 9:28 pm Aries
30th 9:19 am Taurus

December 1941
2nd 9:59 pm Gemini
5th 10:20 am Cancer
7th 9:41 pm Leo
10th 7:08 am Virgo
12th 1:41 pm Libra
14th 4:47 pm Scorpio
16th 5:08 pm Sagittarius
18th 4:30 pm Capricorn
20th 4:59 pm Aquarius
22nd 8:37 pm Pisces
25th 4:28 am Aries
27th 3:46 pm Taurus
30th 4:27 am Gemini

January 1942
1st 4:40 pm Cancer
4th 3:32 am Leo
6th 12:39 pm Virgo
8th 7:47 pm Libra
11th 0:24 am Scorpio
13th 2:30 am Sagittarius
15th 3:07 am Capricorn
17th 3:54 am Aquarius
19th 6:48 am Pisces
21st 1:14 pm Aries
23rd 11:21 pm Taurus
26th 11:45 am Gemini
29th 0:04 am Cancer
31st 10:35 am Leo

February 1942
2nd 6:56 pm Virgo
5th 1:18 am Libra
7th 5:55 am Scorpio
9th 9:06 am Sagittarius
11th 11:18 am Capricorn
13th 1:30 pm Aquarius
15th 4:55 pm Pisces
17th 10:47 pm Aries
20th 8:01 am Taurus
22nd 7:48 pm Gemini
25th 8:15 am Cancer
27th 7:05 pm Leo

March 1942
2nd 3:06 am Virgo
4th 8:21 am Libra
6th 11:49 am Scorpio
8th 2:29 pm Sagittarius
10th 5:10 pm Capricorn
12th 8:32 pm Aquarius
15th 1:10 am Pisces
17th 7:44 am Aries
19th 4:41 pm Taurus
22nd 4:02 am Gemini
24th 4:32 pm Cancer
27th 4:03 am Leo
29th 12:33 pm Virgo
31st 5:34 pm Libra

April 1942
2nd 7:55 pm Scorpio
4th 9:05 pm Sagittarius
6th 10:43 pm Capricorn
9th 1:58 am Aquarius
11th 7:21 am Pisces
13th 2:51 pm Aries
16th 0:18 am Taurus
18th 11:39 am Gemini
21st 0:10 am Cancer
23rd 12:19 pm Leo
25th 10:01 pm Virgo
28th 3:49 am Libra
30th 5:58 am Scorpio

May 1942			June 1942			July 1942			August 1942		
2nd	6:04 am	Sagittarius	2nd	4:05 pm	Aquarius	2nd	3:49 am	Pisces	3rd	1:49 am	Taurus
4th	6:09 am	Capricorn	4th	7:18 pm	Pisces	4th	9:16 am	Aries	5th	12:56 pm	Gemini
6th	8:01 am	Aquarius	7th	2:14 am	Aries	6th	6:25 pm	Taurus	8th	1:31 am	Cancer
8th	12:48 pm	Pisces	9th	12:18 pm	Taurus	9th	6:12 am	Gemini	10th	1:37 pm	Leo
10th	8:32 pm	Aries	12th	0:12 am	Gemini	11th	6:51 pm	Cancer	13th	0:09 am	Virgo
13th	6:38 am	Taurus	14th	12:49 pm	Cancer	14th	7:07 am	Leo	15th	8:29 am	Libra
15th	6:16 pm	Gemini	17th	1:18 am	Leo	16th	6:06 pm	Virgo	17th	2:35 pm	Scorpio
18th	6:49 am	Cancer	19th	12:29 pm	Virgo	19th	2:50 am	Libra	19th	6:32 pm	Sagittarius
20th	7:19 pm	Leo	21st	9:01 pm	Libra	21st	8:56 am	Scorpio	21st	8:44 pm	Capricorn
23rd	6:04 am	Virgo	24th	1:49 am	Scorpio	23rd	11:53 am	Sagittarius	23rd	10:07 pm	Aquarius
25th	1:15 pm	Libra	26th	3:06 am	Sagittarius	25th	12:36 pm	Capricorn	25th	11:55 pm	Pisces
27th	4:26 pm	Scorpio	28th	2:30 am	Capricorn	27th	12:39 pm	Aquarius	28th	3:40 am	Aries
29th	4:38 pm	Sagittarius	30th	2:02 am	Aquarius	29th	1:53 pm	Pisces	30th	10:33 am	Taurus
31st	3:47 pm	Capricorn				31st	5:50 am	Aries			

September 1942			October 1942			November 1942			December 1942		
1st	8:41 pm	Gemini	1st	5:04 pm	Cancer	3rd	1:18 am	Virgo	2nd	6:51 pm	Libra
4th	9:00 am	Cancer	4th	5:33 am	Leo	5th	9:16 am	Libra	5th	0:07 am	Scorpio
6th	9:14 pm	Leo	6th	4:10 pm	Virgo	7th	1:22 pm	Scorpio	7th	1:32 am	Sagittarius
9th	7:28 am	Virgo	8th	11:33 pm	Libra	9th	2:45 pm	Sagittarius	9th	1:08 am	Capricorn
11th	3:01 pm	Libra	11th	3:45 am	Scorpio	11th	3:19 pm	Capricorn	11th	0:57 am	Aquarius
13th	8:18 pm	Scorpio	13th	6:10 am	Sagittarius	13th	4:51 pm	Aquarius	13th	2:59 am	Pisces
15th	11:58 pm	Sagittarius	15th	8:13 am	Capricorn	15th	8:30 pm	Pisces	15th	8:09 am	Aries
18th	2:47 am	Capricorn	17th	11:03 am	Aquarius	18th	2:32 am	Aries	17th	4:20 pm	Taurus
20th	5:27 am	Aquarius	19th	3:06 pm	Pisces	20th	10:39 am	Taurus	20th	2:47 am	Gemini
22nd	8:35 am	Pisces	21st	8:36 pm	Aries	22nd	8:35 pm	Gemini	22nd	2:57 pm	Cancer
24th	12:59 pm	Aries	24th	3:52 am	Taurus	25th	8:17 am	Cancer	25th	3:35 am	Leo
26th	7:35 pm	Taurus	26th	1:20 pm	Gemini	27th	9:09 pm	Leo	27th	4:07 pm	Virgo
29th	5:06 am	Gemini	29th	0:59 am	Cancer	30th	9:25 am	Virgo	30th	2:41 am	Libra
			31st	1:46 pm	Leo						

January 1943			February 1943			March 1943			April 1943		
1st	9:32 am	Scorpio	1st	11:14 pm	Capricorn	1st	7:17 am	Capricorn	1st	6:28 pm	Pisces
3rd	12:28 pm	Sagittarius	3rd	11:11 pm	Aquarius	3rd	8:56 am	Aquarius	3rd	9:18 pm	Aries
5th	12:33 pm	Capricorn	5th	11:09 pm	Pisces	5th	9:56 am	Pisces	6th	1:39 am	Taurus
7th	11:45 am	Aquarius	8th	1:01 am	Aries	7th	11:46 am	Aries	8th	8:46 am	Gemini
9th	12:09 pm	Pisces	10th	6:22 am	Taurus	9th	3:58 pm	Taurus	10th	7:04 pm	Cancer
11th	3:27 pm	Aries	12th	3:29 pm	Gemini	11th	11:39 pm	Gemini	13th	7:39 am	Leo
13th	10:24 pm	Taurus	15th	3:25 am	Cancer	14th	10:53 am	Cancer	15th	7:59 pm	Virgo
16th	8:42 am	Gemini	17th	4:18 pm	Leo	16th	11:42 pm	Leo	18th	5:39 am	Libra
18th	8:54 pm	Cancer	20th	4:19 am	Virgo	19th	11:41 am	Virgo	20th	12:01 pm	Scorpio
21st	9:43 am	Leo	22nd	2:28 pm	Libra	21st	9:21 pm	Libra	22nd	3:55 pm	Sagittarius
23rd	10:02 pm	Virgo	24th	10:24 pm	Scorpio	24th	4:23 am	Scorpio	24th	6:40 pm	Capricorn
26th	8:44 am	Libra	27th	3:58 am	Sagittarius	26th	9:22 am	Sagittarius	26th	9:22 pm	Aquarius
28th	4:46 pm	Scorpio				28th	1:04 pm	Capricorn	29th	0:36 am	Pisces
30th	9:32 pm	Sagittarius				30th	3:57 pm	Aquarius			

May 1943			June 1943			July 1943			August 1943		
1st	4:40 am	Aries	2nd	0:31 am	Gemini	1st	5:15 pm	Cancer	3rd	0:44 am	Virgo
3rd	9:60 am	Taurus	4th	10:48 am	Cancer	4th	5:40 am	Leo	5th	12:48 pm	Libra
5th	5:18 pm	Gemini	6th	11:03 pm	Leo	6th	6:43 pm	Virgo	7th	10:39 pm	Scorpio
8th	3:19 am	Cancer	9th	12:01 pm	Virgo	9th	6:41 am	Libra	10th	5:04 am	Sagittarius
10th	3:40 pm	Leo	11th	11:21 pm	Libra	11th	3:34 pm	Scorpio	12th	8:05 am	Capricorn
13th	4:20 am	Virgo	14th	6:54 am	Scorpio	13th	8:34 pm	Sagittarius	14th	8:34 am	Aquarius
15th	2:40 pm	Libra	16th	10:32 am	Sagittarius	15th	10:05 pm	Capricorn	16th	8:07 am	Pisces
17th	9:18 pm	Scorpio	18th	11:29 am	Capricorn	17th	9:46 pm	Aquarius	18th	8:36 am	Aries
20th	0:33 am	Sagittarius	20th	11:36 am	Aquarius	19th	9:32 pm	Pisces	20th	11:46 am	Taurus
22nd	2:01 am	Capricorn	22nd	12:42 pm	Pisces	21st	11:10 pm	Aries	22nd	6:38 pm	Gemini
24th	3:25 am	Aquarius	24th	3:58 pm	Aries	24th	3:56 am	Taurus	25th	5:09 am	Cancer
26th	6:01 am	Pisces	26th	9:54 pm	Taurus	26th	12:08 pm	Gemini	27th	5:49 pm	Leo
28th	10:20 am	Aries	29th	6:30 am	Gemini	28th	11:04 pm	Cancer	30th	6:47 pm	Virgo
30th	4:26 pm	Taurus				31st	11:44 am	Leo			

September 1943			October 1943			November 1943			December 1943		
1st	6:31 pm	Libra	1st	10:02 am	Scorpio	2nd	3:36 am	Capricorn	1st	1:01 am	Aquarius
4th	4:19 am	Scorpio	3rd	5:01 pm	Sagittarius	4th	7:09 am	Aquarius	3rd	3:36 pm	Pisces
6th	11:34 am	Sagittarius	5th	10:10 pm	Capricorn	6th	10:15 am	Pisces	5th	7:01 pm	Aries
8th	4:09 pm	Capricorn	8th	1:39 am	Aquarius	8th	1:11 pm	Aries	7th	11:30 pm	Taurus
10th	6:15 pm	Aquarius	10th	3:43 am	Pisces	10th	4:33 pm	Taurus	10th	5:34 am	Gemini
12th	6:45 pm	Pisces	12th	5:12 am	Aries	12th	9:31 pm	Gemini	12th	1:49 pm	Cancer
14th	7:09 am	Aries	14th	7:27 am	Taurus	15th	5:24 am	Cancer	15th	0:36 am	Leo
16th	9:15 am	Taurus	16th	12:11 pm	Gemini	17th	4:28 pm	Leo	17th	1:20 pm	Virgo
19th	2:43 am	Gemini	18th	8:29 pm	Cancer	20th	5:20 am	Virgo	20th	1:54 am	Libra
21st	12:13 pm	Cancer	21st	8:13 am	Leo	22nd	5:15 pm	Libra	22nd	11:39 am	Scorpio
24th	0:33 am	Leo	23rd	9:08 pm	Virgo	25th	2:07 am	Scorpio	24th	5:39 pm	Sagittarius
26th	1:29 pm	Virgo	26th	8:33 am	Libra	27th	7:31 am	Sagittarius	26th	8:22 pm	Capricorn
29th	0:56 am	Libra	28th	5:11 pm	Scorpio	29th	10:41 am	Capricorn	28th	9:21 pm	Aquarius
			30th	11:14 pm	Sagittarius				30th	10:17 pm	Pisces

January 1944

2nd	0:35 am	Aries
4th	5:02 am	Taurus
6th	11:48 am	Gemini
8th	8:49 pm	Cancer
11th	7:59 am	Leo
13th	8:39 pm	Virgo
16th	9:26 am	Libra
18th	8:24 pm	Scorpio
21st	3:49 am	Sagittarius
23rd	7:22 am	Capricorn
25th	8:07 am	Aquarius
27th	7:49 am	Pisces
29th	8:18 am	Aries
31st	11:13 am	Taurus

February 1944

2nd	5:22 pm	Gemini
5th	2:42 am	Cancer
7th	2:22 pm	Leo
10th	3:07 am	Virgo
12th	3:53 pm	Libra
15th	3:21 am	Scorpio
17th	12:08 pm	Sagittarius
19th	5:28 pm	Capricorn
21st	7:23 pm	Aquarius
23rd	7:07 pm	Pisces
25th	6:33 pm	Aries
27th	7:40 pm	Taurus

March 1944

1st	0:06 am	Gemini
3rd	8:42 am	Cancer
5th	8:20 pm	Leo
8th	9:19 am	Virgo
10th	9:55 pm	Libra
13th	9:10 am	Scorpio
15th	6:29 pm	Sagittarius
18th	1:12 am	Capricorn
20th	4:53 am	Aquarius
22nd	5:56 am	Pisces
24th	5:42 am	Aries
26th	6:04 am	Taurus
28th	9:04 am	Gemini
30th	4:04 pm	Cancer

April 1944

2nd	2:56 am	Leo
4th	3:49 pm	Virgo
7th	4:22 am	Libra
9th	3:10 pm	Scorpio
12th	0:04 am	Sagittarius
14th	6:54 am	Capricorn
16th	11:44 am	Aquarius
18th	2:26 pm	Pisces
20th	3:35 pm	Aries
22nd	4:31 pm	Taurus
24th	7:03 pm	Gemini
27th	0:49 am	Cancer
29th	10:40 am	Leo

May 1944

1st	11:05 pm	Virgo
4th	11:38 am	Libra
6th	10:18 pm	Scorpio
9th	6:26 am	Sagittarius
11th	12:32 pm	Capricorn
13th	5:08 pm	Aquarius
15th	8:34 pm	Pisces
17th	11:03 pm	Aries
20th	1:16 am	Taurus
22nd	4:30 am	Gemini
24th	10:09 am	Cancer
26th	7:07 pm	Leo
29th	6:59 am	Virgo
31st	7:37 pm	Libra

June 1944

3rd	6:29 am	Scorpio
5th	2:25 pm	Sagittarius
7th	7:41 pm	Capricorn
9th	11:12 pm	Aquarius
12th	1:50 am	Pisces
14th	4:42 am	Aries
16th	7:54 am	Taurus
18th	12:14 pm	Gemini
20th	6:32 pm	Cancer
23rd	3:27 am	Leo
25th	2:59 pm	Virgo
28th	3:39 am	Libra
30th	3:07 pm	Scorpio

July 1944

2nd	11:38 pm	Sagittarius
5th	4:40 am	Capricorn
7th	7:13 am	Aquarius
9th	8:40 am	Pisces
11th	10:22 am	Aries
13th	1:21 pm	Taurus
15th	6:14 pm	Gemini
18th	1:23 am	Cancer
20th	10:55 am	Leo
22nd	10:24 pm	Virgo
25th	11:06 am	Libra
27th	11:16 pm	Scorpio
30th	8:44 am	Sagittarius

August 1944

1st	2:37 pm	Capricorn
3rd	5:07 pm	Aquarius
5th	5:34 pm	Pisces
7th	5:45 pm	Aries
9th	7:23 pm	Taurus
11th	11:39 pm	Gemini
14th	7:07 am	Cancer
16th	5:11 pm	Leo
19th	5:03 am	Virgo
21st	5:45 pm	Libra
24th	6:11 am	Scorpio
26th	4:47 pm	Sagittarius
29th	0:12 am	Capricorn
31st	3:42 am	Aquarius

September 1944

2nd	4:13 am	Pisces
4th	3:27 am	Aries
6th	3:30 am	Taurus
8th	6:18 am	Gemini
10th	12:52 pm	Cancer
12th	10:51 pm	Leo
15th	11:01 am	Virgo
17th	11:48 pm	Libra
20th	12:11 pm	Scorpio
22nd	11:17 pm	Sagittarius
25th	7:51 am	Capricorn
27th	1:04 pm	Aquarius
29th	2:53 pm	Pisces

October 1944

1st	2:28 pm	Aries
3rd	1:49 pm	Taurus
5th	3:05 pm	Gemini
7th	7:58 pm	Cancer
10th	5:04 am	Leo
12th	5:05 pm	Virgo
15th	5:53 am	Libra
17th	6:02 pm	Scorpio
20th	4:49 am	Sagittarius
22nd	1:45 pm	Capricorn
24th	8:17 pm	Aquarius
26th	11:53 pm	Pisces
29th	0:53 am	Aries
31st	0:45 am	Taurus

November 1944

2nd	1:29 am	Gemini
4th	5:07 am	Cancer
6th	12:48 pm	Leo
8th	11:58 pm	Virgo
11th	12:42 pm	Libra
14th	0:47 am	Scorpio
16th	10:50 am	Sagittarius
18th	7:18 pm	Capricorn
21st	1:46 am	Aquarius
23rd	6:16 am	Pisces
25th	8:54 am	Aries
27th	10:22 am	Taurus
29th	11:57 am	Gemini

December 1944

1st	3:21 pm	Cancer
3rd	9:53 pm	Leo
6th	8:06 am	Virgo
8th	8:28 pm	Libra
11th	8:40 am	Scorpio
13th	6:48 pm	Sagittarius
16th	2:20 am	Capricorn
18th	7:41 am	Aquarius
20th	11:38 am	Pisces
22nd	2:42 pm	Aries
24th	5:25 pm	Taurus
26th	8:26 pm	Gemini
29th	0:43 am	Cancer
31st	7:22 am	Leo

January 1945

2nd	4:50 am	Virgo
5th	4:43 am	Libra
7th	5:09 pm	Scorpio
10th	3:51 am	Sagittarius
12th	11:22 am	Capricorn
14th	3:53 pm	Aquarius
16th	6:26 pm	Pisces
18th	8:22 pm	Aries
20th	10:49 pm	Taurus
23rd	2:37 am	Gemini
25th	8:08 am	Cancer
27th	3:35 pm	Leo
30th	1:09 am	Virgo

February 1945

1st	12:46 pm	Libra
4th	1:20 am	Scorpio
6th	12:53 pm	Sagittarius
8th	9:27 pm	Capricorn
11th	2:09 am	Aquarius
13th	3:51 am	Pisces
15th	4:13 am	Aries
17th	5:07 am	Taurus
19th	8:05 am	Gemini
21st	1:46 pm	Cancer
23rd	10:00 pm	Leo
26th	8:15 am	Virgo
28th	7:57 pm	Libra

March 1945

3rd	8:32 am	Scorpio
5th	8:43 pm	Sagittarius
8th	6:32 am	Capricorn
10th	12:34 pm	Aquarius
12th	2:44 pm	Pisces
14th	2:30 pm	Aries
16th	1:57 pm	Taurus
18th	3:09 pm	Gemini
20th	7:35 pm	Cancer
23rd	3:34 am	Leo
25th	2:13 pm	Virgo
28th	2:15 am	Libra
30th	2:51 pm	Scorpio

April 1945

2nd	3:07 am	Sagittarius
4th	1:48 pm	Capricorn
6th	9:28 pm	Aquarius
9th	1:10 am	Pisces
11th	1:37 am	Aries
13th	0:39 am	Taurus
15th	0:31 am	Gemini
17th	3:16 am	Cancer
19th	9:56 am	Leo
21st	8:05 pm	Virgo
24th	8:16 am	Libra
26th	8:52 pm	Scorpio
29th	8:55 am	Sagittarius

May 1945

1st	7:39 pm	Capricorn
4th	4:03 am	Aquarius
6th	9:16 am	Pisces
8th	11:21 am	Aries
10th	11:24 am	Taurus
12th	11:16 am	Gemini
14th	12:57 pm	Cancer
16th	6:01 pm	Leo
19th	2:57 am	Virgo
21st	2:43 pm	Libra
24th	3:21 am	Scorpio
26th	3:09 pm	Sagittarius
29th	1:23 am	Capricorn
31st	9:32 am	

June 1945

2nd	3:22 pm	Pisces
4th	6:48 pm	Aries
6th	8:22 pm	Taurus
8th	9:15 pm	Gemini
10th	11:03 pm	Cancer
13th	3:22 am	Leo
15th	11:12 am	Virgo
17th	10:06 pm	Libra
20th	10:35 am	Scorpio
22nd	10:27 pm	Sagittarius
25th	8:13 am	Capricorn
27th	3:34 pm	Aquarius
29th	8:51 pm	Pisces

July 1945

2nd	0:30 am	Aries
4th	3:04 am	Taurus
6th	5:21 am	Gemini
8th	8:14 am	Cancer
10th	12:48 pm	Leo
12th	8:01 pm	Virgo
15th	6:14 am	Libra
17th	6:29 pm	Scorpio
20th	6:33 am	Sagittarius
22nd	4:25 pm	Capricorn
24th	11:17 pm	Aquarius
27th	3:26 am	Pisces
29th	6:09 am	Aries
31st	8:31 am	Taurus

August 1945

2nd	11:27 am	Gemini
4th	3:26 pm	Cancer
6th	8:54 pm	Leo
9th	4:26 am	Virgo
11th	2:24 pm	Libra
14th	2:24 am	Scorpio
16th	2:54 pm	Sagittarius
19th	1:30 am	Capricorn
21st	8:26 am	Aquarius
23rd	12:02 pm	Pisces
25th	1:30 pm	Aries
27th	2:36 pm	Taurus
29th	4:50 pm	Gemini
31st	9:02 pm	Cancer

September 1945
3rd   3:22 am Leo
5th 11:40 am Virgo
7th   9:51 pm Libra
10th   9:49 am Scorpio
12th 10:37 pm Sagittarius
15th 10:07 am Capricorn
17th   6:15 pm Aquarius
19th 10:17 pm Pisces
21st 11:10 pm Aries
23rd 10:53 pm Taurus
25th 11:31 pm Gemini
28th   2:40 am Cancer
30th   8:50 am Leo

January 1946
2nd 12:07 pm Capricorn
4th   9:36 am Aquarius
7th   4:45 am Pisces
9th   9:53 am Aries
11th   1:23 pm Taurus
13th   3:42 pm Gemini
15th   5:33 pm Cancer
17th   8:05 pm Leo
20th   0:40 am Virgo
22nd   8:35 am Libra
24th   7:40 pm Scorpio
27th   8:24 am Sagittarius
29th   8:15 pm Capricorn

May 1946
2nd   8:04 pm Gemini
4th   8:23 pm Cancer
6th 11:05 pm Leo
9th   4:60 am Virgo
11th   1:55 pm Libra
14th   1:08 am Scorpio
16th   1:47 pm Sagittarius
19th   2:41 am Capricorn
21st   2:29 pm Aquarius
23rd 11:39 pm Pisces
26th   5:01 am Aries
28th   7:01 am Taurus
30th   6:54 am Gemini

September 1946
2nd   5:32 pm Sagittarius
5th   6:22 am Capricorn
7th   5:38 pm Aquarius
10th   1:44 am Pisces
12th   6:47 am Aries
14th 10:03 am Taurus
16th 12:47 pm Gemini
18th   3:44 pm Cancer
20th   7:15 pm Leo
22nd 11:39 pm Virgo
25th   5:44 am Libra
27th   2:17 pm Scorpio
30th   1:33 am Sagittarius

January 1947
2nd   1:05 am Taurus
4th   3:24 am Gemini
6th   3:27 am Cancer
8th   2:53 am Leo
10th   3:47 am Virgo
12th   7:59 am Libra
14th   4:19 pm Scorpio
17th   4:04 am Sagittarius
19th   5:09 pm Capricorn
22nd   5:35 am Aquarius
24th   4:21 pm Pisces
27th   1:10 am Aries
29th   7:42 am Taurus
31st 11:48 am Gemini

October 1945
2nd   5:35 pm Virgo
5th   4:19 am Libra
7th   4:26 pm Scorpio
10th   5:18 am Sagittarius
12th   5:31 pm Capricorn
15th   3:05 am Aquarius
17th   8:27 am Pisces
19th 10:05 am Aries
21st   9:30 am Taurus
23rd   8:53 am Gemini
25th 10:15 am Cancer
27th   2:60 pm Leo
29th 11:12 pm Virgo

February 1946
1st   5:20 am Aquarius
3rd 11:28 am Pisces
5th   3:37 pm Aries
7th   6:46 pm Taurus
9th   9:46 pm Gemini
12th   1:00 am Cancer
14th   4:51 am Leo
16th 10:06 am Virgo
18th   5:38 pm Libra
21st   4:04 am Scorpio
23rd   4:39 pm Sagittarius
26th   4:58 am Capricorn
28th   2:28 pm Aquarius

June 1946
1st   6:31 am Cancer
3rd   7:44 am Leo
5th 12:02 pm Virgo
7th   7:59 pm Libra
10th   7:06 am Scorpio
12th   7:52 pm Sagittarius
15th   8:38 am Capricorn
17th   8:14 pm Aquarius
20th   5:40 am Pisces
22nd 12:15 pm Aries
24th   3:52 pm Taurus
26th   5:06 pm Gemini
28th   5:12 pm Cancer
30th   5:51 pm Leo

October 1946
2nd   2:29 pm Capricorn
5th   2:27 am Aquarius
7th 11:03 am Pisces
9th   4:01 pm Aries
11th   6:19 pm Taurus
13th   7:37 pm Gemini
15th   9:23 pm Cancer
18th   0:35 am Leo
20th   5:38 am Virgo
22nd 12:36 pm Libra
24th   9:43 pm Scorpio
27th   9:06 am Sagittarius
29th   9:50 pm Capricorn

February 1947
2nd   1:36 pm Cancer
4th   2:01 pm Leo
6th   2:45 pm Virgo
8th   5:43 pm Libra
11th   0:27 am Scorpio
13th 11:17 am Sagittarius
16th   0:10 am Capricorn
18th 12:35 pm Aquarius
20th 10:57 pm Pisces
23rd   6:55 am Aries
25th   1:05 pm Taurus
27th   5:45 pm Gemini

November 1945
1st 10:08 am Libra
3rd 10:29 pm Scorpio
6th 11:18 am Sagittarius
8th 11:36 pm Capricorn
11th   9:55 am Aquarius
13th   5:01 pm Pisces
15th   8:21 pm Aries
17th   8:46 pm Taurus
19th   8:04 pm Gemini
21st   8:15 pm Cancer
23rd 11:11 pm Leo
26th   6:02 am Virgo
28th   4:20 pm Libra

March 1946
2nd   8:22 pm Pisces
4th 11:23 pm Aries
7th   1:08 am Taurus
9th   3:13 am Gemini
11th   6:31 am Cancer
13th 11:16 am Leo
15th   5:33 pm Virgo
18th   1:42 am Libra
20th 12:07 pm Scorpio
23rd   0:31 am Sagittarius
25th   1:15 pm Capricorn
27th 11:50 pm Aquarius
30th   6:20 am Pisces

July 1946
2nd   8:48 pm Virgo
5th   3:24 am Libra
7th   1:45 pm Scorpio
10th   2:20 am Sagittarius
12th   3:04 pm Capricorn
15th   2:17 am Aquarius
17th 11:13 am Pisces
19th   5:57 pm Aries
21st 10:15 pm Taurus
24th   1:19 am Gemini
26th   2:45 am Cancer
28th   3:59 am Leo
30th   6:37 am Virgo

November 1946
1st 10:35 am Aquarius
3rd   8:31 pm Pisces
6th   2:27 am Aries
8th   4:48 am Taurus
10th   5:08 am Gemini
12th   5:18 am Cancer
14th   6:55 am Leo
16th 11:09 am Virgo
18th   6:15 pm Libra
21st   3:59 am Scorpio
23rd   3:46 pm Sagittarius
26th   4:39 am Capricorn
28th   5:29 pm Aquarius

March 1947
1st   8:59 pm Cancer
3rd 11:00 pm Leo
6th   0:47 am Virgo
8th   3:54 am Libra
10th   9:55 am Scorpio
12th   7:34 pm Sagittarius
15th   7:59 am Capricorn
17th   8:34 pm Aquarius
20th   6:53 am Pisces
22nd   2:18 pm Aries
24th   7:27 pm Taurus
26th 11:15 pm Gemini
29th   2:56 am Cancer
31st   5:23 am Leo

December 1945
1st   4:42 am Scorpio
3rd   5:28 pm Sagittarius
6th   5:22 am Capricorn
8th   3:31 pm Aquarius
10th 11:20 pm Pisces
13th   4:12 am Aries
15th   6:27 am Taurus
17th   7:02 am Gemini
19th   7:30 am Cancer
21st   9:35 am Leo
23rd   2:49 pm Virgo
25th 11:45 pm Libra
28th 11:43 am Scorpio
31st   0:32 am Sagittarius

April 1946
1st   9:12 am Aries
3rd   9:55 am Taurus
5th 10:27 am Gemini
7th 12:25 pm Cancer
9th   4:40 pm Leo
11th 11:19 pm Virgo
14th   8:15 am Libra
16th   7:04 pm Scorpio
19th   7:32 am Sagittarius
21st   8:27 pm Capricorn
24th   7:53 am Aquarius
26th   3:49 pm Pisces
28th   7:42 pm Aries
30th   8:29 pm Taurus

August 1946
1st 12:11 pm Libra
3rd   9:24 pm Scorpio
6th   9:37 am Sagittarius
8th 10:23 pm Capricorn
11th   9:20 am Aquarius
13th   5:39 pm Pisces
15th 11:39 pm Aries
18th   3:59 am Taurus
20th   7:23 am Gemini
22nd 10:07 am Cancer
24th 12:41 pm Leo
26th   3:57 pm Virgo
28th   9:17 pm Libra
31st   5:52 am Scorpio

December 1946
1st   4:28 am Pisces
3rd 11:59 am Aries
5th   3:44 pm Taurus
7th   4:27 pm Gemini
9th   3:51 pm Cancer
11th   3:50 pm Leo
13th   6:12 pm Virgo
16th   0:08 am Virgo
18th   9:46 am Scorpio
20th   9:49 pm Sagittarius
23rd 10:49 am Capricorn
25th 11:30 pm Aquarius
28th 10:41 am Pisces
30th   7:29 pm Aries

April 1947
2nd   8:32 am Virgo
4th 12:42 pm Libra
6th   6:59 pm Scorpio
9th   4:14 am Sagittarius
11th   4:09 pm Capricorn
14th   4:50 am Aquarius
16th   3:43 pm Pisces
18th 11:24 pm Aries
21st   3:53 am Taurus
23rd   6:26 am Gemini
25th   8:22 am Cancer
27th 10:45 am Leo
29th   2:17 pm Virgo

May 1947
- 1st 7:24 pm Libra
- 4th 2:37 am Scorpio
- 6th 12:12 pm Sagittarius
- 8th 11:54 pm Capricorn
- 11th 12:39 pm Aquarius
- 14th 0:19 am Pisces
- 16th 8:51 am Aries
- 18th 1:46 pm Taurus
- 20th 3:49 pm Gemini
- 22nd 4:26 pm Cancer
- 24th 5:10 pm Leo
- 26th 7:52 pm Virgo
- 29th 0:53 am Libra
- 31st 8:45 am Scorpio

June 1947
- 2nd 6:55 pm Sagittarius
- 5th 6:52 am Capricorn
- 7th 7:38 pm Aquarius
- 10th 7:44 am Pisces
- 12th 5:30 pm Aries
- 14th 11:46 pm Taurus
- 17th 2:20 am Gemini
- 19th 2:32 am Cancer
- 21st 2:07 am Leo
- 23rd 3:03 am Virgo
- 25th 6:55 am Libra
- 27th 2:21 pm Scorpio
- 30th 0:46 am Sagittarius

July 1947
- 2nd 1:03 pm Capricorn
- 5th 1:49 am Aquarius
- 7th 2:01 pm Pisces
- 10th 0:34 am Aries
- 12th 8:08 am Taurus
- 14th 12:12 pm Gemini
- 16th 1:12 pm Cancer
- 18th 12:35 pm Leo
- 20th 12:24 pm Virgo
- 22nd 2:39 pm Libra
- 24th 8:44 pm Scorpio
- 27th 6:42 am Sagittarius
- 29th 7:02 pm Capricorn

August 1947
- 1st 7:49 am Aquarius
- 3rd 7:48 pm Pisces
- 6th 6:18 am Aries
- 8th 2:40 pm Taurus
- 10th 8:16 pm Gemini
- 12th 10:49 pm Cancer
- 14th 11:06 pm Leo
- 16th 10:50 pm Virgo
- 19th 0:05 am Libra
- 21st 4:48 am Scorpio
- 23rd 1:39 pm Sagittarius
- 26th 1:31 am Capricorn
- 28th 2:16 pm Aquarius
- 31st 2:03 am Pisces

September 1947
- 2nd 12:01 pm Aries
- 4th 8:09 pm Taurus
- 7th 2:19 am Gemini
- 9th 6:11 am Cancer
- 11th 8:02 am Leo
- 13th 8:53 am Virgo
- 15th 10:21 am Libra
- 17th 2:17 pm Scorpio
- 19th 9:51 pm Sagittarius
- 22nd 8:60 am Aquarius
- 24th 9:36 pm Aquarius
- 27th 9:22 am Pisces
- 29th 6:56 pm Aries

October 1947
- 2nd 2:15 am Taurus
- 4th 7:42 am Gemini
- 6th 11:46 am Cancer
- 8th 2:41 pm Leo
- 10th 4:58 pm Virgo
- 12th 7:33 pm Libra
- 14th 11:48 pm Scorpio
- 17th 6:57 am Sagittarius
- 19th 5:17 pm Capricorn
- 22nd 5:39 am Aquarius
- 24th 5:44 pm Pisces
- 27th 3:30 am Aries
- 29th 10:13 am Taurus
- 31st 2:34 pm Gemini

November 1947
- 2nd 5:32 pm Cancer
- 4th 8:04 pm Leo
- 6th 10:55 pm Virgo
- 9th 2:44 am Libra
- 11th 8:07 am Scorpio
- 13th 3:38 pm Sagittarius
- 16th 1:39 am Capricorn
- 18th 1:47 pm Aquarius
- 21st 2:17 am Pisces
- 23rd 12:50 pm Aries
- 25th 8:04 pm Taurus
- 27th 11:55 pm Gemini
- 30th 1:31 am Cancer

December 1947
- 2nd 2:32 am Leo
- 4th 4:26 am Virgo
- 6th 8:17 am Libra
- 8th 2:27 pm Scorpio
- 10th 10:50 pm Sagittarius
- 13th 9:17 am Capricorn
- 15th 9:17 pm Aquarius
- 18th 9:59 am Pisces
- 20th 9:35 pm Aries
- 23rd 6:07 am Taurus
- 25th 10:42 am Gemini
- 27th 12:00 pm Cancer
- 29th 11:43 am Leo
- 31st 11:52 am Virgo

January 1948
- 2nd 2:15 pm Libra
- 4th 7:53 pm Scorpio
- 7th 4:42 am Sagittarius
- 9th 3:43 pm Capricorn
- 12th 3:55 am Aquarius
- 14th 4:35 pm Pisces
- 17th 4:42 am Aries
- 19th 2:38 pm Taurus
- 21st 8:50 pm Gemini
- 23rd 11:22 pm Cancer
- 25th 10:59 pm Leo
- 27th 9:58 pm Virgo
- 29th 10:31 pm Libra

February 1948
- 1st 2:29 am Scorpio
- 3rd 10:30 am Sagittarius
- 5th 9:30 pm Capricorn
- 8th 9:59 am Aquarius
- 10th 10:37 pm Pisces
- 13th 10:36 am Aries
- 15th 9:07 pm Taurus
- 18th 4:53 am Gemini
- 20th 9:04 am Cancer
- 22nd 10:03 am Leo
- 24th 9:23 am Virgo
- 26th 9:10 am Libra
- 28th 11:30 am Scorpio

March 1948
- 1st 5:45 pm Sagittarius
- 4th 3:52 am Capricorn
- 6th 4:14 pm Aquarius
- 9th 4:51 am Pisces
- 11th 4:31 pm Aries
- 14th 2:39 am Taurus
- 16th 10:41 am Gemini
- 18th 4:11 pm Cancer
- 20th 6:56 pm Leo
- 22nd 7:42 pm Virgo
- 24th 8:02 pm Libra
- 26th 9:50 pm Scorpio
- 29th 2:48 am Sagittarius
- 31st 11:37 am Capricorn

April 1948
- 2nd 11:18 pm Aquarius
- 5th 11:54 am Pisces
- 7th 11:27 pm Aries
- 10th 8:55 am Taurus
- 12th 4:17 pm Gemini
- 14th 9:39 pm Cancer
- 17th 1:14 am Leo
- 19th 3:29 am Virgo
- 21st 5:17 am Libra
- 23rd 7:53 am Scorpio
- 25th 12:36 pm Sagittarius
- 27th 8:23 pm Capricorn
- 30th 7:17 am Aquarius

May 1948
- 2nd 7:44 pm Pisces
- 5th 7:25 am Aries
- 7th 4:44 pm Taurus
- 9th 11:19 pm Gemini
- 12th 3:35 am Cancer
- 14th 6:37 am Leo
- 16th 9:14 am Virgo
- 18th 12:08 pm Libra
- 20th 3:58 pm Scorpio
- 22nd 9:23 pm Sagittarius
- 25th 5:10 am Capricorn
- 27th 3:33 pm Aquarius
- 30th 3:46 am Pisces

June 1948
- 1st 3:53 pm Aries
- 4th 1:42 am Taurus
- 6th 8:01 am Gemini
- 8th 11:24 am Cancer
- 10th 1:11 pm Leo
- 12th 2:49 pm Virgo
- 14th 5:35 pm Libra
- 16th 10:03 pm Scorpio
- 19th 4:29 am Sagittarius
- 21st 12:53 pm Capricorn
- 23rd 11:15 pm Aquarius
- 26th 11:24 am Pisces
- 28th 11:56 pm Aries

July 1948
- 1st 10:35 am Taurus
- 3rd 5:43 pm Gemini
- 5th 9:04 pm Cancer
- 7th 9:51 pm Leo
- 9th 10:04 pm Virgo
- 11th 11:30 pm Libra
- 14th 3:30 am Scorpio
- 16th 10:14 am Sagittarius
- 18th 7:15 pm Capricorn
- 21st 6:04 am Aquarius
- 23rd 6:13 pm Pisces
- 26th 6:55 am Aries
- 28th 6:31 pm Taurus
- 31st 2:59 am Gemini

August 1948
- 2nd 7:15 am Cancer
- 4th 8:11 am Leo
- 6th 7:33 am Virgo
- 8th 7:33 am Libra
- 10th 10:01 am Scorpio
- 12th 3:53 pm Sagittarius
- 15th 0:51 am Capricorn
- 17th 12:03 pm Aquarius
- 20th 0:22 am Pisces
- 22nd 1:04 pm Aries
- 25th 1:03 am Taurus
- 27th 10:34 am Gemini
- 29th 4:29 pm Cancer
- 31st 6:38 pm Leo

September 1948
- 2nd 6:20 pm Virgo
- 4th 5:38 pm Libra
- 6th 6:38 pm Scorpio
- 8th 10:52 pm Sagittarius
- 11th 6:59 am Capricorn
- 13th 5:59 pm Aquarius
- 16th 6:26 am Pisces
- 18th 7:02 pm Aries
- 21st 6:44 am Taurus
- 23rd 4:38 pm Gemini
- 25th 11:47 pm Cancer
- 28th 3:33 am Leo
- 30th 4:40 am Virgo

October 1948
- 2nd 4:32 am Libra
- 4th 5:02 am Scorpio
- 6th 7:60 am Sagittarius
- 8th 2:37 pm Capricorn
- 11th 0:42 am Aquarius
- 13th 1:04 pm Pisces
- 16th 1:36 am Aries
- 18th 12:52 pm Taurus
- 20th 10:14 pm Gemini
- 23rd 5:18 am Cancer
- 25th 10:07 am Leo
- 27th 12:51 pm Virgo
- 29th 2:16 pm Libra
- 31st 3:34 pm Scorpio

November 1948
- 2nd 6:15 pm Sagittarius
- 4th 11:42 pm Capricorn
- 7th 8:46 am Aquarius
- 9th 8:34 pm Pisces
- 12th 9:12 am Aries
- 14th 8:22 pm Taurus
- 17th 4:59 am Gemini
- 19th 11:08 am Cancer
- 21st 3:31 pm Leo
- 23rd 6:47 pm Virgo
- 25th 9:33 pm Libra
- 28th 0:19 am Scorpio
- 30th 3:55 am Sagittarius

December 1948
- 2nd 9:22 am Capricorn
- 4th 5:37 pm Aquarius
- 7th 4:48 am Pisces
- 9th 5:30 pm Aries
- 12th 5:07 am Taurus
- 14th 1:40 pm Gemini
- 16th 6:59 pm Cancer
- 18th 10:02 pm Leo
- 21st 0:19 am Virgo
- 23rd 2:60 am Libra
- 25th 6:40 am Scorpio
- 27th 11:31 am Sagittarius
- 29th 5:49 pm Capricorn

January 1949
1st 2:10 am Aquarius
3rd 1:02 pm Pisces
6th 1:41 am Aries
8th 2:01 pm Taurus
10th 11:32 pm Gemini
13th 4:54 am Cancer
15th 7:07 am Leo
17th 7:54 am Virgo
19th 9:07 am Libra
21st 12:03 pm Scorpio
23rd 5:11 pm Sagittarius
26th 0:23 am Capricorn
28th 9:30 am Aquarius
30th 8:27 pm Pisces

May 1949
2nd 12:40 pm Cancer
4th 7:07 pm Leo
6th 11:10 pm Virgo
9th 1:07 am Libra
11th 1:54 am Scorpio
13th 2:59 am Sagittarius
15th 6:02 am Capricorn
17th 12:24 pm Aquarius
19th 10:27 pm Pisces
22nd 11:02 am Aries
24th 11:42 pm Taurus
27th 10:22 am Gemini
29th 6:35 pm Cancer

September 1949
1st 12:08 pm Capricorn
3rd 7:39 pm Aquarius
6th 5:27 am Pisces
8th 5:13 pm Aries
11th 6:11 am Taurus
13th 6:44 pm Gemini
16th 4:48 am Cancer
18th 10:59 am Leo
20th 1:30 pm Virgo
22nd 1:41 pm Libra
24th 1:23 pm Scorpio
26th 2:25 pm Sagittarius
28th 6:10 pm Capricorn

January 1950
3rd 6:53 am Cancer
5th 1:55 pm Leo
7th 7:05 pm Virgo
9th 11:08 pm Libra
12th 2:28 am Scorpio
14th 5:17 am Sagittarius
16th 8:09 am Capricorn
18th 12:12 pm Aquarius
20th 6:46 pm Pisces
23rd 4:41 am Aries
25th 5:09 pm Taurus
28th 5:42 am Gemini
30th 3:47 pm Cancer

May 1950
1st 11:36 am Scorpio
3rd 10:54 am Sagittarius
5th 11:14 am Capricorn
7th 2:28 pm Aquarius
9th 9:37 pm Pisces
12th 8:21 am Aries
14th 8:59 pm Taurus
17th 9:51 am Gemini
19th 9:49 pm Cancer
22nd 8:03 am Leo
24th 3:46 pm Virgo
26th 8:24 pm Libra
28th 9:60 pm Scorpio
30th 9:44 pm Sagittarius

February 1949
2nd 9:06 am Aries
4th 9:57 pm Taurus
7th 8:35 am Gemini
9th 3:17 pm Cancer
11th 5:58 pm Leo
13th 6:05 pm Virgo
15th 5:46 pm Libra
17th 6:57 pm Scorpio
19th 10:51 pm Sagittarius
22nd 5:53 am Capricorn
24th 3:27 pm Aquarius
27th 2:55 am Pisces

June 1949
1st 0:35 am Leo
3rd 4:51 am Virgo
5th 7:55 am Libra
7th 10:12 am Scorpio
9th 12:25 pm Sagittarius
11th 3:43 pm Capricorn
13th 9:28 pm Aquarius
16th 6:42 am Pisces
18th 6:46 pm Aries
21st 7:28 am Taurus
23rd 6:16 pm Gemini
26th 1:60 am Cancer
28th 6:58 am Leo
30th 10:25 am Virgo

October 1949
1st 1:14 am Aquarius
3rd 11:21 am Pisces
5th 11:28 pm Aries
8th 12:25 pm Taurus
11th 1:02 am Gemini
13th 11:47 am Cancer
15th 7:32 pm Leo
17th 11:43 pm Virgo
20th 0:48 am Libra
22nd 0:19 am Scorpio
24th 0:08 am Sagittarius
26th 2:13 am Capricorn
28th 7:56 am Aquarius
30th 5:25 pm Pisces

February 1950
1st 10:34 pm Leo
4th 2:36 am Virgo
6th 5:20 am Libra
8th 7:52 am Scorpio
10th 10:53 am Sagittarius
12th 2:47 pm Capricorn
14th 7:60 pm Aquarius
17th 3:14 am Pisces
19th 1:04 pm Aries
22nd 1:13 am Taurus
24th 2:02 pm Gemini
27th 1:02 am Cancer

June 1950
1st 9:29 pm Capricorn
3rd 11:19 pm Aquarius
6th 5:02 am Pisces
8th 2:48 pm Aries
11th 3:13 am Taurus
13th 4:04 pm Gemini
16th 3:42 am Cancer
18th 1:34 pm Leo
20th 9:29 pm Virgo
23rd 3:07 am Libra
25th 6:15 am Scorpio
27th 7:24 am Sagittarius
29th 7:50 am Capricorn

March 1949
1st 3:36 pm Aries
4th 4:32 am Taurus
6th 4:01 pm Gemini
9th 0:21 am Cancer
11th 4:30 am Leo
13th 5:23 am Virgo
15th 4:41 am Libra
17th 4:28 am Scorpio
19th 6:36 am Sagittarius
21st 12:09 pm Capricorn
23rd 9:11 pm Aquarius
26th 8:50 am Pisces
28th 9:42 pm Aries
31st 10:27 am Taurus

July 1949
2nd 1:21 pm Libra
4th 4:22 pm Scorpio
6th 7:45 pm Sagittarius
9th 0:02 am Capricorn
11th 6:12 am Aquarius
13th 3:04 pm Pisces
16th 2:42 am Aries
18th 3:34 pm Taurus
21st 2:55 am Gemini
23rd 10:46 am Cancer
25th 3:16 pm Leo
27th 5:35 pm Virgo
29th 7:19 pm Libra
31st 9:45 pm Scorpio

November 1949
2nd 5:36 am Aries
4th 6:35 am Taurus
7th 6:53 am Gemini
9th 5:33 pm Cancer
12th 1:58 am Leo
14th 7:38 am Virgo
16th 10:32 am Libra
18th 11:30 am Scorpio
20th 11:18 am Sagittarius
22nd 12:26 pm Capricorn
24th 4:30 pm Aquarius
27th 0:37 am Pisces
29th 12:21 pm Aries

March 1950
1st 8:27 am Leo
3rd 12:22 pm Virgo
5th 2:00 pm Libra
7th 2:57 pm Scorpio
9th 4:41 pm Sagittarius
11th 8:09 pm Capricorn
14th 1:53 am Aquarius
16th 10:02 am Pisces
18th 8:21 pm Aries
21st 8:33 am Taurus
23rd 9:28 pm Gemini
26th 9:13 am Cancer
28th 6:02 pm Leo
30th 11:01 pm Virgo

July 1950
1st 9:25 am Aquarius
3rd 1:58 pm Pisces
5th 10:26 pm Aries
8th 10:16 am Taurus
10th 11:01 pm Gemini
13th 10:30 am Cancer
15th 7:51 pm Leo
18th 3:04 am Virgo
20th 8:32 am Libra
22nd 12:24 pm Scorpio
24th 2:53 pm Sagittarius
26th 4:39 pm Capricorn
28th 6:57 pm Aquarius
30th 11:19 pm Pisces

April 1949
2nd 10:02 pm Gemini
5th 7:07 am Cancer
7th 12:55 pm Leo
9th 3:28 pm Virgo
11th 3:47 pm Libra
13th 3:29 pm Scorpio
15th 4:28 pm Sagittarius
17th 8:19 pm Capricorn
20th 4:02 am Aquarius
22nd 3:10 pm Pisces
25th 3:60 am Aries
27th 4:39 pm Taurus
30th 3:45 am Gemini

August 1949
3rd 1:26 am Sagittarius
5th 6:37 am Capricorn
7th 1:37 pm Aquarius
9th 10:47 pm Pisces
12th 10:20 am Aries
14th 11:17 am Taurus
17th 11:19 am Gemini
19th 8:11 pm Cancer
22nd 1:07 am Leo
24th 2:55 am Virgo
26th 3:24 am Libra
28th 4:21 am Scorpio
30th 7:03 am Sagittarius

December 1949
2nd 1:23 am Taurus
4th 1:27 pm Gemini
6th 11:31 pm Cancer
9th 7:25 am Leo
11th 1:27 pm Virgo
13th 5:42 pm Libra
15th 8:12 pm Scorpio
17th 9:33 pm Sagittarius
19th 11:02 pm Capricorn
22nd 2:28 am Aquarius
24th 9:26 am Pisces
26th 8:08 pm Aries
29th 8:58 am Taurus
31st 9:13 pm Gemini

April 1950
2nd 0:42 am Libra
4th 0:37 am Scorpio
6th 0:38 am Sagittarius
8th 2:32 am Capricorn
10th 7:28 am Aquarius
12th 3:41 pm Pisces
15th 2:32 am Aries
17th 3:01 pm Taurus
20th 3:54 am Gemini
22nd 4:01 pm Cancer
25th 1:55 am Leo
27th 8:25 am Virgo
29th 11:21 am Libra

August 1950
2nd 7:06 am Aries
4th 6:08 pm Taurus
7th 6:43 am Gemini
9th 6:25 pm Cancer
12th 3:34 am Leo
14th 10:00 am Virgo
16th 2:28 pm Libra
18th 5:49 pm Scorpio
20th 8:35 pm Sagittarius
22nd 11:23 pm Capricorn
25th 2:53 am Aquarius
27th 8:05 am Pisces
29th 3:48 pm Aries

September 1950
1st   2:18 am Taurus
3rd   2:45 am Gemini
6th   2:52 am Cancer
8th 12:29 pm Leo
10th 6:52 am Virgo
12th 10:27 pm Libra
15th 0:26 am Scorpio
17th 2:12 am Sagittarius
19th 4:50 am Capricorn
21st 9:02 am Aquarius
23rd 3:11 pm Pisces
25th 11:31 pm Aries
28th 10:09 am Taurus
30th 10:27 pm Gemini

January 1951
2nd   3:53 pm Scorpio
4th   5:35 pm Sagittarius
6th   5:32 pm Capricorn
8th   5:39 pm Aquarius
10th 7:60 pm Pisces
13th 2:09 am Aries
15th 12:15 pm Taurus
18th 0:36 am Gemini
20th 1:06 pm Cancer
23rd 0:13 am Leo
25th 9:24 am Virgo
27th 4:44 pm Libra
29th 10:02 pm Scorpio

May 1951
2nd 11:29 am Aries
4th   8:47 pm Taurus
7th   7:51 am Gemini
9th   8:13 pm Cancer
12th 8:48 am Leo
14th 7:42 pm Virgo
17th 3:04 am Libra
19th 6:21 am Scorpio
21st 6:43 am Sagittarius
23rd 6:10 am Capricorn
25th 6:47 am Aquarius
27th 10:12 am Pisces
29th 4:57 pm Aries

September 1951
3rd   5:31 am Libra
5th 11:47 am Scorpio
7th   4:10 pm Sagittarius
9th   7:05 pm Capricorn
11th 9:12 pm Aquarius
13th 11:21 pm Pisces
16th 2:48 am Aries
18th 8:45 am Taurus
20th 5:49 pm Gemini
23rd 5:35 am Cancer
25th 6:07 pm Leo
28th 5:03 am Virgo
30th 1:05 pm Libra

January 1952
1st   2:13 am Pisces
3rd   5:47 am Aries
5th 12:49 pm Taurus
7th 10:44 pm Gemini
10th 10:36 am Cancer
12th 11:19 pm Leo
15th 11:59 am Virgo
17th 11:19 pm Libra
20th 7:39 am Scorpio
22nd 12:16 pm Sagittarius
24th 1:36 pm Capricorn
26th 1:07 pm Aquarius
28th 12:50 pm Pisces
30th 2:39 pm Aries

October 1950
3rd 10:57 am Cancer
5th   9:39 pm Leo
8th   4:50 am Virgo
10th 8:25 am Libra
12th 9:30 am Scorpio
14th 9:47 am Sagittarius
16th 10:60 am Capricorn
18th 2:31 am Aquarius
20th 8:55 pm Pisces
23rd 5:60 am Aries
25th 5:04 pm Taurus
28th 5:22 am Gemini
30th 6:03 pm Cancer

February 1951
1st   1:17 am Sagittarius
3rd   2:53 am Capricorn
5th   4:06 am Aquarius
7th   6:33 am Pisces
9th 11:48 am Aries
11th 8:37 pm Taurus
14th 8:19 am Gemini
16th 8:51 pm Cancer
19th 7:60 am Leo
21st 4:41 pm Virgo
23rd 11:01 pm Libra
26th 3:32 am Scorpio
28th 6:50 am Sagittarius

June 1951
1st   2:35 am Taurus
3rd   2:04 pm Gemini
6th   2:32 am Cancer
8th   3:10 pm Leo
11th 2:44 am Virgo
13th 11:25 am Libra
15th 4:11 pm Scorpio
17th 5:23 pm Sagittarius
19th 4:39 pm Capricorn
21st 4:09 pm Aquarius
23rd 5:54 pm Pisces
25th 11:15 pm Aries
28th 8:21 am Taurus
30th 7:53 pm Gemini

October 1951
2nd   6:21 pm Scorpio
4th   9:47 pm Sagittarius
7th   0:30 am Capricorn
9th   3:20 am Aquarius
11th 6:48 am Pisces
13th 11:21 am Aries
15th 5:39 pm Taurus
18th 2:22 am Gemini
20th 1:45 pm Cancer
23rd 2:25 am Leo
25th 1:58 pm Virgo
27th 10:24 pm Libra
30th 3:08 am Scorpio

February 1952
1st   7:55 am Taurus
4th   4:59 am Gemini
6th   4:46 pm Cancer
9th   5:37 am Leo
11th 6:02 pm Virgo
14th 4:58 am Libra
16th 1:42 pm Scorpio
18th 7:41 pm Sagittarius
20th 10:49 pm Capricorn
22nd 11:49 pm Aquarius
25th 0:02 am Pisces
27th 1:13 am Aries
29th 5:05 am Taurus

November 1950
2nd   5:35 am Leo
4th   2:16 pm Virgo
6th   7:07 pm Libra
8th   8:27 pm Scorpio
10th 7:52 pm Sagittarius
12th 7:29 pm Capricorn
14th 9:17 pm Aquarius
17th 2:40 am Pisces
19th 11:43 am Aries
21st 11:08 pm Taurus
24th 11:38 am Gemini
27th 0:12 am Cancer
29th 11:59 am Leo

March 1951
2nd   9:30 am Capricorn
4th 12:13 pm Aquarius
6th   3:49 pm Pisces
8th   9:19 pm Aries
11th 5:35 am Taurus
13th 4:38 pm Gemini
16th 5:06 am Cancer
18th 4:43 pm Leo
21st 1:40 am Virgo
23rd 7:19 am Libra
25th 10:35 am Scorpio
27th 12:42 pm Sagittarius
29th 2:53 pm Capricorn
31st 6:05 pm Aquarius

July 1951
3rd   8:28 am Cancer
5th   8:59 pm Leo
8th   8:32 am Virgo
10th 6:01 pm Libra
13th 0:17 am Scorpio
15th 3:00 am Sagittarius
17th 3:13 am Capricorn
19th 2:44 am Aquarius
21st 3:31 am Pisces
23rd 7:28 am Aries
25th 3:12 pm Taurus
28th 2:09 am Gemini
30th 2:43 pm Cancer

November 1951
1st   5:19 am Sagittarius
3rd   6:41 am Capricorn
5th   8:46 am Aquarius
7th 12:26 pm Pisces
9th   5:54 pm Aries
12th 1:08 am Taurus
14th 10:17 am Gemini
16th 9:28 pm Cancer
19th 10:11 am Leo
21st 10:34 pm Virgo
24th 8:04 am Libra
26th 1:27 pm Scorpio
28th 3:17 pm Sagittarius
30th 3:23 pm Capricorn

March 1952
2nd 12:42 pm Gemini
4th 11:40 pm Cancer
7th 12:31 pm Leo
10th 0:53 pm Virgo
12th 11:15 am Libra
14th 7:20 pm Scorpio
17th 1:15 am Sagittarius
19th 5:18 am Capricorn
21st 7:54 am Aquarius
23rd 9:40 am Pisces
25th 11:37 am Aries
27th 3:10 pm Taurus
29th 9:37 pm Gemini

December 1950
1st   9:51 pm Virgo
4th   4:26 am Libra
6th   7:15 am Scorpio
8th   7:16 am Sagittarius
10th 6:20 am Capricorn
12th 6:40 am Aquarius
14th 10:18 am Pisces
16th 6:04 pm Aries
19th 5:12 am Taurus
21st 5:49 pm Gemini
24th 6:17 am Cancer
26th 5:43 pm Leo
29th 3:39 am Virgo
31st 11:16 am Libra

April 1951
2nd 10:46 pm Pisces
5th   5:18 am Aries
7th   1:55 pm Taurus
10th 0:42 am Gemini
12th 1:05 pm Cancer
15th 1:18 am Leo
17th 11:03 am Virgo
19th 5:10 pm Libra
21st 7:54 pm Scorpio
23rd 8:41 pm Sagittarius
25th 9:22 pm Capricorn
27th 11:33 pm Aquarius
30th 4:15 am Pisces

August 1951
2nd   3:07 am Leo
4th   2:16 pm Virgo
6th 11:35 pm Libra
9th   6:21 am Scorpio
11th 10:26 am Sagittarius
13th 12:15 pm Capricorn
15th 12:53 pm Aquarius
17th 1:55 pm Pisces
19th 5:02 pm Aries
21st 11:27 pm Taurus
24th 9:30 am Gemini
26th 9:44 pm Cancer
29th 10:08 am Leo
31st 8:50 pm Virgo

December 1951
2nd   3:48 pm Aquarius
4th   6:12 pm Pisces
6th 11:19 pm Aries
9th   7:07 am Taurus
11th 4:56 pm Gemini
14th 4:23 am Cancer
16th 5:05 pm Leo
19th 5:50 am Virgo
21st 4:36 pm Libra
23rd 11:39 pm Scorpio
26th 2:26 am Sagittarius
28th 2:24 am Capricorn
30th 1:37 am Aquarius

April 1952
1st   7:42 am Cancer
3rd   8:10 pm Leo
6th   8:40 am Virgo
8th   6:55 pm Libra
11th 2:14 am Scorpio
13th 7:07 am Sagittarius
15th 10:42 am Capricorn
17th 1:44 pm Aquarius
19th 4:41 pm Pisces
21st 7:58 pm Aries
24th 0:16 am Taurus
26th 6:44 am Gemini
28th 4:10 pm Cancer

May 1952
1st   4:14 am Leo
3rd   4:56 pm Virgo
6th   3:38 am Libra
8th 10:45 am Scorpio
10th   2:49 pm Sagittarius
12th   5:10 pm Capricorn
14th   7:15 pm Aquarius
16th 10:07 pm Pisces
19th   2:09 am Aries
21st   7:32 am Taurus
23rd   2:41 pm Gemini
26th   0:06 am Cancer
28th 12:01 pm Leo
31st   0:58 am Virgo

September 1952
1st   8:60 am Aquarius
3rd   8:60 am Pisces
5th   9:01 am Aries
7th 10:53 am Taurus
9th   4:10 pm Gemini
12th   1:25 am Cancer
14th   1:40 pm Leo
17th   2:42 am Virgo
19th   2:40 pm Libra
22nd   0:43 am Scorpio
24th   8:31 am Sagittarius
26th   2:03 pm Capricorn
28th   5:21 pm Aquarius
30th   6:51 pm Pisces

January 1953
1st   9:18 pm Leo
4th   9:42 am Virgo
6th 10:35 pm Libra
9th   9:39 am Scorpio
11th   5:09 pm Sagittarius
13th   8:53 pm Capricorn
15th   9:57 pm Aquarius
17th 10:08 pm Pisces
19th 11:11 pm Aries
22nd   2:23 am Taurus
24th   8:26 am Gemini
26th   5:10 pm Cancer
29th   4:08 am Leo
31st   4:36 pm Virgo

May 1953
3rd   3:55 am Capricorn
5th   9:11 am Aquarius
7th 12:45 pm Pisces
9th   2:48 pm Aries
11th   4:14 pm Taurus
13th   6:31 pm Gemini
15th 11:17 pm Cancer
18th   7:51 am Leo
20th   7:33 pm Virgo
23rd   8:16 am Libra
25th   7:31 pm Scorpio
28th   4:07 am Sagittarius
30th 10:16 am Capricorn

September 1953
2nd   3:33 am Cancer
4th   1:09 pm Leo
7th   0:48 am Virgo
9th   1:28 pm Libra
12th   2:06 am Scorpio
14th   1:30 pm Sagittarius
16th 10:20 pm Capricorn
19th   3:28 am Aquarius
21st   5:04 am Pisces
23rd   4:31 am Aries
25th   3:47 am Taurus
27th   5:05 am Gemini
29th 10:01 am Cancer

June 1952
2nd 12:21 pm Libra
4th   8:17 pm Scorpio
7th   0:22 am Sagittarius
9th   1:47 am Aquarius
11th   2:29 am Aquarius
13th   4:04 am Pisces
15th   7:34 am Aries
17th   1:14 pm Taurus
19th   9:05 pm Gemini
22nd   7:07 am Cancer
24th   7:03 pm Leo
27th   8:05 am Virgo
29th   8:16 pm Libra

October 1952
2nd   7:34 pm Aries
4th   9:06 pm Taurus
7th   1:15 am Gemini
9th   9:20 am Cancer
11th   8:50 pm Leo
14th   9:49 am Virgo
16th   9:44 pm Libra
19th   7:07 am Scorpio
21st   2:10 pm Sagittarius
23rd   7:27 pm Capricorn
25th 11:27 pm Aquarius
28th   2:22 am Pisces
30th   4:34 am Aries

February 1953
3rd   5:31 am Libra
5th   5:18 pm Scorpio
8th   2:18 am Sagittarius
10th   7:27 am Capricorn
12th   9:12 am Aquarius
14th   8:58 am Pisces
16th   8:34 am Aries
18th   9:56 am Taurus
20th   2:33 pm Gemini
22nd 10:49 pm Cancer
25th 10:09 am Leo
27th 10:53 pm Virgo

June 1953
1st   2:44 pm Aquarius
3rd   6:12 pm Pisces
5th   9:03 pm Aries
7th 11:41 pm Taurus
10th   3:05 am Gemini
12th   8:23 am Cancer
14th   4:31 pm Leo
17th   3:38 am Virgo
19th   4:17 pm Libra
22nd   3:56 am Scorpio
24th 12:44 pm Sagittarius
26th   6:27 pm Capricorn
28th   9:53 pm Aquarius

October 1953
1st   6:57 pm Leo
4th   6:42 am Virgo
6th   7:28 pm Libra
9th   7:56 am Scorpio
11th   7:19 pm Sagittarius
14th   4:49 am Capricorn
16th 11:29 am Aquarius
18th   2:51 pm Pisces
20th   3:24 pm Aries
22nd   2:48 pm Taurus
24th   3:09 pm Gemini
26th   6:27 pm Cancer
29th   1:56 am Leo
31st   1:06 pm Virgo

July 1952
2nd   5:20 am Scorpio
4th 10:21 am Sagittarius
6th 12:00 pm Capricorn
8th 11:55 am Aquarius
10th 12:04 pm Pisces
12th   2:03 pm Aries
14th   6:50 pm Taurus
17th   2:40 am Gemini
19th   1:08 pm Cancer
22nd   1:21 am Leo
24th   2:24 pm Virgo
27th   2:52 am Libra
29th 12:58 pm Scorpio
31st   7:33 pm Sagittarius

November 1952
1st   6:50 am Taurus
3rd 11:07 am Gemini
5th   6:15 pm Cancer
8th   4:58 am Leo
10th   5:47 pm Virgo
13th   5:54 am Libra
15th   3:15 pm Scorpio
17th   9:32 pm Sagittarius
20th   1:39 am Capricorn
22nd   4:51 am Aquarius
24th   7:55 am Pisces
26th 11:10 am Aries
28th   2:56 pm Taurus
30th   7:55 pm Gemini

March 1953
2nd 11:41 am Libra
4th 11:32 pm Scorpio
7th   9:16 am Sagittarius
9th   4:07 pm Capricorn
11th   7:35 pm Aquarius
13th   8:16 pm Pisces
15th   7:40 pm Aries
17th   7:48 pm Taurus
19th 10:37 pm Gemini
22nd   5:33 am Cancer
24th   4:18 pm Leo
27th   5:06 am Virgo
29th   5:51 pm Libra

July 1953
1st   0:10 am Pisces
3rd   2:25 am Aries
5th   5:26 am Taurus
7th   9:46 am Gemini
9th   3:59 pm Cancer
12th   0:29 am Leo
14th 11:31 am Virgo
17th   0:04 am Libra
19th 12:14 pm Scorpio
21st   9:57 pm Sagittarius
24th   4:04 am Sagittarius
26th   7:01 am Aquarius
28th   8:07 am Pisces
30th   8:59 am Aries

November 1953
3rd   1:51 am Libra
5th   2:10 pm Scorpio
8th   1:07 am Sagittarius
10th 10:16 am Capricorn
12th   5:29 pm Aquarius
14th 10:16 pm Pisces
17th   0:34 am Aries
19th   1:44 am Taurus
21st   1:56 am Gemini
23rd   4:34 am Cancer
25th 10:45 am Leo
27th   8:43 pm Virgo
30th   9:06 am Libra

August 1952
2nd 10:25 pm Capricorn
4th 10:40 pm Aquarius
6th 10:06 pm Pisces
8th 10:35 pm Aries
11th   1:47 am Taurus
13th   8:42 am Gemini
15th   6:55 pm Cancer
18th   7:21 am Leo
20th   8:23 pm Virgo
23rd   8:40 am Libra
25th   7:09 pm Scorpio
28th   2:51 am Sagittarius
30th   7:19 am Capricorn

December 1952
3rd   3:10 am Cancer
5th   1:24 pm Leo
8th   1:58 am Virgo
10th   2:32 pm Libra
13th   0:39 am Scorpio
15th   6:55 am Sagittarius
17th 10:15 am Capricorn
19th 12:02 pm Aquarius
21st   1:48 pm Pisces
23rd   4:33 pm Aries
25th   8:48 pm Taurus
28th   2:50 am Gemini
30th 10:57 am Cancer

April 1953
1st   5:19 am Scorpio
3rd   2:57 pm Sagittarius
5th 10:29 pm Capricorn
8th   3:26 am Aquarius
10th   5:48 am Pisces
12th   6:19 am Aries
14th   6:35 am Taurus
16th   8:33 am Gemini
18th   2:00 pm Cancer
20th 11:29 pm Leo
23rd 11:54 am Virgo
26th   0:42 am Libra
28th 11:50 am Scorpio
30th   8:52 pm Sagittarius

August 1953
1st 11:02 am Taurus
3rd   3:16 pm Gemini
5th 10:03 pm Cancer
8th   7:20 am Leo
10th   6:36 pm Virgo
13th   7:09 am Libra
15th   7:43 pm Scorpio
18th   6:27 am Sagittarius
20th   1:47 pm Capricorn
22nd   5:25 pm Aquarius
24th   6:10 pm Pisces
26th   5:47 pm Aries
28th   6:14 pm Taurus
30th   9:10 pm Gemini

December 1953
2nd   9:30 pm Scorpio
5th   8:06 am Sagittarius
7th   4:30 pm Capricorn
9th 10:59 pm Aquarius
12th   3:44 am Pisces
14th   7:05 am Aries
16th   9:22 am Taurus
18th 11:30 am Gemini
20th   2:44 pm Cancer
22nd   8:25 pm Leo
25th   5:26 am Virgo
27th   5:11 pm Libra
30th   5:41 am Scorpio

January 1954
- 1st   4:37 pm Sagittarius
- 4th   0:45 am Capricorn
- 6th   6:07 am Aquarius
- 8th   9:42 am Pisces
- 10th 12:28 am Aries
- 12th   3:12 pm Taurus
- 14th   6:31 pm Gemini
- 16th 11:02 am Cancer
- 19th   5:27 am Leo
- 21st   2:16 pm Virgo
- 24th   1:31 am Libra
- 26th   2:01 pm Scorpio
- 29th   1:40 am Sagittarius
- 31st 10:21 am Capricorn

February 1954
- 2nd   3:34 pm Aquarius
- 4th   6:02 pm Pisces
- 6th   7:15 pm Aries
- 8th   8:49 pm Taurus
- 10th 11:55 pm Gemini
- 13th   5:13 am Cancer
- 15th 12:39 pm Leo
- 17th 10:02 pm Virgo
- 20th   9:17 am Libra
- 22nd   9:44 pm Scorpio
- 25th   9:57 am Sagittarius
- 27th   7:54 pm Capricorn

March 1954
- 2nd   2:05 am Aquarius
- 4th   4:29 am Pisces
- 6th   4:40 am Aries
- 8th   4:35 am Taurus
- 10th   6:11 am Gemini
- 12th 10:42 am Cancer
- 14th   6:20 pm Leo
- 17th   4:22 am Virgo
- 19th   3:59 pm Libra
- 22nd   4:27 am Scorpio
- 24th   4:55 pm Sagittarius
- 27th   3:52 am Capricorn
- 29th 11:32 am Aquarius
- 31st   3:12 pm Pisces

April 1954
- 2nd   3:37 pm Aries
- 4th   2:44 pm Taurus
- 6th   2:45 pm Gemini
- 8th   5:33 pm Cancer
- 11th   0:06 am Leo
- 13th 10:06 am Virgo
- 15th   9:59 pm Libra
- 18th 10:34 am Scorpio
- 20th 10:56 pm Sagittarius
- 23rd 10:09 am Capricorn
- 25th   6:50 pm Aquarius
- 28th   0:22 am Pisces
- 30th   2:08 am Aries

May 1954
- 2nd   1:44 am Taurus
- 4th   1:08 am Gemini
- 6th   2:33 am Cancer
- 8th   7:34 am Leo
- 10th   4:27 pm Virgo
- 13th   4:04 am Libra
- 15th   4:43 pm Scorpio
- 18th   4:54 am Sagittarius
- 20th   3:48 pm Capricorn
- 23rd   0:48 am Aquarius
- 25th   7:06 am Pisces
- 27th 10:28 am Aries
- 29th 11:33 am Taurus
- 31st 11:44 am Gemini

June 1954
- 2nd 12:51 pm Cancer
- 4th   4:40 pm Leo
- 7th   0:08 am Virgo
- 9th 11:01 am Libra
- 11th 11:30 pm Scorpio
- 14th 11:37 am Sagittarius
- 16th 10:04 pm Capricorn
- 19th   6:25 am Aquarius
- 21st 12:35 pm Pisces
- 23rd   4:42 pm Aries
- 25th   7:09 pm Taurus
- 27th   8:44 pm Gemini
- 29th 10:38 pm Cancer

July 1954
- 2nd   2:19 am Leo
- 4th   9:01 am Virgo
- 6th   6:57 pm Libra
- 9th   7:04 am Scorpio
- 11th   7:19 pm Sagittarius
- 14th   5:38 am Capricorn
- 16th   1:16 pm Aquarius
- 18th   6:33 pm Pisces
- 20th 10:09 pm Aries
- 23rd   0:54 am Taurus
- 25th   3:32 am Gemini
- 27th   6:45 am Cancer
- 29th 11:15 am Leo
- 31st   5:54 pm Virgo

August 1954
- 3rd   3:17 am Libra
- 5th   3:04 pm Scorpio
- 8th   3:31 am Sagittarius
- 10th   2:16 pm Capricorn
- 12th   9:53 pm Aquarius
- 15th   2:17 am Pisces
- 17th   4:39 am Aries
- 19th   6:29 am Taurus
- 21st   8:50 am Gemini
- 23rd 12:54 pm Cancer
- 25th   6:26 pm Leo
- 28th   1:46 am Virgo
- 30th 11:16 am Libra

September 1954
- 1st 10:50 pm Scorpio
- 4th 11:32 am Sagittarius
- 6th 11:09 pm Capricorn
- 9th   7:26 am Aquarius
- 11th 11:51 am Pisces
- 13th   1:21 pm Aries
- 15th   1:47 pm Taurus
- 17th   2:59 pm Gemini
- 19th   6:17 pm Cancer
- 22nd   0:06 am Leo
- 24th   8:14 am Virgo
- 26th   6:14 pm Libra
- 29th   5:55 am Scorpio

October 1954
- 1st   6:43 pm Sagittarius
- 4th   7:02 am Capricorn
- 6th   4:41 pm Aquarius
- 8th 10:16 pm Pisces
- 10th 11:58 pm Aries
- 12th 11:33 pm Taurus
- 14th 11:10 pm Gemini
- 17th   0:50 am Cancer
- 19th   5:44 am Leo
- 21st   1:48 pm Virgo
- 24th   0:12 am Libra
- 26th 12:12 pm Scorpio
- 29th   1:01 am Sagittarius
- 31st   1:35 pm Capricorn

November 1954
- 3rd   0:23 am Aquarius
- 5th   7:30 am Pisces
- 7th 10:37 am Aries
- 9th 10:47 am Taurus
- 11th   9:53 am Gemini
- 13th 10:05 am Cancer
- 15th   1:09 pm Leo
- 17th   7:55 pm Virgo
- 20th   6:03 am Libra
- 22nd   6:14 pm Scorpio
- 25th   7:01 am Sagittarius
- 27th   7:24 pm Capricorn
- 30th   6:18 am Aquarius

December 1954
- 2nd   2:35 pm Pisces
- 4th   7:33 pm Aries
- 6th   9:22 pm Taurus
- 8th   9:16 pm Gemini
- 10th   9:08 pm Cancer
- 12th 10:49 pm Leo
- 15th   3:57 am Virgo
- 17th 12:56 pm Libra
- 20th   0:43 am Scorpio
- 22nd   1:34 pm Sagittarius
- 25th   1:40 am Capricorn
- 27th 11:58 am Aquarius
- 29th   8:08 pm Pisces

January 1955
- 1st   1:55 am Aries
- 3rd   5:23 am Taurus
- 5th   7:03 am Gemini
- 7th   8:02 am Cancer
- 9th   9:45 am Leo
- 11th   1:48 pm Virgo
- 13th   9:17 pm Libra
- 16th   8:15 am Scorpio
- 18th   9:01 pm Sagittarius
- 21st   9:06 am Capricorn
- 23rd   6:55 pm Aquarius
- 26th   2:11 am Pisces
- 28th   7:19 am Aries
- 30th 11:05 am Taurus

February 1955
- 1st   2:03 pm Gemini
- 3rd   4:37 pm Cancer
- 5th   7:30 pm Leo
- 7th 11:42 pm Virgo
- 10th   6:37 am Libra
- 12th   4:41 pm Scorpio
- 15th   5:06 am Sagittarius
- 17th   5:32 pm Capricorn
- 20th   3:30 am Aquarius
- 22nd 10:04 am Pisces
- 24th   2:04 pm Aries
- 26th   4:46 pm Taurus
- 28th   7:26 pm Gemini

March 1955
- 2nd 10:41 pm Cancer
- 5th   2:51 am Leo
- 7th   8:12 am Virgo
- 9th   3:24 pm Libra
- 12th   1:05 am Scorpio
- 14th   1:14 pm Sagittarius
- 17th   1:50 am Capricorn
- 19th 12:41 pm Aquarius
- 21st   7:41 pm Pisces
- 23rd 11:08 pm Aries
- 26th   0:31 am Taurus
- 28th   1:42 am Gemini
- 30th   4:07 am Cancer

April 1955
- 1st   8:23 am Leo
- 3rd   2:33 pm Virgo
- 5th 10:35 pm Libra
- 8th   8:41 am Scorpio
- 10th   8:44 pm Sagittarius
- 13th   9:40 am Capricorn
- 15th   9:20 pm Aquarius
- 18th   5:24 am Pisces
- 20th   9:25 am Aries
- 22nd 10:27 am Taurus
- 24th 10:25 am Gemini
- 26th 11:12 am Cancer
- 28th   2:12 pm Leo
- 30th   7:59 pm Virgo

May 1955
- 3rd   4:28 am Libra
- 5th   3:06 pm Scorpio
- 8th   3:19 am Sagittarius
- 10th   4:19 pm Capricorn
- 13th   4:28 am Aquarius
- 15th   1:48 pm Pisces
- 17th   7:18 pm Aries
- 19th   9:10 pm Taurus
- 21st   8:57 pm Gemini
- 23rd   8:34 pm Cancer
- 25th   9:55 pm Leo
- 28th   2:17 am Virgo
- 30th 10:12 am Libra

June 1955
- 1st   8:55 pm Scorpio
- 4th   9:25 am Sagittarius
- 6th 10:21 pm Capricorn
- 9th 10:28 am Aquarius
- 11th   8:31 pm Pisces
- 14th   3:21 am Aries
- 16th   6:47 am Taurus
- 18th   7:36 am Gemini
- 20th   7:18 am Cancer
- 22nd   7:41 am Leo
- 24th 10:32 am Virgo
- 26th   5:01 pm Libra
- 29th   3:06 am Scorpio

July 1955
- 1st   3:36 pm Sagittarius
- 4th   4:30 am Capricorn
- 6th   4:17 pm Aquarius
- 9th   2:09 am Pisces
- 11th   9:31 am Aries
- 13th   2:17 pm Taurus
- 15th   4:42 pm Gemini
- 17th   5:31 pm Cancer
- 19th   6:07 pm Leo
- 21st   8:09 pm Virgo
- 24th   1:18 am Libra
- 26th 10:23 am Scorpio
- 28th 10:25 pm Sagittarius
- 31st 11:18 am Capricorn

August 1955
- 2nd 10:51 pm Aquarius
- 5th   8:02 am Pisces
- 7th   2:59 pm Aries
- 9th   8:04 pm Taurus
- 11th 11:34 pm Gemini
- 14th   1:53 am Cancer
- 16th   3:36 am Leo
- 18th   6:02 am Virgo
- 20th 10:40 am Libra
- 22nd   6:42 pm Scorpio
- 25th   6:05 am Sagittarius
- 27th   6:56 pm Capricorn
- 30th   6:33 am Aquarius

September 1955
1st   3:20 pm Pisces
3rd   9:24 pm Aries
6th   1:38 am Taurus
8th   4:50 am Gemini
10th 8:03 am Cancer
12th 11:05 am Leo
14th 2:37 pm Virgo
16th 7:40 pm Libra
19th 3:22 am Scorpio
21st 2:15 pm Sagittarius
24th 3:02 am Capricorn
26th 3:05 pm Aquarius
29th 0:13 am Pisces

October 1955
1st   5:45 am Aries
3rd   8:51 am Taurus
5th 10:50 am Gemini
7th   1:25 pm Cancer
9th   4:44 pm Leo
11th 9:13 pm Virgo
14th 3:16 am Libra
16th 11:29 am Scorpio
18th 10:09 pm Sagittarius
21st 10:54 am Capricorn
23rd 11:34 pm Aquarius
26th 9:33 am Pisces
28th 3:43 pm Aries
30th 6:28 pm Taurus

November 1955
1st   7:23 pm Gemini
3rd   8:13 pm Cancer
5th 10:20 pm Leo
8th   2:38 am Virgo
10th 9:19 am Libra
12th 6:15 pm Scorpio
15th 5:19 am Sagittarius
17th 6:02 pm Capricorn
20th 6:58 am Aquarius
22nd 6:08 pm Pisces
25th 1:47 am Aries
27th 5:24 am Taurus
29th 6:11 am Gemini

December 1955
1st   5:49 am Cancer
3rd   6:11 am Leo
5th   8:55 am Virgo
7th   2:53 pm Libra
9th 12:00 pm Scorpio
12th 11:36 am Sagittarius
15th 0:24 am Capricorn
17th 1:20 pm Aquarius
20th 1:02 am Pisces
22nd 10:01 am Aries
24th 3:28 pm Taurus
26th 5:31 pm Gemini
28th 5:17 pm Cancer
30th 4:39 pm Leo

January 1956
1st   5:35 pm Virgo
3rd   9:46 pm Libra
6th   6:03 am Scorpio
8th   5:35 pm Sagittarius
11th 6:33 am Capricorn
13th 7:18 pm Aquarius
16th 6:47 am Pisces
18th 4:15 pm Aries
20th 11:11 pm Taurus
23rd 3:05 am Gemini
25th 4:19 am Cancer
27th 4:07 am Leo
29th 4:21 am Virgo
31st 7:01 am Libra

February 1956
2nd   1:38 pm Scorpio
5th   0:12 am Sagittarius
7th   1:07 pm Capricorn
10th 1:51 am Aquarius
12th 12:49 pm Pisces
14th 9:49 pm Aries
17th 4:47 am Taurus
19th 9:48 am Gemini
21st 12:48 pm Cancer
23rd 2:10 pm Leo
25th 3:07 pm Virgo
27th 5:25 pm Libra
29th 10:45 pm Scorpio

March 1956
3rd   8:13 am Sagittarius
5th   8:33 pm Capricorn
8th   9:16 am Aquarius
10th 8:08 pm Pisces
13th 4:25 am Aries
15th 10:30 am Taurus
17th 3:10 pm Gemini
19th 6:47 pm Cancer
21st 9:32 pm Leo
23rd 11:53 pm Virgo
26th 3:02 am Libra
28th 8:23 am Scorpio
30th 4:50 pm Sagittarius

April 1956
2nd   4:38 am Capricorn
4th   5:23 pm Aquarius
7th   4:33 am Pisces
9th 12:42 pm Aries
11th 6:00 pm Taurus
13th 9:30 pm Gemini
16th 0:14 am Cancer
18th 3:00 am Leo
20th 6:18 am Virgo
22nd 10:39 am Libra
24th 4:48 pm Scorpio
27th 1:26 am Sagittarius
29th 12:46 pm Capricorn

May 1956
2nd   1:29 am Aquarius
4th   1:11 pm Pisces
6th 10:05 pm Aries
9th   3:22 am Taurus
11th 5:59 am Gemini
13th 7:20 am Cancer
15th 8:53 am Leo
17th 11:43 am Virgo
19th 4:27 pm Libra
21st 11:27 pm Scorpio
24th 8:49 am Sagittarius
26th 8:12 pm Capricorn
29th 8:53 am Aquarius
31st 9:09 pm Pisces

June 1956
3rd   7:01 am Aries
5th   1:16 pm Taurus
7th   4:06 pm Gemini
9th   4:41 pm Cancer
11th 4:47 pm Leo
13th 6:07 pm Virgo
15th 10:00 pm Libra
18th 5:05 am Scorpio
20th 2:59 pm Sagittarius
23rd 2:44 am Capricorn
25th 3:26 pm Aquarius
28th 3:54 am Pisces
30th 2:39 pm Aries

July 1956
2nd 10:25 pm Taurus
5th   2:24 am Gemini
7th   3:20 am Cancer
9th   2:43 am Leo
11th 2:36 am Virgo
13th 4:58 am Libra
15th 11:02 am Scorpio
17th 8:40 pm Sagittarius
20th 8:42 am Capricorn
22nd 9:28 pm Aquarius
25th 9:50 am Pisces
27th 8:53 pm Aries
30th 5:37 am Taurus

August 1956
1st 11:12 am Gemini
3rd   1:29 pm Cancer
5th   1:27 pm Leo
7th 12:53 pm Virgo
9th   1:57 pm Libra
11th 6:25 pm Scorpio
14th 3:01 am Sagittarius
16th 2:49 pm Capricorn
19th 3:38 am Aquarius
21st 3:45 pm Pisces
24th 2:30 am Aries
26th 11:21 am Taurus
28th 5:57 pm Gemini
30th 9:51 pm Cancer

September 1956
1st 11:14 pm Leo
3rd 11:22 pm Virgo
6th   0:05 am Libra
8th   3:30 am Scorpio
10th 10:51 am Sagittarius
12th 9:46 pm Capricorn
15th 10:27 am Aquarius
17th 10:33 pm Pisces
20th 8:46 am Aries
22nd 5:00 pm Taurus
24th 11:26 pm Gemini
27th 3:50 am Cancer
29th 6:48 am Leo

October 1956
1st   8:25 am Virgo
3rd 10:06 am Libra
5th   1:25 pm Scorpio
7th   7:51 pm Sagittarius
10th 5:51 am Capricorn
12th 6:10 pm Aquarius
15th 6:23 am Pisces
17th 4:33 pm Aries
20th 0:07 am Taurus
22nd 5:28 am Gemini
24th 9:22 am Cancer
26th 12:27 pm Leo
28th 3:11 pm Virgo
30th 6:12 pm Libra

November 1956
1st 10:27 pm Scorpio
4th   5:00 am Sagittarius
6th   2:30 pm Capricorn
9th   2:22 am Aquarius
11th 2:51 pm Pisces
14th 1:36 am Aries
16th 9:09 am Taurus
18th 1:43 pm Gemini
20th 4:16 pm Cancer
22nd 6:11 pm Leo
24th 8:34 pm Virgo
27th 0:11 am Libra
29th 5:37 am Scorpio

December 1956
1st   1:03 pm Sagittarius
3rd 10:38 pm Capricorn
6th 10:19 am Aquarius
8th 10:59 pm Pisces
11th 10:34 am Aries
13th 7:13 pm Taurus
16th 0:07 am Gemini
18th 1:52 am Cancer
20th 2:12 am Leo
22nd 2:58 am Virgo
24th 5:43 am Libra
26th 11:12 am Scorpio
28th 7:22 pm Sagittarius
31st 5:40 am Capricorn

January 1957
2nd   5:26 pm Aquarius
5th   6:06 am Pisces
7th   6:21 pm Aries
10th 4:24 am Taurus
12th 10:39 am Gemini
14th 1:01 pm Cancer
16th 12:50 pm Leo
18th 12:08 pm Virgo
20th 1:02 pm Libra
22nd 5:07 pm Scorpio
25th 0:54 am Sagittarius
27th 11:34 am Capricorn
29th 11:42 pm Aquarius

February 1957
1st 12:21 pm Pisces
4th   0:44 am Aries
6th 11:34 am Taurus
8th   7:32 pm Gemini
10th 11:40 pm Cancer
13th 0:19 am Leo
14th 11:18 pm Virgo
16th 10:51 pm Libra
19th 1:07 am Scorpio
21st 7:28 am Sagittarius
23rd 5:29 pm Capricorn
26th 5:42 am Aquarius
28th 6:25 pm Pisces

March 1957
3rd   6:30 am Aries
5th   5:19 pm Taurus
8th   2:02 am Gemini
10th 7:42 am Cancer
12th 10:08 am Leo
14th 10:19 am Virgo
16th 10:03 am Libra
18th 11:20 am Scorpio
20th 3:59 pm Sagittarius
23rd 0:35 am Capricorn
25th 12:18 pm Aquarius
28th 0:58 am Pisces
30th 12:52 pm Aries

April 1957
1st 11:10 pm Taurus
4th   7:28 am Gemini
6th   1:35 pm Cancer
8th   5:21 pm Leo
10th 7:12 pm Virgo
12th 8:09 pm Libra
14th 9:46 pm Scorpio
17th 1:45 am Sagittarius
19th 9:13 am Capricorn
21st 7:55 pm Aquarius
24th 8:22 am Pisces
26th 8:20 pm Aries
29th 6:15 am Taurus

May 1957
1st 1:43 pm Gemini
3rd 7:06 pm Cancer
5th 10:53 pm Leo
8th 1:36 am Virgo
10th 3:57 am Libra
12th 6:50 am Scorpio
14th 11:17 am Sagittarius
16th 6:17 pm Capricorn
19th 4:14 am Aquarius
21st 4:22 pm Pisces
24th 4:32 am Aries
26th 2:39 pm Taurus
28th 9:45 pm Gemini
31st 2:04 am Cancer

June 1957
2nd 4:45 am Leo
4th 6:59 am Virgo
6th 9:47 am Libra
8th 1:43 pm Scorpio
10th 7:11 pm Sagittarius
13th 2:38 am Capricorn
15th 12:27 pm Aquarius
18th 0:16 am Pisces
20th 12:45 pm Aries
22nd 11:39 pm Taurus
25th 7:02 am Gemini
27th 10:56 am Cancer
29th 12:30 pm Leo

July 1957
1st 1:25 pm Virgo
3rd 3:18 pm Libra
5th 7:12 pm Scorpio
8th 1:22 am Sagittarius
10th 9:37 am Capricorn
12th 7:43 pm Aquarius
15th 7:34 am Pisces
17th 8:13 pm Aries
20th 7:54 am Taurus
22nd 4:29 pm Gemini
24th 9:02 pm Cancer
26th 10:15 pm Leo
28th 9:59 pm Virgo
30th 10:21 pm Libra

August 1957
2nd 1:02 am Scorpio
4th 6:51 am Sagittarius
6th 3:25 pm Capricorn
9th 2:01 am Aquarius
11th 2:03 pm Pisces
14th 2:46 am Aries
16th 2:59 pm Taurus
19th 0:51 am Gemini
21st 6:45 am Cancer
23rd 8:47 am Leo
25th 8:27 am Virgo
27th 7:46 am Libra
29th 8:51 am Scorpio
31st 1:12 pm Sagittarius

September 1957
2nd 9:07 pm Capricorn
5th 7:51 am Aquarius
7th 8:04 pm Pisces
10th 8:45 am Aries
12th 8:57 pm Taurus
15th 7:23 am Gemini
17th 2:45 pm Cancer
19th 6:28 pm Leo
21st 7:11 pm Virgo
23rd 6:35 pm Libra
25th 6:44 pm Scorpio
27th 9:30 pm Sagittarius
30th 4:03 am Capricorn

October 1957
2nd 2:07 pm Aquarius
5th 2:18 am Pisces
7th 2:56 pm Aries
10th 2:47 am Taurus
12th 12:58 pm Gemini
14th 8:53 pm Cancer
17th 1:59 am Leo
19th 4:23 am Virgo
21st 5:04 am Libra
23rd 5:35 am Scorpio
25th 7:38 am Sagittarius
27th 12:48 pm Capricorn
29th 9:35 pm Aquarius

November 1957
1st 9:20 am Pisces
3rd 10:01 pm Aries
6th 9:36 am Taurus
8th 7:07 pm Gemini
11th 2:23 am Cancer
13th 7:34 am Leo
15th 11:05 am Virgo
17th 1:25 pm Libra
19th 3:20 pm Scorpio
21st 5:55 pm Sagittarius
23rd 10:33 pm Capricorn
26th 6:22 am Aquarius
28th 5:20 pm Pisces

December 1957
1st 5:57 am Aries
3rd 5:47 pm Taurus
6th 2:58 am Gemini
8th 9:13 am Cancer
10th 1:22 pm Leo
12th 4:28 pm Virgo
14th 7:23 pm Libra
16th 10:36 pm Scorpio
19th 2:33 am Sagittarius
21st 7:52 am Capricorn
23rd 3:23 pm Aquarius
26th 1:44 am Pisces
28th 2:14 pm Aries
31st 2:37 am Taurus

January 1958
2nd 12:18 pm Gemini
4th 6:19 pm Cancer
6th 9:21 pm Leo
8th 10:59 pm Virgo
11th 0:52 am Libra
13th 4:04 am Scorpio
15th 8:53 am Sagittarius
17th 3:16 pm Capricorn
19th 11:24 pm Aquarius
22nd 9:45 am Pisces
24th 10:04 pm Aries
27th 10:55 am Taurus
29th 9:47 pm Gemini

February 1958
1st 4:38 am Cancer
3rd 7:35 am Leo
5th 8:12 am Virgo
7th 8:28 am Libra
9th 10:08 am Scorpio
11th 2:16 pm Sagittarius
13th 8:57 pm Capricorn
16th 5:53 am Aquarius
18th 4:42 pm Pisces
21st 5:03 am Aries
23rd 6:05 pm Taurus
26th 5:50 am Gemini
28th 2:12 pm Cancer

March 1958
2nd 6:24 pm Leo
4th 7:14 pm Virgo
6th 6:37 pm Libra
8th 6:38 pm Scorpio
10th 8:59 pm Sagittarius
13th 2:38 am Capricorn
15th 11:31 am Aquarius
17th 10:42 pm Pisces
20th 11:17 am Aries
23rd 0:16 am Taurus
25th 12:17 pm Gemini
27th 9:52 pm Cancer
30th 3:44 am Leo

April 1958
1st 5:59 am Virgo
3rd 5:54 am Libra
5th 5:19 am Scorpio
7th 6:11 am Sagittarius
9th 10:07 am Capricorn
11th 5:45 pm Aquarius
14th 4:40 am Pisces
16th 5:23 pm Aries
19th 6:15 am Taurus
21st 6:01 pm Gemini
24th 3:44 am Cancer
26th 10:39 am Leo
28th 2:37 pm Virgo
30th 4:05 pm Libra

May 1958
2nd 4:14 pm Scorpio
4th 4:46 pm Sagittarius
6th 7:24 pm Capricorn
9th 1:31 am Aquarius
11th 11:30 am Pisces
13th 11:58 pm Aries
16th 12:48 pm Gemini
19th 0:13 am Gemini
21st 9:19 am Cancer
23rd 4:11 pm Leo
25th 8:58 pm Virgo
27th 11:55 pm Libra
30th 1:34 am Scorpio

June 1958
1st 2:55 am Sagittarius
3rd 5:26 am Capricorn
5th 10:40 am Aquarius
7th 7:27 pm Pisces
10th 7:22 am Aries
12th 8:12 pm Taurus
15th 7:28 am Gemini
17th 3:50 pm Cancer
19th 10:03 pm Leo
22nd 2:21 am Virgo
24th 5:41 am Libra
26th 8:30 am Scorpio
28th 11:12 am Sagittarius
30th 2:35 pm Capricorn

July 1958
2nd 7:47 pm Aquarius
5th 3:59 am Pisces
7th 3:20 pm Aries
10th 4:08 am Taurus
12th 3:43 pm Gemini
15th 0:14 am Cancer
17th 5:28 am Leo
19th 8:41 am Virgo
21st 11:12 am Libra
23rd 1:58 pm Scorpio
25th 5:26 pm Sagittarius
27th 9:53 pm Capricorn
30th 3:54 am Aqiarius

August 1958
1st 12:14 pm Pisces
3rd 11:14 pm Aries
6th 12:04 pm Taurus
9th 0:16 am Gemini
11th 9:19 am Cancer
13th 2:39 pm Leo
15th 5:05 pm Virgo
17th 6:16 pm Libra
19th 7:50 pm Scorpio
21st 10:48 pm Sagittarius
24th 3:40 am Capricorn
26th 10:30 am Aquarius
28th 7:27 pm Pisces
31st 6:36 am Aries

September 1958
2nd 7:23 pm Taurus
5th 8:04 am Gemini
7th 6:19 pm Cancer
10th 0:41 am Leo
12th 3:19 am Virgo
14th 3:45 am Libra
16th 3:51 am Scorpio
18th 5:19 am Sagittarius
20th 9:17 am Capricorn
22nd 4:06 pm Aquarius
25th 1:34 am Pisces
27th 1:08 pm Aries
30th 1:58 am Taurus

October 1958
2nd 2:48 pm Gemini
5th 1:50 am Cancer
7th 9:46 am Leo
9th 1:46 pm Virgo
11th 2:42 pm Libra
13th 2:13 pm Scorpio
15th 2:13 pm Sagittarius
17th 4:28 pm Capricorn
19th 10:07 pm Aquarius
22nd 7:22 am Pisces
24th 7:12 pm Aries
27th 8:07 am Taurus
29th 8:49 pm Gemini

November 1958
1st 8:06 am Cancer
3rd 4:59 pm Leo
5th 10:44 pm Virgo
8th 1:16 am Libra
10th 1:30 am Scorpio
12th 1:04 am Sagittarius
14th 1:57 am Capricorn
16th 5:59 am Aquarius
18th 2:02 pm Pisces
21st 1:29 am Aries
23rd 2:31 pm Taurus
26th 2:59 am Gemini
28th 1:48 pm Cancer
30th 10:39 pm Leo

December 1958
3rd 5:15 am Virgo
5th 9:27 am Libra
7th 11:26 am Scorpio
9th 12:02 pm Sagittarius
11th 12:51 pm Capricorn
13th 3:45 pm Aquarius
15th 10:16 pm Pisces
18th 8:50 am Aries
20th 9:39 pm Taurus
23rd 10:07 am Gemini
25th 8:31 pm Cancer
28th 4:32 am Leo
30th 10:38 am Virgo

January 1959
- 1st 3:19 pm Libra
- 3rd 6:41 pm Scorpio
- 5th 8:57 pm Sagittarius
- 7th 10:52 pm Capricorn
- 10th 1:54 am Aquarius
- 12th 7:46 am Pisces
- 14th 5:13 am Aries
- 17th 5:34 am Taurus
- 19th 6:15 pm Gemini
- 22nd 4:45 am Cancer
- 24th 12:12 pm Leo
- 26th 5:12 pm Virgo
- 28th 8:55 pm Libra
- 31st 0:07 am Scorpio

February 1959
- 2nd 3:13 am Sagittarius
- 4th 6:31 am Capricorn
- 6th 10:44 am Aquarius
- 8th 4:55 pm Pisces
- 11th 1:56 am Aries
- 13th 1:48 pm Taurus
- 16th 2:40 am Gemini
- 18th 1:48 pm Cancer
- 20th 9:38 pm Leo
- 23rd 2:07 am Virgo
- 25th 4:29 am Libra
- 27th 6:16 am Scorpio

March 1959
- 1st 8:36 am Sagittarius
- 3rd 12:09 pm Capricorn
- 5th 5:19 pm Aquarius
- 8th 0:26 am Pisces
- 10th 9:57 am Aries
- 12th 9:37 pm Taurus
- 15th 10:31 am Gemini
- 17th 10:27 pm Cancer
- 20th 7:19 am Leo
- 22nd 12:25 pm Virgo
- 24th 2:25 pm Libra
- 26th 2:55 pm Scorpio
- 28th 3:35 pm Sagittarius
- 30th 5:53 pm Capricorn

April 1959
- 1st 10:43 pm Aquarius
- 4th 6:25 am Pisces
- 6th 4:35 pm Aries
- 9th 4:31 am Taurus
- 11th 5:25 pm Gemini
- 14th 5:46 am Cancer
- 16th 3:51 pm Leo
- 18th 10:27 pm Virgo
- 21st 1:20 am Libra
- 23rd 1:35 am Scorpio
- 25th 1:01 am Sagittarius
- 27th 1:36 am Capricorn
- 29th 5:01 am Aquarius

May 1959
- 1st 12:04 pm Pisces
- 3rd 10:19 pm Aries
- 6th 10:39 am Taurus
- 8th 11:34 pm Gemini
- 11th 11:55 am Cancer
- 13th 10:39 pm Leo
- 16th 6:34 am Virgo
- 18th 11:02 am Libra
- 20th 12:21 pm Scorpio
- 22nd 11:52 am Sagittarius
- 24th 11:29 am Capricorn
- 26th 1:17 pm Aquarius
- 28th 6:47 pm Pisces
- 31st 4:21 am Aries

June 1959
- 2nd 4:38 pm Taurus
- 5th 5:35 am Gemini
- 7th 5:43 pm Cancer
- 10th 4:16 am Leo
- 12th 12:45 pm Virgo
- 14th 6:38 pm Libra
- 16th 9:37 pm Scorpio
- 18th 10:14 pm Sagittarius
- 20th 10:02 pm Capricorn
- 22nd 11:02 pm Aquarius
- 25th 3:12 am Pisces
- 27th 11:34 am Aries
- 29th 11:12 pm Taurus

July 1959
- 2nd 12:04 pm Gemini
- 5th 0:04 am Cancer
- 7th 10:05 am Leo
- 9th 6:13 pm Virgo
- 12th 0:26 am Libra
- 14th 4:31 am Scorpio
- 16th 6:39 am Sagittarius
- 18th 7:42 am Capricorn
- 20th 9:09 am Aquarius
- 22nd 12:46 pm Pisces
- 24th 7:57 pm Aries
- 27th 6:44 am Taurus
- 29th 7:23 pm Gemini

August 1959
- 1st 7:21 am Cancer
- 3rd 5:06 pm Leo
- 6th 0:29 am Virgo
- 8th 5:55 am Libra
- 10th 9:58 am Scorpio
- 12th 12:57 pm Sagittarius
- 14th 3:19 pm Capricorn
- 16th 5:55 pm Aquarius
- 18th 10:00 pm Pisces
- 21st 4:54 am Aries
- 23rd 3:01 pm Taurus
- 26th 3:18 am Gemini
- 28th 3:30 pm Cancer
- 31st 1:33 am Leo

September 1959
- 2nd 8:27 am Virgo
- 4th 12:54 pm Libra
- 6th 3:53 pm Scorpio
- 8th 6:20 pm Sagittarius
- 10th 9:05 pm Capricorn
- 13th 0:44 am Aquarius
- 15th 5:56 am Pisces
- 17th 1:19 pm Aries
- 19th 11:11 pm Taurus
- 22nd 11:16 am Gemini
- 24th 11:50 pm Cancer
- 27th 10:32 am Leo
- 29th 6:01 pm Virgo

October 1959
- 1st 10:07 pm Libra
- 3rd 11:53 pm Scorpio
- 6th 0:54 am Sagittarius
- 8th 2:39 am Capricorn
- 10th 6:14 am Aquarius
- 12th 12:09 pm Pisces
- 14th 8:21 pm Aries
- 17th 6:40 am Taurus
- 19th 6:39 pm Gemini
- 22nd 7:21 am Cancer
- 24th 7:02 pm Leo
- 27th 3:46 am Virgo
- 29th 8:37 am Libra
- 31st 10:11 am Scorpio

November 1959
- 2nd 10:03 am Sagittarius
- 4th 10:10 am Capricorn
- 6th 12:19 pm Aquarius
- 8th 5:39 pm Pisces
- 11th 2:10 am Aries
- 13th 1:06 pm Taurus
- 16th 1:15 am Gemini
- 18th 1:55 pm Cancer
- 21st 2:02 am Leo
- 23rd 12:03 pm Virgo
- 25th 6:37 pm Libra
- 27th 9:20 pm Scorpio
- 29th 9:11 pm Sagittarius

December 1959
- 1st 8:14 pm Capricorn
- 3rd 8:38 pm Aquarius
- 6th 0:16 am Pisces
- 8th 8:04 am Aries
- 10th 6:57 pm Taurus
- 13th 7:25 am Gemini
- 15th 8:00 pm Cancer
- 18th 7:56 am Leo
- 20th 6:27 pm Virgo
- 23rd 2:27 am Libra
- 25th 6:57 am Scorpio
- 27th 8:13 am Sagittarius
- 29th 7:39 am Capricorn
- 31st 7:20 am Aquarius

January 1960
- 2nd 9:26 am Pisces
- 4th 3:28 pm Aries
- 7th 1:24 am Taurus
- 9th 1:46 pm Gemini
- 12th 2:24 am Cancer
- 14th 1:59 pm Leo
- 17th 0:04 am Virgo
- 19th 8:10 am Libra
- 21st 1:55 pm Scorpio
- 23rd 4:50 pm Sagittarius
- 25th 5:58 pm Capricorn
- 27th 6:21 pm Aquarius
- 29th 7:59 pm Pisces

February 1960
- 1st 0:41 am Aries
- 3rd 9:21 am Taurus
- 5th 9:01 pm Gemini
- 8th 9:36 am Cancer
- 10th 9:09 pm Leo
- 13th 6:33 am Virgo
- 15th 1:53 pm Libra
- 17th 7:23 pm Scorpio
- 19th 11:12 pm Sagittarius
- 22nd 1:40 am Capricorn
- 24th 3:34 am Aquarius
- 26th 6:06 am Pisces
- 28th 10:42 am Aries

March 1960
- 1st 6:22 pm Taurus
- 4th 5:09 am Gemini
- 6th 5:36 pm Cancer
- 9th 5:23 am Leo
- 11th 2:45 pm Virgo
- 13th 9:19 pm Libra
- 16th 1:37 am Scorpio
- 18th 4:39 am Sagittarius
- 20th 7:16 am Capricorn
- 22nd 10:12 am Aquarius
- 24th 2:05 pm Pisces
- 26th 7:31 pm Aries
- 29th 3:15 am Taurus
- 31st 1:34 pm Gemini

April 1960
- 3rd 1:47 am Cancer
- 5th 1:59 pm Leo
- 8th 0:04 am Virgo
- 10th 6:34 am Libra
- 12th 9:59 am Scorpio
- 14th 11:38 am Sagittarius
- 16th 1:04 pm Capricorn
- 18th 3:34 pm Aquarius
- 20th 7:57 pm Pisces
- 23rd 2:23 am Aries
- 25th 10:53 am Taurus
- 27th 9:16 pm Gemini
- 30th 9:24 am Cancer

May 1960
- 2nd 9:59 pm Leo
- 5th 8:55 am Virgo
- 7th 4:26 pm Libra
- 9th 8:05 pm Scorpio
- 11th 8:55 pm Sagittarius
- 13th 8:53 pm Capricorn
- 15th 9:54 pm Aquarius
- 18th 1:26 am Pisces
- 20th 7:59 am Aries
- 22nd 5:02 pm Taurus
- 25th 3:55 am Gemini
- 27th 4:07 pm Cancer
- 30th 4:50 am Leo

June 1960
- 1st 4:35 pm Virgo
- 4th 1:30 am Libra
- 6th 6:16 am Scorpio
- 8th 7:29 am Sagittarius
- 10th 6:50 am Capricorn
- 12th 6:28 am Aquarius
- 14th 8:24 am Pisces
- 16th 1:48 pm Aries
- 18th 10:35 pm Taurus
- 21st 9:48 am Gemini
- 23rd 10:11 pm Cancer
- 26th 10:50 am Leo
- 28th 10:52 pm Virgo

July 1960
- 1st 8:41 am Libra
- 3rd 3:02 pm Scorpio
- 5th 5:37 pm Sagittarius
- 7th 5:32 pm Capricorn
- 9th 4:45 pm Aquarius
- 11th 5:24 pm Pisces
- 13th 9:10 pm Aries
- 16th 4:51 am Taurus
- 18th 3:43 pm Gemini
- 21st 4:09 am Cancer
- 23rd 4:46 pm Leo
- 26th 4:30 am Virgo
- 28th 2:30 pm Libra
- 30th 9:53 pm Scorpio

August 1960
- 2nd 2:02 am Sagittarius
- 4th 3:24 am Capricorn
- 6th 3:21 am Aquarius
- 8th 3:43 am Pisces
- 10th 6:25 am Aries
- 12th 12:41 pm Taurus
- 14th 10:30 pm Gemini
- 17th 10:43 am Cancer
- 19th 11:18 pm Leo
- 22nd 10:39 am Virgo
- 24th 8:08 pm Libra
- 27th 3:22 am Scorpio
- 29th 8:16 am Sagittarius
- 31st 11:06 am Capricorn

September 1960
2nd   12:34 pm Aquarius
4th   1:53 pm Pisces
6th   4:29 pm Aries
8th   9:46 pm Taurus
11th   6:33 am Gemini
13th   6:12 pm Cancer
16th   6:45 am Leo
18th   6:05 pm Virgo
21st   2:57 am Libra
23rd   9:16 am Scorpio
25th   1:41 pm Sagittarius
27th   4:53 pm Capricorn
29th   7:32 pm Aquarius

October 1960
1st   10:13 pm Pisces
4th   1:47 am Aries
6th   7:11 am Taurus
8th   3:19 pm Gemini
11th   2:19 am Cancer
13th   2:54 pm Leo
16th   2:39 am Virgo
18th 11:27 am Libra
20th   5:03 pm Scorpio
22nd   8:15 pm Sagittarius
24th 10:28 pm Capricorn
27th   0:58 am Aquarius
29th   4:27 am Pisces
31st   9:13 am Aries

November 1960
2nd   3:28 pm Taurus
4th   11:43 pm Gemini
7th   10:27 am Cancer
9th   10:59 pm Leo
12th 11:20 am Virgo
14th   9:05 pm Libra
17th   2:51 am Scorpio
19th   5:15 am Sagittarius
21st   6:03 am Capricorn
23rd   7:07 am Aquarius
25th   9:53 am Pisces
27th   2:54 pm Aries
29th 10:01 pm Taurus

December 1960
2nd   7:02 am Gemini
4th   5:53 pm Cancer
7th   6:20 am Leo
9th   7:12 pm Virgo
12th   6:05 am Libra
14th   1:07 pm Scorpio
16th   4:02 pm Sagittarius
18th   4:15 pm Capricorn
20th   3:52 pm Aquarius
22nd   4:52 pm Pisces
24th   8:37 pm Aries
27th   3:34 am Taurus
29th   1:04 pm Gemini

January 1961
1st   0:22 am Cancer
3rd   12:55 pm Leo
6th   1:47 am Virgo
8th   1:26 pm Libra
10th 10:06 pm Scorpio
13th   2:38 am Sagittarius
15th   3:39 am Capricorn
17th   2:56 am Aquarius
19th   2:33 am Pisces
21st   4:31 am Aries
23rd   9:57 am Taurus
25th   6:54 pm Gemini
28th   6:25 am Cancer
30th   7:06 pm Leo

February 1961
2nd   7:48 am Virgo
4th   7:25 pm Libra
7th   4:48 am Scorpio
9th   10:56 am Sagittarius
11th   1:46 pm Capricorn
13th   2:13 pm Aquarius
15th   1:55 pm Pisces
17th   2:45 pm Aries
19th   6:26 pm Taurus
22nd   1:54 am Gemini
24th 12:52 pm Cancer
27th   1:35 am Leo

March 1961
1st   2:11 pm Virgo
4th   1:21 am Libra
6th   10:21 am Scorpio
8th   5:01 pm Sagittarius
10th   9:18 pm Capricorn
12th 11:30 pm Aquarius
15th   0:26 am Pisces
17th   1:34 am Aries
19th   4:28 am Taurus
21st 10:38 am Gemini
23rd   8:24 pm Cancer
26th   8:49 am Leo
28th   9:31 pm Virgo
31st   8:19 am Libra

April 1961
2nd   4:35 pm Scorpio
4th   10:35 pm Sagittarius
7th   2:52 am Capricorn
9th   6:02 am Aquarius
11th   8:32 am Pisces
13th 10:57 am Aries
15th   2:20 pm Taurus
17th   7:58 pm Gemini
20th   4:53 am Cancer
22nd   4:45 pm Leo
25th   5:30 am Virgo
27th   4:33 pm Libra
30th   0:29 am Scorpio

May 1961
2nd   5:24 am Sagittarius
4th   8:40 am Capricorn
6th   11:25 am Aquarius
8th   2:24 pm Pisces
10th   5:57 pm Aries
12th 10:25 pm Taurus
15th   4:36 am Gemini
17th   1:21 pm Cancer
20th   0:45 am Leo
22nd   1:38 pm Virgo
25th   1:17 am Libra
27th   9:30 am Scorpio
29th   2:08 pm Sagittarius
31st   4:20 pm Capricorn

June 1961
2nd   5:47 pm Aquarius
4th   7:52 pm Pisces
6th   11:25 pm Aries
9th   4:39 am Taurus
11th 11:44 am Gemini
13th   8:51 pm Cancer
16th   8:17 am Leo
18th   9:11 pm Virgo
21st   9:29 am Libra
23rd   6:47 pm Scorpio
26th   0:05 am Sagittarius
28th   1:50 am Capricorn
30th   2:18 am Aquarius

July 1961
2nd   2:55 am Pisces
4th   5:16 am Aries
6th   10:06 am Taurus
8th   5:31 pm Gemini
11th   3:15 am Cancer
13th   2:58 pm Leo
16th   3:54 am Virgo
18th   4:35 pm Libra
21st   3:01 am Scorpio
23rd   9:35 am Sagittarius
25th 12:24 pm Capricorn
27th 12:40 pm Aquarius
29th 12:15 pm Pisces
31st   1:01 pm Aries

August 1961
2nd   4:25 pm Taurus
4th   11:06 pm Gemini
7th   8:59 am Cancer
9th   9:01 pm Leo
12th 10:01 am Virgo
14th 10:43 pm Libra
17th   9:41 am Scorpio
19th   5:40 pm Sagittarius
21st 10:05 pm Capricorn
23rd 11:24 pm Aquarius
25th 11:02 pm Pisces
27th 10:49 pm Aries
30th   0:37 am Taurus

September 1961
1st   5:56 am Gemini
3rd   3:04 pm Cancer
6th   3:01 am Leo
8th   4:05 pm Virgo
11th   4:32 am Libra
13th   3:21 pm Scorpio
15th 11:54 pm Sagittarius
18th   5:38 am Capricorn
20th   8:40 am Aquarius
22nd   9:34 am Pisces
24th   9:41 am Aries
26th 10:46 am Taurus
28th   2:36 pm Gemini
30th 10:19 pm Cancer

October 1961
3rd   9:44 am Leo
5th   10:45 pm Virgo
8th   11:01 am Libra
10th   9:19 pm Scorpio
13th   5:19 am Sagittarius
15th 11:21 am Capricorn
17th   3:34 pm Aquarius
19th   6:08 pm Pisces
21st   7:34 am Aries
23rd   9:07 pm Taurus
26th   0:23 am Gemini
28th   7:06 am Cancer
30th   5:32 pm Leo

November 1961
2nd   6:16 am Virgo
4th   6:40 pm Libra
7th   4:37 pm Scorpio
9th   11:47 am Sagittarius
11th   4:58 pm Capricorn
13th   8:59 pm Aquarius
16th   0:19 am Pisces
18th   3:10 am Aries
20th   6:03 am Taurus
22nd 10:01 am Gemini
24th   4:24 pm Cancer
27th   2:01 am Leo
29th   2:24 pm Virgo

December 1961
2nd   3:06 am Libra
4th   1:24 pm Scorpio
6th   8:21 pm Sagittarius
9th   0:31 am Capricorn
11th   3:12 am Aquarius
13th   5:42 am Pisces
15th   8:45 am Aries
17th 12:40 pm Taurus
19th   5:49 pm Gemini
22nd   0:49 am Cancer
24th 10:28 am Leo
26th 10:29 pm Virgo
29th 11:24 am Libra
31st 10:40 pm Scorpio

January 1962
3rd   6:19 am Sagittarius
5th   10:19 am Capricorn
7th   11:58 am Aquarius
9th   12:55 pm Pisces
11th   2:37 pm Aries
13th   6:05 pm Taurus
15th 11:42 pm Gemini
18th   7:42 am Cancer
20th   5:52 pm Leo
23rd   5:54 am Virgo
25th   6:51 pm Libra
28th   6:50 am Scorpio
30th   3:54 pm Sagittarius

February 1962
1st   9:07 pm Capricorn
3rd   10:56 pm Aquarius
5th   10:52 pm Pisces
7th   10:51 pm Aries
10th   0:36 am Taurus
12th   5:22 am Gemini
14th   1:24 pm Cancer
17th   0:04 am Leo
19th 12:28 pm Virgo
22nd   1:21 am Libra
24th   1:34 pm Scorpio
26th 11:45 pm Sagittarius

March 1962
1st   6:33 am Capricorn
3rd   9:47 am Aquarius
5th   10:14 am Pisces
7th   9:34 am Aries
9th   9:45 am Taurus
11th 12:41 pm Gemini
13th   7:30 pm Cancer
16th   5:58 am Leo
18th   6:35 pm Virgo
21st   7:28 am Libra
23rd   7:28 pm Scorpio
26th   5:48 am Sagittarius
28th   1:41 pm Capricorn
30th   6:41 pm Aquarius

April 1962
1st   8:42 pm Pisces
3rd   8:40 pm Aries
5th   8:27 pm Taurus
7th   10:02 pm Gemini
10th   3:14 am Cancer
12th 12:39 pm Leo
15th   0:57 am Virgo
17th   1:54 pm Libra
20th   1:37 am Scorpio
22nd 11:26 am Sagittarius
24th   7:19 pm Capricorn
27th   1:08 am Aquarius
29th   4:39 am Pisces

May 1962		
1st	6:12 am	Aries
3rd	6:50 am	Taurus
5th	8:21 am	Gemini
7th	12:34 pm	Cancer
9th	8:39 pm	Leo
12th	8:12 am	Virgo
14th	9:04 pm	Libra
17th	8:42 am	Scorpio
19th	6:01 pm	Sagittarius
22nd	1:08 am	Capricorn
24th	6:30 am	Aquarius
26th	10:28 am	Pisces
28th	1:15 pm	Aries
30th	3:17 pm	Taurus

June 1962		
1st	5:43 pm	Gemini
3rd	9:50 pm	Cancer
6th	5:26 am	Leo
8th	4:14 pm	Virgo
11th	4:51 am	Libra
13th	4:43 pm	Scorpio
16th	2:03 am	Sagittarius
18th	8:28 am	Capricorn
20th	12:47 pm	Aquarius
22nd	3:59 pm	Pisces
24th	6:44 pm	Aries
26th	9:35 pm	Taurus
29th	1:10 am	Gemini

July 1962		
1st	6:23 am	Cancer
3rd	2:00 pm	Leo
6th	0:22 am	Virgo
8th	12:48 pm	Libra
11th	1:05 am	Scorpio
13th	10:55 am	Sagittarius
15th	5:28 pm	Capricorn
17th	9:07 pm	Aquarius
19th	11:00 pm	Pisces
22nd	0:35 am	Aries
24th	2:50 am	Taurus
26th	7:00 am	Gemini
28th	1:05 pm	Cancer
30th	9:24 pm	Leo

August 1962		
2nd	7:50 am	Virgo
4th	8:18 pm	Libra
7th	8:54 am	Scorpio
9th	7:46 pm	Sagittarius
12th	3:14 am	Capricorn
14th	7:03 am	Aquarius
16th	8:16 am	Pisces
18th	8:27 am	Aries
20th	9:24 am	Taurus
22nd	12:33 pm	Gemini
24th	6:38 pm	Cancer
27th	3:32 am	Leo
29th	2:38 pm	Virgo

September 1962		
1st	3:02 am	Libra
3rd	3:46 pm	Scorpio
6th	3:25 am	Sagittarius
8th	12:15 pm	Capricorn
10th	5:21 pm	Aquarius
12th	6:59 pm	Pisces
14th	6:33 pm	Aries
16th	6:04 pm	Taurus
18th	7:32 pm	Gemini
21st	0:26 am	Cancer
23rd	9:11 am	Leo
25th	8:32 pm	Virgo
28th	9:09 am	Libra
30th	9:49 pm	Scorpio

October 1962		
3rd	9:38 am	Sagittarius
5th	7:32 pm	Capricorn
8th	2:19 am	Aquarius
10th	5:25 am	Pisces
12th	5:38 am	Aries
14th	4:45 am	Taurus
16th	4:54 am	Gemini
18th	8:10 am	Cancer
20th	3:35 pm	Leo
23rd	2:31 am	Virgo
25th	3:13 pm	Libra
28th	3:48 am	Scorpio
30th	3:18 pm	Sagittarius

November 1962		
2nd	1:17 am	Capricorn
4th	8:58 am	Aquarius
6th	1:47 pm	Pisces
8th	3:42 pm	Aries
10th	3:44 pm	Taurus
12th	3:47 pm	Gemini
14th	5:52 pm	Cancer
16th	11:40 pm	Leo
19th	9:36 am	Virgo
21st	9:58 pm	Libra
24th	10:30 am	Scorpio
26th	9:41 pm	Sagittarius
29th	6:58 am	Capricorn

December 1962		
1st	2:23 pm	Aquarius
3rd	7:52 pm	Pisces
5th	11:16 pm	Aries
8th	0:59 am	Taurus
10th	2:07 am	Gemini
12th	4:24 am	Cancer
14th	9:24 am	Leo
16th	6:02 pm	Virgo
19th	5:41 am	Libra
21st	6:16 pm	Scorpio
24th	5:29 am	Sagittarius
26th	2:14 pm	Capricorn
28th	8:41 pm	Aquarius
31st	1:19 am	Pisces

January 1963		
2nd	4:47 am	Aries
4th	7:34 am	Taurus
6th	10:16 am	Gemini
8th	1:44 pm	Cancer
10th	7:03 pm	Leo
13th	3:08 am	Virgo
15th	2:06 pm	Libra
18th	2:33 am	Scorpio
20th	2:16 pm	Sagittarius
22nd	11:23 pm	Capricorn
25th	5:11 am	Aquarius
27th	8:33 am	Pisces
29th	10:43 am	Aries
31st	12:56 pm	Taurus

February 1963		
2nd	4:06 pm	Gemini
4th	8:42 pm	Cancer
7th	3:08 am	Leo
9th	11:39 am	Virgo
11th	10:19 pm	Libra
14th	10:37 am	Scorpio
16th	10:54 pm	Sagittarius
19th	8:54 am	Capricorn
21st	3:18 pm	Aquarius
23rd	6:13 pm	Pisces
25th	7:04 pm	Aries
27th	7:40 pm	Taurus

March 1963		
1st	9:40 pm	Gemini
4th	2:09 am	Cancer
6th	9:18 am	Leo
8th	6:35 pm	Virgo
11th	5:36 am	Libra
13th	5:52 pm	Scorpio
16th	6:26 am	Sagittarius
18th	5:31 pm	Capricorn
21st	1:19 am	Aquarius
23rd	4:60 am	Pisces
25th	5:35 am	Aries
27th	4:58 am	Taurus
29th	5:16 am	Gemini
31st	8:18 am	Cancer

April 1963		
2nd	2:49 pm	Leo
5th	0:22 am	Virgo
7th	11:51 am	Libra
10th	0:14 am	Scorpio
12th	12:48 pm	Sagittarius
15th	0:27 am	Capricorn
17th	9:30 am	Aquarius
19th	2:48 pm	Pisces
21st	4:25 pm	Aries
23rd	3:50 pm	Taurus
25th	3:09 pm	Gemini
27th	4:32 pm	Cancer
29th	9:26 pm	Leo

May 1963		
2nd	6:16 am	Virgo
4th	5:43 pm	Libra
7th	6:16 am	Scorpio
9th	6:43 pm	Sagittarius
12th	6:13 am	Capricorn
14th	3:48 pm	Aquarius
16th	10:32 pm	Pisces
19th	1:46 am	Aries
21st	2:21 am	Taurus
23rd	1:55 am	Gemini
25th	2:31 am	Cancer
27th	6:03 am	Leo
29th	1:27 pm	Virgo

June 1963		
1st	0:10 am	Libra
3rd	12:38 pm	Scorpio
6th	1:02 am	Sagittarius
8th	12:05 pm	Capricorn
10th	9:22 pm	Aquarius
13th	4:20 am	Pisces
15th	8:44 am	Aries
17th	10:53 am	Taurus
19th	11:45 am	Gemini
21st	12:51 pm	Cancer
23rd	3:50 pm	Leo
25th	9:58 pm	Virgo
28th	7:43 am	Libra
30th	7:48 pm	Scorpio

July 1963		
3rd	8:10 am	Sagittarius
5th	7:02 pm	Capricorn
8th	3:35 am	Aquarius
10th	9:51 am	Pisces
12th	2:15 pm	Aries
14th	5:15 pm	Taurus
16th	7:28 pm	Gemini
18th	9:47 pm	Cancer
21st	1:16 am	Leo
23rd	7:11 am	Virgo
25th	4:06 pm	Libra
28th	3:38 am	Scorpio
30th	4:06 pm	Sagittarius

August 1963		
2nd	3:11 am	Capricorn
4th	11:22 am	Aquarius
6th	4:44 pm	Pisces
8th	8:07 pm	Aries
10th	10:39 pm	Taurus
13th	1:17 am	Gemini
15th	4:41 am	Cancer
17th	9:20 am	Leo
19th	3:44 pm	Virgo
22nd	0:27 am	Libra
24th	11:41 am	Scorpio
27th	0:14 am	Sagittarius
29th	11:53 am	Capricorn
31st	8:35 pm	Aquarius

September 1963		
3rd	1:37 am	Pisces
5th	3:52 am	Aries
7th	5:04 am	Taurus
9th	6:49 am	Gemini
11th	10:12 am	Cancer
13th	3:33 pm	Leo
15th	10:49 pm	Virgo
18th	8:03 am	Libra
20th	7:12 pm	Scorpio
23rd	7:51 am	Sagittarius
25th	8:15 pm	Capricorn
28th	5:58 am	Aquarius
30th	11:40 am	Pisces

October 1963		
2nd	1:44 pm	Aries
4th	1:50 pm	Taurus
6th	2:01 pm	Gemini
8th	4:04 pm	Cancer
10th	8:55 pm	Leo
13th	4:36 am	Virgo
15th	2:27 pm	Libra
18th	1:53 am	Scorpio
20th	2:33 pm	Sagittarius
23rd	3:20 am	Capricorn
25th	2:15 pm	Aquarius
27th	9:35 pm	Pisces
30th	9:39 am	Aries

November 1963		
1st	0:42 am	Taurus
2nd	11:49 pm	Gemini
5th	0:08 am	Cancer
7th	3:26 am	Leo
9th	10:17 am	Virgo
11th	8:09 pm	Libra
14th	7:57 am	Scorpio
16th	8:41 pm	Sagittarius
19th	9:22 am	Capricorn
21st	8:50 pm	Aquarius
24th	5:28 am	Pisces
26th	10:19 am	Aries
28th	11:46 am	Taurus
30th	11:15 am	Gemini

December 1963		
2nd	10:48 am	Cancer
4th	12:26 pm	Leo
6th	5:30 pm	Virgo
9th	2:23 am	Libra
11th	2:05 pm	Scorpio
14th	2:52 am	Sagittarius
16th	3:20 pm	Capricorn
19th	2:28 am	Aquarius
21st	11:25 am	Pisces
23rd	5:37 pm	Aries
25th	8:55 pm	Taurus
27th	9:57 pm	Gemini
29th	10:08 pm	Cancer
31st	11:09 pm	Leo

January 1964
3rd	2:49 am	Virgo
5th	10:14 am	Libra
7th	9:04 pm	Scorpio
10th	9:47 am	Sagittarius
12th	10:12 pm	Capricorn
15th	8:44 am	Aquarius
17th	5:01 pm	Pisces
19th	11:10 pm	Aries
22nd	3:23 am	Taurus
24th	6:03 am	Gemini
26th	7:52 am	Cancer
28th	9:47 am	Leo
30th	1:13 pm	Virgo

February 1964
1st	7:28 pm	Libra
4th	5:14 am	Scorpio
6th	5:34 pm	Sagittarius
9th	6:07 am	Capricorn
11th	4:35 pm	Aquarius
14th	0:07 am	Pisces
16th	5:08 am	Aries
18th	8:44 am	Taurus
20th	11:48 am	Gemini
22nd	2:50 pm	Cancer
24th	6:12 pm	Leo
26th	10:30 pm	Virgo
29th	4:49 am	Libra

March 1964
2nd	1:57 pm	Scorpio
5th	1:46 am	Sagittarius
7th	2:32 pm	Capricorn
10th	1:33 am	Aquarius
12th	9:00 am	Pisces
14th	1:11 pm	Aries
16th	3:30 pm	Taurus
18th	5:27 pm	Gemini
20th	8:13 pm	Cancer
23rd	0:16 am	Leo
25th	5:43 am	Virgo
27th	12:50 pm	Libra
29th	10:04 pm	Scorpio

April 1964
1st	9:42 am	Sagittarius
3rd	10:37 pm	Capricorn
6th	10:19 am	Aquarius
8th	6:42 pm	Pisces
10th	11:07 pm	Aries
13th	0:36 am	Taurus
15th	1:05 am	Gemini
17th	2:23 am	Cancer
19th	5:42 am	Leo
21st	11:20 am	Virgo
23rd	7:09 pm	Libra
26th	5:03 am	Scorpio
28th	4:47 pm	Sagittarius

May 1964
1st	5:42 am	Capricorn
3rd	6:04 pm	Aquarius
6th	3:40 am	Pisces
8th	9:11 am	Aries
10th	11:05 am	Taurus
12th	11:01 am	Gemini
14th	10:56 am	Cancer
16th	12:36 pm	Leo
18th	5:06 pm	Virgo
21st	0:40 am	Libra
23rd	11:01 am	Scorpio
25th	11:04 pm	Sagittarius
28th	12:00 pm	Capricorn
31st	0:32 am	Aquarius

June 1964
2nd	10:57 am	Pisces
4th	5:50 pm	Aries
6th	9:18 pm	Taurus
8th	9:49 pm	Gemini
10th	9:17 pm	Cancer
12th	9:37 pm	Leo
15th	0:27 am	Virgo
17th	6:57 am	Libra
19th	4:52 pm	Scorpio
22nd	5:05 am	Sagittarius
24th	6:01 pm	Capricorn
27th	6:20 am	Aquarius
29th	4:54 pm	Pisces

July 1964
2nd	0:52 am	Aries
4th	5:40 am	Taurus
6th	7:41 am	Gemini
8th	7:57 am	Cancer
10th	8:04 am	Leo
12th	9:49 am	Virgo
14th	2:47 pm	Libra
16th	11:33 pm	Scorpio
19th	11:30 am	Sagittarius
22nd	0:28 am	Capricorn
24th	12:28 pm	Aquarius
26th	10:36 pm	Pisces
29th	6:23 am	Aries
31st	11:57 am	Taurus

August 1964
2nd	3:27 pm	Gemini
4th	5:13 pm	Cancer
6th	6:12 pm	Leo
8th	7:52 pm	Virgo
10th	11:53 pm	Libra
13th	7:36 am	Scorpio
15th	6:45 pm	Sagittarius
18th	7:38 am	Capricorn
20th	7:37 pm	Aquarius
23rd	5:11 am	Pisces
25th	12:13 pm	Aries
27th	5:22 pm	Taurus
29th	9:17 pm	Gemini

September 1964
1st	0:15 am	Cancer
3rd	2:38 am	Leo
5th	5:15 am	Virgo
7th	9:24 am	Libra
9th	4:24 pm	Scorpio
12th	2:49 am	Sagittarius
14th	3:29 pm	Capricorn
17th	3:45 am	Aquarius
19th	1:18 pm	Pisces
21st	7:42 pm	Aries
23rd	11:46 pm	Taurus
26th	2:46 am	Gemini
28th	5:40 am	Cancer
30th	8:54 am	Leo

October 1964
2nd	12:45 pm	Virgo
4th	5:47 pm	Libra
7th	0:59 am	Scorpio
9th	11:06 am	Sagittarius
11th	11:34 pm	Capricorn
14th	12:13 pm	Aquarius
16th	10:32 pm	Pisces
19th	5:02 am	Aries
21st	8:22 am	Taurus
23rd	10:04 am	Gemini
25th	11:39 am	Cancer
27th	2:17 pm	Leo
29th	6:27 pm	Virgo

November 1964
1st	0:24 am	Libra
3rd	8:28 am	Scorpio
5th	6:46 pm	Sagittarius
8th	7:08 am	Capricorn
10th	8:09 pm	Aquarius
13th	7:26 am	Pisces
15th	3:05 pm	Aries
17th	6:55 pm	Taurus
19th	7:58 pm	Gemini
21st	8:04 pm	Cancer
23rd	9:00 pm	Leo
26th	0:02 am	Virgo
28th	5:57 am	Libra
30th	2:34 pm	Scorpio

December 1964
3rd	1:24 am	Sagittarius
5th	1:55 pm	Capricorn
8th	2:58 am	Aquarius
10th	2:57 pm	Pisces
13th	0:13 am	Aries
15th	5:29 am	Taurus
17th	7:18 am	Gemini
19th	7:02 am	Cancer
21st	6:34 am	Leo
23rd	7:46 am	Virgo
25th	12:10 pm	Libra
27th	8:12 pm	Scorpio
30th	7:22 am	Sagittarius

January 1965
1st	8:06 pm	Capricorn
4th	9:03 am	Aquarius
6th	9:05 pm	Pisces
9th	7:05 am	Aries
11th	2:05 pm	Taurus
13th	5:44 pm	Gemini
15th	6:32 pm	Cancer
17th	5:58 pm	Leo
19th	5:58 pm	Virgo
21st	8:31 pm	Libra
24th	3:03 am	Scorpio
26th	1:34 pm	Sagittarius
29th	2:21 am	Capricorn
31st	3:16 pm	Aquarius

February 1965
3rd	2:55 am	Pisces
5th	12:41 pm	Aries
7th	8:22 pm	Taurus
10th	1:36 am	Gemini
12th	4:12 am	Cancer
14th	4:53 am	Leo
16th	5:08 am	Virgo
18th	6:50 am	Libra
20th	11:51 am	Scorpio
22nd	8:58 pm	Sagittarius
25th	9:16 am	Capricorn
27th	10:13 pm	Aquarius

March 1965
2nd	9:34 am	Pisces
4th	6:43 pm	Aries
7th	1:50 am	Taurus
9th	7:12 am	Gemini
11th	11:01 am	Cancer
13th	1:22 pm	Leo
15th	2:57 pm	Virgo
17th	5:07 pm	Libra
19th	9:34 pm	Scorpio
22nd	5:39 am	Sagittarius
24th	5:09 pm	Capricorn
27th	5:56 am	Aquarius
29th	5:28 pm	Pisces

April 1965
1st	2:17 am	Aries
3rd	8:25 am	Taurus
5th	12:53 pm	Gemini
7th	4:22 pm	Cancer
9th	7:24 pm	Leo
11th	10:15 pm	Virgo
14th	1:39 am	Libra
16th	6:45 am	Scorpio
18th	2:35 pm	Sagittarius
21st	1:25 am	Capricorn
23rd	2:03 pm	Aquarius
26th	2:00 am	Pisces
28th	11:06 am	Aries
30th	4:59 pm	Taurus

May 1965
2nd	8:25 pm	Gemini
4th	10:38 pm	Cancer
7th	0:49 am	Leo
9th	3:48 am	Virgo
11th	8:05 am	Libra
13th	2:12 pm	Scorpio
15th	10:32 pm	Sagittarius
18th	9:21 am	Capricorn
20th	9:50 pm	Aquarius
23rd	10:12 am	Pisces
25th	8:16 pm	Aries
28th	2:47 am	Taurus
30th	5:56 am	Gemini

June 1965
1st	7:04 am	Cancer
3rd	7:48 am	Leo
5th	9:36 am	Virgo
7th	1:33 pm	Libra
9th	8:05 pm	Scorpio
12th	5:12 am	Sagittarius
14th	4:21 pm	Capricorn
17th	4:52 am	Aquarius
19th	5:28 pm	Pisces
22nd	4:27 am	Aries
24th	12:11 pm	Taurus
26th	4:13 pm	Gemini
28th	5:17 pm	Cancer
30th	4:50 pm	Leo

July 1965
2nd	5:14 pm	Virgo
4th	7:45 pm	Libra
7th	1:40 am	Scorpio
9th	10:56 am	Sagittarius
11th	10:30 pm	Capricorn
14th	11:07 am	Aquarius
16th	11:44 pm	Pisces
19th	11:09 am	Aries
21st	8:11 pm	Taurus
24th	1:47 am	Gemini
26th	3:52 am	Cancer
28th	3:37 am	Leo
30th	2:57 am	Virgo

August 1965
1st	3:57 am	Libra
3rd	8:26 am	Scorpio
5th	4:53 pm	Sagittarius
8th	4:23 am	Capricorn
10th	5:08 pm	Aquarius
13th	5:37 am	Pisces
15th	4:55 pm	Aries
18th	2:27 am	Taurus
20th	9:17 am	Gemini
22nd	1:00 pm	Cancer
24th	1:59 pm	Leo
26th	1:38 pm	Virgo
28th	1:57 pm	Libra
30th	4:50 pm	Scorpio

September 1965		
1st	11:60 pm	Sagittarius
4th	10:54 am	Capricorn
6th	11:34 am	Aquarius
9th	11:35 am	Pisces
11th	10:50 pm	Aries
14th	7:54 am	Taurus
16th	3:03 pm	Gemini
18th	8:00 pm	Cancer
20th	10:35 pm	Leo
22nd	11:31 pm	Virgo
25th	0:17 am	Libra
27th	2:50 am	Scorpio
29th	8:47 am	Sagittarius

October 1965		
1st	6:31 pm	Capricorn
4th	6:49 am	Aquarius
6th	7:12 pm	Pisces
9th	5:51 am	Aries
11th	2:15 pm	Taurus
13th	8:39 pm	Gemini
16th	1:26 am	Cancer
18th	4:50 am	Leo
20th	7:14 am	Virgo
22nd	9:24 am	Libra
24th	12:37 pm	Scorpio
26th	6:14 pm	Sagittarius
29th	3:09 am	Capricorn
31st	2:51 pm	Aquarius

November 1965		
3rd	3:23 am	Pisces
5th	2:19 pm	Aries
7th	10:30 pm	Taurus
10th	3:52 am	Gemini
12th	7:28 am	Cancer
14th	10:14 am	Leo
16th	12:55 pm	Virgo
18th	4:11 pm	Libra
20th	8:39 pm	Scorpio
23rd	2:59 am	Sagittarius
25th	11:49 am	Capricorn
27th	11:06 pm	Aquarius
30th	11:40 am	Pisces

December 1965		
2nd	11:23 pm	Aries
5th	8:07 am	Taurus
7th	1:24 pm	Gemini
9th	3:55 pm	Cancer
11th	5:08 pm	Leo
13th	6:37 pm	Virgo
15th	9:34 pm	Libra
18th	2:42 am	Scorpio
20th	10:04 am	Sagittarius
22nd	7:29 pm	Capricorn
25th	6:46 am	Aquarius
27th	7:18 pm	Pisces
30th	7:38 am	Aries

January 1966		
1st	5:42 pm	Taurus
4th	0:07 am	Gemini
6th	2:39 am	Cancer
8th	2:50 am	Leo
10th	2:37 am	Virgo
12th	3:57 am	Libra
14th	8:13 am	Scorpio
16th	3:42 am	Sagittarius
19th	1:45 am	Capricorn
21st	1:27 pm	Aquarius
24th	1:59 am	Pisces
26th	2:32 pm	Aries
29th	1:41 am	Taurus
31st	9:38 am	Gemini

February 1966		
2nd	1:35 pm	Cancer
4th	2:11 pm	Leo
6th	1:13 pm	Virgo
8th	12:56 pm	Libra
10th	3:20 pm	Scorpio
12th	9:35 pm	Sagittarius
15th	7:27 am	Capricorn
17th	7:26 pm	Aquarius
20th	8:05 am	Pisces
22nd	8:29 pm	Aries
25th	7:51 am	Taurus
27th	4:59 pm	Gemini

March 1966		
1st	10:48 pm	Cancer
4th	0:56 am	Leo
6th	0:36 am	Virgo
7th	11:49 pm	Libra
10th	0:48 am	Scorpio
12th	5:22 am	Sagittarius
14th	1:50 pm	Capricorn
17th	1:35 am	Aquarius
19th	2:18 pm	Pisces
22nd	2:33 am	Aries
24th	1:29 pm	Taurus
26th	10:41 pm	Gemini
29th	5:21 am	Cancer
31st	9:08 am	Leo

April 1966		
2nd	10:29 am	Virgo
4th	10:41 am	Libra
6th	11:35 am	Scorpio
8th	2:59 pm	Sagittarius
10th	10:03 pm	Capricorn
13th	8:44 am	Aquarius
15th	9:12 pm	Pisces
18th	9:25 am	Aries
20th	7:57 pm	Taurus
23rd	4:24 am	Gemini
25th	10:45 am	Cancer
27th	3:06 pm	Leo
29th	5:47 pm	Virgo

May 1966		
1st	7:31 pm	Libra
3rd	9:24 pm	Scorpio
6th	0:53 am	Sagittarius
8th	7:17 am	Capricorn
10th	4:54 pm	Aquarius
13th	4:55 am	Pisces
15th	5:13 pm	Aries
18th	3:45 am	Taurus
20th	11:35 am	Gemini
22nd	4:57 pm	Cancer
24th	8:35 pm	Leo
26th	11:21 pm	Virgo
29th	1:59 am	Libra
31st	5:12 am	Scorpio

June 1966		
2nd	9:41 am	Sagittarius
4th	4:13 pm	Capricorn
7th	1:23 am	Aquarius
9th	12:58 pm	Pisces
12th	1:26 am	Aries
14th	12:26 pm	Taurus
16th	8:23 pm	Gemini
19th	1:03 am	Cancer
21st	3:27 am	Leo
23rd	5:08 am	Virgo
25th	7:24 am	Libra
27th	11:06 am	Scorpio
29th	4:33 pm	Sagittarius

July 1966		
1st	11:51 pm	Capricorn
4th	9:16 am	Aquarius
6th	8:40 pm	Pisces
9th	9:15 am	Aries
11th	9:01 pm	Taurus
14th	5:46 am	Gemini
16th	10:38 am	Cancer
18th	12:24 pm	Leo
20th	12:47 pm	Virgo
22nd	1:41 pm	Libra
24th	4:35 pm	Scorpio
26th	10:06 pm	Sagittarius
29th	6:06 am	Capricorn
31st	4:03 pm	Aquarius

August 1966		
3rd	3:35 am	Pisces
5th	4:14 pm	Aries
8th	4:36 am	Taurus
10th	2:33 pm	Gemini
12th	8:38 pm	Cancer
14th	10:49 pm	Leo
16th	10:35 pm	Virgo
18th	10:05 pm	Libra
20th	11:23 pm	Scorpio
23rd	3:53 am	Sagittarius
25th	11:40 am	Capricorn
27th	9:56 pm	Aquarius
30th	9:48 am	Pisces

September 1966		
1st	10:27 pm	Aries
4th	10:57 am	Taurus
6th	9:50 pm	Gemini
9th	5:23 am	Cancer
11th	8:57 am	Leo
13th	9:24 am	Virgo
15th	8:36 am	Libra
17th	8:38 am	Scorpio
19th	11:27 am	Sagittarius
21st	5:56 pm	Capricorn
24th	3:48 am	Aquarius
26th	3:48 pm	Pisces
29th	4:29 am	Aries

October 1966		
1st	4:45 pm	Taurus
4th	3:42 am	Gemini
6th	12:08 pm	Cancer
8th	5:21 pm	Leo
10th	7:25 pm	Virgo
12th	7:30 pm	Libra
14th	7:24 pm	Scorpio
16th	9:01 pm	Sagittarius
19th	1:58 am	Capricorn
21st	10:46 am	Aquarius
23rd	10:21 pm	Pisces
26th	11:02 am	Aries
28th	11:04 pm	Taurus
31st	9:25 am	Gemini

November 1966		
2nd	5:40 pm	Cancer
4th	11:35 pm	Leo
7th	3:08 am	Virgo
9th	4:54 am	Libra
11th	5:56 am	Scorpio
13th	7:41 am	Sagittarius
15th	11:43 am	Capricorn
17th	7:08 pm	Aquarius
20th	5:55 am	Pisces
22nd	6:32 pm	Aries
25th	6:35 am	Taurus
27th	4:28 pm	Gemini
29th	11:49 pm	Cancer

December 1966		
2nd	4:59 am	Leo
4th	8:46 am	Virgo
6th	11:42 am	Libra
8th	2:18 pm	Scorpio
10th	5:15 pm	Sagittarius
12th	9:34 pm	Capricorn
15th	4:23 am	Aquarius
17th	2:22 pm	Pisces
20th	2:40 am	Aries
22nd	3:06 pm	Taurus
25th	1:14 am	Gemini
27th	7:55 am	Cancer
29th	11:55 am	Leo
31st	2:33 pm	Virgo

January 1967		
2nd	5:04 pm	Libra
4th	8:17 pm	Scorpio
7th	0:28 am	Sagittarius
9th	5:55 am	Capricorn
11th	1:10 pm	Aquarius
13th	10:46 pm	Pisces
16th	10:49 am	Aries
18th	11:40 pm	Taurus
21st	10:34 am	Gemini
23rd	5:48 pm	Cancer
25th	9:20 pm	Leo
27th	10:37 pm	Virgo
29th	11:34 pm	Libra

February 1967		
1st	1:45 am	Scorpio
3rd	5:58 am	Sagittarius
5th	12:14 pm	Capricorn
7th	8:19 pm	Aquarius
10th	6:21 am	Pisces
12th	6:19 pm	Aries
15th	7:18 am	Taurus
17th	7:13 pm	Gemini
20th	3:46 am	Cancer
22nd	8:01 am	Leo
24th	9:03 am	Virgo
26th	8:47 am	Libra
28th	9:14 am	Scorpio

March 1967		
2nd	11:58 am	Sagittarius
4th	5:38 pm	Capricorn
7th	2:04 am	Aquarius
9th	12:44 pm	Pisces
12th	0:53 am	Aries
14th	1:54 pm	Taurus
17th	2:18 am	Gemini
19th	12:06 pm	Cancer
21st	6:01 pm	Leo
23rd	8:06 pm	Virgo
25th	7:49 pm	Libra
27th	7:13 pm	Scorpio
29th	8:11 pm	Sagittarius

April 1967		
1st	0:11 am	Capricorn
3rd	7:52 am	Aquarius
5th	6:30 pm	Pisces
8th	6:56 am	Aries
10th	7:54 pm	Taurus
13th	8:12 am	Gemini
15th	6:33 pm	Cancer
18th	1:53 am	Leo
20th	5:39 am	Virgo
22nd	6:39 am	Libra
24th	6:20 am	Scorpio
26th	6:31 am	Sagittarius
28th	8:59 am	Capricorn
30th	3:02 pm	Aquarius

May 1967
3rd   0:48 am Pisces
5th   1:10 pm Aries
8th   2:09 am Taurus
10th 2:03 pm Gemini
13th 0:09 am Cancer
15th 7:46 am Leo
17th 12:48 pm Virgo
19th 3:27 pm Libra
21st 4:29 pm Scorpio
23rd 5:08 pm Sagittarius
25th 7:01 pm Capricorn
27th 11:46 pm Aquarius
30th 8:22 am Pisces

June 1967
1st   8:08 pm Aries
4th   9:03 am Taurus
6th   8:49 pm Gemini
9th   6:14 am Cancer
11th 1:16 pm Leo
13th 6:21 pm Virgo
15th 9:57 pm Libra
18th 0:25 am Scorpio
20th 2:20 am Sagittarius
22nd 4:48 am Capricorn
24th 9:15 am Aquarius
26th 4:53 pm Pisces
29th 3:54 am Aries

July 1967
1st   4:42 pm Taurus
4th   4:36 am Gemini
6th   1:42 pm Cancer
8th   7:56 pm Leo
11th 0:07 am Virgo
13th 3:19 am Libra
15th 6:17 am Scorpio
17th 9:23 am Sagittarius
19th 12:50 pm Capricorn
21st 6:01 pm Aquarius
24th 1:28 am Pisces
26th 12:02 pm Aries
29th 0:41 am Taurus
31st 12:56 pm Gemini

August 1967
2nd   10:30 pm Cancer
5th   4:23 am Leo
7th   7:34 am Virgo
9th   9:34 am Libra
11th 11:45 am Scorpio
13th 2:54 pm Sagittarius
15th 7:19 pm Capricorn
18th 1:17 am Aquarius
20th 9:20 am Pisces
22nd 7:48 pm Aries
25th 8:21 am Taurus
27th 9:07 pm Gemini
30th 7:30 am Cancer

September 1967
1st   2:02 pm Leo
3rd   5:04 pm Virgo
5th   6:02 pm Libra
7th   6:45 pm Scorpio
9th   8:41 pm Sagittarius
12th 0:43 am Capricorn
14th 7:10 am Aquarius
16th 3:55 pm Pisces
19th 2:46 am Aries
21st 3:19 pm Taurus
24th 4:19 am Gemini
26th 3:42 pm Cancer
28th 11:42 pm Leo

October 1967
1st• 3:37 am Virgo
3rd   4:34 am Libra
5th   4:15 am Scorpio
7th   4:34 am Sagittarius
9th   7:08 am Capricorn
11th 12:49 pm Aquarius
13th 9:39 pm Pisces
16th 8:58 am Aries
18th 9:40 pm Taurus
21st 10:36 am Gemini
23rd 10:27 pm Cancer
26th 7:36 am Leo
28th 1:14 pm Virgo
30th 3:27 pm Libra

November 1967
1st   3:26 pm Scorpio
3rd   2:54 pm Sagittarius
5th   3:50 pm Capricorn
7th   7:49 pm Aquarius
10th 3:45 am Pisces
12th 3:01 pm Aries
15th 3:52 am Taurus
17th 4:39 pm Gemini
20th 4:11 am Cancer
22nd 1:43 pm Leo
24th 8:44 pm Virgo
27th 0:48 am Libra
29th 2:13 am Scorpio

December 1967
1st   2:11 am Sagittarius
3rd   2:27 am Capricorn
5th   5:03 am Aquarius
7th   11:26 am Pisces
9th   9:45 pm Aries
12th 10:32 am Taurus
14th 11:18 pm Gemini
17th 10:20 am Cancer
19th 7:19 pm Leo
22nd 2:20 am Virgo
24th 7:24 am Libra
26th 10:34 am Scorpio
28th 12:08 pm Sagittarius
30th 1:14 pm Capricorn

January 1968
1st   3:29 pm Aquarius
3rd   8:40 pm Pisces
6th   5:50 am Aries
8th   6:05 pm Taurus
11th 6:54 am Gemini
13th 5:51 pm Cancer
16th 2:09 am Leo
18th 8:10 am Virgo
20th 12:46 pm Libra
22nd 4:27 pm Scorpio
24th 7:25 pm Sagittarius
26th 9:57 pm Capricorn
29th 1:08 am Aquarius
31st 6:21 am Pisces

February 1968
2nd   2:44 pm Aries
5th   2:16 am Taurus
7th   3:08 pm Gemini
10th 2:33 am Cancer
12th 10:47 am Leo
14th 4:01 pm Virgo
16th 7:22 pm Libra
18th 10:00 pm Scorpio
21st 0:49 am Sagittarius
23rd 4:13 am Capricorn
25th 8:40 am Aquarius
27th 2:46 pm Pisces
29th 11:16 pm Aries

March 1968
3rd   10:29 am Taurus
5th   11:17 pm Gemini
8th   11:18 am Cancer
10th 8:26 pm Leo
13th 1:51 am Virgo
15th 4:23 am Libra
17th 5:34 am Scorpio
19th 6:57 am Sagittarius
21st 9:39 am Capricorn
23rd 2:20 pm Aquarius
25th 9:16 pm Pisces
28th 6:34 am Aries
30th 5:55 pm Taurus

April 1968
2nd   6:41 am Gemini
4th   7:12 pm Cancer
7th   5:25 am Leo
9th   12:00 pm Virgo
11th 2:58 pm Libra
13th 3:32 pm Scorpio
15th 3:26 pm Sagittarius
17th 4:28 pm Capricorn
19th 7:50 pm Aquarius
22nd 2:47 am Pisces
24th 12:34 pm Aries
27th 0:22 am Taurus
29th 1:10 pm Gemini

May 1968
2nd   1:50 am Cancer
4th   12:50 pm Leo
6th   8:57 pm Virgo
9th   1:20 am Libra
11th 2:29 am Scorpio
13th 1:54 am Sagittarius
15th 1:33 am Capricorn
17th 3:27 am Aquarius
19th 8:59 am Pisces
21st 6:18 pm Aries
24th 6:17 am Taurus
26th 7:12 pm Gemini
29th 7:41 am Cancer
31st 6:52 pm Leo

June 1968
3rd   3:50 am Virgo
5th   9:44 am Libra
7th   12:25 pm Scorpio
9th   12:40 pm Sagittarius
11th 12:09 pm Capricorn
13th 12:53 pm Aquarius
15th 4:49 pm Pisces
18th 0:51 am Aries
20th 12:27 pm Taurus
23rd 1:23 am Gemini
25th 1:41 pm Cancer
28th 0:31 am Leo
30th 9:22 am Virgo

July 1968
2nd   4:06 pm Libra
4th   8:18 pm Scorpio
6th   10:04 pm Sagittarius
8th   10:24 pm Capricorn
10th 11:04 pm Aquarius
13th 2:05 am Pisces
15th 8:57 am Aries
17th 7:33 pm Taurus
20th 8:13 am Gemini
22nd 8:31 pm Cancer
25th 6:53 am Leo
27th 3:07 pm Virgo
29th 9:31 pm Libra

August 1968
1st   2:10 am Scorpio
3rd   5:09 am Sagittarius
5th   6:57 am Capricorn
7th   8:39 am Aquarius
9th   11:50 am Pisces
11th 5:57 pm Aries
14th 3:37 am Taurus
16th 3:52 pm Gemini
19th 4:13 am Cancer
21st 2:36 pm Leo
23rd 10:19 pm Virgo
26th 3:43 am Libra
28th 7:37 am Scorpio
30th 10:40 am Sagittarius

September 1968
1st   1:22 pm Capricorn
3rd   4:30 pm Aquarius
5th   8:29 pm Pisces
8th   2:51 am Aries
10th 12:08 pm Taurus
12th 11:54 pm Gemini
15th 12:27 pm Cancer
17th 11:25 pm Leo
20th 7:11 am Virgo
22nd 11:57 am Libra
24th 2:37 pm Scorpio
26th 4:31 pm Sagittarius
28th 6:46 pm Capricorn
30th 10:11 pm Aquarius

October 1968
3rd   3:22 am Pisces
5th   10:37 am Aries
7th   8:07 pm Taurus
10th 7:44 am Gemini
12th 8:24 pm Cancer
15th 8:05 am Leo
17th 4:54 pm Virgo
19th 10:04 pm Libra
22nd 0:06 am Scorpio
24th 0:32 am Sagittarius
26th 1:15 am Capricorn
28th 3:45 am Aquarius
30th 8:58 am Pisces

November 1968
1st   4:53 pm Aries
4th   3:02 am Taurus
6th   2:48 pm Gemini
9th   3:26 am Cancer
11th 3:43 pm Leo
14th 1:53 am Virgo
16th 8:21 am Libra
18th 11:01 am Scorpio
20th 11:03 am Sagittarius
22nd 10:24 am Capricorn
24th 11:08 am Aquarius
26th 2:58 pm Pisces
28th 10:27 pm Aries

December 1968
1st   9:00 am Taurus
3rd   9:05 pm Gemini
6th   9:42 am Cancer
8th   10:02 pm Leo
11th 8:54 am Virgo
13th 5:04 pm Libra
15th 9:30 pm Scorpio
17th 10:27 pm Sagittarius
19th 9:33 pm Capricorn
21st 9:03 pm Aquarius
23rd 11:02 pm Pisces
26th 5:08 am Aries
28th 3:01 pm Taurus
31st 3:12 am Gemini

January 1969		February 1969		March 1969		April 1969	
2nd	3:52 pm Cancer	1st	10:28 am Leo	3rd	4:06 am Virgo	1st	8:02 pm Libra
5th	3:53 am Leo	3rd	8:41 pm Virgo	5th	11:32 am Libra	4th	0:24 am Scorpio
7th	2:39 pm Virgo	6th	4:59 am Libra	7th	4:55 pm Scorpio	6th	2:59 am Sagittarius
9th	11:32 pm Libra	8th	11:16 am Scorpio	9th	8:48 pm Sagittarius	8th	5:05 am Capricorn
12th	5:29 am Scorpio	10th	3:20 pm Sagittarius	11th	11:41 pm Capricorn	10th	7:49 am Aquarius
14th	8:15 am Sagittarius	12th	5:27 pm Capricorn	14th	2:10 am Aquarius	12th	11:44 am Pisces
16th	8:38 am Capricorn	14th	6:32 pm Aquarius	16th	5:07 am Pisces	14th	5:15 pm Aries
18th	8:20 am Aquarius	16th	8:05 pm Pisces	18th	9:32 am Aries	17th	0:44 am Taurus
20th	9:27 am Pisces	18th	11:49 pm Aries	20th	4:24 pm Taurus	19th	10:31 am Gemini
22nd	1:50 pm Aries	21st	7:06 am Taurus	23rd	2:13 am Gemini	21st	10:17 pm Cancer
24th	10:16 pm Taurus	23rd	5:44 pm Gemini	25th	2:18 pm Cancer	24th	10:50 am Leo
27th	9:56 am Gemini	26th	6:12 am Cancer	28th	2:36 am Leo	26th	9:56 pm Virgo
29th	10:37 pm Cancer	28th	6:12 pm Leo	30th	12:51 pm Virgo	29th	5:42 am Libra

May 1969		June 1969		July 1969		August 1969	
1st	9:46 am Scorpio	1st	9:08 pm Capricorn	1st	6:53 am Aquarius	1st	7:58 am Aries
3rd	11:18 am Sagittarius	3rd	9:07 pm Aquarius	3rd	7:33 am Pisces	4th	2:05 am Taurus
5th	11:60 am Capricorn	5th	11:16 pm Pisces	5th	11:23 am Aries	6th	11:53 am Gemini
7th	1:32 pm Aquarius	8th	4:41 am Aries	7th	6:58 pm Taurus	8th	11:58 pm Cancer
9th	5:08 pm Pisces	10th	1:10 pm Taurus	10th	5:33 am Gemini	11th	12:38 pm Leo
11th	11:09 pm Aries	12th	11:48 pm Gemini	12th	5:48 pm Cancer	14th	0:33 am Virgo
14th	7:30 am Taurus	15th	11:54 am Cancer	15th	6:29 am Leo	16th	10:48 am Libra
16th	5:43 pm Gemini	18th	0:34 am Leo	17th	6:41 pm Virgo	18th	6:52 pm Scorpio
19th	5:31 am Cancer	20th	12:51 pm Virgo	20th	5:16 am Libra	21st	0:12 am Sagittarius
21st	6:12 pm Leo	22nd	11:03 pm Libra	22nd	12:58 pm Scorpio	23rd	2:47 am Capricorn
24th	6:04 am Virgo	25th	5:27 am Scorpio	24th	5:05 pm Sagittarius	25th	3:36 am Aquarius
26th	3:02 pm Libra	27th	7:55 am Sagittarius	26th	6:06 pm Capricorn	27th	4:04 am Pisces
28th	8:03 pm Scorpio	29th	7:44 am Capricorn	28th	5:35 pm Aquarius	29th	6:01 am Aries
30th	9:29 pm Sagittarius			30th	5:34 pm Pisces	31st	10:55 am Taurus

September 1969		October 1969		November 1969		December 1969	
2nd	7:26 am Gemini	2nd	2:55 pm Cancer	1st	11:35 am Leo	1st	8:11 am Virgo
5th	6:57 am Cancer	5th	3:24 am Leo	3rd	12:00 pm Virgo	3rd	7:13 pm Libra
7th	7:35 pm Leo	7th	3:19 pm Virgo	6th	9:54 am Libra	6th	2:28 am Scorpio
10th	7:18 am Virgo	10th	0:48 am Libra	8th	4:13 pm Scorpio	8th	5:40 am Sagittarius
12th	4:50 pm Libra	12th	7:16 am Scorpio	10th	7:28 pm Sagittarius	10th	6:21 am Capricorn
15th	0:25 am Scorpio	14th	11:32 am Sagittarius	12th	9:09 pm Capricorn	12th	6:30 am Aquarius
17th	5:40 am Sagittarius	16th	2:35 pm Capricorn	14th	10:53 pm Aquarius	14th	8:00 am Pisces
19th	9:12 am Capricorn	18th	5:22 pm Aquarius	17th	1:53 am Pisces	16th	12:01 pm Aries
21st	11:30 am Aquarius	20th	8:26 pm Pisces	19th	6:34 am Aries	18th	6:38 pm Taurus
23rd	1:23 pm Pisces	23rd	0:18 am Aries	21st	12:54 pm Taurus	21st	3:29 am Gemini
25th	3:57 pm Aries	25th	5:34 am Taurus	23rd	9:00 pm Gemini	23rd	2:11 pm Cancer
27th	8:30 pm Taurus	27th	1:03 pm Gemini	26th	7:12 am Cancer	26th	2:22 am Leo
30th	4:08 am Gemini	29th	11:13 pm Cancer	28th	7:23 pm Leo	28th	3:19 pm Virgo
						31st	3:16 am Libra

January 1970		February 1970		March 1970		April 1970	
2nd	11:56 am Scorpio	1st	1:48 am Sagittarius	2nd	12:50 pm Capricorn	3rd	0:02 am Pisces
4th	4:28 pm Sagittarius	3rd	4:19 am Capricorn	4th	2:32 pm Aquarius	5th	1:33 am Aries
6th	5:27 pm Capricorn	5th	4:18 am Aquarius	6th	2:49 pm Pisces	7th	4:04 am Taurus
8th	4:49 pm Aquarius	7th	3:39 am Pisces	8th	3:20 pm Aries	9th	9:07 am Gemini
10th	4:42 pm Pisces	9th	4:21 am Aries	10th	5:48 pm Taurus	11th	5:37 pm Cancer
12th	6:52 pm Aries	11th	8:05 am Taurus	12th	11:38 pm Gemini	14th	5:16 am Leo
15th	0:22 am Taurus	13th	3:34 pm Gemini	15th	9:23 am Cancer	16th	6:08 pm Virgo
17th	9:11 am Gemini	16th	2:19 am Cancer	17th	9:40 pm Leo	19th	5:33 am Libra
19th	8:15 pm Cancer	18th	2:56 pm Leo	20th	10:29 am Virgo	21st	2:13 pm Scorpio
22nd	8:41 am Leo	21st	3:43 am Virgo	22nd	9:57 pm Libra	23rd	8:15 pm Sagittarius
24th	9:32 am Virgo	23rd	3:28 pm Libra	25th	7:08 am Scorpio	26th	0:27 am Capricorn
27th	9:40 am Libra	26th	1:22 am Scorpio	27th	2:05 pm Sagittarius	28th	3:43 am Aquarius
29th	7:32 pm Scorpio	28th	8:35 am Sagittarius	29th	6:59 pm Capricorn	30th	6:38 am Pisces
				31st	10:08 pm Aquarius		

May 1970		June 1970		July 1970		August 1970	
2nd	9:34 am Aries	3rd	2:11 am Gemini	2nd	5:25 pm Cancer	1st	10:48 am Leo
4th	1:08 pm Taurus	5th	10:30 am Cancer	5th	4:27 am Leo	3rd	11:36 pm Virgo
6th	6:21 pm Gemini	7th	9:19 pm Leo	7th	5:11 pm Virgo	6th	12:30 pm Libra
9th	2:20 am Cancer	10th	10:02 am Virgo	10th	6:01 am Libra	8th	11:56 pm Scorpio
11th	1:25 pm Leo	12th	10:28 pm Libra	12th	4:36 pm Scorpio	11th	8:02 am Sagittarius
14th	2:11 am Virgo	15th	7:58 am Scorpio	14th	11:24 pm Sagittarius	13th	12:19 pm Capricorn
16th	2:00 pm Libra	17th	1:35 pm Sagittarius	17th	2:19 am Capricorn	15th	1:28 pm Aquarius
18th	10:49 pm Scorpio	19th	4:03 pm Capricorn	19th	2:45 am Aquarius	17th	1:02 pm Pisces
21st	4:10 am Sagittarius	21st	5:02 pm Aquarius	21st	2:39 am Pisces	19th	12:54 pm Aries
23rd	7:13 am Capricorn	23rd	6:14 pm Pisces	23rd	3:46 am Aries	21st	2:51 pm Taurus
25th	9:28 am Aquarius	25th	8:55 pm Aries	25th	7:24 am Taurus	23rd	8:07 pm Gemini
27th	12:02 pm Pisces	28th	1:37 am Taurus	27th	1:58 pm Gemini	26th	5:00 am Cancer
29th	3:29 pm Aries	30th	8:28 am Gemini	29th	11:15 pm Cancer	28th	4:40 pm Leo
31st	8:05 pm Taurus					31st	5:38 am Virgo

September 1970
2nd   6:25 pm Libra
5th   5:53 am Scorpio
7th   2:54 pm Sagittarius
9th   8:48 pm Capricorn
11th 11:33 pm Aquarius
13th 11:57 pm Pisces
15th 11:35 pm Aries
18th 0:20 am Taurus
20th 4:06 am Gemini
22nd 11:46 am Cancer
24th 10:54 am Leo
27th 11:54 am Virgo
30th 0:34 am Libra

October 1970
2nd   11:34 am Scorpio
4th   8:31 pm Sagittarius
7th   3:09 am Capricorn
9th   7:23 am Aquarius
11th 9:28 am Pisces
13th 10:12 am Aries
15th 11:02 am Taurus
17th 1:48 pm Gemini
19th 8:02 pm Cancer
22nd 6:15 am Leo
24th 6:57 pm Virgo
27th 7:35 am Libra
29th 6:12 pm Scorpio

November 1970
1st   2:24 am Sagittarius
3rd   8:31 am Capricorn
5th   1:08 pm Aquarius
7th   4:31 pm Pisces
9th   6:51 pm Aries
11th 8:50 pm Taurus
13th 11:48 pm Gemini
16th 5:26 am Cancer
18th 2:39 pm Leo
21st 2:51 am Virgo
23rd 3:38 pm Libra
26th 2:23 am Scorpio
28th 9:58 am Sagittarius
30th 3:04 pm Capricorn

December 1970
2nd   6:43 pm Aquarius
4th   9:56 pm Pisces
7th   1:03 am Aries
9th   4:26 am Taurus
11th 8:36 am Gemini
13th 2:36 pm Cancer
15th 11:21 pm Leo
18th 11:06 am Virgo
21st 0:02 am Libra
23rd 11:22 am Scorpio
25th 7:23 pm Sagittarius
28th 0:02 am Capricorn
30th 2:24 am Aquarius

January 1971
1st   4:08 am Pisces
3rd   6:29 am Aries
5th   10:04 am Taurus
7th   3:11 pm Gemini
9th   10:11 pm Cancer
12th 7:27 am Leo
14th 6:58 pm Virgo
17th 7:51 am Libra
19th 8:01 pm Scorpio
22nd 5:10 am Sagittarius
24th 10:27 am Capricorn
26th 12:33 pm Aquarius
28th 1:02 pm Pisces
30th 1:39 pm Aries

February 1971
1st   3:54 pm Taurus
3rd   8:38 pm Gemini
6th   4:10 am Cancer
8th   2:10 pm Leo
11th 1:59 am Virgo
13th 2:51 pm Libra
16th 3:20 am Scorpio
18th 1:40 pm Sagittarius
20th 8:33 pm Capricorn
22nd 11:43 pm Aquarius
25th 0:05 am Pisces
26th 11:30 pm Aries
28th 11:55 pm Taurus

March 1971
3rd   3:05 am Gemini
5th   9:52 am Cancer
7th   7:48 pm Leo
10th 8:13 am Virgo
12th 9:07 pm Libra
15th 9:30 am Scorpio
17th 8:23 pm Sagittarius
20th 4:34 am Capricorn
22nd 9:24 am Aquarius
24th 11:04 am Pisces
26th 10:45 am Aries
28th 10:19 am Taurus
30th 11:50 am Gemini

April 1971
1st   4:56 pm Cancer
4th   2:07 am Leo
6th   2:19 pm Virgo
9th   3:18 am Libra
11th 3:28 pm Scorpio
14th 2:04 am Sagittarius
16th 10:35 am Capricorn
18th 4:44 pm Aquarius
20th 8:06 pm Pisces
22nd 9:09 pm Aries
24th 9:07 pm Taurus
26th 10:01 pm Gemini
29th 1:45 am Cancer

May 1971
1st   9:40 am Leo
3rd   9:05 pm Virgo
6th   9:59 am Libra
8th   10:05 pm Scorpio
11th 8:07 am Sagittarius
13th 4:09 pm Capricorn
15th 10:20 pm Aquarius
18th 2:40 am Pisces
20th 5:11 am Aries
22nd 6:32 am Taurus
24th 8:05 am Gemini
26th 11:33 am Cancer
28th 6:20 pm Leo
31st 4:51 am Virgo

June 1971
2nd   5:27 pm Libra
5th   5:35 am Scorpio
7th   3:26 pm Sagittarius
9th   10:45 pm Capricorn
12th 4:03 am Aquarius
14th 8:02 am Pisces
16th 11:06 am Aries
18th 1:40 pm Taurus
20th 4:27 am Gemini
22nd 8:34 pm Cancer
25th 3:15 am Leo
27th 1:10 pm Virgo
30th 1:23 am Libra

July 1971
2nd   1:43 pm Scorpio
4th   11:60 pm Sagittarius
7th   7:01 am Capricorn
9th   11:25 am Aquarius
11th 2:15 pm Pisces
13th 4:35 pm Aries
15th 7:13 pm Taurus
17th 10:49 pm Gemini
20th 3:50 am Cancer
22nd 11:21 am Leo
24th 9:12 pm Virgo
27th 9:13 am Libra
29th 9:49 pm Scorpio

August 1971
1st   8:45 am Sagittarius
3rd   4:28 pm Capricorn
5th   8:45 pm Aquarius
7th   10:35 pm Pisces
9th   11:27 pm Aries
12th 0:57 am Taurus
14th 4:15 am Gemini
16th 9:54 am Cancer
18th 6:02 pm Leo
21st 4:22 am Virgo
23rd 4:24 pm Libra
26th 5:09 am Scorpio
28th 4:54 pm Sagittarius
31st 1:52 am Capricorn

September 1971
2nd   6:59 am Aquarius
4th   8:48 am Pisces
6th   8:44 am Aries
8th   8:41 am Taurus
10th 10:31 am Gemini
12th 3:26 pm Cancer
14th 11:39 pm Leo
17th 10:32 am Virgo
19th 10:49 pm Libra
22nd 11:34 am Scorpio
24th 11:44 pm Sagittarius
27th 9:49 am Capricorn
29th 4:34 pm Aquarius

October 1971
1st   7:33 pm Pisces
3rd   7:39 pm Aries
5th   6:44 pm Taurus
7th   6:56 pm Gemini
9th   10:12 pm Cancer
12th 5:34 am Leo
14th 4:18 pm Virgo
17th 4:48 am Libra
19th 5:31 pm Scorpio
22nd 5:32 am Sagittarius
24th 4:03 pm Capricorn
27th 0:11 am Aquarius
29th 4:53 am Pisces
31st 6:24 am Aries

November 1971
2nd   5:56 am Taurus
4th   5:31 am Gemini
6th   7:20 am Cancer
8th   1:02 pm Leo
10th 10:45 pm Virgo
13th 11:05 am Libra
15th 11:50 pm Scorpio
18th 11:28 am Sagittarius
20th 9:36 pm Capricorn
23rd 5:50 am Aquarius
25th 11:44 am Pisces
27th 2:50 pm Aries
29th 4:06 pm Taurus

December 1971
1st   4:26 pm Gemini
3rd   5:55 pm Cancer
5th   10:18 pm Leo
8th   6:44 am Virgo
10th 6:21 pm Libra
13th 7:00 am Scorpio
15th 6:35 pm Sagittarius
18th 4:05 am Capricorn
20th 11:30 am Aquarius
22nd 5:09 pm Pisces
24th 9:08 pm Aries
26th 11:45 pm Taurus
29th 1:38 am Gemini
31st 4:03 am Cancer

January 1972
2nd   8:26 am Leo
4th   3:54 pm Virgo
7th   2:34 am Libra
9th   3:03 pm Scorpio
12th 2:55 am Sagittarius
14th 12:51 pm Capricorn
16th 7:01 pm Aquarius
18th 11:27 pm Pisces
21st 2:36 am Aries
23rd 5:18 am Taurus
25th 8:16 am Gemini
27th 12:05 pm Cancer
29th 5:25 pm Leo

February 1972
1st   0:56 am Virgo
3rd   11:09 am Libra
5th   11:18 pm Scorpio
8th   11:33 am Sagittarius
10th 9:48 pm Capricorn
13th 4:33 am Aquarius
15th 8:07 am Pisces
17th 9:51 am Aries
19th 11:14 am Taurus
21st 1:39 pm Gemini
23rd 5:56 pm Cancer
26th 0:17 am Leo
28th 8:43 am Virgo

March 1972
1st   7:03 pm Libra
4th   7:02 am Scorpio
6th   7:36 pm Sagittarius
9th   6:46 am Capricorn
11th 2:37 pm Aquarius
13th 6:36 pm Pisces
15th 7:35 pm Aries
17th 7:29 pm Taurus
19th 8:15 pm Gemini
21st 11:27 pm Cancer
24th 5:50 am Leo
26th 2:51 pm Virgo
29th 1:44 am Libra
31st 1:51 pm Scorpio

April 1972
3rd   2:29 am Sagittarius
5th   2:18 pm Capricorn
7th   11:37 pm Aquarius
10th 4:54 am Pisces
12th 6:30 am Aries
14th 5:55 am Taurus
16th 5:20 am Gemini
18th 6:50 am Cancer
20th 11:53 am Leo
22nd 8:26 pm Virgo
25th 7:36 am Libra
27th 7:58 pm Scorpio
30th 8:32 am Sagittarius

May 1972
2nd 8:29 pm Capricorn
5th 6:32 am Aquarius
7th 1:23 pm Pisces
9th 4:31 pm Aries
11th 4:46 pm Taurus
13th 3:59 pm Gemini
15th 4:21 pm Cancer
17th 7:42 pm Leo
20th 2:59 am Virgo
22nd 1:40 pm Libra
25th 2:01 am Scorpio
27th 2:34 pm Sagittarius
30th 2:13 am Capricorn

June 1972
1st 12:13 pm Aquarius
3rd 7:51 pm Pisces
6th 0:29 am Aries
8th 2:14 am Taurus
10th 2:26 am Gemini
12th 2:48 am Cancer
14th 5:15 am Leo
16th .11:09 am Virgo
18th 8:40 pm Libra
21st 8:44 am Scorpio
23rd 9:15 pm Sagittarius
26th 8:35 am Capricorn
28th 6:01 pm Aquarius

July 1972
1st 1:19 am Pisces
3rd 6:21 am Aries
5th 9:24 am Taurus
7th 11:06 am Gemini
9th 12:33 pm Cancer
11th 3:11 pm Leo
13th 8:19 pm Virgo
16th 4:53 am Libra
18th 4:16 pm Scorpio
21st 4:46 am Sagittarius
23rd 4:08 pm Capricorn
26th 1:08 am Aquarius
28th 7:28 am Pisces
30th 11:51 am Aries

August 1972
1st 2:59 pm Taurus
3rd 5:36 pm Gemini
5th 8:21 pm Cancer
7th 11:58 pm Leo
10th 5:27 am Virgo
12th 1:32 pm Libra
15th 0:20 am Scorpio
17th 12:48 pm Sagittarius
20th 0:39 am Capricorn
22nd 9:38 am Aquarius
24th 3:26 pm Pisces
26th 6:40 pm Aries
28th 8:45 pm Taurus
30th 10:58 pm Gemini

September 1972
2nd 2:14 am Cancer
4th 6:57 am Leo
6th 1:19 pm Virgo
8th 9:39 pm Libra
11th 8:19 am Scorpio
13th 8:44 pm Sagittarius
16th 9:05 am Capricorn
18th 7:02 pm Aquarius
21st 1:09 am Pisces
23rd 3:44 am Aries
25th 4:28 am Taurus
27th 5:17 am Gemini
29th 7:42 am Cancer

October 1972
1st 12:30 pm Leo
3rd 7:34 pm Virgo
6th 4:38 am Libra
8th 3:31 pm Scorpio
11th 3:54 am Sagittarius
13th 4:44 pm Capricorn
16th 3:49 am Aquarius
18th 11:07 am Pisces
20th 2:18 pm Aries
22nd 2:36 pm Taurus
24th 2:06 pm Gemini
26th 2:49 pm Cancer
28th 6:17 pm Leo
31st 1:01 am Virgo

November 1972
2nd 10:29 am Libra
4th 9:48 pm Scorpio
7th 10:19 am Sagittarius
9th 11:11 pm Capricorn
12th 11:00 am Aquarius
14th 7:54 pm Pisces
17th 0:43 am Aries
19th 1:52 am Taurus
21st 1:06 am Gemini
23rd 0:33 am Cancer
25th 2:14 am Leo
27th 7:29 am Virgo
29th 4:19 pm Libra

December 1972
2nd 3:44 am Scorpio
4th 4:24 pm Sagittarius
7th 5:06 am Capricorn
9th 4:53 pm Aquarius
12th 2:32 am Pisces
14th 8:55 am Aries
16th 11:54 am Taurus
18th 12:65 pm Gemini
20th 11:59 am Cancer
22nd 12:40 pm Leo
24th 4:08 pm Virgo
26th 11:22 pm Libra
29th 10:13 am Scorpio
31st 10:51 pm Sagittarius

January 1973
3rd 11:29 am Capricorn
5th 10:48 am Aquarius
8th 8:01 am Pisces
10th 2:55 am Aries
12th 7:23 am Taurus
14th 9:41 am Gemini
16th 10:39 am Cancer
18th 11:40 am Leo
21st 2:26 am Virgo
23rd 8:21 am Libra
25th 5:55 am Scorpio
28th 6:10 am Sagittarius
30th 6:52 am Capricorn

February 1973
2nd 5:52 am Aquarius
4th 2:19 pm Pisces
6th 8:28 pm Aries
9th 0:53 am Taurus
11th 4:10 am Gemini
13th 6:45 am Cancer
15th 9:14 am Leo
17th 12:35 pm Virgo
19th 6:02 pm Libra
22nd 2:37 am Scorpio
24th 2:14 pm Sagittarius
27th 3:03 am Capricorn

March 1973
1st 2:18 am Aquarius
3rd 10:30 pm Pisces
6th 3:35 am Aries
8th 6:51 am Taurus
10th 9:32 am Gemini
12th 12:31 pm Cancer
14th 4:09 pm Leo
16th 8:44 pm Virgo
19th 2:50 am Libra
21st 11:19 am Scorpio
23rd 10:26 pm Sagittarius
26th 11:15 am Capricorn
28th 11:13 am Aquarius
31st 7:50 am Pisces

April 1973
2nd 12:43 am Aries
4th 2:56 pm Taurus
6th 4:12 pm Gemini
8th 6:06 pm Cancer
10th 9:33 pm Leo
13th 2:47 am Virgo
15th 9:53 am Libra
17th 6:53 pm Scorpio
20th 6:04 am Sagittarius
22nd 6:50 pm Capricorn
25th 7:19 am Aquarius
27th 5:06 pm Pisces
29th 10:52 pm Aries

May 1973
2nd 1:01 am Taurus
4th 1:15 am Gemini
6th 1:35 am Cancer
8th 3:39 am Leo
10th 8:16 am Virgo
12th 3:34 pm Libra
15th 1:11 am Scorpio
17th 12:44 pm Sagittarius
20th 1:30 am Capricorn
22nd 2:16 pm Aquarius
25th 1:06 am Pisces
27th 8:09 am Aries
29th 11:24 am Taurus
31st 11:51 am Gemini

June 1973
2nd 11:23 am Cancer
4th 11:53 am Leo
6th 2:57 pm Virgo
8th 9:19 pm Libra
11th 6:54 am Scorpio
13th 6:45 pm Sagittarius
16th 7:37 am Capricorn
18th 8:19 pm Aquarius
21st 7:26 am Pisces
23rd 3:45 pm Aries
25th 8:35 pm Taurus
27th 10:17 pm Gemini
29th 10:09 pm Cancer

July 1973
1st 9:57 pm Leo
3rd 11:32 pm Virgo
6th 4:27 am Libra
8th 1:10 pm Scorpio
11th 0:49 am Sagittarius
13th 1:47 pm Capricorn
16th 2:15 am Aquarius
18th 1:06 pm Pisces
20th 9:44 pm Aries
23rd 3:39 am Taurus
25th 6:57 am Gemini
27th 8:11 am Cancer
29th 8:32 am Leo
31st 9:40 am Virgo

August 1973
2nd 1:19 pm Libra
4th 8:39 pm Scorpio
7th 7:39 am Sagittarius
9th 8:31 pm Capricorn
12th 8:51 am Aquarius
14th 7:13 pm Pisces
17th 3:17 am Aries
19th 9:13 am Taurus
21st 1:26 pm Gemini
23rd 4:08 pm Cancer
25th 5:51 pm Leo
27th 7:36 pm Virgo
29th 10:54 pm Libra

September 1973
1st 5:22 am Scorpio
3rd 3:28 pm Sagittarius
6th 4:02 am Capricorn
8th 4:28 pm Aquarius
11th 2:39 am Pisces
13th 9:53 am Aries
15th 2:59 pm Taurus
17th 6:49 pm Gemini
19th 10:02 pm Cancer
22nd 0:58 am Leo
24th 4:01 am Virgo
26th 8:05 am Libra
28th 2:25 pm Scorpio
30th 11:48 pm Sagittarius

October 1973
3rd 12:04 pm Capricorn
6th 0:50 am Aquarius
8th 11:19 am Pisces
10th 6:26 pm Aries
12th 10:36 pm Taurus
15th 1:09 am Gemini
17th 3:29 am Cancer
19th 6:26 am Leo
21st 10:21 am Virgo
23rd 3:32 pm Libra
25th 10:31 pm Scorpio
28th 8:02 am Sagittarius
30th 7:5? pm Capricorn

November 1973
2nd 8:59 am Aquarius
4th 8:26 pm Pisces
7th 4:18 am Aries
9th 8:22 am Taurus
11th 9:59 am Gemini
13th 10:48 am Cancer
15th 12:23 pm Leo
17th 3:45 pm Virgo
19th 9:17 pm Libra
22nd 5:09 am Scorpio
24th 3:15 pm Sagittarius
27th 3:15 am Capricorn
29th 4:18 pm Aquarius

December 1973
2nd 4:32 am Pisces
4th 1:46 pm Aries
6th 7:06 pm Taurus
8th 8:57 pm Gemini
10th 8:53 pm Cancer
12th 8:47 pm Leo
14th 10:23 pm Virgo
17th 2:55 am Libra
19th 10:48 am Scorpio
21st 9:22 pm Sagittarius
24th 9:43 am Capricorn
26th 10:45 pm Aquarius
29th 11:08 am Pisces
31st 9:33 pm Aries

January 1974		February 1974		March 1974		April 1974	
3rd	4:35 am Taurus	1st	4:51 pm Gemini	3rd	2:50 am Cancer	1st	11:40 am Leo
5th	7:57 am Gemini	3rd	7:04 pm Cancer	5th	4:49 am Leo	3rd	1:57 pm Virgo
7th	8:26 am Cancer	5th	7:11 pm Leo	7th	5:35 am Virgo	5th	4:25 pm Libra
9th	7:44 am Leo	7th	6:53 pm Virgo	9th	6:56 am Libra	7th	8:28 pm Scorpio
11th	7:47 am Virgo	9th	8:14 pm Libra	11th	10:46 am Scorpio	10th	3:30 am Sagittarius
13th	10:28 am Libra	12th	0:59 am Scorpio	13th	6:24 pm Sagittarius	12th	1:60 pm Capricorn
15th	4:59 pm Scorpio	14th	10:05 am Sagittarius	16th	5:42 am Capricorn	15th	2:34 am Aquarius
18th	3:14 am Sagittarius	16th	10:16 pm Capricorn	18th	6:37 pm Aquarius	17th	2:41 pm Pisces
20th	3:48 pm Capricorn	19th	11:20 am Aquarius	21st	6:30 am Pisces	20th	0:20 am Aries
23rd	4:49 am Aquarius	21st	11:15 pm Pisces	23rd	3:59 pm Aries	22nd	6:50 am Taurus
25th	4:59 pm Pisces	24th	9:11 am Aries	25th	11:09 pm Taurus	24th	11:08 am Gemini
28th	3:31 am Aries	26th	5:10 pm Taurus	28th	4:32 am Gemini	26th	2:17 pm Cancer
30th	11:37 am Taurus	28th	11:10 pm Gemini	30th	8:38 am Cancer	28th	5:04 pm Leo
						30th	7:50 pm Virgo

May 1974		June 1974		July 1974		August 1974	
2nd	11:39 pm Libra	1st	11:13 am Scorpio	1st	1:22 am Sagittarius	2nd	6:47 am Aquarius
5th	4:45 am Scorpio	3rd	7:24 pm Sagittarius	3rd	12:22 pm Capricorn	4th	7:26 pm Pisces
7th	12:09 pm Sagittarius	6th	5:50 am Capricorn	6th	0:41 am Aquarius	7th	7:14 am Aries
9th	10:16 pm Capricorn	8th	6:04 pm Aquarius	8th	1:25 pm Pisces	9th	5:10 pm Taurus
12th	10:36 am Aquarius	11th	6:43 am Pisces	11th	1:10 am Aries	12th	0:16 am Gemini
14th	11:04 pm Pisces	13th	5:50 pm Aries	13th	10:17 am Taurus	14th	3:47 am Cancer
17th	9:15 am Aries	16th	1:45 am Taurus	15th	3:50 pm Gemini	16th	4:26 am Leo
19th	4:07 pm Taurus	18th	5:55 am Gemini	17th	5:53 pm Cancer	18th	3:45 am Virgo
21st	7:52 pm Gemini	20th	7:19 am Cancer	19th	5:43 pm Leo	20th	3:48 am Libra
23rd	9:45 pm Cancer	22nd	7:30 am Leo	21st	5:12 pm Virgo	22nd	6:43 am Scorpio
25th	11:12 pm Leo	24th	8:15 am Virgo	23rd	6:23 pm Libra	24th	1:40 pm Sagittarius
28th	1:26 am Virgo	26th	11:02 am Libra	25th	10:47 pm Scorpio	27th	0:16 am Capricorn
30th	5:17 am Libra	28th	4:43 pm Scorpio	28th	7:03 am Sagittarius	29th	12:53 pm Aquarius
				30th	6:12 pm Capricorn		

September 1974		October 1974		November 1974		December 1974	
1st	1:30 am Pisces	3rd	4:38 am Taurus	1st	6:22 pm Gemini	1st	6:21 am Cancer
3rd	12:56 pm Aries	5th	11:59 am Gemini	3rd	11:01 pm Cancer	3rd	8:32 am Leo
5th	10:51 pm Taurus	7th	5:28 pm Cancer	6th	2:30 am Leo	5th	10:42 am Virgo
8th	6:34 am Gemini	9th	9:02 pm Leo	8th	5:19 am Virgo	7th	1:45 pm Libra
10th	11:37 am Cancer	11th	10:57 pm Virgo	10th	8:01 am Libra	9th	6:16 pm Scorpio
12th	1:52 pm Leo	14th	0:12 am Libra	12th	11:28 am Scorpio	12th	0:35 am Sagittarius
14th	2:13 pm Virgo	16th	2:27 am Scorpio	14th	4:44 pm Sagittarius	14th	9:09 am Capricorn
16th	2:22 pm Libra	18th	7:21 am Sagittarius	17th	0:45 am Capricorn	16th	7:52 pm Aquarius
18th	4:20 pm Scorpio	20th	3:50 pm Capricorn	19th	11:43 am Aquarius	19th	8:14 am Pisces
20th	9:48 pm Sagittarius	23rd	3:22 am Aquarius	22nd	0:14 am Pisces	21st	8:36 pm Aries
23rd	7:26 am Capricorn	25th	3:57 pm Pisces	24th	11:57 am Aries	24th	6:42 am Taurus
25th	7:39 pm Aquarius	28th	3:12 am Aries	26th	9:04 pm Taurus	26th	1:12 pm Gemini
28th	8:13 am Pisces	30th	11:57 am Taurus	29th	2:57 am Gemini	28th	4:13 pm Cancer
30th	7:25 am Aries					30th	5:05 pm Leo

January 1975		February 1975		March 1975		April 1975	
1st	5:35 pm Virgo	2nd	5:58 am Scorpio	1st	2:40 pm Scorpio	2nd	11:13 am Capricorn
3rd	7:25 pm Libra	4th	12:16 pm Sagittarius	3rd	7:10 pm Sagittarius	4th	9:45 pm Aquarius
5th	11:39 pm Scorpio	6th	9:44 pm Capricorn	6th	3:41 am Capricorn	7th	10:16 am Pisces
8th	6:43 am Sagittarius	9th	9:18 am Aquarius	8th	3:11 pm Aquarius	9th	10:44 pm Aries
10th	4:01 pm Capricorn	11th	9:47 pm Pisces	11th	3:49 am Pisces	12th	9:51 am Taurus
13th	3:04 am Aquarius	14th	10:22 am Aries	13th	4:18 pm Aries	14th	7:13 pm Gemini
15th	3:26 pm Pisces	16th	10:09 pm Taurus	16th	3:53 am Taurus	17th	2:27 am Cancer
18th	4:04 am Aries	19th	7:31 am Gemini	18th	1:40 pm Gemini	19th	7:11 am Leo
20th	3:17 pm Taurus	21st	1:14 pm Cancer	20th	8:47 pm Cancer	21st	9:40 am Virgo
22nd	11:23 pm Gemini	23rd	3:09 pm Leo	23rd	0:31 am Leo	23rd	10:41 am Libra
25th	3:20 am Cancer	25th	2:36 pm Virgo	25th	1:21 am Virgo	25th	11:43 am Scorpio
27th	3:50 am Leo	27th	1:43 pm Libra	27th	0:53 am Libra	27th	2:25 pm Sagittarius
29th	3:16 am Virgo			29th	1:10 am Scorpio	29th	8:12 pm Capricorn
31st	3:17 am Libra			31st	4:13 am Sagittarius		

May 1975		June 1975		July 1975		August 1975	
2nd	5:36 am Aquarius	1st	1:33 am Pisces	3rd	9:51 am Taurus	2nd	3:50 am Gemini
4th	5:35 pm Pisces	3rd	2:01 pm Aries	5th	6:55 pm Gemini	4th	10:11 am Cancer
7th	6:01 am Aries	6th	1:19 am Taurus	8th	0:22 am Cancer	6th	12:40 pm Leo
9th	5:00 pm Taurus	8th	3:17 am Gemini	10th	2:49 am Leo	8th	12:53 pm Virgo
12th	1:43 am Gemini	10th	6:43 am Cancer	12th	3:56 am Virgo	10th	12:54 pm Libra
14th	8:05 am Cancer	12th	9:10 pm Leo	14th	5:24 am Libra	12th	2:34 pm Scorpio
16th	12:35 pm Leo	14th	11:40 pm Virgo	16th	8:26 am Scorpio	14th	7:02 pm Sagittarius
18th	3:44 pm Virgo	16th	2:59 pm Libra	18th	1:35 pm Sagittarius	17th	2:26 am Capricorn
20th	6:04 pm Libra	19th	7:37 pm Scorpio	20th	8:46 pm Capricorn	19th	12:11 pm Aquarius
22nd	8:26 pm Scorpio	21st	1:59 am Sagittarius	23rd	5:58 am Aquarius	21st	11:32 pm Pisces
24th	11:51 pm Sagittarius	23rd	10:34 pm Capricorn	25th	4:50 pm Pisces	24th	12:02 am Aries
27th	5:35 am Capricorn	25th	9:35 am Aquarius	28th	5:27 am Aries	27th	0:44 am Taurus
29th	2:14 pm Aquarius	28th	10:03 am Pisces	30th	5:53 pm Taurus	29th	11:49 am Gemini
		30th	pm Aries			31st	7:33 pm Cancer

September 1975		October 1975		November 1975		December 1975	
2nd 11:08 pm	Leo	2nd 10:00 am	Virgo	2nd 8:10 pm	Scorpio	2nd 7:37 am	Sagittarius
4th 11:30 pm	Virgo	4th 9:41 am	Libra	4th 9:13 pm	Sagittarius	4th 11:04 am	Capricorn
6th 10:38 pm	Libra	6th 9:13 am	Scorpio	7th 0:47 am	Capricorn	6th 5:18 pm	Aquarius
8th 10:47 pm	Scorpio	8th 10:42 am	Sagittarius	9th 8:06 am	Aquarius	9th 2:55 am	Pisces
11th 1:41 am	Sagittarius	10th 3:35 pm	Capricorn	11th 6:45 pm	Pisces	11th 3:09 pm	Aries
13th 8:15 am	Capricorn	13th 0:10 am	Aquarius	14th 7:17 am	Aries	14th 3:40 am	Taurus
15th 5:53 pm	Aquarius	15th 11:42 am	Pisces	16th 7:37 pm	Taurus	16th 2:10 pm	Gemini
18th 5:32 am	Pisces	18th 0:20 am	Aries	19th 6:12 am	Gemini	18th 9:49 pm	Cancer
20th 6:08 pm	Aries	20th 12:42 pm	Taurus	21st 2:33 pm	Cancer	21st 2:53 am	Leo
23rd 6:43 am	Taurus	22nd 11:52 pm	Gemini	23rd 8:47 pm	Leo	23rd 6:27 am	Virgo
25th 6:12 pm	Gemini	25th 8:54 am	Cancer	26th 1:05 am	Virgo	25th 9:27 am	Libra
28th 3:05 am	Cancer	27th 3:16 pm	Leo	28th 3:47 am	Libra	27th 12:29 pm	Scorpio
30th 8:16 am	Leo	29th 6:44 pm	Virgo	30th 5:38 am	Scorpio	29th 3:55 pm	Sagittarius
		31st 7:55 pm	Libra			31st 8:19 pm	Capricorn

January 1976		February 1976		March 1976		April 1976	
3rd 2:35 am	Aquarius	1st 7:50 pm	Pisces	2nd 2:24 pm	Aries	1st 9:34 am	Taurus
5th 11:40 am	Pisces	4th 7:20 am	Aries	5th 3:19 am	Taurus	3rd 10:15 pm	Gemini
7th 11:22 pm	Aries	6th 8:14 pm	Taurus	7th 3:55 pm	Gemini	6th 9:04 am	Cancer
10th 12:09 pm	Taurus	9th 8:13 am	Gemini	10th 1:58 am	Cancer	8th 4:33 pm	Leo
12th 11:21 pm	Gemini	11th 4:55 pm	Cancer	12th 7:52 am	Leo	10th 8:15 pm	Virgo
15th 6:57 am	Cancer	13th 9:31 pm	Leo	14th 9:56 am	Virgo	12th 8:54 pm	Libra
17th 11:13 am	Leo	15th 10:50 pm	Virgo	16th 9:45 am	Libra	14th 8:16 pm	Scorpio
19th 1:25 pm	Virgo	17th 11:15 pm	Libra	18th 9:22 am	Scorpio	16th 8:18 pm	Sagittarius
21st 3:12 pm	Libra	20th 0:15 am	Scorpio	20th 10:39 am	Sagittarius	18th 10:45 pm	Capricorn
23rd 5:50 pm	Scorpio	22nd 3:20 am	Sagittarius	22nd 2:54 pm	Capricorn	21st 4:51 am	Aquarius
25th 9:52 pm	Sagittarius	24th 8:58 am	Capricorn	24th 10:20 pm	Aquarius	23rd 2:31 pm	Pisces
28th 3:25 am	Capricorn	26th 4:50 pm	Aquarius	27th 8:35 am	Pisces	26th 2:36 am	Aries
30th 10:38 am	Aquarius	29th 2:44 am	Pisces	29th 8:35 am	Aries	28th 3:36 pm	Taurus

May 1976		June 1976		July 1976		August 1976	
1st 4:02 am	Gemini	2nd 4:35 am	Leo	1st 3:44 pm	Virgo	2nd 3:56 am	Scorpio
3rd 2:51 pm	Cancer	4th 10:17 am	Virgo	3rd 7:33 pm	Libra	4th 7:04 am	Sagittarius
5th 11:08 pm	Leo	6th 1:56 pm	Libra	5th 10:32 pm	Scorpio	6th 10:56 am	Capricorn
8th 4:18 am	Virgo	8th 3:57 pm	Scorpio	8th 1:06 am	Sagittarius	8th 3:59 pm	Aquarius
10th 6:37 am	Libra	10th 5:07 pm	Sagittarius	10th 3:50 am	Capricorn	10th 11:00 pm	Pisces
12th 7:03 am	Scorpio	12th 6:47 pm	Capricorn	12th 7:57 am	Aquarius	13th 8:52 am	Aries
14th 7:06 am	Sagittarius	14th 10:32 pm	Aquarius	14th 2:41 pm	Pisces	15th 9:06 pm	Taurus
16th 8:37 am	Capricorn	17th 5:49 am	Pisces	17th 0:40 am	Aries	18th 9:52 am	Gemini
18th 1:10 pm	Aquarius	19th 4:35 pm	Aries	19th 1:11 pm	Taurus	20th 8:31 pm	Cancer
20th 9:30 pm	Pisces	22nd 5:22 am	Taurus	22nd 1:40 am	Gemini	23rd 3:28 am	Leo
23rd 9:09 am	Aries	24th 5:35 pm	Gemini	24th 11:35 am	Cancer	25th 7:01 am	Virgo
25th 10:08 pm	Taurus	27th 3:27 am	Cancer	26th 6:16 pm	Leo	27th 8:42 am	Libra
28th 10:19 am	Gemini	29th 10:36 am	Leo	28th 10:22 pm	Virgo	29th 10:06 am	Scorpio
30th 8:37 pm	Cancer			31st 1:13 am	Libra	31st 12:32 pm	Sagittarius

September 1976		October 1976		November 1976		December 1976	
2nd 4:32 pm	Capricorn	2nd 3:51 am	Aquarius	3rd 4:47 am	Aries	2nd 11:42 pm	Taurus
4th 10:20 pm	Aquarius	4th 12:12 pm	Pisces	5th 5:23 pm	Taurus	5th 12:36 pm	Gemini
7th 6:14 am	Pisces	6th 10:51 pm	Aries	8th 6:20 am	Gemini	8th 0:21 am	Cancer
9th 4:20 pm	Aries	9th 11:12 am	Taurus	10th 6:27 pm	Cancer	10th 10:09 am	Leo
12th 4:31 am	Taurus	12th 0:14 am	Gemini	13th 4:34 am	Leo	12th 5:53 pm	Virgo
14th 5:31 pm	Gemini	14th 12:21 pm	Cancer	15th 11:40 am	Virgo	14th 11:13 pm	Libra
17th 5:03 am	Cancer	16th 9:49 pm	Leo	17th 3:30 pm	Libra	17th 2:02 am	Scorpio
19th 1:06 pm	Leo	19th 3:23 am	Virgo	19th 4:29 pm	Scorpio	19th 2:54 am	Sagittarius
21st 5:13 pm	Virgo	21st 5:24 am	Libra	21st 4:06 pm	Sagittarius	21st 3:14 am	Capricorn
23rd 6:27 pm	Libra	23rd 5:17 am	Scorpio	23rd 4:09 pm	Capricorn	23rd 4:53 am	Aquarius
25th 6:34 pm	Scorpio	25th 4:52 am	Sagittarius	25th 6:36 pm	Aquarius	25th 9:43 am	Pisces
27th 7:24 pm	Sagittarius	27th 5:50 am	Capricorn	28th 0:50 am	Pisces	27th 6:37 pm	Aries
29th 10:15 pm	Capricorn	29th 10:11 am	Aquarius	30th 11:06 am	Aries	30th 6:45 am	Taurus
		31st 5:56 pm	Pisces				

January 1977		February 1977		March 1977		April 1977	
1st 7:43 pm	Gemini	3rd 0:13 am	Leo	2nd 9:22 am	Leo	1st 1:25 am	Virgo
4th 7:10 am	Cancer	5th 6:17 am	Virgo	4th 3:16 pm	Virgo	3rd 4:39 am	Libra
6th 4:19 pm	Leo	7th 10:36 am	Libra	6th 6:35 pm	Libra	5th 5:41 am	Scorpio
8th 11:24 pm	Virgo	9th 2:04 pm	Scorpio	8th 8:39 pm	Scorpio	7th 6:12 am	Sagittarius
11th 4:47 am	Libra	11th 5:12 pm	Sagittarius	10th 10:43 pm	Sagittarius	9th 7:45 am	Capricorn
13th 8:43 am	Scorpio	13th 8:15 pm	Capricorn	13th 1:42 am	Capricorn	11th 11:28 am	Aquarius
15th 11:18 am	Sagittarius	15th 11:46 pm	Aquarius	15th 6:03 am	Aquarius	13th 5:52 pm	Pisces
17th 1:04 pm	Capricorn	18th 4:49 am	Pisces	17th 12:09 pm	Pisces	16th 2:54 am	Aries
19th 3:17 pm	Aquarius	20th 12:28 pm	Aries	19th 8:25 pm	Aries	18th 2:04 pm	Taurus
21st 7:35 pm	Pisces	22nd 11:06 pm	Taurus	22nd 7:08 am	Taurus	21st 2:38 am	Gemini
24th 3:24 am	Aries	25th 11:51 am	Gemini	24th 7:40 pm	Gemini	23rd 3:24 pm	Cancer
26th 2:43 pm	Taurus	28th 0:04 am	Cancer	27th 8:15 am	Cancer	26th 2:43 am	Leo
29th 3:38 am	Gemini			29th 6:38 pm	Leo	28th 10:48 am	Virgo
31st 3:18 pm	Cancer					30th 3:09 pm	Libra

May 1977
2nd   4:22 pm Scorpio
4th   4:01 pm Sagittarius
6th   3:59 pm Capricorn
8th   6:05 pm Aquarius
10th 11:29 pm Pisces
13th 8:33 am Aries
15th 8:05 pm Taurus
18th 8:50 am Gemini
20th 9:35 am Cancer
23rd 9:10 am Leo
25th 6:27 pm Virgo
28th 0:29 am Libra
30th 2:55 am Scorpio

September 1977
2nd   0:51 am Taurus
4th   12:28 pm Gemini
7th   1:02 am Cancer
9th   12:10 pm Leo
11th 8:33 pm Virgo
14th 2:07 am Libra
16th 5:45 am Scorpio
18th 8:29 am Sagittarius
20th 11:05 am Capricorn
22nd 2:14 pm Aquarius
24th 6:32 pm Pisces
27th 0:41 am Aries
29th 9:24 am Taurus

January 1978
1st   2:27 pm Libra
3rd   8:32 pm Scorpio
5th   11:02 pm Sagittarius
7th   10:54 pm Capricorn
9th   10:06 pm Aquarius
11th 10:52 pm Pisces
14th 3:09 am Aries
16th 11:37 am Taurus
18th 11:08 pm Gemini
21st 11:51 am Cancer
24th 0:04 am Leo
26th 10:54 am Virgo
28th 8:07 pm Libra
31st 3:02 am Scorpio

May 1978
1st   9:03 am Pisces
3rd   2:29 am Aries
5th   9:53 am Taurus
8th   7:22 am Gemini
10th 6:44 am Cancer
13th 7:16 am Leo
15th 7:14 pm Virgo
18th 4:22 am Libra
20th 9:35 am Sagittarius
22nd 11:28 am Sagittarius
24th 11:43 am Capricorn
26th 12:15 pm Aquarius
28th 2:42 pm Pisces
30th 7:56 pm Aries

September 1978
1st   8:47 am Virgo
4th   7:14 am Libra
6th   3:36 pm Scorpio
8th   9:38 pm Sagittarius
11th 1:19 am Capricorn
13th 3:08 am Aquarius
15th 4:10 am Pisces
17th 5:52 am Aries
19th 9:47 am Taurus
21st 4:50 pm Gemini
24th 3:33 am Cancer
26th 4:01 pm Leo
29th 4:10 am Virgo

June 1977
1st   2:54 am Sagittarius
3rd   2:09 am Capricorn
5th   2:47 am Aquarius
7th   6:42 am Pisces
9th   2:40 pm Aries
12th 1:57 am Taurus
14th 2:51 pm Gemini
17th 3:28 am Cancer
19th 2:50 pm Leo
22nd 0:28 am Virgo
24th 7:30 am Libra
26th 11:36 am Scorpio
28th 12:58 pm Sagittarius
30th 12:48 pm Capricorn

October 1977
1st   8:34 am Gemini
4th   9:09 am Cancer
6th   8:57 pm Leo
9th   5:55 am Virgo
11th 11:25 am Libra
13th 2:09 pm Scorpio
15th 3:28 pm Sagittarius
17th 4:53 pm Capricorn
19th 7:38 pm Aquarius
22nd 0:25 am Pisces
24th 7:37 am Aries
26th 4:54 pm Taurus
29th 4:07 am Gemini
31st 4:41 pm Cancer

February 1978
2nd   7:11 am Sagittarius
4th   8:48 am Capricorn
6th   9:06 am Aquarius
8th   9:52 am Pisces
10th 1:03 pm Aries
12th 7:54 pm Taurus
15th 6:27 am Gemini
17th 6:56 pm Cancer
20th 7:09 am Leo
22nd 5:39 pm Virgo
25th 2:03 am Libra
27th 8:27 am Scorpio

June 1978
2nd   3:52 am Taurus
4th   1:56 pm Gemini
7th   1:31 am Cancer
9th   2:08 pm Leo
12th 2:34 am Virgo
14th 12:51 pm Libra
16th 7:24 pm Scorpio
18th 9:50 pm Sagittarius
20th 9:52 pm Capricorn
22nd 9:11 pm Aquarius
24th 9:59 pm Pisces
27th 1:56 am Aries
29th 9:26 am Taurus

October 1978
1st   2:14 pm Libra
3rd   9:47 pm Scorpio
6th   3:06 am Sagittarius
8th   6:51 am Capricorn
10th 9:42 am Aquarius
12th 12:13 pm Pisces
14th 3:06 am Aries
16th 7:23 pm Taurus
19th 2:05 am Gemini
21st 11:55 am Cancer
24th 0:04 am Leo
26th 12:29 pm Virgo
28th 10:51 pm Libra
31st 5:49 am Scorpio

July 1977
2nd   1:01 pm Aquarius
4th   3:38 pm Pisces
6th   10:06 pm Aries
9th   8:37 am Taurus
11th 9:15 pm Gemini
14th 9:48 am Cancer
16th 8:51 pm Leo
19th 5:56 am Virgo
21st 1:06 pm Libra
23rd 6:10 pm Scorpio
25th 9:03 pm Sagittarius
27th 10:14 pm Capricorn
29th 11:04 pm Aquarius

November 1977
3rd   5:01 am Leo
5th   3:12 pm Virgo
7th   9:50 pm Libra
10th 0:42 am Scorpio
12th 1:04 am Sagittarius
14th 0:52 am Capricorn
16th 2:22 am Aquarius
18th 6:02 am Pisces
20th 1:17 pm Aries
22nd 11:09 pm Taurus
25th 10:49 am Gemini
27th 11:20 pm Cancer
30th 11:51 am Leo

March 1978
1st   1:00 pm Sagittarius
3rd   3:57 pm Capricorn
5th   5:51 pm Aquarius
7th   7:47 pm Pisces
9th   11:10 pm Aries
12th 5:21 am Taurus
14th 2:52 pm Gemini
17th 2:50 am Cancer
19th 3:11 pm Leo
22nd 1:50 am Virgo
24th 9:40 am Libra
26th 3:00 pm Scorpio
28th 6:38 pm Sagittarius
30th 9:25 pm Capricorn

July 1978
1st   7:40 pm Gemini
4th   7:35 am Cancer
6th   8:13 pm Leo
9th   8:42 am Virgo
11th 7:46 pm Libra
14th 3:43 am Scorpio
16th 7:44 am Sagittarius
18th 8:30 am Capricorn
20th 7:44 am Aquarius
22nd 7:31 am Pisces
24th 9:52 am Aries
26th 3:56 pm Taurus
29th 1:33 am Gemini
31st 1:30 pm Cancer

November 1978
2nd   10:02 am Sagittarius
4th   12:40 pm Capricorn
6th   3:04 pm Aquarius
8th   6:07 pm Pisces
10th 10:12 pm Aries
13th 3:36 am Taurus
15th 10:48 am Gemini
17th 8:16 pm Cancer
20th 8:10 am Leo
22nd 8:56 pm Virgo
25th 8:03 am Libra
27th 3:33 pm Scorpio
29th 7:20 pm Sagittarius

August 1977
1st   1:26 am Pisces
3rd   6:59 am Aries
5th   4:21 pm Taurus
8th   4:30 am Gemini
10th 5:03 pm Cancer
13th 3:55 am Leo
15th 12:24 pm Virgo
17th 6:48 pm Libra
19th 11:36 pm Scorpio
22nd 3:03 am Sagittarius
24th 5:29 am Capricorn
26th 7:41 am Aquarius
28th 10:50 am Pisces
30th 4:15 pm Aries

December 1977
2nd   11:03 pm Virgo
5th   7:13 am Libra
7th   11:27 am Scorpio
9th   12:18 pm Sagittarius
11th 11:28 am Capricorn
13th 11:06 am Aquarius
15th 1:16 pm Pisces
17th 7:16 pm Aries
20th 4:57 am Taurus
22nd 4:53 pm Gemini
25th 5:29 am Cancer
27th 5:51 pm Leo
30th 5:11 am Virgo

April 1978
2nd   0:05 am Aquarius
4th   3:21 am Pisces
6th   7:55 am Aries
8th   2:25 pm Taurus
10th 11:29 pm Gemini
13th 11:01 am Cancer
15th 11:32 pm Leo
18th 10:41 am Virgo
20th 6:51 pm Libra
22nd 11:41 pm Scorpio
25th 2:01 am Sagittarius
27th 3:30 am Capricorn
29th 5:31 am Aquarius

August 1978
3rd   2:11 am Leo
5th   2:28 pm Virgo
8th   1:28 am Libra
10th 10:07 am Scorpio
12th 3:38 pm Sagittarius
14th 5:59 pm Capricorn
16th 6:14 pm Aquarius
18th 6:07 pm Pisces
20th 7:32 pm Aries
23rd 0:06 am Taurus
25th 8:36 am Gemini
27th 7:59 pm Cancer
30th 8:39 am Leo

December 1978
1st   8:44 pm Capricorn
3rd   9:36 pm Aquarius
5th   11:36 pm Pisces
8th   3:41 am Aries
10th 9:53 am Taurus
12th 5:57 pm Gemini
15th 3:51 am Cancer
17th 3:38 pm Leo
20th 4:32 am Virgo
22nd 4:35 pm Libra
25th 1:30 am Scorpio
27th 6:03 am Sagittarius
29th 7:13 am Capricorn
31st 6:55 am Aquarius

January 1979		February 1979		March 1979		April 1979	
2nd	7:12 am Pisces	2nd	10:05 pm Taurus	2nd	7:14 am Taurus	3rd	6:27 am Cancer
4th	9:47 am Aries	5th	5:37 am Gemini	4th	1:04 pm Gemini	5th	5:59 pm Leo
6th	3:23 pm Taurus	7th	4:08 pm Cancer	6th	10:36 pm Cancer	8th	6:52 am Virgo
8th	11:43 pm Gemini	10th	4:28 am Leo	9th	10:49 am Leo	10th	6:45 pm Libra
11th	10:16 am Cancer	12th	5:18 pm Virgo	11th	11:44 pm Virgo	13th	4:15 am Scorpio
13th	10:17 pm Leo	15th	5:35 am Libra	14th	11:40 am Libra	15th	11:16 am Sagittarius
16th	11:10 am Virgo	17th	4:09 pm Scorpio	16th	9:50 pm Scorpio	17th	4:22 pm Capricorn
18th	11:40 pm Libra	19th	11:51 pm Sagittarius	19th	5:36 am Sagittarius	19th	8:01 pm Aquarius
21st	9:45 am Scorpio	22nd	3:58 am Capricorn	21st	10:53 am Capricorn	21st	10:41 pm Pisces
23rd	4:02 pm Sagittarius	24th	5:10 am Aquarius	23rd	1:50 pm Aquarius	24th	0:52 am Aries
25th	6:23 pm Capricorn	26th	4:53 am Pisces	25th	3:04 pm Pisces	26th	3:30 am Taurus
27th	6:11 pm Aquarius	28th	4:57 am Aries	27th	3:49 pm Aries	28th	7:53 am Gemini
29th	5:27 pm Pisces			29th	5:40 pm Taurus	30th	3:16 pm Cancer
31st	6:15 pm Aries			31st	10:09 pm Gemini		

May 1979		June 1979		July 1979		August 1979	
3rd	1:57 am Leo	1st	10:41 pm Virgo	1st	7:06 pm Libra	2nd	10:03 pm Sagittarius
5th	2:41 pm Virgo	4th	11:08 am Libra	4th	5:53 am Scorpio	5th	2:21 am Capricorn
8th	2:48 am Libra	6th	9:03 pm Scorpio	6th	12:50 pm Sagittarius	7th	3:27 am Aquarius
10th	12:07 pm Scorpio	9th	3:14 am Sagittarius	8th	4:04 pm Capricorn	9th	3:06 am Pisces
12th	6:23 pm Sagittarius	11th	6:23 am Capricorn	10th	4:59 pm Aquarius	11th	3:12 am Aries
14th	10:27 pm Capricorn	13th	8:08 am Aquarius	12th	5:26 pm Pisces	13th	5:26 am Taurus
17th	1:26 am Aquarius	15th	9:59 am Pisces	14th	7:00 pm Aries	15th	10:47 am Gemini
19th	4:19 am Pisces	17th	12:56 pm Aries	16th	10:45 pm Taurus	17th	7:21 pm Cancer
21st	7:31 am Aries	19th	5:21 pm Taurus	19th	5:03 am Gemini	20th	6:32 am Leo
23rd	11:22 am Taurus	21st	11:24 pm Gemini	21st	1:44 pm Cancer	22nd	7:13 pm Virgo
25th	4:31 pm Gemini	24th	7:27 am Cancer	24th	0:32 am Leo	25th	8:13 am Libra
27th	11:51 pm Cancer	26th	5:50 pm Leo	26th	1:02 pm Virgo	27th	8:11 pm Scorpio
30th	10:11 am Leo	29th	6:15 am Virgo	29th	2:05 am Libra	30th	5:36 am Sagittarius
				31st	1:42 pm Scorpio		

September 1979		October 1979		November 1979		December 1979	
1st	11:28 am Capricorn	3rd	0:23 am Pisces	1st	10:08 am Aries	2nd	11:02 pm Gemini
3rd	1:55 pm Aquarius	5th	0:27 am Aries	3rd	11:16 am Taurus	5th	4:03 am Cancer
5th	2:02 pm Pisces	7th	0:45 am Taurus	5th	1:30 pm Gemini	7th	12:13 pm Leo
7th	1:31 pm Aries	9th	3:09 am Gemini	7th	6:27 pm Cancer	9th	11:32 pm Virgo
9th	2:17 pm Taurus	11th	9:14 am Cancer	10th	3:16 am Leo	12th	12:27 pm Libra
11th	5:59 pm Gemini	13th	7:13 pm Leo	12th	3:21 pm Virgo	15th	0:08 am Scorpio
14th	1:27 am Cancer	16th	7:51 am Virgo	15th	4:15 am Libra	17th	8:32 am Sagittarius
16th	12:28 pm Leo	18th	8:44 pm Libra	17th	3:26 pm Scorpio	19th	1:51 pm Capricorn
19th	1:15 am Virgo	21st	8:00 am Scorpio	19th	11:56 pm Sagittarius	21st	5:12 pm Aquarius
21st	2:10 pm Libra	23rd	5:07 pm Sagittarius	22nd	6:00 am Capricorn	23rd	7:50 pm Pisces
24th	1:55 am Scorpio	26th	0:11 am Capricorn	24th	10:35 am Aquarius	25th	10:40 pm Aries
26th	11:33 am Sagittarius	28th	5:15 am Aquarius	26th	2:16 pm Pisces	28th	2:08 am Taurus
28th	6:36 pm Capricorn	30th	8:26 am Pisces	28th	5:16 pm Aries	30th	6:34 am Gemini
30th	10:48 pm Aquarius			30th	7:54 pm Taurus		

January 1980		February 1980		March 1980		April 1980	
1st	12:33 pm Cancer	2nd	3:23 pm Virgo	3rd	10:40 am Libra	2nd	5:21 am Scorpio
3rd	8:49 pm Leo	5th	4:04 am Libra	5th	11:24 pm Scorpio	4th	4:34 pm Sagittarius
6th	7:50 am Virgo	7th	4:43 pm Scorpio	8th	10:35 am Sagittarius	7th	1:41 am Capricorn
8th	8:37 pm Libra	10th	3:15 am Sagittarius	10th	6:59 pm Capricorn	9th	7:56 am Aquarius
11th	8:50 am Scorpio	12th	10:06 am Capricorn	12th	11:46 pm Aquarius	11th	11:03 am Pisces
13th	6:12 pm Sagittarius	14th	1:14 pm Aquarius	15th	1:10 am Pisces	13th	11:39 am Aries
15th	11:51 pm Capricorn	16th	1:52 pm Pisces	17th	0:41 am Aries	15th	11:12 am Taurus
18th	2:25 am Aquarius	18th	1:45 pm Aries	19th	0:13 am Taurus	17th	11:47 am Gemini
20th	3:33 am Pisces	20th	2:39 pm Taurus	21st	1:49 am Gemini	19th	3:18 pm Cancer
22nd	4:54 am Aries	22nd	6:03 pm Gemini	23rd	7:00 am Cancer	21st	10:54 pm Leo
24th	7:36 am Taurus	25th	0:36 am Cancer	25th	4:02 pm Leo	24th	10:14 am Virgo
26th	12:14 pm Gemini	27th	10:14 am Leo	28th	3:53 am Virgo	26th	11:11 pm Libra
28th	7:05 pm Cancer	29th	9:54 pm Virgo	30th	4:49 pm Libra	29th	11:34 am Scorpio
31st	4:11 am Leo						

May 1980		June 1980		July 1980		August 1980	
1st	10:23 pm Sagittarius	2nd	7:28 pm Aquarius	2nd	5:48 am Pisces	2nd	4:58 pm Taurus
4th	7:13 am Capricorn	5th	0:10 am Pisces	4th	8:48 am Aries	4th	8:12 pm Gemini
6th	2:01 pm Aquarius	7th	3:23 am Aries	6th	11:32 am Taurus	7th	1:14 am Cancer
8th	6:31 pm Pisces	9th	5:30 am Taurus	8th	2:36 pm Gemini	9th	8:28 am Leo
10th	8:44 pm Aries	11th	7:25 am Gemini	10th	6:48 pm Cancer	11th	5:58 pm Virgo
12th	9:25 pm Taurus	13th	10:35 am Cancer	13th	1:04 am Leo	14th	5:33 am Libra
14th	10:09 pm Gemini	15th	4:26 pm Leo	15th	10:15 am Virgo	16th	6:14 pm Scorpio
17th	0:53 am Cancer	18th	1:49 am Virgo	17th	9:55 pm Libra	19th	6:04 am Sagittarius
19th	7:19 am Leo	20th	1:56 pm Libra	20th	10:30 am Scorpio	21st	3:06 pm Capricorn
21st	5:35 pm Virgo	23rd	2:27 am Scorpio	22nd	9:40 pm Sagittarius	23rd	8:30 pm Aquarius
24th	6:12 am Libra	25th	12:58 pm Sagittarius	25th	5:42 am Capricorn	25th	10:42 pm Pisces
26th	6:37 pm Scorpio	27th	8:45 pm Capricorn	27th	10:32 am Aquarius	27th	11:12 pm Aries
29th	5:04 am Sagittarius	30th	2:03 am Aquarius	29th	1:10 pm Pisces	29th	11:42 pm Taurus
31st	1:13 pm Capricorn			31st	2:55 pm Aries		

September 1980
1st 1:53 am Gemini
3rd 6:44 am Cancer
5th 2:26 pm Leo
8th 0:32 am Virgo
10th 12:24 pm Libra
13th 1:07 am Scorpio
15th 1:26 pm Sagittarius
17th 11:45 pm Capricorn
20th 6:26 am Aquarius
22nd 9:22 am Pisces
24th 9:36 am Aries
26th 8:55 am Taurus
28th 9:25 am Gemini
30th 12:51 pm Cancer

October 1980
2nd 7:59 pm Leo
5th 6:20 am Virgo
7th 6:31 pm Libra
10th 7:15 am Scorpio
12th 7:38 pm Sagittarius
15th 6:34 am Capricorn
17th 2:49 pm Aquarius
19th 7:28 pm Pisces
21st 8:40 pm Aries
23rd 7:55 pm Taurus
25th 7:19 pm Gemini
27th 9:02 pm Cancer
30th 2:40 am Leo

November 1980
1st 12:21 pm Virgo
4th 0:30 am Libra
6th 1:18 pm Scorpio
9th 1:25 am Sagittarius
11th 12:13 pm Capricorn
13th 9:08 pm Aquarius
16th 3:18 am Pisces
18th 6:18 am Aries
20th 6:48 am Taurus
22nd 6:29 am Gemini
24th 7:23 am Cancer
26th 11:28 am Leo
28th 7:40 pm Virgo

December 1980
1st 7:14 am Libra
3rd 7:59 pm Scorpio
6th 7:55 am Sagittarius
8th 6:09 pm Capricorn
11th 2:34 am Aquarius
13th 8:50 am Pisces
15th 1:18 pm Aries
17th 3:33 pm Taurus
19th 4:40 pm Gemini
21st 6:05 pm Cancer
23rd 9:35 pm Leo
26th 4:35 am Virgo
28th 3:06 pm Libra
31st 3:34 am Scorpio

January 1981
2nd 3:38 pm Sagittarius
5th 1:39 am Capricorn
7th 9:09 am Aquarius
9th 2:39 pm Pisces
11th 6:42 pm Aries
13th 9:45 pm Taurus
16th 0:17 am Gemini
18th 3:09 am Cancer
20th 7:24 am Leo
22nd 2:06 pm Virgo
24th 11:44 pm Libra
27th 11:48 am Scorpio
30th 0:10 am Sagittarius

February 1981
1st 10:31 am Capricorn
3rd 5:51 pm Aquarius
5th 10:20 pm Pisces
8th 1:02 am Aries
10th 3:12 am Taurus
12th 5:53 am Gemini
14th 9:46 am Cancer
16th 3:14 pm Leo
18th 10:34 pm Virgo
21st 8:14 am Libra
23rd 7:55 pm Scorpio
26th 8:26 am Sagittarius
28th 7:43 pm Capricorn

March 1981
3rd 3:47 am Aquarius
5th 8:07 am Pisces
7th 9:45 am Aries
9th 10:23 am Taurus
11th 11:46 am Gemini
13th 3:10 pm Cancer
15th 9:05 pm Leo
18th 5:22 am Virgo
20th 3:33 pm Libra
23rd 3:15 am Scorpio
25th 3:51 pm Sagittarius
28th 3:51 am Capricorn
30th 1:09 pm Aquarius

April 1981
1st 6:37 pm Pisces
3rd 8:22 pm Aries
5th 8:03 pm Taurus
7th 7:50 pm Gemini
9th 9:35 pm Cancer
12th 2:39 am Leo
14th 10:59 am Virgo
16th 9:38 pm Libra
19th 9:40 am Scorpio
21st 10:15 pm Sagittarius
24th 10:30 am Capricorn
26th 8:56 pm Aquarius
29th 3:54 am Pisces

May 1981
1st 6:53 am Aries
3rd 6:58 am Taurus
5th 6:03 am Gemini
7th 6:22 am Cancer
9th 9:46 am Leo
11th 4:59 pm Virgo
14th 3:25 am Libra
16th 3:39 pm Scorpio
19th 4:14 am Sagittarius
21st 4:19 pm Capricorn
24th 2:59 am Aquarius
26th 11:01 am Pisces
28th 3:39 pm Aries
30th 5:08 pm Taurus

June 1981
1st 4:49 pm Gemini
3rd 4:43 pm Cancer
5th 6:47 pm Leo
8th 0:26 am Virgo
10th 9:59 am Libra
12th 9:55 pm Scorpio
15th 10:32 am Sagittarius
17th 10:21 pm Capricorn
20th 8:34 am Aquarius
22nd 4:42 pm Pisces
24th 10:18 pm Aries
27th 1:16 am Taurus
29th 2:22 am Gemini

July 1981
1st 2:59 am Cancer
3rd 4:51 am Leo
5th 9:32 am Virgo
7th 5:45 pm Libra
10th 5:02 am Scorpio
12th 5:35 pm Sagittarius
15th 5:18 am Capricorn
17th 2:50 pm Aquarius
19th 10:25 pm Pisces
22nd 3:44 am Aries
24th 7:18 am Taurus
26th 9:42 am Gemini
28th 11:43 am Cancer
30th 2:25 pm Leo

August 1981
1st 6:58 pm Virgo
4th 2:26 am Libra
6th 1:01 pm Scorpio
9th 1:23 am Sagittarius
11th 1:17 pm Capricorn
13th 10:56 pm Aquarius
16th 5:32 am Pisces
18th 9:48 am Aries
20th 12:45 pm Taurus
22nd 3:20 pm Gemini
24th 6:18 pm Cancer
26th 10:12 pm Leo
29th 3:35 am Virgo
31st 11:07 am Libra

September 1981
2nd 9:13 pm Scorpio
5th 9:24 am Sagittarius
7th 9:48 pm Capricorn
10th 7:54 am Aquarius
12th 2:29 pm Pisces
14th 5:53 pm Aries
16th 7:30 pm Taurus
18th 9:01 pm Gemini
20th 11:40 pm Cancer
23rd 4:11 am Leo
25th 10:32 am Virgo
27th 6:43 pm Libra
30th 4:56 am Scorpio

October 1981
2nd 5:01 pm Sagittarius
5th 5:47 am Capricorn
7th 4:57 pm Aquarius
10th 0:32 am Pisces
12th 3:59 am Aries
14th 4:43 am Taurus
16th 4:43 am Gemini
18th 5:55 am Cancer
20th 9:39 am Leo
22nd 4:07 pm Virgo
25th 0:56 am Libra
27th 11:40 am Scorpio
29th 11:50 pm Sagittarius

November 1981
1st 12:46 pm Capricorn
4th 0:50 am Aquarius
6th 9:46 am Pisces
8th 2:33 pm Aries
10th 3:41 pm Taurus
12th 3:00 pm Gemini
14th 2:40 pm Cancer
16th 4:36 pm Leo
18th 9:55 pm Virgo
21st 6:34 am Libra
23rd 5:38 pm Scorpio
26th 6:01 am Sagittarius
28th 6:52 pm Capricorn

December 1981
1st 7:07 am Aquarius
3rd 5:13 pm Pisces
5th 11:49 pm Aries
8th 2:29 am Taurus
10th 2:29 am Gemini
12th 1:42 am Cancer
14th 2:09 am Leo
16th 5:41 am Virgo
18th 1:03 pm Libra
20th 11:38 pm Scorpio
23rd 12:11 pm Sagittarius
26th 0:58 am Capricorn
28th 12:51 pm Aquarius
30th 11:01 pm Pisces

January 1982
2nd 6:29 am Aries
4th 10:57 am Taurus
6th 12:46 pm Gemini
8th 1:01 pm Cancer
10th 1:24 pm Leo
12th 3:42 pm Virgo
14th 9:19 pm Libra
17th 6:48 am Scorpio
19th 6:50 pm Sagittarius
22nd 7:49 am Capricorn
24th 7:22 pm Aquarius
27th 4:47 am Pisces
29th 11:55 am Aries
31st 5:02 pm Taurus

February 1982
2nd 8:19 pm Gemini
4th 10:17 pm Cancer
6th 11:50 pm Leo
9th 2:16 am Virgo
11th 7:05 am Libra
13th 3:20 pm Scorpio
16th 2:44 am Sagittarius
18th 3:34 pm Capricorn
21st 3:11 am Aquarius
23rd 12:04 pm Pisces
25th 6:14 pm Aries
27th 10:32 pm Taurus

March 1982
2nd 1:49 am Gemini
4th 4:49 am Cancer
6th 7:51 am Leo
8th 11:29 am Virgo
10th 4:37 pm Libra
13th 0:17 am Scorpio
15th 11:05 am Sagittarius
17th 11:46 pm Capricorn
20th 11:48 am Aquarius
22nd 8:57 pm Pisces
25th 2:35 am Aries
27th 5:38 am Taurus
29th 7:44 am Gemini
31st 10:10 am Cancer

April 1982
2nd 1:39 pm Leo
4th 6:20 pm Virgo
7th 0:26 am Libra
9th 8:37 am Scorpio
11th 7:08 pm Sagittarius
14th 7:42 am Capricorn
16th 8:16 pm Aquarius
19th 6:15 am Pisces
21st 12:17 pm Aries
23rd 2:55 pm Taurus
25th 3:48 pm Gemini
27th 4:44 pm Cancer
29th 7:10 pm Leo

May 1982
1st 11:44 pm Virgo
4th 6:34 am Libra
6th 3:26 pm Scorpio
9th 2:18 am Sagittarius
11th 2:51 pm Capricorn
14th 3:44 am Aquarius
16th 2:42 pm Pisces
18th 10:03 pm Aries
21st 1:20 am Taurus
23rd 1:54 am Gemini
25th 1:38 am Cancer
27th 2:28 am Leo
29th 5:46 am Virgo
31st 12:06 pm Libra

June 1982
2nd 9:12 pm Scorpio
5th 8:33 am Sagittarius
7th 9:11 pm Capricorn
10th 10:06 am Aquarius
12th 9:43 pm Pisces
15th 6:16 am Aries
17th 11:01 am Taurus
19th 12:31 pm Gemini
21st 12:13 pm Cancer
23rd 11:50 am Leo
25th 1:41 pm Virgo
27th 6:34 pm Libra
30th 3:03 am Scorpio

July 1982
2nd 2:27 pm Sagittarius
5th 3:15 am Capricorn
7th 4:01 pm Aquarius
10th 3:33 am Pisces
12th 12:45 pm Aries
14th 6:56 pm Taurus
16th 10:03 pm Gemini
18th 10:46 pm Cancer
20th 10:36 pm Leo
22nd 11:21 pm Virgo
25th 2:47 am Libra
27th 10:04 am Scorpio
29th 8:49 pm Sagittarius

August 1982
1st 9:36 am Capricorn
3rd 10:17 pm Aquarius
6th 9:21 am Pisces
8th 6:20 pm Aries
11th 1:00 am Taurus
13th 5:21 am Gemini
15th 7:39 am Cancer
17th 8:42 am Leo
19th 9:44 am Virgo
21st 12:27 pm Libra
23rd 6:25 pm Scorpio
26th 4:13 am Sagittarius
28th 4:41 pm Capricorn
31st 5:22 am Aquarius

September 1982
2nd 4:07 pm Pisces
5th 0:24 am Aries
7th 6:26 am Taurus
9th 10:57 am Gemini
11th 2:18 pm Cancer
3th 4:46 pm Leo
15th 6:50 pm Virgo
17th 10:05 pm Libra
20th 3:36 am Scorpio
22nd 12:35 pm Sagittarius
25th 0:32 am Capricorn
27th 1:19 pm Aquarius
30th 0:19 am Pisces

October 1982
2nd 8:02 am Aries
4th 1:07 pm Taurus
6th 4:38 pm Gemini
8th 7:40 pm Cancer
10th 10:45 pm Leo
13th 2:10 am Virgo
15th 6:26 am Libra
17th 12:26 pm Scorpio
19th 9:05 pm Sagittarius
22nd 8:41 am Capricorn
24th 9:36 pm Aquarius
27th 9:08 am Pisces
29th 5:21 pm Aries
31st 10:03 pm Taurus

November 1982
3rd 0:23 am Gemini
5th 1:58 am Cancer
7th 4:12 am Leo
9th 7:43 am Virgo
11th 12:48 pm Libra
13th 7:44 pm Scorpio
16th 4:55 am Sagittarius
18th 4:23 pm Capricorn
21st 5:21 am Aquarius
23rd 5:41 pm Pisces
26th 3:04 am Aries
28th 8:28 am Taurus
30th 10:34 am Gemini

December 1982
2nd 10:58 am Cancer
4th 11:29 am Leo
6th 1:37 pm Virgo
8th 6:14 pm Libra
11th 1:35 am Scorpio
13th 11:30 am Sagittarius
15th 11:16 pm Capricorn
18th 12:13 pm Aquarius
21st 0:36 am Pisces
23rd 11:30 am Aries
25th 6:33 pm Taurus
27th 9:48 pm Gemini
29th 10:12 pm Cancer
31st 9:33 pm Leo

January 1983
2nd 9:51 pm Virgo
5th 0:45 am Libra
7th 7:20 am Scorpio
9th 5:16 pm Sagittarius
12th 5:27 am Capricorn
14th 6:26 pm Aquarius
17th 7:01 am Pisces
19th 6:05 pm Aries
22nd 2:34 am Taurus
24th 7:36 am Gemini
26th 9:24 am Cancer
28th 9:09 am Leo
30th 8:38 am Virgo

February 1983
1st 9:53 am Libra
3rd 2:37 pm Scorpio
5th 11:29 pm Sagittarius
8th 11:35 am Capricorn
11th 0:41 am Aquarius
13th 12:50 pm Pisces
15th 11:46 pm Aries
18th 8:28 am Taurus
20th 2:48 pm Gemini
22nd 6:29 pm Cancer
24th 7:46 pm Leo
26th 7:49 pm Virgo
28th 8:31 pm Libra

March 1983
2nd 11:51 pm Scorpio
5th 7:18 am Sagittarius
7th 6:30 pm Capricorn
10th 7:29 am Aquarius
12th 7:44 pm Pisces
15th 5:58 am Aries
17th 2:02 pm Taurus
19th 8:18 pm Gemini
22nd 0:53 am Cancer
24th 3:43 am Leo
26th 5:19 am Virgo
28th 6:50 am Libra
30th 10:02 am Scorpio

April 1983
1st 4:24 pm Sagittarius
4th 2:30 am Capricorn
6th 3:06 pm Aquarius
9th 3:29 am Pisces
11th 1:32 pm Aries
13th 8:56 pm Taurus
16th 2:12 am Gemini
18th 6:12 am Cancer
20th 9:25 am Leo
22nd 12:11 pm Virgo
24th 3:04 pm Libra
26th 7:07 pm Scorpio
29th 1:29 am Sagittarius

May 1983
1st 11:04 am Capricorn
3rd 11:09 pm Aquarius
6th 11:41 am Pisces
8th 10:14 pm Aries
11th 5:33 am Taurus
13th 9:59 am Gemini
15th 12:45 pm Cancer
17th 3:00 pm Leo
19th 5:37 pm Virgo
21st 9:12 pm Libra
24th 2:18 am Scorpio
26th 9:30 am Sagittarius
28th 7:09 pm Capricorn
31st 7:01 am Aquarius

June 1983
2nd 7:42 pm Pisces
5th 6:55 am Aries
7th 2:59 pm Taurus
9th 7:34 pm Gemini
11th 9:30 pm Cancer
13th 10:21 pm Leo
15th 11:37 pm Virgo
18th 2:38 am Libra
20th 8:02 am Scorpio
22nd 3:57 pm Sagittarius
25th 2:09 am Capricorn
27th 2:07 pm Aquarius
30th 2:51 am Pisces

July 1983
2nd 2:44 pm Aries
5th 0:05 am Taurus
7th 5:37 am Gemini
9th 7:47 am Cancer
11th 7:53 am Leo
13th 7:45 am Virgo
15th 9:15 am Libra
17th 1:43 pm Scorpio
19th 9:32 pm Sagittarius
22nd 8:12 am Capricorn
24th 8:26 pm Aquarius
27th 9:10 am Pisces
29th 9:21 pm Aries

August 1983
1st 7:33 am Taurus
3rd 2:38 pm Gemini
5th 6:06 pm Cancer
7th 6:35 pm Leo
9th 5:50 pm Virgo
11th 5:55 pm Libra
13th 8:46 pm Scorpio
16th 3:36 am Sagittarius
18th 2:01 pm Capricorn
21st 2:26 am Aquarius
23rd 3:09 pm Pisces
26th 3:07 am Aries
28th 1:35 pm Taurus
30th 9:47 pm Gemini

September 1983
2nd 2:51 am Cancer
4th 4:45 am Leo
6th 4:36 am Virgo
8th 4:16 am Libra
10th 5:54 am Scorpio
12th 11:14 am Sagittarius
14th 8:35 pm Capricorn
17th 8:45 am Aquarius
19th 9:29 pm Pisces
22nd 9:09 am Aries
24th 7:11 pm Taurus
27th 3:23 am Gemini
29th 9:21 am Cancer

October 1983
1st 12:52 pm Leo
3rd 2:14 pm Virgo
5th 2:44 pm Libra
7th 4:11 pm Scorpio
9th 8:24 pm Sagittarius
12th 4:33 am Capricorn
14th 4:03 pm Aquarius
17th 4:40 am Pisces
19th 4:16 pm Aries
22nd 1:46 am Taurus
24th 9:07 am Gemini
26th 2:45 pm Cancer
28th 6:49 pm Leo
30th 9:32 pm Virgo

November 1983
1st 11:32 pm Libra
4th 1:55 am Scorpio
6th 4:14 am Sagittarius
8th 1:37 pm Capricorn
11th 0:21 am Aquarius
13th 12:41 pm Pisces
16th 0:37 am Aries
18th 10:04 am Taurus
20th 4:42 pm Gemini
22nd 9:09 pm Cancer
25th 0:19 am Leo
27th 3:03 am Virgo
29th 5:57 am Libra

December 1983
1st 9:44 am Scorpio
3rd 2:50 pm Sagittarius
5th 10:30 pm Capricorn
8th 8:44 am Aquarius
10th 8:54 pm Pisces
13th 9:15 am Aries
15th 7:31 pm Taurus
18th 2:23 am Gemini
20th 6:00 am Cancer
22nd 7:43 am Leo
24th 9:03 am Virgo
26th 11:22 am Libra
28th 3:29 pm Scorpio
30th 9:44 pm Sagittarius

January 1984
- 2nd 6:11 am Capricorn
- 4th 4:32 am Aquarius
- 7th 4:35 am Pisces
- 9th 5:15 pm Aries
- 12th 4:34 am Taurus
- 14th 12:35 pm Gemini
- 16th 4:43 am Cancer
- 18th 5:48 pm Leo
- 20th 5:37 pm Virgo
- 22nd 6:11 am Libra
- 24th 9:07 am Scorpio
- 27th 3:14 am Sagittarius
- 29th 12:15 am Capricorn
- 31st 11:10 pm Aquarius

February 1984
- 3rd 11:23 am Pisces
- 6th 0:04 am Aries
- 8th 12:03 pm Taurus
- 10th 9:37 pm Gemini
- 13th 3:19 am Cancer
- 15th 5:07 am Leo
- 17th 4:32 am Virgo
- 19th 3:42 am Libra
- 21st 4:48 am Scorpio
- 23rd 9:28 am Sagittarius
- 25th 5:52 pm Capricorn
- 28th 5:03 am Aquarius

March 1984
- 1st 5:30 pm Pisces
- 4th 6:07 am Aries
- 6th 6:08 pm Taurus
- 9th 4:28 am Gemini
- 11th 11:43 am Cancer
- 13th 3:17 pm Leo
- 15th 3:44 pm Virgo
- 17th 2:54 pm Libra
- 19th 2:54 pm Scorpio
- 21st 5:46 pm Sagittarius
- 24th 0:36 am Capricorn
- 26th 11:10 am Aquarius
- 28th 11:36 pm Pisces
- 31st 12:12 am Aries

April 1984
- 2nd 11:54 am Taurus
- 5th 10:01 am Gemini
- 7th 5:56 pm Cancer
- 9th 11:01 pm Leo
- 12th 1:10 am Virgo
- 14th 1:30 am Libra
- 16th 1:42 am Scorpio
- 18th 3:46 am Sagittarius
- 20th 9:16 am Capricorn
- 22nd 6:30 pm Aquarius
- 25th 6:26 am Pisces
- 27th 7:00 pm Aries
- 30th 6:27 am Taurus

May 1984
- 2nd 3:59 pm Gemini
- 4th 11:25 pm Cancer
- 7th 4:41 am Leo
- 9th 7:58 am Virgo
- 11th 9:52 am Libra
- 13th 11:24 am Scorpio
- 15th 1:54 pm Sagittarius
- 17th 6:46 pm Capricorn
- 20th 2:57 am Aquarius
- 22nd 2:10 pm Pisces
- 25th 2:38 am Aries
- 27th 2:10 pm Taurus
- 29th 11:21 pm Gemini

June 1984
- 1st 5:50 am Cancer
- 3rd 10:16 am Leo
- 5th 1:25 pm Virgo
- 7th 4:02 pm Libra
- 9th 6:48 pm Scorpio
- 11th 10:26 pm Sagittarius
- 14th 3:51 am Capricorn
- 16th 11:45 am Aquarius
- 18th 10:19 pm Pisces
- 21st 10:49 am Aries
- 23rd 10:37 pm Taurus
- 26th 7:59 am Gemini
- 28th 2:04 pm Cancer
- 30th 5:27 pm Leo

July 1984
- 2nd 7:26 pm Virgo
- 4th 9:26 pm Libra
- 7th 0:28 am Scorpio
- 9th 5:04 am Sagittarius
- 11th 11:25 am Capricorn
- 13th 7:43 pm Aquarius
- 16th 6:12 am Pisces
- 18th 6:26 pm Aries
- 21st 6:51 am Taurus
- 23rd 5:06 pm Gemini
- 25th 11:44 pm Cancer
- 28th 2:39 am Leo
- 30th 3:28 am Virgo

August 1984
- 1st 4:04 am Libra
- 3rd 6:07 am Scorpio
- 5th 10:33 am Sagittarius
- 7th 5:27 pm Capricorn
- 10th 2:26 am Aquarius
- 12th 1:14 pm Pisces
- 15th 1:27 am Aries
- 17th 2:11 pm Taurus
- 20th 1:30 am Gemini
- 22nd 9:14 am Cancer
- 24th 12:55 pm Leo
- 26th 1:31 pm Virgo
- 28th 12:59 pm Libra
- 30th 1:27 pm Scorpio

September 1984
- 1st 4:34 pm Sagittarius
- 3rd 10:55 pm Capricorn
- 6th 8:13 am Aquarius
- 8th 7:25 pm Pisces
- 11th 7:46 am Aries
- 13th 8:32 pm Taurus
- 16th 8:22 am Gemini
- 18th 5:32 pm Cancer
- 20th 10:47 pm Leo
- 23rd 0:19 am Virgo
- 24th 11:41 pm Libra
- 26th 11:04 pm Scorpio
- 29th 0:31 am Sagittarius

October 1984
- 1st 5:31 am Capricorn
- 3rd 2:07 pm Aquarius
- 6th 1:18 am Pisces
- 8th 1:50 pm Aries
- 11th 2:27 am Taurus
- 13th 2:12 pm Gemini
- 15th 12:00 am Cancer
- 18th 6:38 am Leo
- 20th 9:52 am Virgo
- 22nd 10:31 am Libra
- 24th 10:11 am Scorpio
- 26th 10:49 am Sagittarius
- 28th 2:11 pm Capricorn
- 30th 9:16 pm Aquarius

November 1984
- 2nd 7:52 am Pisces
- 4th 8:21 pm Aries
- 7th 8:52 am Taurus
- 9th 8:09 pm Gemini
- 12th 5:28 am Cancer
- 14th 12:30 pm Leo
- 16th 5:04 pm Virgo
- 18th 7:28 pm Libra
- 20th 8:31 pm Scorpio
- 22nd 9:35 pm Sagittarius
- 25th 0:19 am Capricorn
- 27th 6:12 am Aquarius
- 29th 3:38 pm Pisces

December 1984
- 2nd 3:43 am Aries
- 4th 4:20 pm Taurus
- 7th 3:23 am Gemini
- 9th 11:53 am Cancer
- 11th 6:06 pm Leo
- 13th 10:35 pm Virgo
- 16th 1:52 am Libra
- 18th 4:27 am Scorpio
- 20th 7:00 am Sagittarius
- 22nd 10:24 am Capricorn
- 24th 3:52 pm Aquarius
- 27th 0:20 am Pisces
- 29th 11:52 am Aries

January 1985
- 1st 0:36 am Taurus
- 3rd 11:57 am Gemini
- 5th 8:16 pm Cancer
- 8th 1:28 am Leo
- 10th 4:40 am Virgo
- 12th 7:14 am Libra
- 14th 10:09 am Scorpio
- 16th 1:50 pm Sagittarius
- 18th 6:31 pm Capricorn
- 21st 0:39 am Aquarius
- 23rd 9:06 am Pisces
- 25th 8:06 pm Aries
- 28th 8:53 am Taurus
- 30th 9:00 pm Gemini

February 1985
- 2nd 5:56 am Cancer
- 4th 10:58 am Leo
- 6th 1:08 pm Virgo
- 8th 2:13 pm Libra
- 10th 3:52 pm Scorpio
- 12th 7:12 pm Sagittarius
- 15th 0:27 am Capricorn
- 17th 7:39 am Aquarius
- 19th 4:40 pm Pisces
- 22nd 3:45 am Aries
- 24th 4:28 pm Taurus
- 27th 5:09 am Gemini

March 1985
- 1st 3:19 pm Cancer
- 3rd 9:27 pm Leo
- 5th 11:44 pm Virgo
- 7th 11:49 pm Libra
- 9th 11:47 pm Scorpio
- 12th 1:31 am Sagittarius
- 14th 5:58 am Capricorn
- 16th 1:14 pm Aquarius
- 18th 10:50 pm Pisces
- 21st 10:21 am Aries
- 23rd 11:07 pm Taurus
- 26th 12:01 pm Gemini
- 28th 11:13 pm Cancer
- 31st 6:47 am Leo

April 1985
- 2nd 10:21 am Virgo
- 4th 10:53 am Libra
- 6th 10:13 am Scorpio
- 8th 10:22 am Sagittarius
- 10th 1:03 pm Capricorn
- 12th 7:06 pm Aquarius
- 15th 4:32 am Pisces
- 17th 4:19 am Aries
- 20th 5:11 am Taurus
- 22nd 5:59 pm Gemini
- 25th 5:23 am Cancer
- 27th 2:06 pm Leo
- 29th 7:21 pm Virgo

May 1985
- 1st 9:21 pm Libra
- 3rd 9:17 pm Scorpio
- 5th 8:58 pm Sagittarius
- 7th 10:13 pm Capricorn
- 10th 2:41 am Aquarius
- 12th 10:50 am Pisces
- 14th 10:26 am Aries
- 17th 11:23 am Taurus
- 19th 12:00 pm Gemini
- 22nd 11:01 am Cancer
- 24th 7:50 pm Leo
- 27th 2:04 am Virgo
- 29th 5:37 am Libra
- 31st 7:05 am Scorpio

June 1985
- 2nd 7:34 am Sagittarius
- 4th 8:37 am Capricorn
- 6th 11:58 am Aquarius
- 8th 6:51 pm Pisces
- 11th 5:26 am Aries
- 13th 6:12 pm Taurus
- 16th 6:43 am Gemini
- 18th 5:19 pm Cancer
- 21st 1:31 am Leo
- 23rd 7:29 am Virgo
- 25th 11:44 am Libra
- 27th 2:34 pm Scorpio
- 29th 4:29 pm Sagittarius

July 1985
- 1st 6:23 pm Capricorn
- 3rd 9:38 pm Aquarius
- 6th 3:44 am Pisces
- 8th 1:24 pm Aries
- 11th 1:44 am Taurus
- 13th 2:21 pm Gemini
- 16th 0:53 am Cancer
- 18th 8:22 am Leo
- 20th 1:26 pm Virgo
- 22nd 5:09 pm Libra
- 24th 8:16 pm Scorpio
- 26th 11:12 pm Sagittarius
- 29th 2:21 am Capricorn
- 31st 6:28 am Aquarius

August 1985
- 2nd 12:37 pm Pisces
- 4th 9:44 pm Aries
- 7th 9:42 am Taurus
- 9th 10:31 pm Gemini
- 12th 9:24 am Cancer
- 14th 4:53 pm Leo
- 16th 9:14 pm Virgo
- 18th 11:43 pm Libra
- 21st 1:51 am Scorpio
- 23rd 4:37 am Sagittarius
- 25th 8:26 am Capricorn
- 27th 1:33 pm Aquarius
- 29th 8:25 pm Pisces

September 1985		October 1985		November 1985		December 1985	
1st	5:43 am Aries	1st	0:34 am Taurus	2nd	8:29 am Cancer	2nd	0:59 am Leo
3rd	5:28 pm Taurus	3rd	1:35 pm Gemini	4th	7:01 pm Leo	4th	9:09 am Virgo
6th	6:26 am Gemini	6th	1:58 am Cancer	7th	2:17 am Virgo	6th	2:28 pm Libra
8th	6:07 pm Cancer	8th	11:28 am Leo	9th	5:48 am Libra	8th	4:54 pm Scorpio
11th	2:25 am Leo	10th	5:05 pm Virgo	11th	6:30 am Scorpio	10th	5:12 pm Sagittarius
13th	6:49 am Virgo	12th	7:10 pm Libra	13th	5:54 am Sagittarius	12th	5:02 pm Capricorn
15th	8:33 am Libra	14th	7:12 pm Scorpio	15th	5:57 am Capricorn	14th	6:20 pm Aquarius
17th	9:17 am Scorpio	16th	7:07 pm Sagittarius	17th	8:32 am Aquarius	16th	10:52 pm Pisces
19th	10:43 am Sagittarius	18th	8:37 pm Capricorn	19th	2:48 pm Pisces	19th	7:42 am Aries
21st	1:52 pm Capricorn	21st	0:55 am Aquarius	22nd	0:44 am Aries	21st	7:42 pm Taurus
23rd	7:13 pm Aquarius	23rd	8:31 am Pisces	24th	1:08 pm Taurus	24th	8:44 am Gemini
26th	2:51 am Pisces	25th	6:48 pm Aries	27th	2:07 am Gemini	26th	8:42 pm Cancer
28th	12:44 pm Aries	28th	6:50 am Taurus	29th	2:20 pm Cancer	29th	6:42 am Leo
		30th	7:58 pm Gemini			31st	2:40 pm Virgo

January 1986		February 1986		March 1986		April 1986	
2nd	8:43 pm Libra	1st	6:18 am Scorpio	2nd	2:53 pm Sagittarius	3rd	3:13 am Aquarius
5th	0:44 am Scorpio	3rd	9:31 am Sagittarius	4th	5:57 pm Capricorn	5th	9:06 am Pisces
7th	2:47 am Sagittarius	5th	12:02 pm Capricorn	6th	9:43 pm Aquarius	7th	5:14 pm Aries
9th	3:43 am Capricorn	7th	2:38 pm Aquarius	9th	2:50 am Pisces	10th	3:37 am Taurus
11th	5:05 am Aquarius	9th	6:36 pm Pisces	11th	10:07 am Aries	12th	3:52 pm Gemini
13th	8:45 am Pisces	12th	1:22 am Aries	13th	8:06 pm Taurus	15th	4:42 am Cancer
15th	4:09 am Aries	14th	11:42 am Taurus	16th	8:24 am Gemini	17th	4:06 pm Leo
18th	3:16 am Taurus	17th	0:18 am Gemini	18th	9:05 pm Cancer	20th	0:25 am Virgo
20th	4:12 pm Gemini	19th	12:38 pm Cancer	21st	7:35 am Leo	22nd	4:48 am Libra
23rd	4:14 am Cancer	21st	10:25 pm Leo	23rd	2:36 pm Virgo	24th	6:15 am Scorpio
25th	1:45 pm Leo	24th	4:58 am Virgo	25th	6:22 pm Libra	26th	6:18 am Sagittarius
27th	8:51 pm Virgo	26th	9:07 am Libra	27th	8:06 pm Scorpio	28th	6:45 am Capricorn
30th	2:09 am Libra	28th	12:06 pm Scorpio	29th	9:22 pm Sagittarius	30th	9:11 am Aquarius
				31st	11:26 pm Capricorn		

May 1986		June 1986		July 1986		August 1986	
2nd	2:35 pm Pisces	1st	4:46 am Aries	3rd	10:33 am Gemini	2nd	6:03 am Cancer
4th	11:01 pm Aries	3rd	3:48 pm Taurus	5th	11:20 pm Cancer	4th	5:24 pm Leo
7th	10:00 am Taurus	6th	4:26 am Gemini	8th	10:52 am Leo	7th	2:44 am Virgo
9th	10:25 pm Gemini	8th	5:14 pm Cancer	10th	8:47 pm Virgo	9th	10:02 am Libra
12th	11:17 am Cancer	11th	5:09 am Leo	13th	4:37 am Libra	11th	3:34 pm Scorpio
14th	11:14 pm Leo	13th	3:14 pm Virgo	15th	9:53 am Scorpio	13th	7:14 pm Sagittarius
17th	8:41 am Virgo	15th	10:37 pm Libra	17th	12:30 pm Sagittarius	15th	9:21 pm Capricorn
19th	2:36 pm Libra	18th	2:34 am Scorpio	19th	1:08 pm Capricorn	17th	10:44 pm Aquarius
21st	4:59 pm Scorpio	20th	3:34 am Sagittarius	21st	1:20 pm Aquarius	20th	0:52 am Pisces
23rd	4:55 pm Sagittarius	22nd	3:00 am Capricorn	23rd	3:03 pm Pisces	22nd	5:30 am Aries
25th	4:15 pm Capricorn	24th	2:53 am Aquarius	25th	8:06 pm Aries	24th	1:40 pm Taurus
27th	5:05 pm Aquarius	26th	5:18 am Pisces	28th	5:14 am Taurus	27th	1:01 am Gemini
29th	8:58 pm Pisces	28th	11:41 am Aries	30th	5:20 pm Gemini	29th	1:38 pm Cancer
		30th	9:55 pm Taurus				

September 1986		October 1986		November 1986		December 1986	
1st	1:07 am Leo	3rd	1:03 am Libra	1st	2:16 pm Scorpio	1st	2:07 am Sagittarius
3rd	10:02 am Virgo	5th	4:34 am Scorpio	3rd	3:18 pm Sagittarius	3rd	1:29 am Capricorn
5th	4:32 pm Libra	7th	6:48 am Sagittarius	5th	3:51 pm Capricorn	5th	1:24 am Aquarius
7th	9:11 pm Scorpio	9th	8:54 am Capricorn	7th	5:31 pm Aquarius	7th	3:52 am Pisces
10th	0:41 am Sagittarius	11th	11:47 am Aquarius	9th	9:30 pm Pisces	9th	9:55 am Aries
12th	3:27 am Capricorn	13th	4:05 pm Pisces	12th	4:16 am Aries	11th	7:12 pm Taurus
14th	6:07 am Aquarius	15th	10:14 pm Aries	14th	1:26 pm Taurus	14th	6:42 am Gemini
16th	9:29 am Pisces	18th	6:37 am Taurus	17th	0:26 am Gemini	16th	7:09 pm Cancer
18th	2:36 pm Aries	20th	5:15 pm Gemini	19th	12:46 pm Cancer	19th	7:43 am Leo
20th	10:25 pm Taurus	23rd	5:36 am Cancer	22nd	1:24 am Leo	21st	7:28 pm Virgo
23rd	9:15 am Gemini	25th	6:00 pm Leo	24th	12:41 pm Virgo	24th	4:50 am Libra
25th	9:44 pm Cancer	28th	4:18 am Virgo	26th	8:57 pm Libra	26th	11:00 am Scorpio
28th	9:36 am Leo	30th	11:00 am Libra	29th	1:13 am Scorpio	28th	1:14 pm Sagittarius
30th	6:55 pm Virgo					30th	12:53 pm Capricorn

January 1987		February 1987		March 1987		April 1987	
1st	11:58 am Aquarius	2nd	2:12 am Aries	1st	12:41 pm Aries	2nd	12:20 pm Gemini
3rd	12:43 pm Pisces	4th	8:50 am Taurus	3rd	6:16 pm Taurus	4th	11:34 pm Cancer
5th	4:57 pm Aries	6th	7:26 pm Gemini	6th	3:28 am Gemini	7th	12:02 pm Leo
8th	1:16 am Taurus	9th	7:56 am Cancer	8th	3:25 pm Cancer	9th	11:29 pm Virgo
10th	12:42 pm Gemini	11th	8:22 pm Leo	11th	3:55 am Leo	12th	8:02 am Libra
13th	1:19 am Cancer	14th	7:25 am Virgo	13th	2:53 pm Virgo	14th	1:39 pm Scorpio
15th	1:45 pm Leo	16th	4:43 pm Libra	15th	11:36 pm Libra	16th	5:01 pm Sagittarius
18th	1:14 am Virgo	19th	0:05 am Scorpio	18th	5:56 am Scorpio	18th	7:22 pm Capricorn
20th	11:05 am Libra	21st	5:08 am Sagittarius	20th	10:30 am Sagittarius	20th	9:45 pm Aquarius
22nd	6:28 pm Scorpio	23rd	7:55 am Capricorn	22nd	1:47 pm Capricorn	23rd	1:03 am Pisces
24th	10:35 pm Sagittarius	25th	9:08 am Aquarius	24th	4:18 pm Aquarius	25th	5:42 am Aries
26th	11:42 pm Capricorn	27th	10:09 am Pisces	26th	6:47 pm Pisces	27th	12:08 pm Taurus
28th	11:17 pm Aquarius			28th	10:13 pm Aries	29th	8:45 pm Gemini
30th	11:26 pm Pisces			31st	3:49 am Taurus		

May 1987

2nd	7:41 am	Cancer
4th	8:07 pm	Leo
7th	8:05 am	Virgo
9th	5:26 pm	Libra
11th	11:09 pm	Scorpio
14th	1:42 am	Sagittarius
16th	2:38 am	Capricorn
18th	3:45 am	Aquarius
20th	6:27 am	Pisces
22nd	11:27 am	Aries
24th	6:41 pm	Taurus
27th	3:56 am	Gemini
29th	3:01 pm	Cancer

June 1987

1st	3:27 am	Leo
3rd	3:54 pm	Virgo
6th	2:22 am	Libra
8th	9:01 am	Scorpio
10th	11:49 am	Sagittarius
12th	12:04 pm	Capricorn
14th	11:49 am	Aquarius
16th	1:00 pm	Pisces
18th	5:02 pm	Aries
21st	0:10 am	Taurus
23rd	9:58 am	Gemini
25th	9:22 pm	Cancer
28th	9:52 am	Leo
30th	10:33 pm	Virgo

July 1987

3rd	9:50 am	Libra
5th	5:58 pm	Scorpio
7th	10:03 pm	Sagittarius
9th	10:42 pm	Capricorn
11th	9:50 pm	Aquarius
13th	9:38 pm	Pisces
16th	0:02 am	Aries
18th	6:09 am	Taurus
20th	3:36 pm	Gemini
23rd	3:14 am	Cancer
25th	3:50 pm	Leo
28th	4:25 am	Virgo
30th	3:56 pm	Libra

August 1987

2nd	1:08 am	Scorpio
4th	6:42 am	Sagittarius
6th	8:47 am	Capricorn
8th	8:36 am	Aquarius
10th	8:04 am	Pisces
12th	9:14 am	Aries
14th	1:44 pm	Taurus
16th	10:01 pm	Gemini
19th	9:21 am	Cancer
21st	9:58 pm	Leo
24th	10:23 am	Virgo
26th	9:35 pm	Libra
29th	6:47 am	Scorpio
31st	1:20 pm	Sagittarius

September 1987

2nd	5:00 pm	Capricorn
4th	6:19 pm	Aquarius
6th	6:37 pm	Pisces
8th	7:36 pm	Aries
10th	10:57 pm	Taurus
13th	5:59 am	Gemini
15th	4:25 pm	Cancer
18th	4:50 am	Leo
20th	5:13 pm	Virgo
23rd	3:57 am	Libra
25th	12:28 pm	Scorpio
27th	6:48 pm	Sagittarius
29th	11:08 pm	Capricorn

October 1987

2nd	1:50 am	Aquarius
4th	3:39 am	Pisces
6th	5:36 am	Aries
8th	8:50 am	Taurus
10th	3:07 pm	Gemini
13th	0:30 am	Cancer
15th	12:34 pm	Leo
18th	1:06 am	Virgo
20th	11:47 am	Libra
22nd	7:39 pm	Scorpio
25th	0:57 am	Sagittarius
27th	4:32 am	Capricorn
29th	7:27 am	Aquarius
31st	10:20 am	Pisces

November 1987

2nd	1:41 pm	Aries
4th	6:04 pm	Taurus
7th	0:15 am	Gemini
9th	9:12 am	Cancer
11th	8:45 pm	Leo
14th	9:28 am	Virgo
16th	8:46 pm	Libra
19th	4:43 am	Scorpio
21st	9:13 am	Sagittarius
23rd	11:31 am	Capricorn
25th	1:13 pm	Aquarius
27th	3:43 pm	Pisces
29th	7:38 pm	Aries

December 1987

2nd	1:06 am	Taurus
4th	8:16 am	Gemini
6th	5:22 pm	Cancer
9th	4:40 am	Leo
11th	5:29 pm	Virgo
14th	5:36 am	Libra
16th	2:35 pm	Scorpio
18th	7:29 pm	Sagittarius
20th	9:06 pm	Capricorn
22nd	9:21 pm	Aquarius
24th	10:12 pm	Pisces
27th	1:07 am	Aries
29th	6:40 am	Taurus
31st	2:32 pm	Gemini

January 1988

3rd	0:18 am	Cancer
5th	11:49 am	Leo
8th	0:35 am	Virgo
10th	1:13 pm	Libra
12th	11:39 pm	Scorpio
15th	5:53 am	Sagittarius
17th	8:10 am	Capricorn
19th	8:02 am	Aquarius
21st	7:31 am	Pisces
23rd	8:37 am	Aries
25th	12:43 pm	Taurus
27th	8:06 pm	Gemini
30th	6:14 am	Cancer

February 1988

1st	6:08 pm	Leo
4th	6:54 am	Virgo
6th	7:35 pm	Libra
9th	6:38 am	Scorpio
11th	2:30 pm	Sagittarius
13th	6:32 pm	Capricorn
15th	7:23 pm	Aquarius
17th	6:44 pm	Pisces
19th	6:38 pm	Aries
21st	8:54 pm	Taurus
24th	2:45 am	Gemini
26th	12:16 pm	Cancer
29th	0:12 am	Leo

March 1988

2nd	1:07 pm	Virgo
5th	1:33 am	Libra
7th	12:25 pm	Scorpio
9th	8:58 pm	Sagittarius
12th	2:29 am	Capricorn
14th	5:06 am	Aquarius
16th	5:42 am	Pisces
18th	5:47 am	Aries
20th	7:09 am	Taurus
22nd	11:27 am	Gemini
24th	7:30 pm	Cancer
27th	6:55 am	Leo
29th	7:50 pm	Virgo

April 1988

1st	8:04 am	Libra
3rd	6:25 pm	Scorpio
6th	2:29 am	Sagittarius
8th	8:17 am	Capricorn
10th	12:08 pm	Aquarius
12th	2:23 pm	Pisces
14th	3:47 pm	Aries
16th	5:33 pm	Taurus
18th	9:12 pm	Gemini
21st	4:08 am	Cancer
23rd	2:38 pm	Leo
26th	3:17 am	Virgo
28th	3:36 pm	Libra

May 1988

1st	1:39 am	Scorpio
3rd	8:50 am	Sagittarius
5th	1:53 pm	Capricorn
7th	5:36 pm	Aquarius
9th	8:40 pm	Pisces
11th	11:24 pm	Aries
14th	2:23 am	Taurus
16th	6:35 am	Gemini
18th	1:10 pm	Cancer
20th	10:53 pm	Leo
23rd	11:13 am	Virgo
25th	11:50 pm	Libra
28th	10:02 am	Scorpio
30th	4:54 pm	Sagittarius

June 1988

1st	8:59 pm	Capricorn
3rd	11:35 pm	Aquarius
6th	2:02 am	Pisces
8th	5:06 am	Aries
10th	9:05 am	Taurus
12th	2:18 pm	Gemini
14th	9:22 pm	Cancer
17th	7:00 am	Leo
19th	7:04 pm	Virgo
22nd	7:56 am	Libra
24th	6:56 pm	Scorpio
27th	2:15 am	Sagittarius
29th	5:57 am	Capricorn

July 1988

1st	7:31 am	Aquarius
3rd	8:36 am	Pisces
5th	10:42 am	Aries
7th	2:31 pm	Taurus
9th	8:18 pm	Gemini
12th	4:12 am	Cancer
14th	2:15 pm	Leo
17th	2:18 am	Virgo
19th	3:20 pm	Libra
22nd	3:11 am	Scorpio
24th	11:36 am	Sagittarius
26th	4:02 pm	Capricorn
28th	5:22 pm	Aquarius
30th	5:24 pm	Pisces

August 1988

1st	5:57 pm	Aries
3rd	8:28 pm	Taurus
6th	1:45 am	Gemini
8th	9:56 am	Cancer
10th	8:29 pm	Leo
13th	8:48 am	Virgo
15th	9:52 pm	Libra
18th	10:08 am	Scorpio
20th	7:52 pm	Sagittarius
23rd	1:47 am	Capricorn
25th	4:02 am	Aquarius
27th	4:01 am	Pisces
29th	3:31 am	Aries
31st	4:25 am	Taurus

September 1988

2nd	8:17 am	Gemini
4th	3:41 pm	Cancer
7th	2:16 am	Leo
9th	2:49 pm	Virgo
12th	3:51 am	Libra
14th	4:05 pm	Scorpio
17th	2:25 am	Sagittarius
19th	9:40 am	Capricorn
21st	1:38 pm	Aquarius
23rd	2:47 pm	Pisces
25th	2:30 pm	Aries
27th	2:32 pm	Taurus
29th	4:47 pm	Gemini

October 1988

1st	10:39 pm	Cancer
4th	8:33 am	Leo
6th	9:01 pm	Virgo
9th	10:03 am	Libra
11th	9:57 pm	Scorpio
14th	7:57 am	Sagittarius
16th	3:42 pm	Capricorn
18th	9:03 pm	Aquarius
20th	11:58 pm	Pisces
23rd	0:58 am	Aries
25th	1:22 am	Taurus
27th	2:56 am	Gemini
29th	7:33 am	Cancer
31st	4:08 pm	Leo

November 1988

3rd	4:02 am	Virgo
5th	5:03 pm	Libra
8th	4:44 am	Scorpio
10th	2:03 pm	Sagittarius
12th	9:11 pm	Capricorn
15th	2:35 am	Aquarius
17th	6:32 am	Pisces
19th	9:11 am	Aries
21st	11:02 am	Taurus
23rd	1:15 pm	Gemini
25th	5:24 pm	Cancer
28th	0:52 am	Leo
30th	12:02 pm	Virgo

December 1988

3rd	0:57 am	Libra
5th	12:47 pm	Scorpio
7th	9:53 pm	Sagittarius
10th	4:05 am	Capricorn
12th	8:25 am	Aquarius
14th	11:52 am	Pisces
16th	3:03 pm	Aries
18th	6:12 pm	Taurus
20th	9:44 pm	Gemini
23rd	2:36 am	Cancer
25th	10:01 am	Leo
27th	8:28 pm	Virgo
30th	9:09 am	Libra

January 1989
1st 9:33 pm Scorpio
4th 7:07 am Sagittarius
6th 1:09 pm Capricorn
8th 4:29 pm Aquarius
10th 6:31 pm Pisces
12th 8:37 pm Aries
14th 11:38 pm Taurus
17th 3:59 am Gemini
19th 10:01 am Cancer
21st 6:05 pm Leo
24th 4:34 am Virgo
26th 5:02 pm Libra
29th 5:46 am Scorpio
31st 4:24 pm Sagittarius

February 1989
2nd 11:28 pm Capricorn
5th 2:48 am Aquarius
7th 3:52 am Pisces
9th 4:19 am Aries
11th 5:48 am Taurus
13th 9:28 am Gemini
15th 3:45 pm Cancer
18th 0:33 am Leo
20th 11:37 am Virgo
23rd 0:06 am Libra
25th 12:56 pm Scorpio
28th 0:29 am Sagittarius

March 1989
2nd 8:53 am Capricorn
4th 1:31 pm Aquarius
6th 2:56 pm Pisces
8th 2:36 pm Aries
10th 2:29 pm Taurus
12th 4:22 pm Gemini
14th 9:29 pm Cancer
17th 6:17 am Leo
19th 5:42 pm Virgo
22nd 6:24 am Libra
24th 7:11 pm Scorpio
27th 6:52 am Sagittarius
29th 4:22 pm Capricorn
31st 10:45 pm Aquarius

April 1989
3rd 1:36 am Pisces
5th 1:50 am Aries
7th 1:07 am Taurus
9th 1:32 am Gemini
11th 5:02 am Cancer
13th 12:35 pm Leo
15th 11:40 pm Virgo
18th 12:33 pm Libra
21st 1:14 am Scorpio
23rd 12:38 pm Sagittarius
25th 10:16 pm Capricorn
28th 5:31 am Aquarius
30th 10:00 am Pisces

May 1989
2nd 11:49 am Aries
4th 11:55 am Taurus
6th 12:08 pm Gemini
8th 2:27 pm Cancer
10th 8:27 pm Leo
13th 6:33 am Virgo
15th 7:09 pm Libra
18th 7:47 am Scorpio
20th 6:51 pm Sagittarius
23rd 3:54 am Capricorn
25th 10:59 am Aquarius
27th 4:10 pm Pisces
29th 7:25 pm Aries
31st 8:50 pm Taurus

June 1989
2nd 10:04 pm Gemini
5th 0:19 am Cancer
7th 5:33 am Leo
9th 2:35 pm Virgo
12th 2:32 am Libra
14th 3:11 pm Scorpio
17th 2:12 am Sagittarius
19th 10:39 am Capricorn
21st 4:56 pm Aquarius
23rd 9:37 pm Pisces
26th 1:08 am Aries
28th 3:47 am Taurus
30th 6:10 am Gemini

July 1989
2nd 9:23 am Cancer
4th 2:43 pm Leo
6th 11:06 pm Virgo
9th 10:32 am Libra
11th 11:10 pm Scorpio
14th 10:28 am Sagittarius
16th 6:59 pm Capricorn
19th 0:36 am Aquarius
21st 4:07 am Pisces
23rd 6:42 am Aries
25th 9:13 am Taurus
27th 12:19 pm Gemini
29th 4:35 pm Cancer
31st 10:43 pm Leo

August 1989
3rd 7:22 am Virgo
5th 6:30 pm Libra
8th 7:04 am Scorpio
10th 7:00 pm Sagittarius
13th 4:13 am Capricorn
15th 9:54 am Aquarius
17th 12:43 pm Pisces
19th 1:59 pm Aries
21st 3:14 pm Taurus
23rd 5:43 pm Gemini
25th 10:15 pm Cancer
28th 5:16 am Leo
30th 2:33 pm Virgo

September 1989
2nd 1:49 am Libra
4th 2:24 pm Scorpio
7th 2:50 am Sagittarius
9th 1:08 pm Capricorn
11th 7:59 pm Aquarius
13th 11:06 pm Pisces
15th 11:38 pm Aries
17th 11:23 pm Taurus
20th 0:17 am Gemini
22nd 3:53 am Cancer
24th 10:48 am Leo
26th 8:35 pm Virgo
29th 8:17 am Libra

October 1989
1st 8:54 pm Scorpio
4th 9:29 am Sagittarius
6th 8:43 pm Capricorn
9th 5:02 am Aquarius
11th 9:32 am Pisces
13th 10:38 am Aries
15th 9:53 am Taurus
17th 9:23 am Gemini
19th 11:15 am Cancer
21st 4:52 pm Leo
24th 2:16 am Virgo
26th 2:12 pm Libra
29th 2:56 am Scorpio
31st 3:23 pm Sagittarius

November 1989
3rd 2:47 am Capricorn
5th 12:06 pm Aquarius
7th 6:21 pm Pisces
9th 9:06 pm Aries
11th 9:08 pm Taurus
13th 8:19 pm Gemini
15th 8:54 pm Cancer
18th 0:46 am Leo
20th 8:58 am Virgo
22nd 8:27 pm Libra
25th 9:12 am Scorpio
27th 9:30 pm Sagittarius
30th 8:25 am Capricorn

December 1989
2nd 5:40 pm Aquarius
5th 0:48 am Pisces
7th 5:09 am Aries
9th 6:56 am Taurus
11th 7:15 am Gemini
13th 7:53 am Cancer
15th 10:47 am Leo
17th 5:24 pm Virgo
20th 3:47 am Libra
22nd 4:18 pm Scorpio
25th 4:35 am Sagittarius
27th 3:08 pm Capricorn
29th 11:38 pm Aquarius

January 1990
1st 6:09 am Pisces
3rd 10:54 am Aries
5th 2:03 pm Taurus
7th 4:01 pm Gemini
9th 5:54 pm Cancer
11th 9:04 pm Leo
14th 2:50 am Virgo
16th 12:21 pm Libra
19th 0:16 am Scorpio
21st 12:41 pm Sagittarius
23rd 11:27 pm Capricorn
26th 7:22 am Aquarius
28th 12:48 pm Pisces
30th 4:32 pm Aries

February 1990
1st 7:28 pm Taurus
3rd 10:13 pm Gemini
6th 1:28 am Cancer
8th 5:55 am Leo
10th 12:17 pm Virgo
12th 9:10 pm Libra
15th 8:35 am Scorpio
17th 9:05 pm Sagittarius
20th 8:25 am Capricorn
22nd 4:48 pm Aquarius
24th 9:48 pm Pisces
27th 0:16 am Aries

March 1990
1st 1:44 am Taurus
3rd 3:39 am Gemini
5th 7:06 am Cancer
7th 12:28 pm Leo
9th 7:49 pm Virgo
12th 5:11 am Libra
14th 4:27 pm Scorpio
17th 4:56 am Sagittarius
19th 4:59 pm Capricorn
22nd 2:28 am Aquarius
24th 8:03 am Pisces
26th 10:11 am Aries
28th 10:27 am Taurus
30th 10:46 am Gemini

April 1990
1st 12:55 pm Cancer
3rd 5:53 pm Leo
6th 1:43 am Virgo
8th 11:46 am Libra
10th 11:18 pm Scorpio
13th 11:49 am Sagittarius
16th 0:16 am Capricorn
18th 10:48 am Aquarius
20th 5:53 pm Pisces
22nd 8:56 pm Aries
24th 9:01 pm Taurus
26th 8:13 pm Gemini
28th 8:42 pm Cancer

May 1990
1st 0:09 am Leo
3rd 7:21 am Virgo
5th 5:30 pm Libra
8th 5:24 am Scorpio
10th 5:56 pm Sagittarius
13th 6:21 am Capricorn
15th 5:28 pm Aquarius
18th 1:53 am Pisces
20th 6:28 am Aries
22nd 7:40 am Taurus
24th 7:01 am Gemini
26th 6:38 am Cancer
28th 8:35 am Leo
30th 2:13 pm Virgo

June 1990
1st 11:31 pm Libra
4th 11:24 am Scorpio
6th 12:00 pm Sagittarius
9th 12:11 pm Capricorn
11th 11:09 pm Aquarius
14th 7:57 am Pisces
16th 1:51 pm Aries
18th 4:40 pm Taurus
20th 5:14 pm Gemini
22nd 5:12 pm Cancer
24th 6:29 pm Leo
26th 10:43 pm Virgo
29th 6:51 am Libra

July 1990
1st 6:02 pm Scorpio
4th 6:35 am Sagittarius
6th 6:39 pm Capricorn
9th 5:05 am Aquarius
11th 1:28 pm Pisces
13th 7:35 pm Aries
15th 11:29 pm Taurus
18th 1:32 am Gemini
20th 2:46 am Cancer
22nd 4:33 am Leo
24th 8:23 am Virgo
26th 3:24 pm Libra
29th 1:40 am Scorpio
31st 1:59 pm Sagittarius

August 1990
3rd 2:08 am Capricorn
5th 12:16 pm Aquarius
7th 7:54 pm Pisces
10th 1:15 am Aries
12th 4:56 am Taurus
14th 7:43 am Gemini
16th 10:14 am Cancer
18th 1:15 pm Leo
20th 5:37 pm Virgo
23rd 0:19 am Libra
25th 9:50 am Scorpio
27th 9:59 pm Sagittarius
30th 10:21 am Capricorn

September 1990

1st	8:49 pm	Aquarius
4th	4:03 am	Pisces
6th	8:21 am	Aries
8th	10:56 am	Taurus
10th	1:07 pm	Gemini
12th	3:56 pm	Cancer
14th	7:55 pm	Leo
17th	1:20 am	Virgo
19th	8:38 am	Libra
21st	6:09 pm	Scorpio
24th	5:54 am	Sagittarius
26th	6:37 pm	Capricorn
29th	5:51 am	Aquarius

October 1990

1st	1:37 pm	Pisces
3rd	5:38 am	Aries
5th	7:05 pm	Taurus
7th	7:48 pm	Gemini
9th	9:31 pm	Cancer
12th	1:17 am	Leo
14th	7:24 am	Virgo
16th	3:30 pm	Libra
19th	1:25 am	Scorpio
21st	1:13 pm	Sagittarius
24th	2:04 am	Capricorn
26th	2:11 pm	Aquarius
28th	11:23 pm	Pisces
31st	4:11 am	Aries

November 1990

2nd	5:30 am	Taurus
4th	5:07 am	Gemini
6th	5:10 am	Cancer
8th	7:28 am	Leo
10th	12:52 pm	Virgo
12th	9:10 pm	Libra
15th	7:42 am	Scorpio
17th	7:40 pm	Sagittarius
20th	8:33 am	Capricorn
22nd	9:08 pm	Aquarius
25th	7:27 am	Pisces
27th	2:00 pm	Aries
29th	4:33 pm	Taurus

December 1990

1st	4:21 pm	Gemini
3rd	3:30 pm	Cancer
5th	4:05 pm	Leo
7th	7:42 pm	Virgo
10th	3:02 am	Libra
12th	1:29 pm	Scorpio
15th	1:43 am	Sagittarius
17th	2:35 pm	Capricorn
20th	2:59 am	Aquarius
22nd	1:45 pm	Pisces
24th	9:43 pm	Aries
27th	2:07 am	Taurus
29th	2:24 am	Gemini
31st	3:04 am	Cancer

January 1991

2nd	2:57 am	Leo
4th	5:01 am	Virgo
6th	10:39 am	Libra
8th	8:01 pm	Scorpio
11th	8:07 am	Sagittarius
13th	8:59 pm	Capricorn
16th	9:02 am	Aquarius
18th	7:22 pm	Pisces
21st	3:27 am	Aries
23rd	8:57 am	Taurus
25th	12:04 pm	Gemini
27th	1:23 pm	Cancer
29th	2:05 pm	Leo
31st	3:48 pm	Virgo

February 1991

2nd	8:05 pm	Libra
5th	4:03 am	Scorpio
7th	3:24 pm	Sagittarius
10th	4:14 am	Capricorn
12th	4:13 pm	Aquarius
15th	1:58 am	Pisces
17th	9:09 am	Aries
19th	2:23 pm	Taurus
21st	6:09 pm	Gemini
23rd	8:56 pm	Cancer
25th	11:13 pm	Leo
28th	1:52 am	Virgo

March 1991

2nd	6:06 am	Libra
4th	1:13 pm	Scorpio
6th	11:34 pm	Sagittarius
9th	12:13 pm	Capricorn
12th	0:29 am	Aquarius
14th	10:05 am	Pisces
16th	4:34 pm	Aries
18th	8:39 pm	Taurus
20th	11:36 pm	Gemini
23rd	2:28 am	Cancer
25th	5:44 am	Leo
27th	9:43 am	Virgo
29th	2:52 pm	Libra
31st	10:02 pm	Scorpio

April 1991

3rd	8:02 am	Sagittarius
5th	8:21 pm	Capricorn
8th	8:57 am	Aquarius
10th	7:14 pm	Pisces
13th	1:48 am	Aries
15th	5:03 am	Taurus
17th	6:42 am	Gemini
19th	8:18 am	Cancer
21st	11:06 am	Leo
23rd	3:32 pm	Virgo
25th	9:36 pm	Libra
28th	5:36 am	Scorpio
30th	3:46 pm	Sagittarius

May 1991

3rd	3:56 am	Capricorn
5th	4:50 pm	Aquarius
8th	4:01 am	Pisces
10th	11:29 am	Aries
12th	3:03 pm	Taurus
14th	3:50 pm	Gemini
16th	4:16 pm	Cancer
18th	5:33 pm	Leo
20th	9:02 pm	Virgo
23rd	3:10 am	Libra
25th	11:44 am	Scorpio
27th	10:21 pm	Sagittarius
30th	10:42 am	Capricorn

June 1991

1st	11:42 pm	Aquarius
4th	11:34 am	Pisces
6th	8:22 pm	Aries
9th	1:12 am	Taurus
11th	2:35 am	Gemini
13th	2:16 am	Cancer
15th	2:12 am	Leo
17th	4:05 am	Virgo
19th	9:06 am	Libra
21st	5:21 pm	Scorpio
24th	4:18 am	Sagittarius
26th	4:50 pm	Capricorn
29th	5:46 am	Aquarius

July 1991

1st	5:48 pm	Pisces
4th	3:31 am	Aries
6th	9:48 am	Taurus
8th	12:38 pm	Gemini
10th	1:02 pm	Cancer
12th	12:37 pm	Leo
14th	1:17 pm	Virgo
16th	4:39 pm	Libra
18th	11:41 pm	Scorpio
21st	10:19 am	Sagittarius
23rd	10:57 pm	Capricorn
26th	11:48 am	Aquarius
28th	11:34 pm	Pisces
31st	9:18 am	Aries

August 1991

2nd	4:29 pm	Taurus
4th	8:53 pm	Gemini
6th	10:48 pm	Cancer
8th	11:10 pm	Leo
10th	11:36 pm	Virgo
13th	1:54 am	Libra
15th	7:39 am	Scorpio
17th	5:14 pm	Sagittarius
20th	5:34 am	Capricorn
22nd	6:27 pm	Aquarius
25th	5:49 am	Pisces
27th	2:59 pm	Aries
29th	10:00 pm	Taurus

September 1991

1st	3:03 am	Gemini
3rd	6:19 am	Cancer
5th	8:14 am	Leo
7th	9:39 am	Virgo
9th	11:57 am	Libra
11th	4:48 pm	Scorpio
14th	1:17 am	Sagittarius
16th	1:05 pm	Capricorn
19th	1:56 am	Aquarius
21st	1:17 pm	Pisces
23rd	9:56 pm	Aries
26th	3:59 am	Taurus
28th	8:25 am	Gemini
30th	11:57 am	Cancer

October 1991

2nd	2:50 pm	Leo
4th	5:46 pm	Virgo
6th	9:03 pm	Libra
9th	2:03 am	Scorpio
11th	10:03 am	Sagittarius
13th	9:12 pm	Capricorn
16th	10:04 am	Aquarius
18th	9:52 pm	Pisces
21st	6:30 am	Aries
23rd	11:53 am	Taurus
25th	3:08 pm	Gemini
27th	5:37 pm	Cancer
29th	8:21 pm	Leo
31st	11:48 pm	Virgo

November 1991

3rd	4:14 am	Libra
5th	10:13 am	Scorpio
7th	6:26 pm	Sagittarius
10th	5:20 am	Capricorn
12th	6:08 pm	Aquarius
15th	6:31 am	Pisces
17th	4:04 pm	Aries
19th	9:49 pm	Taurus
22nd	0:23 am	Gemini
24th	1:26 am	Cancer
26th	2:38 am	Leo
28th	5:14 am	Virgo
30th	9:50 am	Libra

December 1991

2nd	4:36 pm	Scorpio
5th	1:34 am	Sagittarius
7th	12:45 pm	Capricorn
10th	1:28 am	Aquarius
12th	2:18 pm	Pisces
15th	1:06 am	Aries
17th	8:05 am	Taurus
19th	11:18 am	Gemini
21st	11:54 am	Cancer
23rd	11:41 am	Leo
25th	12:28 pm	Virgo
27th	3:42 pm	Libra
29th	10:05 pm	Scorpio

Daylight Saving Time

In the United States, Daylight Saving Time (DST), prior to 1986, always began on the last Sunday in April, at 2:00 am (in 1986 Congress passed a law that changed this to the first Sunday in April). It always ends on the last Sunday in October, also at 2:00 am. However, there are a few exceptions. DST was in effect continuously from February 9, 1942 to September 9, 1945 in a wartime effort to reduce the need for artificial light. During the energy crisis of the 1970s it was again extended, so that in 1974 DST was in effect from January 6 to October 27 and in 1975 from February 23 to October 26.

If DST was in effect on the day you were born, you need to add *one less* hour to adjust your birth time to GMT. That is, if you were born on October 12, 1966 at 11:46 pm, in the Eastern Standard Time zone, you would add only *four* hours to your birth time, instead of the usual five. Similarly, if you were born at this time, but in the Mountain Standard Time zone, add six, instead of seven, hours to find GMT.

In some states, such as Arizona, Hawaii, and parts of Indiana, DST is not observed. Thus, the formula remains constant throughout the year in these areas.

SUN SIGNS

Aries (March 21–April 20)

Taurus (April 21–May 20)

Gemini (May 21–June 20)

Cancer (June 21–July 21)

Leo (July 22–August 21)

Virgo (August 22–September 21)

Libra (September 22–October 22)

Scorpio (October 23–November 21)

Sagittarius (November 22–December 20)

Capricorn (December 21–January 19)

Aquarius (January 20–February 18)

Pisces (February 19–March 20)